JOHN DONNE IN CONTEXT

John Donne was a writer of dazzling extremes. He was a notorious rake and eloquent preacher; he wrote poems of tender intimacy and lyrics of gross misogyny. This book offers a comprehensive account of early modern life and culture as it relates to Donne's richly varied body of work. Short, lively, and accessible chapters written by leading experts in early modern studies shed light on Donne's literary career, language, and works as well as explore the social and intellectual contexts of his writing and its reception from the seventeenth to the twenty-first century. These chapters provide the depth of interpretation that Donne demands, and the range of knowledge that his prodigiously learned works elicit. Supported by a chronology of Donne's life and works and a comprehensive bibliography, this volume is a major new contribution to the study and criticism of the age of Donne and his writing.

MICHAEL SCHOENFELDT is John R. Knott, Jr. Collegiate Professor of English at the University of Michigan. His previous publications include *Bodies and Selves in Early Modern England: Physiology and Inwardness in Spenser, Shakespeare, Herbert, and Milton* (Cambridge, 2000), and *The Cambridge Introduction to Shakespeare's Poetry* (Cambridge, 2010); and as editor, *A Companion to Shakespeare's Sonnets* (2007).

JOHN DONNE IN CONTEXT

EDITED BY

MICHAEL SCHOENFELDT

University of Michigan

CAMBRIDGE
UNIVERSITY PRESS

University Printing House, Cambridge CB2 8BS, United Kingdom

One Liberty Plaza, 20th Floor, New York, NY 10006, USA

477 Williamstown Road, Port Melbourne, VIC 3207, Australia

314-321, 3rd Floor, Plot 3, Splendor Forum, Jasola District Centre, New Delhi - 110025, India

79 Anson Road, #06-04/06, Singapore 079906

Cambridge University Press is part of the University of Cambridge.

It furthers the University's mission by disseminating knowledge in the pursuit of education, learning and research at the highest international levels of excellence.

www.cambridge.org
Information on this title: www.cambridge.org/9781009010481
DOI: 10.1017/9781107338593

© Cambridge University Press 2019

First published 2019
First paperback edition 2021

A catalogue record for this publication is available from the British Library

Library of Congress Cataloging in Publication data
NAMES: Schoenfeldt, Michael Carl, editor.
TITLE: John Donne in context / edited by Michael Schoenfeldt.
DESCRIPTION: Cambridge, United Kingdom ; New York, NY : Cambridge University Press,
2019. | Series: Literature in context | Includes bibliographical references and index.
IDENTIFIERS: LCCN 2018052008 | ISBN 9781107043503 (hardback)
SUBJECTS: LCSH: Donne, John, 1572–1631 – Criticism and interpretation. | BISAC: LITERARY
CRITICISM / European / English, Irish, Scottish, Welsh.
CLASSIFICATION: LCC PR2248 .J625 2019 | DDC 821/.3–dc23
LC record available at https://lccn.loc.gov/2018052008

ISBN 978-1-107-04350-3 Hardback
ISBN 978-1-009-01048-1 Paperback

To Patrick

Contents

List of Illustrations   *page* x

Notes on Contributors   xi

Acknowledgments   xviii

Chronology   xx
    Kentston Bauman

List of Abbreviations   xxxv

    Introduction   1
    Michael Schoenfeldt

1 Donne's Literary Career   5
    Patrick Cheney

2 Donne's Texts and Materials   18
    Piers Brown

3 Donne and Print   30
    Katherine Rundell

4 Language   39
    Douglas Trevor

5 Donne's Poetics of Obstruction   50
    Kimberly Johnson

6 Elegies and Satires   58
    Melissa E. Sanchez

7 The Unity of the *Songs and Sonnets*   68
    Richard Strier

8 Divine Poems   85
    David Marno

9   Letters   94
     James Daybell

10   Orality and Performance   110
     Ilona Bell

11   Reading and Interpretation   120
     Katrin Ettenhuber

12   Education   131
     Andrew Wallace

13   Law   139
     Gregory Kneidel

14   Donne's Prisons   149
     Molly Murray

15   Donne and the Natural World   157
     Rebecca Bushnell

16   Money   165
     David Landreth

17   Sexuality   177
     Catherine Bates

18   Donne and the Passions   185
     Christopher Tilmouth

19   Pain   196
     Joseph Campana

20   Medicine   204
     Stephen Pender

21   Science, Alchemy, and the New Philosophy   217
     Margaret Healy

22   Donne and Skepticism   227
     Anita Gilman Sherman

23   The Metaphysics of the Metaphysicals   236
     Gordon Teskey

24   Controversial Prose   247
     Andrew Hadfield

25 Devotional Prose 256
  Brooke Conti

26 The Sermons 266
  Lori Anne Ferrell

27 The Self 276
  Nancy Selleck

28 Portraits 287
  Sarah Howe

29 Donne in the Seventeenth and Eighteenth Centuries 306
  Nicholas D. Nace

30 Donne in the Nineteenth and Twentieth Centuries 318
  James Longenbach

31 Donne in the Twenty-first Century: Thinking Feeling 326
  Linda Gregerson

Further Reading 338
Index 348

Illustrations

1 Frontispiece portrait engraved by William Marshall, from *page* 289
Donne's *Poems* (1635), based on a lost original possibly by
Nicholas Hilliard. Reproduced by permission of Cambridge
University Library.

2 Miniature by Isaac Oliver, watercolour and bodycolour on 294
vellum laid on card, 1616, Royal Collection Trust. © Her
Majesty Queen Elizabeth II 2013.

3 Frontispiece portrait engraved by Matthäus Merian, from 295
Donne's *LXXX Sermons* (1640), based on the miniature by
Isaac Oliver. Reproduced by permission of Cambridge
University Library.

4 Portrait in roundel format, oil on canvas, 1620, Deanery of St. 296
Paul's Cathedral, London. © The Chapter of St. Paul's Cathedral.

5 Frontispiece portrait engraved by Pierre Lombart, from 297
Donne's *Letters* (1651), based on the roundel portrait of 1620.
Reproduced by permission of Cambridge University Library.

6 Marble funeral monument to Donne by Nicholas Stone the 298
Elder, 1631, St. Paul's Cathedral, London. © The Chapter of
St. Paul's Cathedral.

7 Detail of Stone's funeral monument to Donne. © The 299
Chapter of St. Paul's Cathedral.

8 Donne in his shroud, frontispiece portrait engraved by 300
William Marshall, from the *Devotions* (1638). Reproduced by
permission of Cambridge University Library.

9 Donne in his shroud, frontispiece portrait engraved by Martin 301
Droeshout, from *Deaths Duell* (1632). Reproduced by
permission of Cambridge University Library.

Notes on Contributors

CATHERINE BATES is Research Professor at the University of Warwick. She is the author of five monographs on Renaissance literature, most recently *Masculinity and the Hunt: Wyatt to Spenser* (2013), winner of the British Academy Rose Mary Crawshay Prize 2015, and *On Not Defending Poetry: Defence and Indefensibility in Sidney's Defence of Poesy* (2017). She is editor of *The Cambridge Companion to the Epic* (2010) and *A Companion to Renaissance Poetry* (2018), and is currently coediting with Patrick Cheney the *Oxford History of Poetry in English, Volume 4: Sixteenth-Century English Poetry*.

KENTSTON BAUMAN received his PhD in English from the University of Michigan in 2011, and has taught for a number of years at various institutions in Ohio, Michigan, Rhode Island, and Massachusetts. However, taking some inspiration from Donne himself, he is in the midst of a career change, and currently works as a CNA [alternatively you could spell it out as Certified Nursing Assistant] at a long-term care facility in Massachusetts. He hopes to enter a Physician Assistant program in 2019.

ILONA BELL is Clarke Professor of English at Williams College. She is the author of *Elizabethan Women and the Poetry of Courtship* (Cambridge, 1998) and *Elizabeth I: The Voice of a Monarch* (2010), as well as numerous essays on John Donne and other Renaissance poets. She has edited *John Donne: Collected Poetry* (2012), *John Donne: Selected Poems* (2007), and *Pamphilia to Amphilanthus in Manuscript and Print* (2017).

PIERS BROWN is an Assistant Professor of English at Kenyon College, where he teaches Renaissance poetry, Book History, and the History of Science. He is the author of essays on Donne in *RQ*, *SEL*, and elsewhere, and is at work on a book on Donne's reception of early modern astronomy.

REBECCA BUSHNELL is the School of Arts and Sciences Board of Overseers Professor of English at the University of Pennsylvania. Her books include *Prophesying Tragedy: Sign and Voice in Sophocles' Theban Plays* (1988); *Tragedies of Tyrants: Political Thought & Theater in The English Renaissance* (1990); *A Culture of Teaching: Early Modern Humanism in Theory and Practice* (1996); and *Green Desire: Imagining Early Modern English Gardens* (2003). She has also published *A Companion to Tragedy* (2005) and *Tragedy: A Short Introduction* (2007). Her new book is called *Tragic Time in Drama, Film, and Videogames: The Future in the Instant* (2016). Professor Bushnell served at Penn as Dean of the School of Arts and Sciences from 2005–13.

JOSEPH CAMPANA is Alan Dugald McKillop Professor at Rice University where he serves as an editor of *Studies in English Literature 1500–1900*. He is the author of *The Pain of Reformation: Spenser, Vulnerability, and the Ethics of Masculinity* (2012), essays in *PMLA, Modern Philology, ELH*, and *Shakespeare Studies*, and the coeditor of *Renaissance Posthumanism* (2015). Current projects include *The Child's Two Bodies*, a study of sovereignty and childhood in the works of Shakespeare, and a series of essays on creaturely life in the Renaissance.

PATRICK CHENEY is Edwin Erle Sparks Professor of English and Comparative Literature at Penn State. He has written books on the literary careers of Spenser, Marlowe, and Shakespeare with the most recent being *English Authorship and the Early Modern Sublime: Spenser, Marlowe, Shakespeare, Jonson* (Cambridge, 2018).

BROOKE CONTI is Associate Professor of English at Cleveland State University. She is the author of *Confessions of Faith in Early Modern England* (2014) and editor, with Reid Barbour, of the forthcoming edition of Thomas Browne's *Religio Medici* (as part of *The Complete Works of Thomas Browne*). She is currently working on a book on Protestantism and nostalgia from Shakespeare to Milton.

JAMES DAYBELL is Professor of Early Modern British History at Plymouth University, and Fellow of the Royal Historical Society. He is author of *The Material Letter in Early Modern England: Manuscript Letters and the Culture and Practices of Letter-Writing, 1512–1635* (2012), *Women Letter-Writers in Tudor England* (2006); editor of *Early Modern Women's Letter-Writing, 1450–1700* (2001), *Women and Politics in Early Modern England, 1450–1700* (2004), (with Peter Hinds) *Material Readings of Early Modern Culture, 1580–1730* (2010), and (with Andrew

Gordon) *Cultures of Correspondence in Early Modern Britain, 1550–1642* (2016); and has written more than thirty articles and essays on the subjects of early modern letter-writing, women, gender, and politics. He is codirector with Kim McLean-Fiander (University of Victoria, Canada) of the British Academy/Leverhulme-funded project "Women's Early Modern Letters Online," codirector with Svante Norrhem (Lund University) of the AHRC-Research Network "Gender, Politics and Materiality in Early Modern Europe," and coeditor with Adam Smyth (Balliol College, Oxford) of the book series "Material Readings in Early Modern Culture."

KATRIN ETTENHUBER is Fellow and Tutor in English at Pembroke College, Cambridge. She is the author of *Donne's Augustine: Renaissance Cultures of Interpretation* (2011), editor of Volume V of *The Oxford Edition of the Sermons of John Donne* (2015), and coeditor, with Gavin Alexander and Sylvia Adamson, of *Renaissance Figures of Speech* (Cambridge, 2008).

LORI ANNE FERRELL is John D. and Lillian Maguire Distinguished Professor in the Humanities at Claremont Graduate University. Author of many essays on sermon literature, the English-language Bible, and the cultural history of protestant theology, Ferrell has also written *Government by Polemic: James I and the King's Preachers* (1998) and *The Bible and the People* (2008), and has edited, with Peter McCullough, *The English Sermon Revised* (2000) and with David Cressy, *Religion and Society in Early Modern England* (1996 and 2005). She is also the editor of Volume II of *The Oxford Edition of the Sermons of John Donne: Sermons at St. Paul's Cathedral, 1623–1625* (forthcoming).

LINDA GREGERSON is the Caroline Walker Bynum Distinguished University Professor of English at the University of Michigan. She is the editor, with Susan Juster, of *Empires of God: Religious Encounters in the Early Modern Atlantic* (2011) and author of *The Reformation of the Subject: Spenser, Milton, and the English Protestant Epic* (Cambridge, 1995), as well as six books of poetry and a volume of essays on the contemporary American lyric. Her essays on Milton, Spenser, Shakespeare, Wyatt, and Jonson appear in numerous journals and anthologies.

ANDREW HADFIELD is Professor of English at the University of Sussex and current chair of the Society for Renaissance Studies (2016–19). He is the author of *Lying in Early Modern English Culture from the Oath of Supremacy to the Oath of Allegiance* (2017), *Edmund Spenser: A Life* (2012), and *Shakespeare and Republicanism* (Cambridge, 2008), and editor of *The Oxford Handbook of Early Modern Prose* (2013). He is editing the works of Thomas Nashe with Jennifer Richards, Joseph Black, and Cathy Shrank.

MARGARET HEALY is Professor of Literature and Culture in the School of English at the University of Sussex. She is particularly interested in the cultural history of the body and the interfaces between literature, medicine, and science. Healy is the author of *Shakespeare, Alchemy and the Creative Imagination: The Sonnets and A Lover's Complaint* (Cambridge, 2011) and *Fictions of Disease in Early Modern England: Bodies, Plague and Politics* (2001). She is coeditor of a special issue of *Textual Practice* on "Prosthesis in Medieval and Early Modern Culture" (2016), *The Intellectual Culture of the British Country House 1500–1700* (2015), and *Renaissance Transformations: The Making of English Writing 1500–1650* (2009).

SARAH HOWE is a Leverhulme Early Career Fellow at University College London. She has formerly held fellowships at Gonville and Caius College, Cambridge, and the Radcliffe Institute, Harvard University. She is completing a monograph called *The Mind's Eye in Renaissance English Literature*, while working on a new project about early modern illustrated books.

KIMBERLY JOHNSON is Professor of English at Brigham Young University, where she teaches Renaissance literature and creative writing. She is the author of *Made Flesh: Sacrament and Poetics in Post-Reformation England* (2014) and coeditor, with Jay Hopler, of *Before the Door of God: An Anthology of Devotional Poetry* (2013). Her most recent collection of poetry is *Uncommon Prayer* (2014).

GREGORY KNEIDEL is Associate Professor of English at the University of Connecticut. He is the author of *Rethinking the Turn to Religion in Early Modern English Literature: The Poetics of all Believers* (2008) and *John Donne and Early Modern Legal Culture: The End of Equity in the Satyres* (2015). He is also Associate General Editor of *The Variorum Edition of the Poetry of John Donne*.

DAVID LANDRETH is Associate Professor of English at the University of California, Berkeley. He is the author of *The Face of Mammon: The*

Matter of Money in English Renaissance Literature (2012), and of several articles on the literature and culture of early modern England.

JAMES LONGENBACH is the Joseph Gilmore Professor of English at the University of Rochester. His most recent critical works are *The Resistance to Poetry* (2004), *The Virtues of Poetry* (2013), and *How Poems Get Made* (2018); his most recent volumes of poems are *The Iron Key* (2011) and *Earthling* (2017).

DAVID MARNO is Associate Professor of English at the University of California, Berkeley, where he teaches early modern poetry and drama. He is author of *Death Be Not Proud: The Art of Holy Attention* (2016), a study of Donne's *Holy Sonnets* as exercises of attentiveness. He is currently working on a book project, co-authored with Niklaus Largier, on prayer and its literary afterlives.

MOLLY MURRAY is Associate Professor of English at Columbia University. She is the author of *The Poetics of Conversion in Early Modern English Literature* (Cambridge, 2009), and has published essays on early modern literature and culture in *SEL, Huntington Library Quarterly, Renaissance and Reformation*, and numerous edited collections. She is currently completing a monograph on prison writing from More to Milton.

NICHOLAS D. NACE is Assistant Professor of Rhetoric at Hampden-Sydney College in Virginia. He is the editor, with Travis Williams and the late Russ McDonald, of *Shakespeare Up Close* (2012) and, with Charles Altieri, of *The Fate of Difficulty in the Poetry of Our Time* (2017). Though he has written elsewhere on Shakespeare, Herbert, and Milton, his specialty is eighteenth-century literature. He is currently finishing the *Broadview Anthology of Satire* and continuing work on a cultural history of the eighteenth-century novel *Fanny Hill*.

STEPHEN PENDER is Professor of English at the University of Windsor, Canada. With Nancy S. Struever, he has edited *Rhetoric and Medicine in Early Modern Europe* (2012). He has published essays on the history of rhetoric, the history of medicine, and early modern intellect history in *Rhetorica, Early Science and Medicine, The Seventeenth Century, Philosophy & Rhetoric*, and *Intellectual History Review*. He is currently completing a monograph on the passions in early modern medicine, rhetoric, and moral philosophy.

KATHERINE RUNDELL is a Fellow of All Souls College, Oxford, where she teaches Shakespeare. She is the author of six novels for children and a

play about Hector Hugh Munro. She has published articles, largely on
Early Modern literature though also about night-climbing and tightrope
walking, *in Essays in Criticism, The London Review of Books, The New
York Review of Books*, and *The New York Times*.

MELISSA E. SANCHEZ is Associate Professor of English and Core Faculty
of Gender, Sexuality, and Women's Studies at the University of
Pennsylvania. She is the author of *Erotic Subjects: The Sexuality of
Politics in Early Modern English Literature* (2011). She is also the coeditor
of three volumes of essays: *Spenser and "The Human"* (special volume
of *Spenser Studies*, 2015); *Desiring History and Historicizing
Desire* (special issue of *JEMCS*, 2016); and *Rethinking Feminism in
Early Modern Studies: Gender, Race, and Sexuality* (2016).

MICHAEL SCHOENFELDT is the John Knott Professor of English at the
University of Michigan. He is the author of *Prayer and Power: George
Herbert and Renaissance Courtship* (1991), *Bodies and Selves in Early
Modern England* (Cambridge, 1999), and *The Cambridge Introduction
to Shakespeare's Poetry* (2010); and editor of the *Blackwell Companion to
Shakespeare's Sonnets* (2006). He is currently writing a book entitled
Reading Seventeenth-Century Poetry, and researching pain and pleasure
in early modern England.

NANCY SELLECK is Associate Professor of English at the University of
Massachusetts Lowell. She is the author of *The Interpersonal Idiom in
Shakespeare, Donne, and Early Modern Culture* (2008), and is currently
completing a study of the history of soliloquy and the changing relationship of stage and audience in early modern drama.

ANITA GILMAN SHERMAN is an Associate Professor of Literature at
American University in Washington DC. She is the author of
Skepticism and Memory in Shakespeare and Donne (2007) and has pub-
lished essays in journals and edited collections. She is completing a
project tentatively titled *Reimagining Skepticism in Early Modern
English Literature: Problems and Pleasures*.

RICHARD STRIER, Frank L. Sulzberger Distinguished Service Professor
emeritus at the University of Chicago, is the author of *The Unrepentant
Renaissance from Petrarch to Shakespeare to Milton* (2011) – winner of
the Robert Penn Warren-Cleanth Brooks Award for Literary
Criticism – *Resistant Structures: Particularity, Radicalism, and
Renaissance Texts* (1995), and *Love Known: Theology and Experience in*

George Herbert's Poetry (1983). He has coedited a number of interdisciplinary collections, including *Shakespeare and the Law: A Conversation Among Disciplines and Professions* (2013). He has published essays on Shakespeare, Donne, Luther, Montaigne, and Milton, on formalism and historicism, and on twentieth-century poetry and critical theory.

GORDON TESKEY, Professor of English at Harvard University, is author of *Allegory and Violence* (1996), *Delirious Milton* (2006; James Holly Hanford Award), and *The Poetry of John Milton* (2015; James Holly Hanford Award; Christian Gauss Award). He is editor of the Norton Edition of Milton's *Paradise Lost* (2005), which is to appear in a second edition in 2018.

CHRISTOPHER TILMOUTH is a University Senior Lecturer in the Faculty of English, University of Cambridge. He is the author of *Passion's Triumph over Reason: A History of the Moral Imagination from Spenser to Rochester* (2007) and of assorted essays on Shakespeare, Burton, Milton, Rochester, Pope, and Akenside, as well as of studies of British responses to Montaigne and Descartes. He is currently working on a book on eighteenth-century literature and twentieth-/twenty-first-century moral philosophy.

DOUGLAS TREVOR is Professor of English at the University of Michigan and Director of the Helen Zell Writers' Program. He is the author of *The Poetics of Melancholy in Early Modern England* (Cambridge, 2004), the short story collection *A Thin Tear in the Fabric of Space* (2005), and the novel *Girls I Know* (2013). He has published widely on writers ranging from Thomas More to Milton, and is coeditor, with Carla Mazzio, of *Historicism, Psychoanalysis, and Early Modern Culture* (2000). He is presently completing a study of charity in medieval and early modern culture.

ANDREW WALLACE is Associate Professor of English at Carleton University. He is the author of *Virgil's Schoolboys: The Poetics of Pedagogy in Renaissance England* (2010) and coeditor of *Taking Exception to the Law: Materializing Injustice in Early Modern English Literature* (2015). He is currently completing a book on the afterlife of Roman Britain.

Acknowledgments

I would like to begin by thanking Sarah Stanton, who first approached me about taking on this immense project. I think I have forgiven her, and know I will miss working with her. Her successor, Emily Hockley, has repeatedly demonstrated the unfaltering encouragement that bolstered the last stages of the book.

My brilliant colleagues and students at the University of Michigan have been a continual source of support, challenge, and inspiration. I would like to thank in particular Leila Watkins, Andrew Bozio, Kyle Grady, Cordelia Zukerman, Cassie Miura, Angela Heetderks, Amrita Dhar, Steven Mullaney, David Porter, Valerie Traub, Linda Gregerson, and Douglas Trevor. I am pleased to say that I was able to twist the arms of the latter two colleagues to contribute to the collection. Kentston Bauman, a former student, proved a patient and meticulous research assistant throughout the long process of this collection. He also produced a wonderful timeline for the volume. I, and every reader of this volume, should be grateful for his efforts.

The members of the John Donne Society, together with the larger international community of those who read and value Donne, have done so much to foster our knowledge of this estimable writer.

Some of the work for this volume was completed while I was a Visiting Fellow at Trinity College, Cambridge, and I want to thank that remarkable institution for its unparalleled hospitality. I would like to thank in particular Adrian Poole, Joe Moshenska, David Hillman, Katrin Ettenhuber, and David Colclough, who made my time there the occasion of considerable learning as well as great pleasure. Leslie Atzmon has been a model of tenacity and a welcome resource of companionship and commiseration as we both pushed large scholarly projects towards the finish line.

I am grateful to Richard Strier, who applied his appropriately astringent commentary (as he has done for me so many times) to a particularly bloated version of the Introduction.

My thanks, finally, go to all the contributors, who invariably brought such fresh insights to Donne studies, and showed great patience as life interrupted the production of this volume. I am so glad it is "done."

Chronology

Kentston Bauman

1534	Henry VIII completes his break with Rome; Parliament's Act of Supremacy establishes Henry as head of the Protestant Church of England.
1535	Thomas More, Donne's maternal relative, executed for refusing to acknowledge Henry VIII as the Supreme Head of the Anglican Church; the Coverdale Bible published, the first complete Modern English translation of the Bible.
1539	The Great Bible published, the first authorized edition of the Bible in English; Andreas Vesalius publishes *De Humani Corporis Fabrica*, his groundbreaking human anatomy based on dissection; Copernicus publishes *De Revolutionibus Orbium Coelestium*, which argues for a heliocentric, rather than a geocentric, universe.
1547	Henry VIII dies; Edward VI, age nine, becomes king and institutes more radical Protestant reformations.
1549	Book of Common Prayer introduced.
1553	Edward VI dies; Mary I becomes queen and marries the Catholic Prince Philip of Spain (later Philip II of Spain); the Spanish Michael Servetus publishes *Christianismi Restitutio*, the first published description of pulmonary circulation.
1554	Mary I returns the English church to Roman Catholic jurisdiction; Heresy Acts revived, leading to the Marian persecutions of Protestant reformers; many Protestants choose exile to the European continent.
1558	Mary I dies; Elizabeth I becomes queen.
1559	The Act of Uniformity and the Act of Supremacy re-establish the Protestant Church of England.
1560	The Geneva Bible published, the primary Bible used by Donne and Shakespeare.

1562	Thomas Norton and Thomas Sackville's *The Tragedy of Gorboduc* performed, the first English play in blank verse.
1563	John Foxe publishes *Acts and Monuments* (*Foxe's Book of Martyrs*).
1564	William Shakespeare born in Stratford to John and Mary Arden Shakespeare.
1566	Donne's maternal uncle Ellis Heywood accepted into the Society of Jesus in Bavaria, becoming a Jesuit priest.
1567	Mary Queen of Scots imprisoned on suspicion of murdering her husband, Lord Darnley; her infant son is crowned James VI of Scotland; John Brayne builds the Red Lion, England's first professional theater, in Whitechapel.
1568	The Bishops' Bible published; the 1602 edition served as the base text for the Authorized Bible of 1611.
1569	The German-Flemish cartographer Gerardus Mercator publishes a world map which represents sailing courses of constant bearing as straight lines, a cartographic innovation still employed today.
1570	The Flemish cartographer Abraham Ortelius publishes his *Theatrum Orbis Terrarum*, the first modern atlas.
1571	The Thirty-Nine Articles, which defined the doctrine of the Church of England in relation to Calvinist and Roman Catholic practices, finalized.
1572	Donne born in Bread Street, London, to John, warden of the Ironmongers' Company, and Elizabeth Donne; the third of six known children; Ben Jonson born.
1573	The Danish astronomer Tycho Brahe publishes *De Nova Stella*, his observations of a supernova, a "new star" that suddenly appeared on November 11, 1572.
1576	Donne's father dies; mother marries Dr. John Syminges; James Burbage constructs the Theatre, London's first permanent amphitheater, in the suburb of Shoreditch.
1577	Donne's sister Elizabeth likely dies; the first edition of Ralph Holinshed's *The Chronicles of England, Scotland, and Ireland* published.
1577–80	Sir Francis Drake circumnavigates the globe, the second such endeavor (behind the 1519–22 Magellan-Elcano voyage).

1580	Robert Persons and Edmund Campion establish a Jesuit mission in England in the hopes of reconverting the nation to Catholicism.
1581	Donne's maternal uncle, the Jesuit priest Jasper Heywood, assumes control of the Jesuit mission when Campion is executed and Persons exiled to the continent; Donne's sisters Mary and Katherine die.
1583	Sir Humphrey Gilbert lays claim to Newfoundland.
1584	Donne matriculates at Hart Hall, Oxford University, with his younger brother Henry; Anne More born, May 27; Jasper Heywood indicted for treason for being a Catholic priest; Donne and his mother likely visit his uncle in the Tower of London in December.
1585	Donne possibly travels abroad with Henry Stanley, Earl of Derby; his sister Anne marries Avery Copley (who dies in 1591); Jasper Heywood exiled to the continent, eventually dying in Naples in 1598; Sir Walter Ralegh sends John White to found England's first New World colony at Roanoke Island, in modern North Carolina.
1586	Sir Philip Sidney, age 31, dies of a gunshot wound suffered in the Battle of Zutphen against the Spanish.
1587	Mary Queen of Scots executed for plotting to assassinate Elizabeth I; Sir Francis Drake raids the ports of Cádiz and Corunna, destroying 37 Spanish ships; Philip Henslowe builds The Rose theater at Bankside; Thomas Kyd's *The Spanish Tragedy* most likely first performed; the two parts of Christopher Marlowe's *Tamburlaine the Great* first performed.
1587–90	Donne's movements uncertain, possibly at Cambridge University, or, more likely, traveling abroad.
1588	Dr. John Syminges, Donne's stepfather, dies; the Catholic Philip II of Spain attempts to invade England and overthrow the Protestant Elizabeth I; the English defeat the Spanish Armada.
1590	James VI marries Anne of Denmark; Sir Philip Sidney's *Arcadia* published; Edmund Spenser's *The Faerie Queene*, Books I–III published.
1590–91	Donne's mother marries Richard Rainsford.

1591	Donne likely attends Thavie's Inn, an Inn of Chancery designed to prepare students for law school; Sir Philip Sidney's *Astrophel and Stella* published.
1591–92	Shakespeare's first plays performed, including *Two Gentlemen of Verona* and *2* and *3 Henry VI*.
1592	Donne studies law at Lincoln's Inn, one of London's Inns of Court, until 1595 or 1596; while there, Donne likely composes and circulates some verse letters, the first two satires, most of the elegies, and some of the *Songs and Sonnets*; Philip Henslowe begins his diary, which keeps detailed records of his theatrical business transactions; continued until 1604; Christopher Marlowe's *Doctor Faustus* first performed.
1592–94	London's theaters frequently closed during the summers because of the plague.
1593	Donne serves as Master of the Revels at Lincoln's Inn; receives part of his inheritance in June; Donne's brother Henry is caught harboring William Harrington, a Catholic priest, in his rooms at Thavie's Inn; Henry imprisoned at Newgate under horrific conditions where he dies from the plague a month later; the Anglo-Irish Nine Years' War, the largest conflict fought by England in the Elizabethan era, breaks out; George Herbert born in Wales.
1594	Donne receives an additional portion of his and Henry's inheritance; the Catholic priest William Harrington hanged, drawn, and quartered; James VI's first son, Henry, born.
1595	Sir Walter Ralegh, looking for the golden city of El Dorado, explores Guiana in northern South America; Hugh O'Neill, Earl of Tyrone, joins the Irish rebels against the English.
1596	Donne joins the successful military campaign of the Queen's favorite, Robert Devereux, Earl of Essex, to Cádiz; the city sacked and burned, and the Spanish fleet destroyed; James VI's daughter, Elizabeth, born; James Burbage opens the Blackfriars indoor theater; Edmund Spenser's second edition of *The Faerie Queene*, now including Books IV–VI, published.
1597	Donne joins the unsuccessful military campaign of the Earl of Essex and Sir Walter Ralegh to the Azores Islands; the

English suffer heavy losses, and fail to destroy the Spanish fleet or capture any treasure ships; Donne writes "The Storm" and "The Calm" about this expedition; upon returning, Donne becomes secretary to Sir Thomas Egerton, Lord Keeper of the Great Seal, at York House in the Strand.

1598   King Henry IV of France signs the Edict of Nantes, which ends France's religious wars and provides toleration for Protestants.

1599   The Earl of Essex leads a force of 16,000 troops to Ireland; after failing to crush Hugh O'Neill's rebellion and concluding an unfavorable truce, Essex returns to England without the Queen's permission and is confined to house arrest for desertion of duty; Donne's friend, Sir Thomas Egerton the younger, accompanied Essex on this military campaign, dying from wounds suffered in a skirmish; Donne participates in funeral procession by bearing Egerton's sword; John Whitgift, Archbishop of Canterbury, and Richard Bancroft, Bishop of London, sign an order banning satires and other offensive books; some copies rounded up and burned, including works by Thomas Nashe, John Marston, and John Davies; The Theatre closes after the Lord Chamberlain's Men fail to secure a new lease; the Globe Theatre, partially built with timber from The Theatre, opens at Bankside.

1600   Elizabeth I charters the East India Company; James VI's second son, Charles, born; Edward Alleyn and Philip Henslowe construct the Fortune Theater for the Lord Admiral's Men; William Gilbert publishes *De Magnete, Magneticisque Corporibus, et de Magno Magnete Tellure*, which argues that the earth itself is magnetic.

1600–01 Shakespeare's *Hamlet* and *Twelfth Night* likely first performed.

1601   Donne serves as a Member of Parliament for Brackley, Northampton, in the autumn, the seat in the gift from Egerton; composes *Metempsychosis*, and, most likely, some of his prose *Paradoxes*; clandestinely marries Anne More, ward and niece to his employer Egerton, in December; Deprived of office, influence, and revenue streams, the Earl of Essex leads a rebellion into London to force an audience with the Queen; the uprising fails, and Essex is convicted of treason; Essex beheaded on Tower Green, the last person to be executed at the Tower of London.

1601–03   Shakespeare's *Othello* likely first performed.

1602   Donne's father-in-law, Sir George More, incarcerates Donne in Fleet prison in February after Donne finally writes to him of the elopement; Christopher Brooke, who gave the bride away, and Samuel Brooke, who performed the ceremony, also imprisoned; Donne released after a few days to house arrest in London; his service to Egerton terminated; the Court of Audience upholds the validity of the marriage on April 27; after Sir George refuses to support the new couple, Donne and Anne move to Pyrford, Surrey, staying in a house owned by Anne's cousin Francis Wolley; the Bodleian Library at Oxford University opens with a catalogue of around two thousand books.

1603   Donne's daughter Constance born, the first of twelve children; Elizabeth I dies on March 24; James VI of Scotland, Elizabeth I's cousin, becomes king as James I; despite James I's mother's Catholicism, England remains Protestant; Sir Walter Ralegh imprisoned in the Tower of London for his involvement in the Main Plot against James I; released in 1616; Hugh O'Neill surrenders in Ireland in March, signing the Treaty of Mellifont and thus ending the Nine Years' War; John Florio's English translation of Montaigne's *Essays* published.

1603–04   Donne prepares a legal opinion for Sir Robert Cotton on Valdesius' *De Dignitate Regum Regnorumque Hispaniae*; the plague closes London's theaters from mid-1603 to mid-1604.

1604   Donne's second child, John, born; signing of the Treaty of London, which concludes the nineteen-year Anglo-Spanish war; passage across the Atlantic now much safer for England's colonizing interests.

1605   Donne travels to the continent with Sir Walter Chute, visiting Paris and possibly Venice; while abroad, Donne's third child, George, born; discovery of the Gunpowder Plot, a plan by radical Catholics to blow up Parliament and the royal family during opening ceremonies on November 5; Ben Jonson's *The Masque of Blackness* performed in the Banqueting Hall of Whitehall Palace on January 6, the

	first of many entertainment collaborations between Jonson and the stage designer Inigo Jones.
1605–06	Shakespeare's *King Lear* likely first performed.
1606	Donne returns to England in April; moves family to a cottage in Mitcham, Surrey; in the wake of the Gunpowder Plot, Parliament passes the Popish Recusants Act, which requires citizens to take a new Oath of Allegiance that denies the Pope's authority over the king; James I charters the London and Plymouth Companies (collectively known as the Virginia Company) to colonize Virginia.
1607	Donne's fourth child, Francis, born; writes Latin commendatory verses for print edition of Jonson's *Volpone*; Hugh O'Neill and Rory O'Donnell, Earl of Tyrconnell, fearing arrest, flee to the continent with their families; this marks the end of the power of Ireland's Gaelic aristocracy; the London Company establishes Jamestown, England's first permanent New World colony.
1607–11	Donne keeps lodgings in London in the Strand; fruitlessly attempts to gain civil employment, including a vacant position in Elizabeth I's household (June 1607), a secretaryship in Ireland (November 1608), and a secretaryship with the Virginia Company (February 1609).
1608	Donne's fifth child, Lucy, born; writes the controversial *Biathanatos*, his defense of suicide; John Milton born in Bread Street, London; Han Lippershey, a German-Dutch eyeglass maker, produces the first known telescope, which he fails to get a patent for.
1608–09	Donne ill during the winter with chronic neuritis; writes poem sequence *A Litany*; likely writes most of the Holy Sonnets; "The Expiration" published.
1609	Donne's sixth child, Bridget, born; James I determines to secure northern Ireland for the Crown; encourages English and Scottish Protestants to move to Ulster, onto land confiscated from its Gaelic Catholic inhabitants; *Shakespeare's Sonnets* published; the German Johannes Kepler publishes his first two laws of planetary motion, which improve upon Copernicus' heliocentric theory.
1610	Donne publishes his anti-Catholic polemic *Pseudo-Martyr*, which argues English Catholics should take the Oath of Allegiance and those that refuse should not be called

martyrs; dedicated to the Protestant James I; Donne awarded an honorary MA from Oxford University; Elizabeth Drury, daughter of Donne's patrons Sir Robert and Lady Drury, dies; Ben Jonson's *The Alchemist* first performed; Galileo publishes *Sidereus Nuncius*, the first scientific work based on observations of stars and planets made through a telescope.

1611   Donne's seventh child, Mary, born; publishes, anonymously, the anti-Catholic polemic *Ignatius His Conclave* in both Latin and English; publishes, anonymously, the elegies *The First Anniversary* and "A Funeral Elegy," both written for Elizabeth Drury; travels to France with the Drurys, lodging in Amiens; Anne and the children stay with her younger sister Frances on the Isle of Wight; Shakespeare's *The Winter's Tale* and *The Tempest* first performed; Aemelia Lanyer publishes *Salve Deus Rex Judaeorum*; the Authorized Bible (the King James Bible) published.

1611–12   English cartographer John Speed publishes *The Theatre of the Empire of Great Britaine*, a collection of 67 maps of England, Wales, Ireland, and Scotland, including the first set of individual English and Welsh county maps.

1612   Donne and the Drurys travel to Paris, where Donne falls ill, and then to Germany and the Low Countries; while abroad, Anne gives birth to a stillborn child, their eighth; Donne returns to England and moves family to London, staying in a house on Drury Lane owned by the Drurys; publishes the *First* and *Second Anniversaries* and "Break of Day"; James I's eldest son, Prince Henry, dies of typhoid fever.

1613   Donne publishes "Elegy, On the Untimely Death of the Incomparable Prince, Henry"; writes an epithalamion for the Valentine's Day marriage of Princess Elizabeth to Frederick V, Count Palatine of the Rhine; commemorates his visit to Sir Henry Goodyer at Polesworth in "Goodfriday, 1613"; offers his services to Robert Carr, Viscount Rochester (later Earl of Somerset); Donne's ninth child, Nicholas, born; dies within a year; the Globe Theatre burns down during a performance of Shakespeare's *Henry VIII*; Elizabeth Cary publishes *The Tragedy of Mariam, the Fair Queen of Jewry*.

1614   Donne unsuccessfully petitions the Earl of Somerset for the ambassadorship to Venice; serves as a Member of Parliament for Taunton, Somerset; Donne's daughter Mary (May) and son Francis (November) die; the Globe Theatre reopens after being rebuilt; Ben Jonson's *Bartholomew Fair* first performed; John Webster's *The Duchess of Malfi* first performed; John Napier publishes *Mirifici Logarithmorum Canonis Descriptio*, the first description of logarithms.

1615   Donne takes Anglican orders and is ordained deacon and priest on January 23 in St. Paul's by John King, bishop of London; appointed a Royal Chaplain; attends James I on visit to Cambridge, where he is awarded an honorary doctorate of divinity; preaches his first surviving sermon, at Greenwich on April 30; has a cipher entrusted to him for encrypting and decrypting diplomatic correspondence; Donne's tenth child, Margaret, born.

1616   Donne becomes vicar at Keyston in Huntingdon in January and Sevenoaks in Kent in July; Donne's eleventh child, Elizabeth, born; appointed as Reader in Divinity at Lincoln's Inn in October; Shakespeare dies on April 23, in Stratford; George Chapman completes his translations of *The Iliad* and *The Odyssey*, the first complete English translations, publishing them in *The Whole Works of Homer*; Ben Jonson publishes his *Works*, the first folio edition to include commercial plays.

1617   Donne preaches his first sermon at the outdoor pulpit of Paul's Cross on March 24; Anne Donne, age 33, dies on August 15, five days after giving birth to a stillborn baby, their twelfth child; Donne preaches her funeral sermon at St. Clement Danes, his parish church; writes Holy Sonnet 17 (XVII) ("Since she whom I loved"); pardoned by James I, Sir Walter Ralegh conducts a second expedition to South America in search of El Dorado; men under his command attack a Spanish outpost on the Orinoco River; Ralegh's son, Walter, fatally shot during the raid.

1618   The Defenestration of Prague ignites the Bohemian Revolt, which marks the beginning of the Thirty Years' War, a deadly conflict between Protestant and Catholic states in the Holy Roman Empire; Sir Walter Ralegh publicly executed for violating the terms of his pardon and the Treaty of London, an act to appease Spain.

1618–19 The Synod of Dort upholds Calvinism, rejecting Arminian views that challenged reformation standards.

1619 Donne becomes chaplain to James Hay, Viscount Doncaster, and travels with him to Germany, part of an embassy from James I to mediate peace between the Holy Roman Emperor Ferdinand II, a staunch Catholic, and the Bohemian Protestants; in Heidelberg Donne preaches a sermon to Frederick V and Princess Elizabeth; preaches at the Hague, where he is given a medal commemorating the Synod of Dort; writes "A Hymn to Christ, at the Author's Last Going into Germany"; the first record of Africans, as indentured servants, arriving in British North American colonies, in Jamestown; Frederick V and Princess Elizabeth elected King and Queen of Bohemia in November; Johannes Kepler publishes his third law of planetary motion.

1620 Donne returns to London with Doncaster's embassy on January 1; preaches at the wedding of Sir Francis Nethersole and Lucy Goodyer in February; Ferdinand II defeats Frederick V in the Battle of White Mountain on November 8; Frederick and Elizabeth deposed, and sent into exile; The *Mayflower* lands in Massachusetts in November; the Pilgrims explore Cape Cod before founding Plymouth Colony on the mainland in December; Francis Bacon publishes *Novum Organum Scientiarum*, which outlines a new scientific method of acquiring natural knowledge.

1621 Donne elected and installed as Dean of St. Paul's on November 22; moves from Drury Lane to the deanery of St. Paul's; resigns vicarship at Keyston; *The Anniversaries* republished; Lady Mary Wroth publishes her prose romance *The Countess of Montgomery's Urania* and sonnet sequence *Pamphilia to Amphilanthus*; Willebrord Snellius, a Dutch mathematician, discovers Snell's Law, the law of refraction of light.

1622 Donne resigns from his readership at Lincoln's Inn on February 11; appointed Rector of Blunham, Bedfordshire, in the gift of the Earl of Kent; preaches at Hanworth before Doncaster, the Earl of Northumberland, and the Duke of

Buckingham; made an honorary member of the Virginia Company (May 22) and its Council (July 3); appointed a Justice of the Peace for Kent and Bedford, and as judge in the Court of Delegates (an appointment he would regularly fill in subsequent years); James I, to thwart clerical criticism of his policies, issues his "Directions to Preachers," which severely restricts the subjects clergy could address from the pulpit; Donne preaches at Paul's Cross on September 15 in support of this action; James I, impressed with the sermon, orders it published, the first of Donne's sermons to see print; Donne preaches, on November 5, the annual Gunpowder Plot sermon at St. Paul's, which James I also looks at but does not have printed; Donne delivers a sermon before the Virginia Company on November 13 at St. Michael Cornhill, which subsequently becomes Donne's second sermon printed.

1623   Donne preaches a sermon at the consecration of the new chapel at Lincoln's Inn, which he then publishes; gravely ill during the winter; writes *Devotions upon Emergent Occasions*, a series of twenty-three meditations and prayers on sickness, health, and spirituality; arranges the marriage between his daughter Constance and Edward Alleyn, the famous Elizabethan stage actor and founder of Dulwich College, on December 3; Andrew Marvell born; The first edition of Robert Burton's *The Anatomy of Melancholy* published; members of the King's Men publish Shakespeare's plays and poems in the First Folio.

1624   Donne publishes *Devotions upon Emergent Occasions*; appointed Rector at St. Dunstan-in-the-West in March.

1625   Donne composes "A Hymn to the Saints, and to Marquesse Hamilton," one of his last poems; James I dies on March 27; his son Charles I becomes king; Donne delivers the first sermon before the new king on April 3; quarrels with his son-in-law Edward Alleyn over part of the wedding settlement, a supposedly-promised £500 loan; falls ill again and leaves London to escape the plague, staying with Sir John and Lady Danvers in Chelsea; while there writes out many of his sermons; Captain John Powell lands in Barbados and claims the uninhabited island in James I's name; returns two years later to establish a colony.

1626   Donne chosen as prolocutor (president of the lower house) for Charles I's first ecclesiastical Convocation; delivers the annual Lent sermon at court, which subsequently sees print at Charles I's suggestion; becomes governor of the Charterhouse, a London almshouse and school; Constance and Alleyn's wedding settlement revised in June; Edward Alleyn dies on November 21.

1627   Donne's daughter Lucy, age 18, dies; Donne's longtime friends Goodyer (March 18), Lady Bedford (May 31), and Lady Danvers (early June) also die; Donne preaches Lady Danvers' funeral sermon, which is soon printed; William Laud, the influential Dean of the Chapel Royal, has Charles I scrutinize Donne's April 1 sermon for criticism of Laud's ceremonial innovations; Donne cleared; preaches at the wedding of Lady Mary Egerton, daughter of the Earl of Bridgewater, and Richard Herbert, son to Lord Herbert of Cherbury.

1628   William Laud becomes Bishop of London; William Harvey publishes *De Motu Cordis*, the first detailed account of the circulation of the blood.

1629   Charles I, outraged at the passage of three resolutions condemning his financial and religious policies, dissolves Parliament on March 10, thereby instituting eleven years of "personal rule."

1629–33 John Ford's *'Tis Pity She's a Whore* likely first performed.

1630   Donne listed as a candidate for next available bishopric; daughter Constance marries Samuel Harvey in June; Donne and his mother stay with Constance at Aldborough Hatch, Essex; terminally ill, possibly with stomach cancer, writes his will on December 13.

1631   Donne's mother dies in January; Donne returns to London and, on February 25, preaches his last sermon, *Deaths Duell*, before the king's court at Whitehall; poses in his shroud for his monument by Nicholas Stone, which is the only sculpture at St. Paul's to survive, intact, the Great Fire of 1666; Donne dies, age 59, at the deanery on March 31; buried in St. Paul's on April 3; survived by six of his twelve children.

1632   Donne's *Deaths Duell* published; the Puritan William Prynne publishes *Histriomastix*, a critique of professional theater and actors.

1633   *Poems by J.D.*, Donne's first edition of his poetry, published;
            Donne's *Juvenalia: Or Certain Paradoxes and Problems* pub-
            lished; both of these are pirated printings not authorized by
            the Donne estate; William Laud appointed Archbishop of
            Canterbury; vigorously attempts to impose uniformity on
            the Church of England through service reforms and perse-
            cution of Puritans and other religious dissidents; George
            Herbert dies; his collected English poetry published as *The
            Temple*.

1635   The second edition of Donne's *Poems* published, still
            unauthorized, which includes an engraving of Donne, age
            18, by William Marshall.

1637   John Donne the Younger, Donne's eldest son and his lit-
            erary executor, petitions Archbishop William Laud to help
            him gain control of his father's literary property; the French
            philosopher René Descartes publishes *Discourse on the
            Method*.

1639–40   The Bishops' Wars, a series of political and military con-
            flicts that serve as a prelude to the Civil War, take place
            between England and Scotland over the type of govern-
            ance of the Church of Scotland; Charles I and William
            Laud favor the episcopacy (a hierarchical rule with
            bishops and archbishops, who are often seen as ministers
            of the Crown), while much of Scotland favor a
            Presbyterian system (each local church is governed by an
            assembly of elected elders).

1640   Donne's *LXXX Sermons* published by his son, the first of
            three folio volumes containing all one hundred and sixty
            surviving sermons; includes the first printing of Izaak
            Walton's "The Life of Dr. John Donne," the first biogra-
            phy of an English poet; Parliament meets for the first time
            in eleven years for three weeks in the spring, the so-called
            Short Parliament; the Long Parliament, which lasts until
            1660, begins in the fall; Parliament impeaches William
            Laud, who is arrested and accused of being an anti-
            Calvinist Arminian who harbors secret Catholic
            sympathies.

1641   Rebellion breaks out in Ireland in October; several thousand
            English and Scottish Protestant settlers killed; Milton pub-
            lishes his pamphlet *Of Reformation Touching Church*

Discipline in England, his first polemic arguing against the episcopacy.

1642   The English Civil War breaks out when Charles I raises his standard on Castle Hill at Nottingham on August 22, summoning his loyal subjects to join him against his enemies in Parliament; Parliament orders the closure of London's public theaters in September; Isaac Newton born.

1643   On September 15 Charles I signs a ceasefire with Catholic insurgents in Ireland; on September 25 the Parliamentarians enter into an alliance with the Scots; the Italian physicist and mathematician Evangelista Torricelli invents the mercury barometer; the torr, a unit of measurement of pressure, named after him.

1644   Donne's son enters the second volume of his father's sermons at Stationers' Hall, but holds off on publication for fear of persecution from Parliamentarian forces.

1645   William Laud executed for high treason and trying to return England to Rome; Parliament establishes the "New Model Army" to defeat the Royalists, led by Sir Thomas Fairfax and Oliver Cromwell; Milton publishes his *Poems*.

1646   Donne's *Biathanatos* published for the first time, by his son; Charles I surrenders to the Scots, who eventually hand him over to the Parliamentarians; Parliament abolishes the episcopacy.

1647   Beaumont and Fletcher's collected plays published in two folios.

1648   Colonel Thomas Pride purges the Long Parliament on December 6 of all members opposed to the New Model Army's plans to try and execute Charles I; remaining members called the Rump Parliament.

1649   Donne's *Fifty Sermons* published by his son; Charles I executed for high treason, January 30; Parliament abolishes the monarchy and establishes a republic, the Commonwealth of England.

1650   Donne's son finally secures the rights to his father's *Poems*, publishing an edition.

1651   Donne's *Letters to Severall Persons of Honour* and *Essays in Divinity* published by his son; Thomas Hobbes publishes *Leviathan*, his seminal work on the structure of society and legitimate government.

1652   Donne's *Paradoxes, Problems, Essays, Characters* published by his son.

1653   Oliver Cromwell appoints himself as Lord Protector, with powers akin to a monarch.

1658   Oliver Cromwell dies on September 3; his son, Richard, succeeds him as Lord Protector.

1659   Richard Cromwell is overthrown and resigns his position as Lord Protector on May 25.

1660   Donne's *XXVI Sermons* published by his son; Restoration of the monarchy; Charles II crowned king; London's public theaters reopen.

1661   John Donne the Younger dies at his home in Covent Garden; bequeaths his father's manuscripts to Izaak Walton.

1662   Parliament passes the Act of Uniformity, which re-establishes the episcopal Church of England; Margaret Cavendish prints *Plays*, her first collection of dramatic works; Robert Boyle discovers Boyle's Law of Ideal Gas, which states that, under controlled conditions, the pressure of a gas is inversely proportional to the volume occupied by it.

1665   England invades Jamaica and seizes it from Spain, who had ruled it since 1509.

1665   From March to December, the Great Plague of London kills more than 100,000 people, a quarter of the city's inhabitants; Robert Hooke, observing a cork slice under a primitive compound microscope, discovers a honeycomb-like structure; coins the term "cell" to describe these compartments.

1666   The Great Fire of London destroys nearly two-thirds of the city.

1667   The first edition of Milton's *Paradise Lost* published.

1669   Donne's *Poems* published, which now include previously omitted elegies; Francesco Redi, an Italian biologist, becomes the first scientist to challenge the theory of spontaneous generation, demonstrating that maggots come from fly eggs; the Danish scientist Nicolas Steno publishes his *Dissertationis Prodromus*, which outlines the four defining principles of stratigraphy, the science of studying rock layers.

Abbreviations

Unless otherwise indicated, all citations and line numbers for Donne's poetry, as well as the elegies written for him after his death, are taken from Bell, *Collected*.

Bald, *Life*	R. C. Bald, *John Donne: A Life* (New York: Oxford University Press, 1970).
Bell, *Collected*	*John Donne: Collected Poetry*, ed. Ilona Bell (London: Penguin, 2012).
Carey, *Mind*	John Carey, *John Donne: Life, Mind and Art* (Oxford University Press, 1981).
Carew, "Elegy"	Thomas Carew, "An Elegy upon the Death of the Dean of Paul's, Dr John Donne."
CCJD	*The Cambridge Companion to John Donne*, ed. Achsah Guibbory (Cambridge University Press, 2006).
Critical Heritage	*John Donne: The Critical Heritage*, ed. A. J. Smith (London: Routledge and Kegan Paul, 1975).
"Goodfriday, 1613"	Donne, "Goodfriday, 1613. Riding Westward."
Holy Sonnet 2	Donne, Holy Sonnet 2 (IV) ("O my black soul")
Holy Sonnet 3	Donne, Holy Sonnet 3 (VI) ("This is my play's last scene")
Holy Sonnet 4	Donne, Holy Sonnet 4 (VII) ("At the round earth's imagined corners")
Holy Sonnet 10	Donne, Holy Sonnet 10 (XIV) ("Batter my heart")
Holy Sonnet 13	Donne, Holy Sonnet 13 (I) ("Thou hast made me")
Holy Sonnet 18	Donne, Holy Sonnet 18 (XVIII) ("Show me, dear Christ")
Holy Sonnet 19	Donne, Holy Sonnet 19 (XIX) ("O, to vex me")

JDJ	*John Donne Journal*
Letters	John Donne, *Letters to Severall Persons of Honour*, ed. Charles Edmund Merrill (New York: Sturgis & Walton Company, 1910).
Marotti, *Coterie*	Arthur F. Marotti, *John Donne, Coterie Poet* (Madison, WI: University of Wisconsin Press, 1986).
Marotti, *Manuscript*	Arthur F. Marotti, *Manuscript, Print, and the English Renaissance Lyric* (Ithaca, NY: Cornell University Press, 1995).
OHJD	*The Oxford Handbook of John Donne*, ed. Jeanne Shami, Dennis Flynn, and M. Thomas Hester (Oxford, 2011).
Pseudo-Martyr	Donne, *Pseudo-Martyr*, ed. Anthony Raspa (Montreal: McGill-Queen's University Press, 1993).
Sermons	John Donne, *The Sermons of John Donne*, ed. George R. Potter and Evelyn M. Simpson, 10 vols. (Berkeley, CA: University of California Press, 1953–62).
Soliciting	*Soliciting Interpretation: Literary Theory and Seventeenth-Century English Poetry*, eds. Elizabeth Harvey and Katharine Eisaman Maus (University of Chicago Press, 1990).
Walton, *Lives*	Izaak Walton, *The Lives of John Donne, Sir Henry Wotton, Richard Hooker, George Herbert & Robert Sanderson* (Oxford University Press, 1927; reprint 1936).

Introduction

Michael Schoenfeldt

John Donne produced some of the finest writing in any language about the pleasures and mysteries of love and religion. His restless imagination and voracious intellect invested his poetry and prose with an unprecedented dramatic energy and metaphoric intensity. His work is formally inventive, aggressively pushing against the very generic boundaries it enters. Even commonplace sentiments are rendered breathtakingly vivid and witty when filtered through Donne's singular intelligence.

Yet wit and intelligence sometimes come at a cost. Donne can be difficult, deliberately difficult. Even his friends and contemporaries sometimes had trouble understanding his works. Ben Jonson, the Renaissance dramatist and poet, thought "That Donne himself, for not being understood, would perish."[1] And as Nicholas Nace demonstrates in his accomplished essay in this volume, Jonson was nearly a prophet: Donne in fact almost vanishes from the eighteenth-century literary landscape. Whereas the reputation of William Shakespeare, Donne's slightly older contemporary, entails a relatively continuous rise through the centuries, Donne's reputation has risen and fallen violently over time. But as James Longenbach and Linda Gregerson, both practicing poets and critics, demonstrate in the last two essays in the collection, it is impossible to imagine poetry of the last 200 years without the influence and example of Donne. Donne's seesaw reputation over the centuries offers a salutary lesson in the shifting values of literary taste.

Donne was most decidedly a writer of his age, and he is most emphatically a writer for ours. This collection is designed to ensure the lasting defeat of Jonson's portentous prophecy, by making significant elements of Donne's remarkable achievement available to the twenty-first century reader. While Donne's work sometimes requires the help of an expert in the frequently arcane forms of knowledge that Donne relishes, his complexity is never gratuitous. Rather, it is a consequence of his uncompromising effort to honor the full complexity of lived experience. Donne possesses a remarkable eye for tacit connections among apparently unrelated phenomena, and is fascinated by the way that mundane existence and arcane knowledge can be made to gloss each other. Perhaps only Donne would have dared – in a single stanza of a single poem – to compare the parting of lovers to the legs of a compass, separated but still conjoined, and found emotional comfort in that profoundly cerebral comparison ("A Valediction Forbidding Mourning").

Indeed, part of the immense pleasure of reading Donne is coming to apprehend the full impact of his startling metaphors and dense syntax. Donne repeatedly challenges his readers to sustain a level of knowledge and attention few can consistently muster. Even scholars occasionally require assistance in discerning Donne's deeply learned utterances. One of our finest close readers, William Empson, interrupts a discussion of the extravagant textures of Donne's poetry to offer an uncharacteristic apology for the need to give historical context in order to understand the work's aesthetic accomplishment: "I feel I should apologize for so much 'background material,' but with Donne it seems to be mainly doubt about the background which makes a critic reject the arguments from the text of the poems."[2] As Empson's explanation makes clear, Donne's works frequently require knowledge of "background material" in order to comprehend the complex architecture of the works. The essays of this volume were specifically solicited from scholars who possess the necessary expertise in the various genres and modes of knowledge that Donne's work participates in. But none of the essays supplies merely inert background material; rather together they demonstrate boldly and convincingly the ways that scholarly knowledge of Donne and his culture can be mobilized to enhance, and even electrify, our reading of his works. The goal of this collection is to offer fresh interpretations of this immense body of work by supplying the background and contextual information required to appreciate his works fully. The context is explicitly designed not to bury, but rather to uncover, the elaborate, highly referential text of Donne's works. Written in a wide range of genres, for disparate occasions, and repeatedly challenging the interpretive skill of the reader, Donne's works demand an almost unique combination of contextual knowledge and new critical techniques. The reader must continually move outside a poem in order to be able to enter it fully. The poems may be well-wrought urns, but they are urns that contain rather than exclude the essence of the world around them.[3]

This collection, then, aspires to represent the remarkable range of Donne's writings by exploring the various contexts in which he lived and worked. Through a series of concise, pointed essays from an international group of outstanding scholars and critics, Donne's works, and his world, are allowed to come alive. I want Donne's twenty-first-century readers to see that when they are given enough information to understand the particular situation of the writer, the tone of the speaker, the arcane knowledge exploited by Donne, and the formal choices made by the author, even the most difficult texts can yield lasting pleasures. It is hoped that the volume will prove useful to general readers, students, scholars, and teachers in their efforts to understand, appreciate, and enjoy Donne's works. The volume is premised on the idea that Donne's deep originality, what his contemporary Thomas Carew termed his "fresh invention" (28),[4] can be best appreciated amid the various contexts in which his invention flourished.

For all of its range, and the erudition of its numerous contributors, this volume is not exhaustive – no single collection could be for such a sumptuous and substantial body of work. Donne wrote in an extraordinarily wide range of genres and subgenres, from cynical paradoxes that flirt with atheism, materialism, and antifeminism to sermons that stir the devotional soul. He composed caustic satires, poetry of fulsome praise, racy elegies, sincere love poems, devotional meditations, and touching letters of remarkable warmth, wit, and intimacy. This collection aspires to be almost as intellectually promiscuous as Donne himself. It says something about Donne's mind that it requires the expertise of thirty-one scholars to begin to approach the range of his learning and interests. The collection contains essays on Donne's biography and self-representation (Cheney, Howe, Selleck), his chosen media (Brown, Rundell, Trevor, Johnson, Bell), his various genres (Sanchez, Strier, Daybell, Marno, Conti, Ferrell, Hadfield), his education (Ettenhuber, Wallace), his attitude to the natural world (Bushnell), his ideas about emotion and sensation (Tilmouth, Campana), the cultural practices that fascinated him (Landreth, Bates), the institutions that shaped him (Kneidel, Murray), and the ideas that absorbed him (Teskey, Pender, Healy, Sherman). Of course, there is rich overlap among these categories, but this list bestows some sense of the various threads of continuity that unite these scholarly engagements.

The time is ripe for a full and multifaceted reappraisal of John Donne. A major research tool, the *Donne Variorum*, is currently being produced, with several volumes already out. As several of the essays in this collection discuss (see Brown and Rundell), Donne rarely published in print, and when he did, he tended to regret it later. But his works were popular, and circulated widely in manuscript, with variants introduced almost every time the work was copied. He is perhaps best known today for a single line from one of his *Devotions upon Emergent Occasions* – "No man is an Island, entire of itself" – but his pungent and pithy phrasing has been the source of many book titles (Ernest Hemingway's *For Whom the Bell Tolls* and John Gunther's *Death Be Not Proud* among the most famous). While his poems and devotions are generally admired, Donne deserves an even wider audience. Donne's Holy Sonnets were recently at the center of the Pulitzer Prize-winning play *W;t* by Margaret Edson, which mentions prominently the work of one of our contributors (Strier). The new *OHJD* provides a delightful companion for readers of Donne. Donne's fascinating life has been the subject of a biography by John Stubbs, *John Donne: The Reformed Soul* (Norton, 2008). There is a very useful new edition of Donne's poetry from Longman, edited by Robin Robbins (2008, rev. 2010), and another from Penguin (2012), edited by Ilona Bell (another contributor to this volume), which is used whenever relevant in this collection. Of crucial importance to T. S. Eliot and the other modernists, Donne's work remains indispensable to any account of English poetry. His sermons and devotions are some of the richest religious utterances in any language, and continue to permeate the devotional discourse of various religious persuasions.

This volume is designed to help today's readers appreciate the infinite riches of John Donne's remarkable works. The multifaceted format of this volume is tailor-made for exploring the many sides of Donne. At times imperious, at others profoundly vulnerable, Donne's voice is always fresh and compelling; his works speak to us forcefully across the centuries with a power that moves both brain and heart, if we only have ears to hear.

Notes

1. Ben Jonson, *Conversations of Ben Jonson with William Drummond*, ed. Philip Sidney (London: Gay and Bird, 1906), 25.
2. William Empson, "Donne the Space Man," in *Essays on Renaissance Literature*, ed. John Haffenden, 2 vols. (Cambridge University Press, 1993), 1: 114.
3. I refer here to that famous work of New Criticism, Cleanth Brooks, *The Well-Wrought Urn: Studies in the Structure of Poetry* (New York: Harcourt Brace, 1947), which discusses, and takes its title from, Donne's "The Canonization."
4. Carew, "Elegy."

CHAPTER I

Donne's Literary Career

Patrick Cheney

This opening chapter aims to situate Donne in the context of Western ideas of a literary career. In doing so, it relies on recent research to chart fundamentally new territory in Donne criticism, and in the process it challenges the received wisdom about this enigmatic early modern writer. That wisdom takes the 1983 cue of Richard Helgerson to classify Donne as an "amateur" who writes poetry primarily as a "pastime," who eschews "print" publication for "manuscript" circulation, and who finally "repents" of his "youthful" error to serve the state as a preacher in the Church of England.[1] As a result of this narrative, many today view Donne as either a "coterie poet" who rejects the humanist goal of using literature to perform national leadership in service of a Christian eternity, or as a "professional" who turns from poetry to preaching.[2] According to this narrative, Donne differs from the "laureate" authors of his generation, Edmund Spenser, Samuel Daniel, Michael Drayton, George Chapman, and his friend Ben Jonson, who rely on the printing press to write literature throughout their adult lives for serious national and religious ends. In the words of John Carey, "Donne is singular among English poets in that he never refers to his poetry except disparagingly ... [T]he idea of having poetry printed struck him as totally repellent." Rather than having a literary career, Donne "carries on like a disappointed careerist."[3]

The idea of Donne as a careerist traces to Donne himself, making his "ambition" a major topic of criticism. Indeed, the idea is arguably the most famous fact about Donne's life. In a letter dating to 1619, he tells Sir Robert Ker that *Biathanatos* "is a Book written by *Jack Donne*, and not by D[r]. Donne."[4] Judith Scherer Herz shows that Donne first introduced this idea in a 1605 letter to Sir Henry Goodyer: "I am brought to a necessity of printing my Poems ... By this occasion I am made a Rhapsoder of mine own rags ... for I must do this, as a valediction to the world, before I take Orders."[5] Donne never did print a volume of his own verse, but the idea of

his career as moving from Jack Donne to Doctor Donne, the youthful poet
to the mature divine, remains the first principle of Donne criticism.

Usefully, Herz traces the history of this idea: from Donne's own poetry
and prose, to the early editions of his poetry (1633, 1635), to his first
biographer, Izaak Walton (1649), to the key figure of Samuel Taylor
Coleridge (early nineteenth century), and to such heirs as A. B. Grosart
(late nineteenth century), T. S. Eliot (early twentieth century), and Carey
himself (late twentieth century). Yet, as Herz concludes, "much recent
criticism has shown [that] ... Donne could have been interested in
a career without the negative implications of 'careerist,' indeed could have
sought a career as a man of integrity."[6] Even so, Herz's essay illustrates
a fundamental limitation to "the strong biographical emphasis in so much
Donne criticism down to this moment." On the one hand, criticism remains
obsessed with Donne the man, in a methodology that seeks to find *the man
in his works*, either defending or attacking the distinction between "the
person" and "the persona."[7] On the other, criticism neglects Donne as an
author, with a methodology of finding *a writer in his literary fictions*, focusing
on the persona's self-presentation rather than on the person's motivation.
Donne criticism has been so preoccupied with the way "Donne's art (both
his poems and his sermons) expresses the personality – self-advancing,
anxious, unsatisfied," that we have bypassed the way his writings record
a different story.[8] This story, I suggest, finds Donne presenting himself as an
author with a literary career. The two stories should not be confused, but
instead form a paradox that Donne himself bequeaths, for evidence exists for
both. Whereas biographical criticism is concerned with "life, mind, and art"
(Carey's title), criticism on a literary career attends to the facts of his fictions.

Today, critics writing on Donne acknowledge that he had a "career."
Indeed, it is difficult to read a piece of Donne criticism without finding
some reference to the word. Yet few, if any, acknowledge that Donne had
a "literary career."[9] Work on literary careers has been inspired by
Helgerson and Lawrence Lipking, the twin pioneers of "career criticism."
During the past thirty-five years, critics have attended to the literary careers
of Spenser, Marlowe, Shakespeare, Drayton, Jonson, and Milton, but not
Donne. While this is not surprising, it is unfortunate. The reason is that
Donne's authorship intriguingly shows two things simultaneously: first,
that his extant works display a formal interest in Western ideas of a literary
career as they emerge from antiquity during the English Renaissance;
and second, that Donne's works are unique in compelling readers to
overlook – or disparage – that interest. Donne's literary career is that

uncanny thing: a literary career that is not recognizable as a literary career at all.

From Helgerson, Lipking, and others, we may speak of Donne as having a literary career if:

- he aspires to the status of being an "author," the way Spenser and Jonson do, by relying on the medium of print to publish works into maturity – that is to say, without youthful "repentance";
- he self-reflexively places himself in the literary tradition of authorship stemming from Virgil and other classical authors, such as Ovid and Horace, from such continental Renaissance heirs as Petrarch, and from such contemporary "laureates" as Spenser and Jonson;
- he composes a set of works in canonical literary genres, and represents an interest in genre patterns, including the "progress" from one work to another, especially the two dominant versions during the English Renaissance: the Virgilian progression from pastoral to epic, and the Augustinian progression from Petrarchan love poetry to Du Bartasian divine poetry;
- he pursues the political goal of national service to the state; and
- he seeks the literary *telos* of fame.

We may consolidate these criteria as the major constituents for defining an English Renaissance literary career: *print authorship, literary imitation, genre patterning, national service*, and *artistic renown*.

Does Donne qualify as a print-author? Does he imitate other canonical authors? Does he pursue his authorship by representing a pattern of literary forms? Does he provide national leadership to other authors and readers? And does he show an interest in literary fame? Perhaps shockingly, the answer to all these questions is: *yes*. As we shall see, John Donne may not qualify as a "laureate" the way Spenser and Jonson do, but we should not classify him as simply an "amateur," or as a "coterie" and "manuscript" poet, or even as a "professional." To the contrary, the evidence suggests a more complex classification, rendering a composite figure: John Donne is a manuscript coterie poet and professional clergyman who fictionalizes himself as an author with a literary career.

A book-length study would be required to pursue this hypothesis fully. Further research needs to be done. In this chapter, we have time for only brief discussion of the above criteria, but one warrants special attention: Donne's fictions of genre patterning.

* * * *

The 2011 *OHJD* opens with two chapters that call into question the simplistic notion that Donne is a manuscript poet who eschews print for a coterie audience. As Gary A. Stringer puts it, "An emphasis in recent years on Donne's involvement in the manuscript culture of his time has tended to make us forget just how much of his work he actually published." By Stringer's count, "Donne published about 42 per cent of the 3,849 pages of prose he had written."[10] In a follow-up essay, Ernest W. Sullivan writes that "twenty-five rather than five of Donne's poems were published in their entirety (and another six in part) during his lifetime," bringing the total to thirty-one.[11] Central to the present chapter is the set of three poems that Donne published in 1611 and 1612: *The First Anniversary* (1611), "A Funeral Elegy" (1611), and *The Second Anniversary* (1612), a set that is "generally acknowledged to be the greatest long poem between *The Faerie Queene* (1590) and *Paradise Lost* (1667)."[12] The key point is that Donne published – and had published during his lifetime – more poems and prose works than the classification of "amateur," "coterie," or "professional" seems to allow. In particular, it is Donne's "long poem" – evidently, alone among English Renaissance works – that has the privilege of joining the two national epics of England's major "laureates," Edmund Spenser and John Milton.

Equally importantly, Donne leaves a record of his attitude toward print. On the one hand, he is well known to have suffered from "the stigma of print," the idea that gentlemen did not use the printing press to publish their works.[13] In a letter of April 14, 1612, he tells George Garrard, "Of my Anniversaries, the fault that I acknowledge in my self, is to have descended to print any thing in verse, which though it have excuse even in our times, by men who professe, and practise much gravitie, yet I confesse I wonder how I declined to it, and do not pardon my self."[14] On the other hand, in his 1605 letter to Goodyer, Donne announces his plan to collect his poems in a printed edition, "addressing them to my L[ord], Chamberlain [Robert Carr, Earl of Somerset]. This I mean to do forthwith; not for much publique view, but at mine own cost, a few Copies."[15] While the edition did not materialize during his lifetime, Donne is on record for having written about his poems as substantial enough to make up an edition in the manner of such contemporaries as Daniel (1602) and Spenser (1611), well in advance of Jonson's 1616 folio *Workes*. When such an edition of Donne posthumously emerges, first in 1633 and again in 1635, we may understand *Poems, by J.D. With Elegies on the Authors Death* as *fulfilling* his own plan. If we stick to the facts, rather than Donne's attitude toward print or his motives, a different picture emerges: he imagines himself as the author of a printed edition of poetry; and this is the author that his heirs then publish. As Stringer points out, we need to be careful when gauging Donne's disparaging remarks about print: "Donne at various times availed himself of each of the modes of communication available to him, choosing print, oral delivery, or manuscript circulation in accordance with the various meanings he intended for – and felt comfortable in conveying to – particular audiences at particular times ... When he determined to reach the broadest possible audience in the most enduring form, he chose print."[16]

The idea that Donne is a manuscript writer is a myth. The truth is more complicated; periodically, we catch him not only in print but talking about the necessity of print. The public dissemination of Donne's poems and prose works qualifies him as in some sense a print-author. Like the early "laureate" John Skelton, who also eschewed print, Donne went into print often enough to disqualify him as merely a manuscript poet writing for a coterie audience. Donne is something more enigmatic: neither a Spenser nor a Marlowe, a Jonson nor a Sidney. Donne may not have liked print-authorship, but he is on record as being a print-author. Perhaps our binary thinking has made it difficult to get Donne right.

* * * *

Donne's self-conscious imitation of canonical authors in the Western literary tradition has long been well established. In accord with Renaissance practice, he imitates by transforming the authors he read, usually in a rebellious manner.[17] While occasionally we can witness Donne responding to an individual author, as in "The Bait" when he responds to Marlowe in "The Passionate Shepherd to His Love," most often Donne responds more widely to an entire genre. Notably, the *OHJD* includes chapters on nineteen Donne genres, with eleven *poetic*. Indeed, Donne's generic output is "unequalled in excellence and variety by the work of any other English writer."[18] Donne's documented reinvention of so many major Western literary forms supplies one of the most compelling reasons for not relegating Donne to the status of amateur. We may intensify the evidence by recalling his "predilection for writing in meta-genres (that is, genres about genres)."[19] Donne's fictions of genre may be one of his stellar contributions to English literature: "these rhymes, which never had / Mother, want matter, and they only have / A little form, the which their father gave" ("To Mr B. B.," 23–25). As Donne says "To the Countess of Huntingdon ('That unripe side of earth')," "neither will I vex your eyes to see / A sighing ode, nor cross-armed elegy" (21–22). In fact,

Donne's troping of literary form produces one of the most famous lines in English poetry: "We'll build in sonnets pretty rooms" ("The Canonization," 32), the Italian word "sonnet" meaning "room." As Donne's line indicates, for him love-making and *love-making* are one and the same.

In particular, Donne's response to Petrarchan sonneteering is prodigious, exhibited memorably in "The Triple Fool," with its indictment of "whining poetry" (3), but also on display throughout *Songs and Sonnets*, and indeed elsewhere. As countless studies have shown, out of Petrarchism, Donne plucks one of the most important revolutions in the history of English literature: "Metaphysical" poetry. In the words of Michael Schoenfeldt, Donne's secular metaphysical poetry "overtly rejects the Petrarchan rhetoric of idealization and distant worship ... in favor of a celebration of the pleasures and terrors of erotic intimacy."[20]

Several other experimentations in literary forms have been seen as historically important interventions in: *Epigrams* (Donne's earliest verse), jointly responsible with Jonson for "'the epigrammatic transformation' of English poetry in the late sixteenth century," written in response to "two main traditions of classical epigram – Greek and Latin";[21] *Satires*, the first English sequence, written in response to Horace, Juvenal, and Persius; *Elegies*, also a carefully patterned sequence, "unique in the elegiac tradition," written in response to Ovid, Marlowe, Joachim du Bellay, and Joannes Secundus;[22] *Verse Letters*, which Donne "resorted to ... more often than other early modern English writers," written in response to Horace, Ovid, Petrarch, and others but often against Petrarchan sonneteering, as the fourteen-line structure of several letters indicate;[23] *Holy Sonnets*, another carefully structured sequence, "justly famous and hold-[ing] a place among the most powerful expressions of religious longing and anxiety in the English language," written in response to Petrarch, Sidney, and others;[24] *Anniversaries*, one of the most highly regarded works in English, written in response to the genres of "'anatomy' and 'funeral elegy'";[25] *Epicedes* and *Obsequies*, which "pioneer ... the development of a new kind of funeral elegy and a new rhetoric of grief," written in response to the tradition coming out of Greece and Rome;[26] and finally *Epithalamia*, which "bend ... conventional forms to register ... disjunctions and difficulties of merging the individual into the collective," written against Spenser in particular.[27]

When the collective evidence is amassed – spread over such a remarkable array of authors and literary forms – we may need to recall John Donne from relegation and assign to him the status as author with a "literary career."

* * * *

Yet the key piece of evidence comes from Donne's recurrent inscription of genre patterning, and especially its cardinal principle: "progress." Three Donne poems contain this word in their titles: "Love's Progress," from the *Elegies*; *The Progress of the Soul … Metempsychosis*; and *The Second Anniversary*, whose main title is *Of the Progress of the Soul*. In his poetry itself, Donne uses the word "progress" five times ("The Autumnal," 20; "Upon Mr Thomas Coryat's Crudities," 28; *The First Anniversary*, 7; *The Second Anniversary*, 219; and *Metempsychosis*, 1). Additionally, scholars have drawn attention to "the patterning of anatomy and progress" developed in Donne's sermons.[28] Among contemporaries, Joseph Hall dilated on the Donnean principle of progress in his commendatory verse to *The Second Anniversary*, "The Harbinger to the Progress":

> So while thou mak'st her soul's high progress known,
> Thou mak'st a noble progress of thine own,
> From this world's carcass having mounted high
> To that pure life of immortality.   (27–30)

The idea is important, because it connects Donne's fiction about the progress of Elizabeth Drury's soul with Donne's own progress as a literary author.

Among Donne's poems, *Metempsychosis* best exemplifies his interest in Western ideas of a literary career. Intriguingly, the details of the poem itself, which Don Cameron Allen called Donne's "longest and most poetically ambitious work" – a "quasi-epic" with an "epic method"[29] – present Donne as the author of a Virgilian career, while the position of the poem in both the 1633 and 1635 editions presents Donne as the author of a Augustinian career. The poem opens in Virgilian epic fashion:

> I sing the progress of a deathless soul,
> Whom fate, which God made but doth not control,
> Placed in most shapes, all times before the law
> Yoked us, and when, and since, in this I sing.
> And the great world to his aged evening,
> From infant morn through manly noon I draw.
> What the gold Chaldee or silver Persian saw,
> Greek brass or Roman iron is in this one,
> A work t'outwear Seth's pillars, brick and stone,
> And (holy writ excepted) made to yield to none.   (1–10)

The opening phrase, "I sing," self-consciously imitates the opening of Virgil's *Aeneid*, "I sing of the arms and man."[30] Yet Donne's repetition of "I sing" in line 4, and his variation in line 6, "I draw," is unusual in the Virgilian epic tradition, and registers Donne going overboard with the career formula, intimating that this is a "satirical mock-epic."[31]

While the opening lines seriously mock Virgilian epic, the first stanza concludes by imitating Ovid, accommodated to the biblical topic of a "deathless soul": "A work t'outwear Seth's pillars." Ovid concludes the *Metamorphoses* singing, "Still in my better part I shall be borne immortal far beyond the lofty stars and I shall have an undying name" (15.875–76). Instead of climbing to the sky, however, Donne's epic traverses the earth, at once charting the "progress" of the soul from "the great world to his aged evening" and lasting longer than the "brick and stone" of "Seth's pillars." Donne's final phrase, "yield to none," rewrites Ovid's bravado with belligerence. The Ovidian provenance of Donne's *Metempsychosis* is also clear in its title, not merely echoing Ovid's *Metamorphoses* but featuring the Pythagorean doctrine of "The Progress of the Soul" that is the topic of Ovid's final book.

Donne's stanzaic structure indicates that he targets more than the two famed classical epics, for his "ten-line iambic stanza, culminating in a triple-rhyme and an alexandrine, overtakes . . . the metrical intricacy of Spenser's celebrated stanza."[32] Thus, Donne's mock-voice, "I sing," also targets the opening of *The Faerie Queene*: "I . . . sing of Knights and Ladies" (1–5).[33] Repeatedly, critics emphasize Donne's engagement in this work with Spenser. Long ago, Allen called attention to the way Donne responds to Spenser's "epic method," his narration of the "poetic process," and his pattern of "allusiveness."[34] More recently, Elizabeth Harvey argues that "Donne's poem . . . incorporates Spenser's own speculations about the natural historical, philosophical, and medical dimension of souls," while Theresa M. DiPasquale adds that Donne's prefatory "Epistle" to the poem "rejects a Spenserian poetics that would attempt to mould readers into something better than they were before."[35]

What might it mean for an evaluation of Donne's authorship that he so profoundly engages Elizabethan England's premier "laureate"? Such engagement, joined to Donne's much-discussed relation to Jonson, constitutes a key part of any attempt to determine whether the author had a literary career. In the second stanza of *Metempsychosis*, Donne himself inserts the word "career" (his only use of the word in his poetic canon) to refer to the progress of the sun across Europe – what he calls the sun's "loose-reined career / At Tagus, Po, Seine, Thames, and Danon" (15–16), naming the national rivers of poetic inspiration for Italy, France, England, and Germany, with the Thames being Spenser's renowned source of poetic inspiration.

In an important essay, W. H. Herendeen classifies *Metempsychosis* as a "palinode," because Donne's mock epic gestures to the poems printed after it in both the 1633 and 1635 editions: "through . . . links between the 'La Corona' sonnets and *The Progresse of the Soule*, Donne initiates the redefinition of his poetic vocation and effects a transfer from profane to sacred poetic. . . . [H]e makes this profane progress the beginning of a spiritual triumph that carries his readers through the 'Holy Sonnets' and into the rest of the volume."[36] For *La Corona* opens, "do not with a vile crown of frails bays / Reward my muse's white sincerity, / But what thy thorny crown gained, that give me, / A crown of glory" (5–8): Donne fictionalizes a turn from secular laureate to Christian laureate, abandoning earthly fame for divine glory.

The 1635 edition is notable for dividing Donne's poetic canon into genres, and for arranging them in a distinct pattern. That pattern is Du Bartasian, moving from the lower erotic forms, such as *Songs and Sonnets* and *Elegies*, to the higher religious forms, such as the *Anniversaries* and *Divine Poems*. Back in 1622 Roger Tisdale recognized a version of this pattern:

> 'Tis you, deare Sir, that after a soaring flight of many yeeres, have now lighted upon a faire Tree. . . . Yet I must ingenuously confesse . . . that your yong daies were to me of much admiration, as these dayes are now of deserved reverence. . . . I know you doe love pure, and undefiled *Poesie*. . . . And I hope for the love of the Muses (who in your Youth initiated you their Son, and now in your Age have elected you a Patron) you will open the imbraces of favour.[37]

In this "pattern of Donne's career," to borrow A. J. Smith's phrase,[38] the "Learned and Reverend John Donne" moves from an author of youthful poetry worth "admiration" to a revered "Patron" of another poet's poetry. Yet Tisdale does not record merely Donne's change from poet to preacher; he sees Donne at both stages of his career to be a lover of "pure, undefiled Poesie." The idea is important, and joins a good deal of recent work on the dates of composition of Donne's poems, to confirm that Dr. Donne did not abandon the amateur sport of Jack Donne but maintained a vital interest in the art of poetry throughout his adult life. Donne, then, belies his status as an "amateur," for he never "repents."

* * * *

The last two criteria for defining a literary career, national service and artistic fame, may be handled briefly together. The former, in which Donne *writes the nation*, would require a full study, but here we may settle on a few observations. The first is that Donne does address a national audience in his funeral poetry, not merely the *Anniversaries*, but also "Elegy, On the Untimely Death of the Incomparable Prince, Henry," published in 1613. What has not been noticed is that in printing no fewer than four funeral poems, Donne can be seen to usurp Spenser's standing as national funeral poet, which England's New Poet advertises first in the "November" eclogue to *The Shepherardes Calender* (1579), and which he fulfills in such poems as *The Ruines of Time*, *Muiopotmos*, and *Virgils Gnat* from the 1591 *Complaints* volume, in the 1592 *Daphnaida*, and in the 1595 *Astrophel*. As Claude J. Summers reports, "Donne's [Funeral] Elegies are public poems."[39] For instance, the funeral elegy for Prince Henry both begins and ends with Donne presenting himself to the nation as its funeral voice: "Look to me, faith, and look to my faith, God, . . . I were an angel singing what you were" (1, 98). As Summers concludes, "By making [the funeral elegy] . . . a more intellectual and supple genre . . . [Donne] considerably expanded the traditional English elegy."[40]

Second, a longer study could also examine the recurrent ways that Donne's manuscript poetry establishes a curious signature, that of addressing posterity, with "The Canonization" being perhaps the most memorable example. But "Valediction of the Book" inscripts the signature more directly:

> And how posterity shall know it too,
>> How thine may out-endure
>> Sibyl's glory, and obscure
>> Her who from Pindar could allure,
> And her through whose help Lucan is not lame,
> And her whose book (they say) Homer did find, and name.   (4–9)

Donne's references to Pindar, Lucan, and Homer do not merely flatter his mistress, or even evoke poetry from ancient Greece and Rome; specifically, Donne evokes public poetry, and in particular classical epic.

As the passage above makes clear, Donne joins Spenser and other laureates in recurrently representing literary fame. Indeed, the word "fame" appears fifteen times in his poetry, while cognates of "glory" appear another thirty-two, and "immortality" eleven more, bringing the total to fifty-six. The key point Donne makes in "Valediction: of the Book" is that his poetry will make his mistress famous: "This book, as long lived as the elements" (19). No wonder we can catch Donne engraving his "name" in "A Valediction of my Name in the Window" (1) – the word "name" repeated obsessively seven times. As we have seen, *Metempsychosis* is devoted to the concept not merely of living forever but of writing poetry that lasts forever. Even in the *Verse Letters*, which write more habitually on the topic of poetry than any other Donne form, we find a quintessential representation of the poet – the nightingale – blurring the boundaries between artistic fame and Christian glory:

> Here in our nightingales we hear you sing,
> Who so do make the whole year through a spring,
> And save us from the fear of autumn's sting.
>
> ("A Letter Written by Sir H. G. and J. D. *alternis vicibus*," 22–24)

In "To the Countess of Bedford, on New Year's Day," Donne precisely tropes poetic fame while advertising his poetry for posterity:

> I would show future times
> What you were, and teach them to'urge towards such.
> Verse embalms virtue;'and tombs, or thrones of rhymes,
> Preserve frail transitory fame.   (11–14)

Moreover, in "Epitaph on Himself" Donne wittily allies fame with glory: "And for my fame, which I love next my soul" (2). As to be expected, Donne's funeral poetry focuses on fame and glory as consolations for death, and nowhere more memorably than in the *Anniversaries*, presented before the nation: "Verse hath a middle nature: heaven keeps souls, / The grave keeps bodies, verse the fame enrols" (473–74). When Donne concludes *The Second Anniversary* with lines of nearly unparalleled artistic authority, "I am / The trumpet, at whose voice the people came" (527–28), the print-author uses the poetic instrument not merely of the hymn but of Spenserian epic to advertise his national leadership role: simultaneously, he is the verse prophet of Scripture, the herald of royal proclamation, and the laureate poet of fame and glory.

* * * *

To conclude, we may suggest that "posterity" listened to Donne's "trumpet" call, revealing a final reason for thinking this author had a literary career: reception history. The remarkable surge of commendatory verses to the 1633 edition of Donne's poems alone suggests how quickly, if this author did not have a literary career, he was assigned one. Poem after poem throws the "crown of bays" on Donne's hearse, as Thomas Carew does famously ("Elegy," 84). And when Carew delivers the much-quoted "epitaph" (94) to "Dr. John Donne" (title) – "Here lies a king that ruled as he thought fit, / The universal monarchy of wit" (95–96) – we see Donne classified as more than simply "two flamens, . . . Apollo's first, at last the true God's priest" (97–98); he also receives a version of the title given to Colin Clout in the "November" eclogue of Spenser's *Calender*: "The Nightingale is sovereign of song" (25).[41]

Donne may not be Spenser – or Jonson – but he joins such enigmatic writers as Marlowe and Shakespeare in engaging with the discourse of an author's literary career at the very time that the discourse comes into view: the transition from the sixteenth to the seventeenth centuries. Donne was no doubt deeply conflicted over print publication, but in this he was not alone. The evidence of his canon shows that periodically he overcomes the conflict, and it presents him as a print-author, committed to literary imitation, to genre patterning, to national service, and finally to artistic fame *progressing* to Christian glory. Perhaps the topic of Donne's literary career fascinates, not because it is a settled matter, but because it is not.

Notes

1. Richard Helgerson, *Self-Crowned Laureates: Spenser, Jonson, Milton, and the Literary System* (Berkeley, CA: University of California Press, 1983), 30–39.
2. Helgerson, *Self-Crowned*, 7–8.
3. Carey, *Mind*, 69–70, 43.
4. *Letters*, 19.
5. Judith Scherer Herz, "'By Parting Have Joyn'd Here': The Story of the Two (or More) Donnes," in *OHJD*, 733; *Letters*, 170.
6. Herz, "Parting," 739.
7. Herz, "Parting," 738.
8. Carey, *Mind*, 94.
9. The *OHJD* uses the word "career" and its cognates 53 times; the word "vocation," 9; "calling," 3; and "profession," 16. Most often, Donne has a religious career (14 times), but he also has a military career (4), a legal career (3), a diplomatic career (1), and a career in general (19). Nowhere does Donne have a "literary career" or a "poetic career." Thanks to Ted Chelis for these numbers.
10. Gary A. Stringer, "The Composition and Dissemination of Donne's Writings," in *OHJD*, 13.
11. Ernest W. Sullivan II, "John Donne's Seventeenth-Century Readers," in *OHJD*, 29.
12. M. Thomas Hester, "John Donne," in *Oxford Encyclopedia of British Literature*, ed. David Scott Kastan (Oxford University Press, 2006), 191.

13. J. W. Saunders, "The Stigma of Print: A Note on the Social Bases of Tudor Poetry," *Essays in Criticism* 1.2 (1951), 139–64.

14. *Letters*, 206.

15. *Letters*, 170.

16. Stringer, "Composition," 13.

17. Helgerson, *Self-Crowned*, 33.

18. Jeanne Shami, M. Thomas Hester, and Dennis Flynn, "General Introduction," in *OHJD*, 2.

19. Heather Dubrow and M. Thomas Hester, "Introduction" to "Donne's Genres," in *OHJD*, 101.

20. Michael Schoenfeldt, "Metaphysical Poetry," in *The Princeton Encyclopedia of Poetry and Poetics*, ed. Roland Greene, 4th edn (Princeton University Press, 2012), 871.

21. M. Thomas Hester, "The Epigram," in *OHJD*, 105, 107.

22. R. V. Young, "The Elegy," in *OHJD*, 148.

23. Margaret Maurer, "The Verse Letter," in *OHJD*, 209.

24. R. V. Young, "The Religious Sonnet," in *OHJD*, 219.

25. Graham Roebuck, "The Anniversary Poem," in *OHJD*, 274.

26. Claude J. Summers, "The Epicede and Obsequy," in *OHJD*, 286.

27. Camille Wells Slights, "The Epithalamion," in *OHJD*, 307.

28. Roebuck, "Anniversary," 284.

29. Don Cameron Allen, "The Double Journey of John Donne," in *A Tribute to George Coffin Taylor*, ed. Arnold Williams (Chapel Hill, NC: University of North Carolina Press, 1952), 83, 88, 89.

30. Anne Lake Prescott, "Menippean Donne," in *OHJD*, 161.

31. Prescott, "Menippean," 160.

32. Daniel D. Moss, *The Ovidian Vogue: Literary Fashion and Imitative Practice in Late Elizabethan England* (University of Toronto Press, 2014), 168.

33. Edmund Spenser, *The Faerie Queene*, ed. A. C. Hamilton (Harlowe, UK: Pearson Education-Longman, 2001).

34. Allen, "Double," 89, 91.

35. Elizabeth Harvey, "Nomadic Souls: Pythagoras, Spenser, Donne," *Spenser Studies* 22 (2007), 259; Theresa M. DiPasquale, "Donne, Women, and the Spectre of Misogyny," in *OHJD*, 679.

36. W. H. Herendeen, "'I launch at paradise, and saile toward home': *The Progresse of the Soule* as Palinode," *Early Modern Literary Studies* Special Issue 7 (2001), par. 5, http://extra.shu.ac.uk/emls/si-07/herendeen.htm.

37. Rpt. in *Critical Heritage*, 76.

38. *Critical Heritage*, 76.

39. Claude J. Summers, "The Epicede and Obsequy," in *OHJD*, 288.

40. Summers, "Epicede," 297.

41. Edmund Spenser, "November," in *The Shorter Poems of Edmund Spenser*, ed. Richard McCabe (Harmondsworth, UK: Penguin, 1999).

CHAPTER 2

Donne's Texts and Materials

Piers Brown

Donne's poems first became widely available two years after his death, with the printing of *Poems by J.D. With Elegies on the Author's Death* (1633). But neither the title page nor the prefatory matter state clearly who wrote the poems. The "Printer to the Understander" instead introduces the author with "the best warrant that can bee, publique authority, and private friends."[1] In doing so, it suggests both that there is a hesitation in admitting that the eminent Dean Donne was a poet, at the same time that it attests to his poetic reputation – a reputation that preceded the publication of his work. The disjunction between reputation and publication jibes with our modern assumption that printing is synonymous with publication, and that manuscript transmission, by contrast, was a private, pre-print phenomenon. In early modern England, however, publication had a more general meaning – the act of making things known to a public audience – a meaning that included public announcement or the dissemination of scribal copies, as well as print publication. The relationship between manuscript and print is vital to an understanding of the transmission and reception of Donne's texts.

Manuscript, Print, and Performance

The posthumous printing of Donne's work had much in common with other early modern writers, both his contemporaries and authors of previous generations. Courtly poets, such as Sir Thomas Wyatt and Sir Philip Sidney, circulated their poems in manuscript and only saw posthumous – and initially unauthorized – printing. Other famous writers of the period, such as Edmund Spenser, William Shakespeare, and Ben Jonson, used print as one avenue in the pursuit of fame and advancement. For Spenser who, like Donne, sought employment as a secretary, the publication of the *Faerie Queene* (1590, 1596) and other works was intended to gain patronage. Shakespeare wrote primarily for the stage and, while he established his early poetic reputation with the publication of *Venus and Adonis* (1593) and *The Rape of Lucrece* (1594), the printing of his plays was less important than their performance. Only Jonson deliberately published a collection of his *Workes* (1616) during his lifetime – and was mocked for presuming to do so. Yet, both Shakespeare and Jonson also distributed their poems in manuscript: Shakespeare's sonnets, also written during the 1590s, did not see print until 1609, and Jonson's inclusion of poems from "The Forest" in the *Workes* was selected from amongst a much larger body of poetry written for his patrons. The differences between these strategies reflect the particular situations in which each author found himself and the sorts of patronage or profit he pursued.

Donne had been writing for over forty years by his death, and the time between the composition of his earliest works and their late printing produced a textual situation even more complex than that of his contemporaries. His corpus consists of approximately two hundred poems, two hundred and thirty letters, five long prose texts, a series of thirty-five shorter prose pieces, and one hundred and sixty sermons. However, very little of this material is in Donne's own hand: just one verse letter, two epigrams, thirty-eight letters, and a few other documents. These manuscripts stand in direct contrast to the voluminous scribal copies in which his work circulated and its extensive printing during the seventeenth century. By any measure, Donne was the most popular manuscript poet in England of his age, with over 250 extant manuscripts containing more than 5,000 copies of individual texts. Moreover, the half-century following his death saw the printing of almost all of his extant writing, often in multiple editions and formats, from the duodecimos of his poems, juvenalia, and devotions, to the folios of his collected sermons – taken together, a body of work comparable to any but the most prolific of his contemporaries.

The material forms of Donne's texts are vital to his editors and to literary historians. Editors compare manuscript and print in pursuit of original, authorial texts. Sir Herbert Grierson's early twentieth-century edition of Donne's poetry based itself on the first print editions with emendations drawn from manuscript. Since then, Donne's editors have not only used manuscript sources for specific readings, but as copy-texts of their editions. At the same time, advocates of "social text" have explored early modern readers' encounters with his works as they were transmitted, connecting methods of circulation, diffusion, and preservation with the social circumstances in which he worked. The consensus has been that Donne, as Ted-Larry Pebworth puts it, "preferred manuscript circulation to print publication."[2] But this claim underestimates the variety of methods by which Donne's work circulated.

In the early modern period, manuscript and print were in use at the same time: printing reproduced texts at low price in large quantities, but scribal copying was faster and cheaper at producing individual copies. In this context, Donne and his contemporaries chose different methods of reproduction according to their goals for each piece of writing. For many kinds of text, such as Donne's sermons, a print edition offered wide distribution and prestige. For other sorts of writing, and poetry in parti-cular, there was the worry that print meant exposure to the vulgar public – the so-called "stigma of print." However, manuscript was also the most practical method of distributing poems, and the author's own hand gave an impression of intimacy and exclusivity.

Despite this, Donne also wrote poetry for print publication: prefatory poems for Ben Jonson's *Volpone* (1607; reprinted in *Workes*, 1616) and Thomas Coryate's *Crudities* (1611); the *Anniversaries* commemorating Elizabeth Drury (1611–12); and a funeral elegy for Prince Henry, in Joshua Sylvester's *Lachrymae Lachrymarum* (1613). The *Anniversaries* pro-voked complaints by some of his patrons, to which he admitted, "the fault that I acknowledge in my self, is to have descended to print any thing in verse."[3] Donne expresses a similar preference for manuscript in a Latin poem, which claims that manuscripts "should be more greatly praised than that produced by the straining of the press."[4] In both cases, Donne's denigration of print is in part for social reasons: embarrassment over his hyperbolic praise of Elizabeth Drury, in the first case, and that he had to replace a printed book his children had accidentally burnt with a manuscript one, in the second. Thus, when Donne tried – and eventually decided against – organizing a print edition of his poetry, just prior to his ordination in 1614, he planned to print one "not for much publique view, but at mine own cost, a few Copies."[5] Indeed, one way of understanding this episode might be that it was not an attempt at publication at all, but rather an example of printing for private circulation, like that of Donne's contemporary Thomas Milles.[6]

In both print and manuscript, Donne attempted to control access to risqué works, as when he asked Sir Henry Wotton for "an assurance ... that no copy shalbee taken" of the paradoxes enclosed with a letter, because "to my satyrs there belongs some feare & to some elegies & these perhaps, shame."[7] Donne's caution was well judged: his erotic poetry became famous enough that any poem in circulation about a man and a woman going to bed together ran the risk of be attributed to Dr. Donne by those enthusiastic for his work, or being destroyed by those offended by it. The Rosenbach manuscript of Donne's poems, for instance, includes a copy of Donne's "To His Mistress Going to Bed" that is smeared out with ink.[8] Similarly, when the 1633 poems were printed, ten poems, "the five *satires*, and the first, second, Tenth, Eleventh, and Thirteenth *Elegies*," were censored.[9]

Some of Donne's prose works were initially available only in manuscript, including *Essays in Divinity* and his now-lost *Cases of Conscience*. The most closely guarded was *Biathanatos* (c. 1608), his treatise on suicide, about which Donne claimed, "I have always gone so near suppressing it, as that it is onely not burnt: no hand hath passed upon it to copy it, nor many eyes to read it" as it was on a "misinterpretable" subject.[10] While little of Donne's poetry was printed during his lifetime, much of his surviving prose was, because it was directed at a different audience. He saw the controversial *Pseudo-Martyr* (1610), the satiric *Conclave Ignatii* (1611), and its English translation *Ignatius His Conclave* (1611), into print – the latter two texts anonymously. In the years between his ordination and his death, six sermons were printed individually and collected as *Three, Four,* and *Five Sermons* (1623, 1624, 1625, 1626). Most significantly, his *Devotions upon Emergent Occasions* was popular enough to see four editions from 1624–27. Together these make for a substantial print presence that supplemented his reputation as a preacher and a divine.

Donne's writing was also disseminated by performance to literal *audiences*. Donne's sermons were preached in parish churches, at St. Paul's Cross, at court, and in noble households, and only later revised for print publication. These sermons' textual forms can help recover the circumstances of performance: Peter McCullough has shown that some manuscript versions that are punctuated for oral delivery differ significantly from those revised for the printed edition.[11] Notes on the sermons, such as those in the Earl of Bedford's commonplace books, are similarly useful. Donne's poetry could also be recited or set to music. One of Donne's *Songs and Sonnets*, "The Triple Fool," dramatizes this possibility: the poem's speaker complains that he is "two fools ... / For loving, and for saying so / In whining poetry" (1–3), before realizing that he is even more of a fool when "Some man, his art and voice to show, / Doth set and sing my pain" (13–14). This is not merely a poetic conceit. The lyrics "The Expiration," "The Bait," and "The Break of Day" all first saw print during Donne's lifetime in song books: Alfonso Ferrabosco's *Ayres* (1609) and William Corkine's *Second Booke of Ayres* (1612). Even more directly, Izaak Walton recounts that Donne had his "Hymn to God the Father" "set to a most grave and solemn Tune, and to be often sung to the *Organ* by the *Choristers* of St. *Pauls* Church, in his own hearing; especially at the Evening Service."[12] Even if we cannot recapture these forms of transmission completely, they played an important role in the reception of Donne's texts.

Production and Reproduction

Donne's career was a bookish one, during which he was educated at or worked in all of the major centres of communication in early modern England: the universities of Cambridge and Oxford, the Inns of Court, the government of Elizabeth I, and the Anglican Church. Finally, as Dean of St. Paul's, he was responsible for the Cathedral and its precinct – which contained both the country's most important pulpit and the centre of the English book-trade. In each place, Donne depended on his training in the practical humanist methods of reading and digesting texts. While his voluminous notes are now lost, the pencil marginalia in his books helps us understand his reading methods, the results of which are evident in his writing. These humanist skills are also on display in the two extant scribal copies of *Biathanatos* and his Gunpowder sermon of 1622, which Donne has corrected in his own hand.

Donne's letters, however, provide the best material and contextual evidence for how he composed, as well as offering valuable information about the transmission of the writing he often shared with his correspondents. His letters mention his *Paradoxes and Problems*, the satirical booklist *The Courtier's Library*, and his treatise on suicide, *Biathanatos*, and they contain a great deal of evidence for the circulation and reception of his poetry. Donne's verse letters – a hybrid poetic-epistolary form – include the single extant poem in Donne's hand, his verses to Lady Carew. Equally importantly, the letters are also associated with two specific material forms in which his poems circulated – the "separate" (a poem on a half-sheet for enclosure) and the booklet (one or more quires containing a long text or several shorter ones). When Donne speaks, for instance, of "two problemes" accompanied by "another ragge of verses," these texts would probably have been in booklet and separate form, respectively.[13]

Like other early modern authors, Donne probably produced an original draft on loose paper, before making a fair copy, in either a separate or a booklet form, to share with a friend or present to a patron. Meanwhile, the original would be retained for later recopying or reworking. However, while there is evidence that Donne sometimes reworked his poetry, he was not always careful in retaining his drafts, which might, themselves, be sent to other correspondents when he did not have time to make a copy: he writes to Sir Henry Goodyer, "I know not how this paper scaped last week which I send now; I was so sure that I enwrapped it then, that I should be so still, but that I had but one copy."[14] Indeed, as Daniel Starza Smith has shown, Goodyer was eager to acquire the original drafts of Donne's poems for his patrons, as they gained value via their intimate connection with the author.[15]

These material forms had significant effects on our understanding of Donne's work: poems circulating on separates could be casually reordered. By contrast, poems transmitted in a paper booklet might retain their original sequence. Donne's five satires, for instance, are known by number because they circulated in booklet form: we know of five extant groups which contain early copies of these poems accompanied by two verse letters to Christopher Brooke, "The Storm" and "The Calm." A booklet at the Folger Shakespeare library, which contains two of Donne's satires along-side a list of poems "in loose papers" that have been "lent to Mr. Murhouse" that includes ten of Donne's *Songs and Sonnets*, suggests how separates and booklets forms circulated together in the context of the Inns of Court.[16]

It is difficult to date many of Donne's poems. Contextual evidence allows us to assign his satires, and many of the elegies, verse letters and songs and sonnets to his years at university and the Inns of Court. It was once conventional to divide Donne's poems into erotic and satirical verse written by Jack Donne and the divine poetry attributed to Dr. Donne, but these are contrasting personae rather than distinct periods: many of his love lyrics and his Holy Sonnets appear to have been written during the first decade of the seventeenth century, when Donne was newly married to his wife, Anne, and in exile in the countryside. This period, and the years as secretary to Sir Robert Drury, is also when we can date many of his occasional works, including verse letters to patronesses, funeral elegies, epithalamia, and poems like "Goodfriday, 1613." Finally, there are a group of primarily divine poems, such as "A Hymn to God the Father" and "Hymn to God my God, in my Sickness," that can be dated to the years after Donne's ordination.

Most of our manuscript versions of the poems, however, were copied many years after their original composition and as a result are not useful for the purpose of dating. While Izaak Walton exaggerates when he claims that Donne's poems "were facetiously composed and carelessly scattered,"[17] one reason for this impression is that Donne did not create a permanent repository for his poetry – or if he did, he did not retain possession of it.

The "old book" that Donne requested from Goodyer in 1614 might have been such a collection, as could "the Poems, of which you took a promise," that he sends to Sir Robert Ker along with the manuscript of *Biathanatos*.[18] However, as neither collection is extant, we have to cope with a complex array of manuscripts of differing contents and authority.

The different versions of Donne's texts are the result of authorial and scribal practice. Donne's dispersal of copies both before and after revision meant that there were multiple authorial versions of poems in circulation. But misreading, miscopying, or conjectural amendment by professional and amateur scribes also changed the text of the poems. The scale of Donne's circulation magnified the number of variant texts and produced cruxes that sometimes dramatically change readings of a poem. Donne's "To His Mistress Going to Bed" and "The Anagram," the poems with most numerous copies, exist in around seventy manuscript versions. The ongoing *Donne Variorum*, in particular, has put an immense amount of editorial work into identifying the relationships between these versions and their variant readings.

As well as tracking versions of poems and their variants, editors have also attempted to follow the movement of the familiar groups in which Donne's poems are usually organized. Some of these groups, such as the elegies, satires, and Holy Sonnets, bear the names used by Donne and his collectors. Francis Davison records among his "Papers lent" that he had given "John Duns Satyres to my br. Christopher." On the verso of the same note, however, he lists amongst the poetry which he desires: "Satyres, Elegies, Epigrams &c. by John Don." with the intention of asking for "some from Eleaz. Hodgson & Ben: Jonson."[19] But other groups derive from Donne's *Poems* of 1635 or later scholarly naming, and in both cases the relationship between the order we associate with these poems and Donne's arrangement of them is unclear. The Holy Sonnets, for instance, include two overlapping and differently ordered twelve-sonnet sequences, each in multiple witnesses: a sixteen-sonnet version, which includes all the poems in the twelve-sonnet versions; and, in the Westmoreland manuscript, a nineteen-sonnet sequence that includes three unique sonnets not elsewhere available until Sir Edmund Gosse printed them in the nineteenth century.

Gathering and Ordering

Understanding the surviving manuscripts is vital to any attempt at reconstructing the original versions and sequences of Donne's poems. To this end, it is useful to divide the manuscript compilations of his poems into two main groups based upon the processes by which they were put together: collections of poems, usually copied together by a single scribe, and miscellanies, with far more eclectic contents built up over time. The distinction is not a clear-cut one, but it catches important differences in transmission and organization. Collections usually contain large groups of texts by a few authors or Donne alone, and they are often carefully planned and executed scribal manuscripts, such as the Dobell manuscript. But perhaps the distinguishing characteristic is that these manuscripts contain large groups of poems by Donne, suggesting that either the links between them and Donne's circle were close and well established, or that they were copied from the manuscripts of another collector of Donne's work.

Donne's friends were important intermediaries in the transmission of his work. Ben Jonson introduced Donne and his poetry to the Countess of Bedford; Sir Henry Goodyer sent draft copies of poems to the Conway family; and Roland Woodward collected and copied work for the Earl of Westmoreland. Patrons with this sort of access could build large collections of verse, either wholesale – as with the Westmoreland manuscript, which Woodward put together from two other collections – or piecemeal – as in the Conway manuscript, which includes copies of Donne's Somerset "Epithalamion," "Goodfriday, 1613," and "Lovers' Infiniteness" in Goodyer's hand. These collections form the basis for later recopying, as in the case of the Puckering and Dublin manuscripts: they contain an overlapping group of one hundred and twenty-one and one hundred and forty-three poems, copied by the same scribe, as well as the same selection of *Paradoxes and Problems*. Both collections were later supplemented by additional poems, either copied into or bound with the original manuscript. Moreover, each has been copied wholesale as the Denbigh and Norton manuscripts. This is, however, a particularly straightforward case, whereas other manuscripts do not show these clear lines of descent, either because their exemplars are lost or because they were brought together from multiple sources.

By contrast, verse collectors further from Donne's circle usually only had access to individual poems or small groups, which they copied into a miscellany: often a blank, pre-bound "wastebook" or "paper book." Because they were acquired and copied over time, the contents of these miscellanies are often jumbled together, sometimes alongside other writing – accounts, recipes, legal records or notes, and scribbles. But despite failing to preserve poetic sequences, individual poems may bear valuable witness to authorial versions that have otherwise been lost.

The first two editions of Donne's *Poems*, both printed by John Marriot, show the close link between print and these manuscript traditions. The 1633 *Poems* is disordered because it follows multiple manuscript sources containing overlapping sets of Donne's poems. The elegies, for instance, appear in two sections: those drawn from the Balam manuscript (minus three censored poems), and another group in which love elegies appear alongside funeral elegies; the lyrics and verse letters are intermixed; and there are no clear division between secular and divine poems. The 1635 *Poems*, which supplements the first edition with the O'Flahertie manuscript, radically rearranges the poems, setting the order and categories for most modern editions of Donne's poetry. The "Songs and Sonnets" appear as a category for the first time; the elegies and funeral elegies become separate, partially reordered groups; and the "Holy Sonnets" appeared in expanded form, not mixed with the lyric poetry, but in a separate section alongside other "Divine Poems." All these groupings appear enlarged and sometimes refined in later seventeenth-century editions – in 1639, 1649 (reissued 1650 and 1654), and 1669.

Other publications also took advantage of the interest in Donne's work provoked by his death. His final sermon, preached before King Charles, was published as *Deaths Duell* in 1632, and Henry Seyle published two editions of his *Paradoxes and Problems* under the title *Juvenalia* in 1633, and two more editions of the *Devotions* (1634, 1638). In the mid-century, Donne's eldest son, John Donne, Jr., reclaimed control of his father's literary property. While it would be wrong to call him a careful editor, he brought most of his father's remaining works into print, including *Biathanatos* (1646), *Essays in Divinity* (1651), *Paradoxes, Problems, Essayes* (1652), *Letters to Some Persons of Honor* (1651, 1654), as well as the *Tobie Mathew Collection* (1660) of letters, which includes a number by Donne.[20] Most significantly, he saw the folio printings of three collections of sermons that begin with clear reliable texts of *LXXX Sermons* (1640) and *Fifty Sermons* (1649), and work their way through to the error-ridden *XXVI Sermons* (1660). These printed works were the basis of later editions of Donne down to the end of the nineteenth century – but they are not the only forms in which Donne's writings were transmitted in the seventeenth century.

Texts in Transmission

The reception of Donne's writing can best be understood via the bloom of other print and manuscript forms that appeared alongside the collected editions of his work. Robert Chamberlin's printed poetic miscellany

The Harmony of the Muses (1654), for instance, contains seven of Donne's poems, including the first print appearance of the previously censored "To His Mistress Going to Bed"; the *Reliquae Wottonianae* (1654) includes Donne's verse letter "To Sir H[enry] W[otton] at His Going Ambassador to Venice"; and Donne's biographer, Izaak Walton, inserts "The Bait" into his *Compleat Angler* (1653). Donne's writing also appears in manuscript commonplace books, such as the Save manuscript's extracts from forty-five poems, as well as in printed ones, including *The Philosopher's Banquet* (1620, 1621, 1623), *The Academy of Complements* (1645), *The Marrow of Complements* (1655), and *The English Parnassus* (1657). Quotations from these and other collections were reused in literary works, such as Samuel Sheppard's parodic almanac *Merlinus Anonymous* (1653), which deploys 224 lines drawn from over twenty of Donne's poems. And fragments and quotations of Donne's poetry and prose appear in the works by a wide variety of writers including John Webster, Sir John Petty, and William Drummond.

Early modern writers felt free to rework texts. Donne's own poem "The Bait" is a parody of "The Passionate Shepherd to His Love" and its response "The Nymph's Reply." His readers, likewise, rewrote or adapted his poems: "Dr Donne at his Mistris rising" stitches together lines from Donne's "Break of Day" and "Sweet Stay Awhile," a song printed in John Dowland's *A Pilgrimes Solace* (1612).[21] Simon Butteris reworked Donne's "A Valediction Forbidding Mourning," changing the original version's "nine tetrameter quatrains into five pentameter six-line stanzas."[22] Even Donne's friends reused his work, sometimes with his permission: in one letter he asks Sir Henry Goodyer, "whether you ever made any such use of the letter in verse, *A nostre Countesse chez vous.*"[23]

Some of Donne's work reached an audience beyond Britain. The Latin *Conclave Ignatii* (1611) was republished on the continent, making it as far as Prague where Johannes Kepler complained at finding himself satirized. Donne also translated his own text into English for a re-issue to a domestic audience.[24] Donne's foreign transmission can likewise be seen in a small number of translations, the most famous being those of the Dutch poet and statesman Constantijn Huygens (1596–1697). In addition, thirteen of Donne's problems were translated into Latin and printed at Leyden in 1616.[25] Lastly, and perhaps most curiously, is a "*Book of Epigrams: Written in Latin by [Donne], translated into English by J: Maine, D.D.*," which is the only surviving version of the Latin original.[26]

Equally importantly, the printing of Donne's poetry and prose did not mark the end of its manuscript transmission. While the majority of

manuscript collections of Donne's work date from before print versions
were available, the Wase, Capell, Stowe II, and Welden manuscript collections can be dated later, either because of lack of access to the print edition
or in order to obtain poems omitted from the print text. However, print
was also a source of manuscript, as in the Harley Rawlinson manuscript,
which contains "Donnes quaintest conceits" extracted from and listed by
the page number and edition of his poems.[27] Or, printed texts might be
augmented with manuscript: copies of Donne's *Poems* (1633) exist in which
poems have been added in blank spaces, or improved by the addition of
"An Index" of topics.[28]

Perhaps the best example of these print–manuscript hybrids is the
Mapletoft Volume. This printed copy of the 1633 *Poems* contains handwritten corrections and an 80-page manuscript supplement, labelled
"Additions to Dr. Donne in ye Edition, 1669 8vo." Here we see print
derived from manuscript, supplemented by manuscript derived from
print. It is a reminder that editions of Donne's writing, beneath their
seemingly stable surface, consist of layer upon layer of work by editors and
collectors, each annotating and (hopefully) improving the texts we read.
These may be Donne's texts, but they are also the material product of many
other hands.

Notes

1. *Poems* (London, 1633), sig. A2r.
2. Ted-Larry Pebworth, "The Text of Donne's Writings," in *CCJD*, 23.
3. *Letters*, 206.
4. "De libro cum mutuaretur impresso, … D. D. Andrews," trans. Edmund
   Blunden, "Some Seventeenth-Century Latin Poems by English Writers,"
   University of Toronto Quarterly 25.1 (1955), 11.
5. *Letters*, 170.
6. William H. Sherman and Heather Wolfe, "The Department of Hybrid
   Books: Thomas Milles between Manuscript and Print," *Journal of Medieval
   and Early Modern Studies* 45.3 (2015), 457–85.
7. John Donne, *Selected Prose*, eds. Helen Gardner and Timothy Healy (Oxford
   University Press, 1967), 111.
8. Rosenbach Museum & Library, Commonplace book MS 239/22.
9. *A Transcript of the Registers of the Company of Stationers of London*, ed.
   Edward Arber, 5 vols. (London, 1887), 4:285.
10. *Letters*, 19.
11. Peter McCullough, "'Cribrated and Recribrated and Post-Cribrated':
    The Revisionist Contributions of *The Oxford Edition of the Sermons of John
    Donne*," MLA Panel, January 6, 2012.

12. Walton, *Lives*, 62.
13. *Letters*, 76.
14. *Letters*, 26–27.
15. Daniel Starza Smith, *John Donne and the Conway Papers: Patronage and Manuscript Circulation in the Early Seventeenth Century* (Oxford University Press, 2014), 204–05.
16. Folger MS X.d. 580.
17. Walton, *Lives*, 61.
18. *Letters*, 170, 18.
19. Harley Ms. 298, f. 159.
20. *Pseudo-Martyr* (1610) is the one exception.
21. Folger MS V.a. 262, p. 102.
22. See Marotti, *Manuscript*, 152–53.
23. *Letters*, 170.
24. There is also the anonymous manuscript translation, *Ignatius His Closet*.
25. Keynes, *Bibliography* pp. 96–70.
26. This is included as part of Donne's *Paradoxes, Problems, Essayes* (London, 1652).
27. Harley MS 3991. f. 113r.
28. Folger STC 7045 copy 2, 407–08.

CHAPTER 3

Donne and Print

Katherine Rundell

There has been some superb scholarship in recent years – some of it in this volume – which has aimed to complicate the assumption that Donne's work moved neatly from written draft to manuscript circulation to post-humous print publication. This essay aims to extend that complication, and to highlight how easy it is to retroactively read inevitability into the literary trajectories of the poets whose lives we know best. Donne was a coterie poet, but the cursus of his writing life was more made up of compromise and serendipity than the label perhaps suggests. The recent recalibration of Donne's manuscript presence – showing it to be far greater than Grierson, Gardner, and Milgate could have supposed – has widened the scope and breadth of the way we define coterie, but still the idea of the contained, private author is the dominant narrative.[1] Arthur Marotti writes that "Donne was obviously most comfortable when he knew his readers personally and they knew him."[2] It might be, however, that anyone walking through St Paul's Churchyard in the first decades of the seven-teenth century and stopping to browse under the sign of the Boar's Head would have been surprised to hear it said.

This hypothetical customer would have easily been able to purchase Donne's refutation of the Pope's authority in *Pseudo-Martyr*, for its print-run was blockbusting. He would also have been able to buy scatological satire in *Ignatius His Conclave*, copies of which had, by 1611, already made their way to the booksellers of Paris.[3] Printed anonymously, it was none-theless widely known to be by Donne. If the customer had been loitering after 1630, he would have been able to choose from two editions of the *Devotions upon Emergent Occasions*, and six published sermons. And if he had been a frequent visitor to the churchyards at St Paul's and St Dunstan's, he would already have encountered Donne's verse in seven other texts: the epigram 'A Lame Beggar' (also known as 'Zoppo') in Thomas Deloney's *Strange Histories* (1607); 'Amicissimo et Meritissimo Ben Jonson' in *Ben: Jonson his Volpone or the Fox* (1607); 'The Expiration' in Alfonso Ferrabosco's

Ayres (1609); "Upon Mr Thomas Coryat's Crudities," published alongside the *Crudities* themselves in 1611 and reprinted that same year in *The Odcombian Banquet*; 'Break of Day' in *The Second Book Ayres*, collected by William Corkine in 1612; the much-imitated 'Elegy upon the Death of Prince Henry' in Josuah Sylvester's *Lachrymae Lachrymarum* (1613), and 'A Licentious Person', a satiric couplet in Henry Fitzgeffrey's *Satyres and Satyricall Epigrams* (1617).[4] And above all, there were *The First* and *Second Anniversaries*: a lover of Donne would by 1625 have been able to collect up to four different editions of one or both of the poems. John Donne, then, was a print author. This is not to say that the manuscript verse is not the more enticing part of the canon, nor to dismiss the scholarship highlighting Donne's ambivalent attitude to print. Indeed, one of the dangers of emphasising the private over the public Donne is that it damps the thrill of the contrast that must have been a part of owning a manuscript Donne poem: we risk limiting the parameters of reader response for work that *was* intensely personal. "A Nocturnal upon Saint Lucy's Day" would, at any time, have been a thing worth having; to receive it in the wake of the small storm surrounding *Pseudo-Martyr* and *Ignatius His Conclave* would have been doubly extraordinary.

There is an argument to be made for a strategic Donne, a Donne whose early attitude to the print market was not so different from his contemporaries and immediate forerunners. The difficulty is that Walton's *Life* has left us with a narrative of Donne's attitude to his work that is seductive; but it is also impossibly neat, and it is tempting to lose sight of the cultural project involved in reconceptualising Donne's identity. Donne's professed distaste for the print market can usefully be compared to that of Marston or Fletcher, men ambitious for fame who equally took up the anti-print pose. All three were in a liminal social position, and all three took pains to assert their claim to gentility: Marston, for example, writes in his preface to *The Fawn*, 'many shall wonder why I *print* a Comedie . . . Let such know, that it cannot avoide publishing.'[5] Many Donne-narratives give emphasis to the rarefied nature of his connection to Thomas More – an emphasis championed by Donne himself – but in fact Fletcher and Marston had similar beginnings in life; Fletcher, for instance, had the Bishop of London for his father, and his grandfather was a close companion of John Foxe. Marston's Inns of Court mentality is mirrored in Donne's; *Histriomastix* probably started out as a piece to be performed at the Inns for Christmas 1598, and it is not unlikely that Donne would have hosted similar entertainments in his time at Lincoln's Inn. Marston suppressed his name from the title-page of the 1633 collected edition of his plays in the year before his death (by which time he had, like Donne, taken up divine office), but he had undoubtedly sought fame and notoriety in his youth. It may be that this life cursus – of a riotous youth in which the author intends, almost from the beginning, to be self-conscious in maturity – is as useful a frame to understand Donne as the more glamorous and usual focus on his recusancy and religious conversion. It is unlikely that the Donne of the 1590s was clear that he did not want to be a print author; we need to understand life narratives in early modern rather than Romantic terms. It is tempting to map mid-Jacobean conceptions of gentlemanliness backwards onto Donne's world of the late sixteenth and early seventeenth centuries, but in those earlier years these roles were precisely in flux – the Earl of Oxford, after all, wrote anonymously for the Paul's Boys – and were being invented and formed by the writers of the moment.

In this context of thinking of Donne as less uniquely aloof than Walton suggests, it becomes interesting to see how Donne's career up until 1611 maps onto Spenser's of 1589. Like Spenser, Donne was a secretary to a member of the aristocracy (Sir Thomas Egerton; Spenser served Lord Grey) and thereby of ambiguous social position; like Donne, Spenser published anonymously, and both used ludic prefatory material which played with the idea of anonymity. Where Spenser has E. K. in *The Shepherdes Calender* Donne has the "Printer to the Reader" in *Ignatius His Conclave*, which makes claims to reluctance whilst all the time establishing itself as a companion piece to the "other book," *Pseudo-Martyr*, widely known to be by Donne. And, as with Donne, Spenser's narrative has been fixed in a way that allows his early published texts to pass under the critical radar. Joseph Lowenstein encapsulates the problem of retrography:

> when Spenser's pastorals were first published in 1579 his first published verse had been in print for exactly ten years. That the twenty-two sonnets in the *Theatre for Voluptuous Worldlings* are not identified in print as Spenser's should not set them securely outside the circle that includes the poems made canonical … since *The Shepherd's Calender* is similarly anonymous. The anonymity of Spenser's early sonnets was banal in 1569, but the anonymity of his eclogues is made to shimmer in 1579.[6]

In the same way, Donne's anonymous print work is seen as banal, his manuscript verse as shimmering; the two writers, in fact, had very similar run-ups to very different endpoints. Just as the *Faerie Queene* did not look so obviously predictable until it was published, so conversely, in 1612, John Donne coterie poet could not have looked inevitable. As Lowenstein says, we 'ought to steer clear of any account that misses the uncertainties of composition, the mystery of the next thing'.[7]

The most famous reference to Donne's attitude to print is also the one most often cited as conclusive proof of Donne's desire to keep his verse close. Peter Beal writes that we 'have the testimony of Ben Jonson (in his cups) in 1619 that "since he was made Doctor" (in March 1615) Donne "repenteth highlie & seeketh to destroy all his poems"'.[8] The extract, though, is worth quoting in full:

> He affirmed that Donne wrote all his best pieces before he was Twenty five Years of Age. That Conceit of Donne's Transformation or *Metempsychosis*, was, that he sought the Soul of that Apple which Eva pulled, and thereafter made it the Soul of a Bitch, then of a She-wolf, and so of a Woman: His general Purpose was to have brought it into all the Bodies of the Hereticks from the Soul of Cain; and at last left it in the Body of Calvin. He only wrote one Sheet of this, and since he was made Doctor; repented hugely, and resolved to destroy all his Poems.[9]

It is important here that the context is of *Metempsychosis* and the sub-genre of religious satire, and that Jonson is reported at second hand by Drummond of Hawthornden – and is, of course, famously drunk. Jonson is also a rival poet with an agenda: Jonson's gossipy malice suggests he conceived of Donne as a figure with ambitions that might intersect with, and be threatening to, his own – as more of a print-competitor than we might generally assume.

Alongside this reference to Donne's wariness of print, the most important evidence of a retiring and anti-print Donne is in Walton's statement in his 1640 version of the *Life* that Donne's poems 'were facetiously composed', and – he added in the 1658 edition – 'carelessly scattered'.[10] The idea was made more emphatic in the 1670 edition with the addition of the words, 'scattered loosely (God knows too loosely)'.[11] It is significant that these additions come after the 1641 abolition of the Star Chamber; in 'scattering' his verse without commercial ambition, Donne is posited as a foil to the ink-covered mercenary, despite having died before anti-Grub Street invective became fashionable. A second reason to read Walton's picture of Donne with scepticism is the gap between the way Walton talks about his *own* reluctance to print, and his actual output. The 'Introduction to the Reader' in the 1670 edition of Walton's *Lives* avers that 'tis not without some little wonder myself, that I am come to be publicly in print': a wonder that the reader cannot share, given Walton's previous publication of six separate editions of the *Lives* and *The Compleat Angler*, which ran in

five different editions between 1653 and 1676.[12] In the appended letter to the
1676 edition of the *Angler*, Walton writes, 'I did neither undertake, nor write,
nor publish . . . this discourse to please myself'.[13] The reluctant-writer starts to
appear as a useful trope that Walton applied both to himself and to Donne.
This is not to say that the stigma of print did not exist, but when we
remember that King James published his *Reulis and Cautelis* in 1584 and
Lepanto in 1591, it becomes possible that it was more of a pliable trope than an
imperative; perhaps, in some cases, even the hallmark of the print author.

    The most important print moment in Donne's life, though, was the
publication of *The First* and *Second Anniversaries*. Written to mark the
death of Elizabeth Drury, the daughter of Sir Robert Drury, whose patronage Donne is thought to have sought, they are long poems, printed
anonymously, of hyperbolic praise and contempt for the world. The first
version of the text, containing only *The First Anniversary* and 'A Funeral
Elegy', was printed for the prominent St Paul's bookseller Samuel Macham
in 1611 under the title 'An Anatomy of the World'.[14] In 1612 *The Second
Anniversary* was joined to a second edition of the *First* and marginal glosses
were added to both *Anniversaries*, as a kind of running commentary not
unlike those in the Geneva bible. We know that Donne was interested and
anxious as to their reception. In his letter to Goodyer, he writes:

> I hear from *England* many censures of my book, of Mris Drury; if any of
> those censures do but pardon me my descent in Printing any thing in verse,
> (which if they do, they are more charitable than my self; for I do not pardon
> my self, but confesse that I did it against my conscience, that is, against my
> own opinion, that I should not have done so) I doubt not that they will soon
> give over that other part of that indictment, which is that I have said so
> much; for no body can imagine, that I who never saw her, could have any
> other purpose in that, than that when I had received so very good testimony
> of her worthinesse, and was gone down to print verses, it became me to say,
> not what I was sure was just truth, but the best that I could conceive; for that
> had been a new weaknesse in me, to have praised any body in printed verses,
> that had not been capable of the best praise I could give.[15]

    Despite the disavowals ('I did it against my conscience') and disowning of
ambition (surprising, considering the swiftness with which *The Second
Anniversary* followed the *First*), Donne nonetheless had sufficient confidence
in his own prominence to expect the anonymous poems to be recognised as
his own. This was precisely what happened; as soon after publication as 1612,
John Davies of Hereford, in his elegy on Elizabeth Dutton, writes:

> I must confesse a Priest of Phebus, late
> Upon like Text so well did meditate,

> That with a sinlesse Envy I doe runne
> In his Soules Progress, till it al be DONNE.[16]

It also suggests that Donne had clear ideas about the printed verse form as necessitating a different kind of composition from manuscript poetry. These poetic recalibrations include the need an inflated tone, of 'the best praise that I could give'. Jonson is said to have complained that 'if it had been written of ye Virgin Marie, it had been something', to which Donne replied, 'that he had described the Idea of a Woman and not as she was'.[17] Donne, then, merges and conflates Elizabeth with abstract virtue: 'She, of whom th'ancients seemed to prophesy / When they called virtues by the name of she' (*The First Anniversary*, 175–76). If the woman is both Elizabeth Drury and an Idea, she is only half there; the hyperbole acts as protective colouring, an ingenious way of de-personalising the personal. The moment gives an insight into Donne's attitude to print, as something to be carefully negotiated; there is a defensive quality to the hyperbole of the *Anniversaries* that there is not in the more playful exaggerations of, for instance, the quasi-blasphemous 'The Relic': 'Thou shalt be'a Mary Magdalene, and I / A something else thereby' (17–18). Comparison with Spenser is useful here, too; his *Fowre Hymnes*, like the *Anniversaries*, are elaborate praise-pieces of a metaphysical kind, relying on Neo-Platonic analogy and dedicated to women the author had likely never met.[18] The preface to the *Hymnes* states that the poems in their manuscript version became too successful to control; Spenser tries to 'call in the same', 'But being vnable so to doe, by reason that many copies thereof were formerly scattered abroad, I resolued at least to amend, and by way of retractation to reforme them.'[19] This narrative is, like Donne's statements of reluctance, a little undermined by the pomp and beauty of the title pages that accompany both Spenser's and Donne's verse. Both sets of poems seem to be instances of tactical authors using strange and knowingly excessive verse as a way of keeping print work appropriately impersonal.

To say that the *Anniversaries* are strange, though, is not to say that they are not Donne-like. If 'Donne-like' might signify a febrile, baroque, and twisting sensibility, they are more Donne-like than many. They bring into question our sense of *why* Donne was Donne-like, in that his complexity is supposed, in part, to have been elitist; the highly wrought nature of his verse was enabled, Marotti writes, by his faith in the rarefied intellect of his select readership. Donne is supposed to have been unwilling to write for those readers who were not also 'Understanders', and this shaped his work: 'his fondness for dialectic, intellectual complexity, paradox and irony, the appeals to shared attitudes and group interests ... the styles he adopted or invented all relate to the coterie circumstances of his verse'.[20] By that reckoning the *Anniversaries* should be lower in brow than the unpublished verse, and free from the concerns of Donne's coterie. Instead they are amongst the most knotty, allusive, and complex of his texts. To read the *Anniversaries* is to feel that Donne's need for nuance transcends the need to be understood: the poems avow faith in difficulty and lower decibels. The two poems pass through references to Aristotelian logic and Ptolemaic planetary theory to Augustine's discussion of beauty and Pliny's theory of poisonous snakes. The politics of Donne's own set are opaquely present in the poems: in *The Second Anniversary* (9–15) Donne evokes the beheading of the Earl of Essex in 1601 (Donne was, at the time, secretary of the Lord Keeper and therefore closely involved) and links it, via references to 'those two red seas' (10), to Moses, baptism by blood, and the death of Christ, in a form of political coding that evokes the Spenser of *Mother Hubberds Tale*.[21]

The enjambment in both *Anniversaries* is often difficult, and the sense recalcitrant. For instance, in a discourse on physical decay, Donne writes, 'Only death adds to'our length, nor are we grown / In stature to be men, till we are none' (*The First Anniversary*, 145–46). This is very recognisably Donne. The thought is circular and the thrust biblical, evoking, as Robin Robbins points out, Corinthians 15, 'corruption shall put on incorruption'. But the poem twists in the next line, 'But this were light, did our less volume hold / All the old text' (147–48), punning on 'light' as both weightless and of little importance, and, taking one pun to galvanise another, juggling the double meaning of 'volume', the second, bookish meaning of which provokes scripture again in 'All the old text', which evokes Adam's pre-textual knowledge and thereby, self-enfolding, making man back into book.[22] Donne's transformative sensibility is recognisably at work here in the same way as in the other poems in which he makes himself into text, as, for instance, in 'Hymn to God my God, in my Sickness': 'Whil'st my physicians by their love are grown / Cosmographers, and I their map, who lie / Flat on this bed' (6–8). Moreover, in *The First Anniversary* the distinctive vocabulary of transubstantiation evokes other of Donne's poems, and suggests Donne recognised some interplay between published and unpublished verse. In *The First Anniversary*, 'though she could not transubstantiate / All states to gold' (417–18) recalls in 'Twickenham Garden', 'the spider love, which transubstantiates all' (6) and, even more so, in 'To the Countess Huntingdon' ('Man to God's image'), 'She gilded us, but you are gold, and she; / Us she informed, but transubstantiates you' (25–26). If these transliterations across different states of being are amongst the hallmarks of Donne's poetry, then Donne in print is at his most Donnean.

After the first two publications of the *Anniversaries*, of course, there is a shift, and Donne's career from that point on does not resemble the trajectory of a print author. There are many possible explanations for the change: the taking of Holy Orders might have militated against print, and it is possible that the publication of the *Anniversaries* gave Donne a stronger footing in court and thereby an alternative way to disseminate his work. What is fascinating about them is that they mark a moment in which a poet with professional anxieties and strategies is visible. The *Anniversaries* stand as a monument to another kind of poet that Donne might have become. They remind us that no poet's cursus or canon looks obvious or certain until long after the fact, and that, with a poet as intellectually quicksilver as Donne, even the poet's own avowed stances are slippery. It might be best, as Donne writes in "Satire III," to "doubt wisely; in strange way / To stand inquiring right is not to stray" (77–78).

Notes

1. *The Complete Poetry of John Donne*, ed. John T. Shawcross (New York: Doubleday, 1967), lists 157 Donne manuscripts, which doubles the collected total of Grierson, Gardner, and Milgate, who list forty-three between them. Peter Beal, in *Index of English Literary Manuscripts: 1475–1625* (London: Mansell, 1980) lists 219. *The Variorum Edition of the Poetry of John Donne. Vol 6: The Anniversaries and the Epicedes and Obsequies*, eds. Gary Stringer et al. (Bloomington, IN: Indiana University Press, 1995), fifteen years later, lists 239.
2. Marotti, *Coterie*, 9.
3. John Donne, *Ignatius His Conclave*, ed. T. S. Healy (Oxford University Press, 1969), xii.
4. Ernest W. Sullivan, *The Influence of John Donne* (Columbia, MO: University of Missouri Press, 1993), 6.
5. John Marston, *The Fawn* (London, 1606), 4.
6. Joseph Lowenstein, "Spenser's Retrography: Two Episodes in Post-Petrarchan Bibliography," in *Spenser's Life and the Subject of Biography*, eds. Judith Anderson et al. (Amherst, MA: University of Massachusetts Press, 1996), 115.
7. Lowenstein, 'Spencer's,' 115.
8. Peter Beal, 'John Donne and the Circulation of Manuscripts' in *The Cambridge History of the Book in Britain, 1557–1695*, eds. John Barnard and Donald Francis McKenzie (Cambridge University Press, 2002), 123.
9. *Ben Jonson*, eds. C. H. Herford, Percy Simpson, and Evelyn Simpson, 11 vols. (Oxford University Press, 1925–52), 1:136.

10. Izaak Walton, *The Life and Death of Dr Donne* (London, 1658), 75.
11. Izaak Walton, *The Lives of Dr. John Donne, Sir Henry Wotton, Mr. Richard Hooker, Mr. George Herbert* (London, 1670), 75.
12. Walton, *The Lives*, 4.
13. Izaak Walton, *The Compleat Angler, or, the Contemplative Man's Recreation*, (London, 1676), 11.
14. *Variorum*, 38.
15. *Letters*, 64–65.
16. *Critical Heritage*, 67. The reference is to the subtitle of *The Second Anniversary*, "Of the Progress of the Soul."
17. *Variorum*, 240.
18. Spenser's poem is dedicated to 'Ladie Margaret Countesse of Cumberland, and the Ladie Marie Countesse of Warwicke.' Edmund Spenser, *The Fowre Hymnes*, ed. L. Winstanley (Cambridge University Press, 1916), 6.
19. Spenser, *Fowre*, 6.
20. Marotti, *Coterie*, 19.
21. *Variorum*, 464.
22. John Donne, *The Complete Poems*, ed. Robin Robbins (Harlow, UK: Longmans, 2010), 828.

CHAPTER 4

Language

Douglas Trevor

When John Donne's poetry was re-examined by scholars and critics in the early twentieth century, first assembled anew by Herbert Grierson in *The Poems of John Donne* (1912) and subsequently theorized anew – most notably by T. S. Eliot in his essay "The Metaphysical Poets" (1921)[1] – it was Donne's language in particular that drew much attention. For Eliot, borrowing a term from John Dryden, Donne's writing was "metaphysical" in that it could be characterized by "the elaboration (contrasted with the condensation) of a figure of speech to the furthest stage to which ingenuity can carry it." According to Eliot, when the "language" of English poetry in the latter seventeenth century "became more refined, the feeling became more crude." Eliot is thinking here specifically of Dryden and John Milton, whom he terms "masters of diction in our language," but whom he also accuses of having "a dazzling disregard of the soul." "Those who object to the 'artificiality' of Milton or Dryden sometimes tell us to 'look into our hearts and write,'" Eliot observes. "But that is not looking deep enough; Racine or Donne looked into a good deal more than the heart. One must look into the cerebral cortex, the nervous system, and the digestive tracts."[2]

As J. B. Leishman observed in the 1950s, Eliot's view of Donne's language evolved after 1921, such that by the early 1930s he was accusing Donne's verse, along with Dryden and Milton's, of possessing "a manifest fissure between thought and sensibility."[3] Nonetheless, Eliot never did abandon his claim that Donne's verse possesses a "massive music,"[4] and indeed Donne's reputation as a poet from Dryden on is – for better and for worse – tied to his idiosyncratic and striking use of language, not to mention the inventiveness with which this language is poetically arranged. Like Dryden, Samuel Johnson was dismissive of Donne and his contemporaries for being "careless of their diction,"[5] whereas Grierson praised the eventual Dean of Saint Paul's for his "witty language of all the moods of a lover that experience and imagination have taught him to understand – sensuality aerated by a brilliant wit."[6]

Notwithstanding that readers have been divided over the effects of Donne's tonal and stylistic innovativeness as a poet, there has been remarkable agreement over the distinctiveness with which ideas in Donne are "yoked" together with language.[7] Eliot adduces a certain material specificity in Donne's image-making upon which other readers have also remarked. For example, "A bracelet of bright hair about the bone" ("The Relic," 6), with its "telescoping of images and multiplied associations," represents for Eliot an example of the "vitality of . . . language" found not only in Donne but also in the writings of some of his contemporaries, particularly Shakespeare, Middleton, and Webster.[8] Samuel Taylor Coleridge singled out the metaphor of the compass in "A Valediction Forbidding Mourning," along with other turns of phrase in Donne's poems, as pre-eminent examples of "Wonder-exciting vigour, intenseness and peculiarity of thought, using at will the almost boundless stores of a capacious memory, and exercised on subjects, where we have no right to expect it – this is the wit of Donne!"[9] And in a 1981 interview, the Russian poet (and eventual Nobel Prize Laureate) Joseph Brodsky characterized his great admiration for Donne as grounded in part on the Englishman's "translation of heavenly truth into the language of earthly truth, i.e. of eternal phenomena into transient language."[10]

Even without being prompted by such illustrious predecessors, it is not very difficult to produce our own examples of striking Donnean language, and the paradoxes that so often make this language striking in the first place: "Nor ever chaste, except You ravish me" (Holy Sonnet 10, 14); "We 'are tapers too, and at our own cost die" ("The Canonization," 21); "Whil'st my physicians by their love are grown / Cosmographers, and I their map, who lie" ("Hymn to God my God, in my Sickness," 6–7); "Love's mysteries in souls do grow, / But yet the body is his book" ("The Ecstasy," 71–72); and so on. In these instances, and many others, we see Donne juxtaposing opposite states of being, vividly conjuring unusual images, and developing detailed, complex metaphors that evolve – sometimes even dissolve – as they unfold.

How might we account for Donne's unique poetic language, besides simply granting him remarkable skills as a writer and moving on? Eliot's examples of Shakespeare, Middleton, and Webster suggest that – in the hands of many writers at this point in time – English was a distinctly acquisitive language, absorbing words from French and Italian in particular at a dizzying rate throughout the late 1500s and early 1600s.

The linguistic inventiveness of playwrights and poets in this period is but one barometer of the elasticity of English at the end of the Elizabethan era. We might also consider the work of translators such as John Florio, who produced dictionaries and language manuals – books that not only claimed to be able to teach Englishmen and women continental tongues, but that also exposed English readers to foreign words, some of which soon became *Englished*.

Like many of his English contemporaries, Donne was interested in foreign tongues. If we are to believe his first biographer, Izaak Walton, Donne had a "good command" of French and Latin by the age of eleven, and attained "perfection in the learned Languages, *Greek* and *Hebrew*," prior to taking holy orders in 1615.[11] There is no need to question Donne's Latin; he wrote letters, poems, epigrams, and a satire of the Jesuits, *Conclave Ignatii* (*Ignatius His Conclave*), all in that tongue. His proficiency in French also seems likely, although his "perfection" in Greek and Hebrew is harder to prove. But the arresting effects of Donne's poetic language hardly seem dependent upon him being multilingual. Milton, after all, knew even more languages than Donne, but his mature style struck readers such as Dryden and Eliot as far less deliberately witty and playful, far less *metaphysical*, in comparison.

Rather than focusing on languages themselves in order to explain why Donne has sounded so unique to so many readers for so long, it might behoove us instead to consider the various contexts in which Donne came of age. These include his religious and familial upbringing, the social and intellectual world of London that he inhabited as a young man, and the kind of intellectual practices fostered by his study of divinity and conversion to Protestantism. It is in these domains, we might assume, where Donne was first exposed to the rather technical vocabularies of theological, cartographic, medical, and more broadly scientific discourses in the early modern era – discourses that so mark his poetry. In addition, it is through his study of devotional practices, controversialist theology, and law that Donne came to write poems that are both persuasive and argumentative. These factors, along with those intangibles that constitute any great artist's sensibility – including a capacious, even at times radical, intellectual curiosity – all seem to have shaped Donne's utterly original poetic voice.

To begin with the poet's upbringing, Donne was raised as a Catholic in an era in which England was more and more emphatically self-identifying as a Protestant nation. This English, Protestant self-identification was by no means uniform or without internal ruptures. Just as English Catholics and Protestants did not see eye to eye on numerous issues from the ceremonial aspects of church service to the devotional conduct of individual Christians, mainstream Protestants – those who conformed to the Church of England's Book of Common Prayer – did not see eye to eye with Puritans, Anabaptists, or Presbyterians. Protestantism in England, particularly during the first half of Donne's life (roughly 1575 to 1605) was a kaleidoscope, then, of different liturgical, ecclesiastical, and devotional opinions.

So what held England together, in religious terms, during this time? One could argue that after the defeat of the Spanish Armada in 1588, and even more so after the failed Gunpowder Plot of 1605 (itself concocted by English Catholics in the hopes of occasioning an uprising against the Protestant King James), anti-Catholicism was the crucial common ground on which Protestants of all different persuasions congregated. And Donne's family was not just surreptitiously Catholic, as were many families in this period. They were, rather, famously so. Donne's mother, born Elizabeth Heywood, was the granddaughter of the famed Catholic martyr Thomas More's brother-in-law, John Rastell. Jasper Heywood headed the Jesuit mission in England for a brief period of time and was eventually incarcerated in the Tower of London before being shipped off to Europe.[12] Perhaps Donne visited him there, for he recounts witnessing a "Consultation of *Jesuites* in the *Tower*" in his prose tract *Pseudo-Martyr* (1610).[13] Donne's brother, Henry, was imprisoned for lodging a seminary priest and died at Newgate while incarcerated in 1593. The priest in question, William Harrington, was executed, at least in part it seems, because of the testimony provided by Henry under torture. Before that, in 1584, Donne and his brother Henry enrolled at Hart Hall, Oxford, presumably because it provided a more accommodating environment for Catholic boys than other colleges.[14]

While Donne would end up turning against the Jesuits when he published *Pseudo-Martyr* in 1610 and *Ignatius His Conclave* in 1611, his early education might have been influenced by at least one Jesuitical text – a text that circulated well beyond the reach of the order itself (an order, incidentally, that did not send missionaries into England until 1580). Ignatius of Loyola's *Spiritual Exercises* (1548) presents a series of meditations, prayers, and mental exercises, adaptable to Catholic devotees of all ages and educational backgrounds, aimed at fostering new or renewed spiritual vigor in the devotional practices of the reader. Ignatius encourages his followers to visualize specific places and details, both in their meditations and prayers. Hypothetical scenarios are also proposed. "I will imagine a person whom I have never seen or known," the "*Second Rule*" of the "Second Method of Making a Sound and Good Election" begins:

"Desiring all perfection for him or her, I will consider what I would say in order to bring such a one to act and elect for the greater glory of God our Lord and the greater perfection of his or her soul."[15]

The encouragement to practice persuasive speech acts, elsewhere in the *Exercises* described as colloquies that mirror "the way one friend speaks to another," the emphasis on viewing the "whole self as composed of soul and body," the prominence placed upon comparing oneself not just with "other human beings" but also with "the angels and saints in paradise," and the repeated call for specificity in one's mental practices, such that followers of the *Exercises* are said to learn how to contemplate "in detail all the circumstances around them,"[16] all contribute to Donne's poetic language and the frames and conceits of many of his poems. "The Flea," "The Sun Rising," "Lovers' Infiniteness," and "Break of Day," not to mention Holy Sonnets 10 and 13, all aim to persuade their addressees to adopt the speakers' often fantastic, counterintuitive claims. "The Canonization" and "Satire I" both experiment with the colloquy tones of friendly banter. "Witchcraft by a Picture" begins in a classically Ignatian mode ("I fix mine eye on thine, and there / Pity my picture burning in thine eye," 1–2), while Holy Sonnet 9 produces a harrowing picture of Christ while on the cross ("Tears in His eyes quench the amassing light, / Blood fills His frowns," 5–6) that attest to imaginative faculties honed by the *Exercises*. "Air and Angels" proposes a series of comparisons – not just between spirits and the air in which they move but also between male and female love – derivative of Ignatian habits of thought, while "The Ecstasy" regards the human – as did Ignatius – as comprised of spiritual and bodily qualities that are thoroughly mixed together. "I am a little world made cunningly" (Holy Sonnet 15, 1) enacts the Ignatian thought experiment in which the single soul is placed within God's massive creative design, while "A Valediction of My Name in the Window" meditates on the speaker's "ruinous anatomy" (24) before looking forward to a state of "repair" (31), as Ignatius would recommend.

But here we are right to pause, for if Donne's linguistic practices strike us, as they have scholars in the past, as discernibly Ignatian, how are we to account for the equally striking celebration of bodily pleasure and union that runs throughout so much of the *Songs and Sonnets*? Ignatius, after all, insists that his spiritual exercises "will work against their [his readers'] human sensitivities and against their carnal and worldly love,"[17] while Donne's speakers appear more inclined to argue – as in "To His Mistress Going to Bed" – that "As souls unbodied, bodies unclothed must be / To taste whole joys" (34–35). Some readers of Donne have proposed that, with the example from Holy Sonnet 10 offered above ("Nor ever chaste, except You ravish me," 14), "[p]erhaps the Ignatian exercises, with their extraordinary reliance on the power of corporeal images, promoted unsettling formulations of this kind."[18] Perhaps they did, but this does not mean that they alone can account for the all the erotic dimensions of Donne's poetic language. Here it seems that, in addition to his religious studies, Donne read a whole range of largely secular poets, from the ancient Roman writer Ovid, whose work was energetically imitated, and translated, by humanists in the sixteenth century, to Italian poets such as Lodovico Ariosto and Torquato Tasso, to the French Pléiade poets (Pierre de Ronsard, Joachim du Bellay, and others), all of whom were also directly influenced – as was Donne – by Petrarch, the fourteenth-century Italian poet. For these writers, the amorous and the divine *did* intermingle, with constancy toward both often being jointly affirmed. Here is Petrarch, for example, in "Poem 37" of the *Rime Sparse*:

> Every place makes me sad where I do not see those lovely sweet eyes that carried off the keys of my thoughts, which were sweet as long as it pleased God; and – so that harsh exile may weigh me down even more – if I sleep or walk or sit, I call out for nothing else, and all I have seen since them displeases me. (33–40)[19]

And here is Donne in "A Valediction of My Name in the Window":

> Then, as all my souls be
> Emparadised in you (in whom alone
>   I understand, and grow and see),
>   The rafters of my body, bone,
> Being still with you, the muscle, sinew,'and vein,
>   Which tile this house, will come again.   (25–30)

In both examples, the poet in question emphasizes the ocular apprehension of the beloved, insists upon the exclusivity and constancy of the human bond described, and asserts that this bond is animated by – and interfused with – the divine. In response to the often aloof, seemingly uninterested female beloved that we find in Petrarch, Donne's female addresses are often more playfully engaged by his speakers, even if they too typically remain silent. Nonetheless, the declarative insistence in Donne that one can be utterly remade by one's amorous attachment, such that a past without one's beloved is taken to be nearly unthinkable in a poem such as "The Good Morrow" ("I wonder by my troth, what thou and I / Did, till we loved," 1–2), often reminds us of the kind of male speaker we encounter in Petrarch, who is inclined to declare – as in "Poem 20" of the *Rime Sparse* – "I recall the time when I first saw you, such that there will never be another who pleases me" (3–4).

If we attempt, however, to read Donne as a Petrarchan poet, or as an exclusive follower of either Italianate or French sixteenth-century schools of poetry, we find ourselves stymied by the linguistic turns Donne is fond of making that are not fully anticipated by these predecessors. What are we to do, for example, with the second stanza of "The Good Morrow," which seems to abruptly leave the Petrarchan behind with the extended carto-graphic allusion of its second sentence – one that occasions the opportunity for Donne to evoke an image of a balanced, shared love never achieved by Petrarch's lovers in the earthly sphere:

> Let sea-discoverers to new worlds have gone,
> Let maps to others, worlds on worlds have shown,
> Let us possess one world, each hath one, and is one.   (12–14)

This language of maps and "new worlds" might strike us as quintessentially Donnean, and indeed allusions to the cartographic are everywhere in his verse, as are similar references to medicine and science, from the "fantastic ague" (13) of Holy Sonnet 19 to his well-known claim, in *The First Anniversary*, that the "new philosophy calls all in doubt" (205). Where might Donne, beyond evident reading and self-directed intellectual inquiry, have acquired such references? Donne's stepfather, John Syminges, was a prominent Catholic physician and President of the Royal College of Physicians who might have exposed Donne to medical terminology and practice, although we have little evidence of the two having very much contact. We do know, however, that following the completion of his studies at Oxford, Donne spent time first at Thavie's Inn and next at Lincoln's.

The Inns of Court were institutions in London where young men were trained in law, and were afforded the opportunity to mingle with – and learn from – the barristers practicing at this time. But just as importantly as exposing Donne to the world of legal practice and parlance, the Inns of Court were centers where the most avant-garde intellectual subjects of the day were routinely discussed. We know, for example, that a pair of globes, one terrestrial, the other celestial, designed and fabricated by Emery Molyneux, were owned by the Middle Temple as early as 1603, with Richard Hakluyt mentioning that such globes were being constructed as far back as 1589 (Donne's name first appears in the Lincoln's Inn admission record of May 6, 1592 and he appears to have been in residence there for the two years that followed[20]).[21] If Donne had the opportunity to examine these objects, the first of their kind to be made in England, they might very well have further stimulated his interest in cartography. Members of the Inns of Court were actively involved in the Virginia Company, which was chartered by King James in 1606 to establish a colony in North America. Just a few months after the first settlers arrived at what would become Jamestown, Donne appears to have put his name forward to become secretary of the colony (his friend William Strachey ended up securing the appointment).[22] With these biographical details and contexts in mind, we should not be surprised to find Donne, in "To His Mistress Going to Bed," referring to "my America, my new-found-land" (27), or imagining a raindrop creating "a terrestrial galaxy" (6) in "The Primrose," or describing how "On a round ball / A workman that hath copies by can lay / An Europe, Afric, and an Asia" (10–12) in "A Valediction of Weeping." These are details that draw from the world of discovery and science – a world in which Donne had more than a passing interest.

Donne is also interested, both as a poet and a preacher, in utilizing a language of argumentation that we might rightly see as more exacting than in the Ignatian mode we have already examined. This is the language of legal disputation, put to artistic use. Such a form of speech often draws rhetorically from the language of hypothesis in order to establish its argumentative frame, as in the opening of "Goodfriday, 1613":

> Let man's soul be a sphere, and then, in this,
> The'intelligence that moves, devotion is,
> And as the other spheres, by being grown
> Subject to foreign motions, lose their own,
> And being by others hurried every day,
> Scarce in a year their natural form obey,
> Pleasure or business, so, our souls admit
> For their first mover, and are whirled by it.   (1–8)

This literally dizzying sentence combines the language of theology and religion ("man's soul," "first mover," "devotion," etc.) with that of cosmology ("other spheres," "foreign motions," "natural form") to produce a speculative surmise ("Let") regarding the spiritual state of man within a universe in which certain bodies appear to be losing steam ("Scarce in a year their natural form obey"), while other, more divine, entities retain their eminence. Amidst what we might surmise to be a rather serious, scientific-sounding consideration of celestial decay, we discover a "first mover" somewhat playfully whirling around the objects of his creation. The worldview presented here is not simply worldly; it is cosmic and mesmerizing, in part because it draws from discourses that seem to be almost, but not quite, at odds with one another, turning the transcendent (as Brodsky might say) into an earthly language while making the earthly sound sublime.

Eliot observes of Donne that the kind of texts he cites in works such as *Pseudo-Martyr* and *Biathanatos* show "a pronounced taste, even a passion, for theology of the more controversial and legalistic type; for theology, in fact, as it was practised in his time."[23] If we are to believe Donne, it was only after he had "survayed and digested the whole body of Divinity, controverted betweene ours and the Romane Church," that Donne resolved to join the Church of England.[24] In his poetry as well, Donne is fond of making arguments – of convincing an addressee he often imagines as skeptical and leery that whatever he is proposing makes sense, even if it might not sound plausible at first glance. This argumentative outlook is an integral part of Donne's sensibility, one that seizes upon the many attributes of Donne's inquisitive mind in order to make a case that – in poetic terms – is meant both to convince and dazzle. Thus, to return to Coleridge's example, in "A Valediction Forbidding Mourning," Donne seizes upon the compass, perhaps *the* quintessential instrument of early modern exploration, to make the ingenious case that the consequences of the speaker's impending separation from his beloved can be minimized by a close, metaphoric examination of the very tool by which distances were judged in early modern Europe. Referring to their two souls, the speaker says to the addressee:

> If they be two, they are two so
>   As stiff twin compasses are two:
> Thy soul, the fixed foot, makes no show
>   To move, but doth, if the'other do.
>
> And though it in the centre sit,
>   Yet when the other far doth roam,
> It leans, and hearkens after it,
>   And grows erect as that comes home.   (25–32)

The case Donne presents here is counterintuitive but nonetheless simply stated, with the addressee's soul likened matter-of-factly to the foot of a compass. By the end of the poem, the poet has literally and figuratively come full circle, ending where he had "begun" (36). Distance has been overcome, with the speaker having performed an act of consolation that depends upon, of all things, the example of scientific measurement.

Donne's language is all his own. Constituted by theological, devotional, legal, Petrarchan, cartographic, medical, and other discourses, the poet's diction provides the foundation and fodder for his rhetorical efforts at persuasion and argumentation, for his robust image-making, and for his persistent claims for intellectual virtuosity. Drawn from these different – and in the hands of others often presumably competing – modes of speech, Donne's language stitches these different modes together, all in a form of serious play that attests to its creator's irascible, mischievous, and irreverent self.

Notes

1. T. S. Eliot, "The Metaphysical Poets," in *Selected Prose of T. S. Eliot*, ed. Frank Kermode (New York: Harcourt Brace, 1975). Eliot's essay was occasioned by Herbert Grierson's 1921 publication of *Metaphysical Lyrics and Poems of the Seventeenth Century* (Oxford University Press, 1995), which presented Donne's poems within the context of other poetic works from the period.
2. Eliot, "Metaphysical," 60, 64, 66, 66.
3. J. B. Leishman, *The Monarch of Wit: An Analytical and Comparative Study of the Poetry of John Donne* (London: Hutchinson, 1962), 96. Leishman is quoting from T. S. Eliot's essay "Donne in Our Time," in *A Garland for John Donne: 1631–1931*, ed. Theodore Spencer (Gloucester, MA: Peter Smith, 1958), 8.
4. Eliot, "Metaphysical," 67.
5. Samuel Johnson, *The Lives of the Most Eminent English Poets*, 3 vols. (Chicago: Stone and Kimball, 1896), 1:13.
6. Grierson, *Metaphysical*, 5.
7. Johnson, *Lives*, 14.
8. Eliot, "Metaphysical," 60.
9. Samuel Taylor Coleridge, *The Literary Remains of Samuel Taylor Coleridge*, ed. Henry Nelson Coleridge (New York: AMS Press, 1967), 149.
10. Igor Pomeranzev, "Brodsky on Donne: 'The Poet is Engaged in The Translation of One Thing into Another,'" *Radio Free Europe, Radio Liberty*, May 24, 2010, www.rferl.org/.
11. Walton, *Lives*, 23, 46.
12. See John Stubbs, *John Donne: The Reformed Soul* (New York: W. W. Norton, 2008), 16.
13. *Pseudo-Martyr*, 56.
14. Since it lacked a chapel, it was less noticeable at Hart Hall when students did not attend Church of England services. See Alexandra Gajda, "Education as a Courtier," in *OHJD*, 402.
15. Ignatius of Loyola, *Spiritual Exercises, in The Spiritual Exercises and Selected Works*, ed. George E. Ganss (New York: Paulist Press, 1991), 164–65.
16. Ignatius, *Spiritual*, 138, 136, 139, 151.
17. Ignatius, *Spiritual*, 147.

18. William Kerrigan, "The Fearful Accommodations of John Donne," *ELR* 4.3 (1974), 340.
19. Petrarch, *Petrarch's Lyric Poems: The Rime Sparse and Other Lyrics*, trans. and ed. Robert M. Durling (Cambridge, MA: Harvard University Press, 1976), 98.
20. Dennis Flynn, "Donne's Education," in *OHJD*, 422.
21. Helen M. Wallis, "The First English Globe: A Recent Discovery," *The Geographical Journal* 117.3 (1951), 276.
22. Stanley Johnson, "John Donne and the Virginia Company," *ELH* 14.2 (1947), 127.
23. T. S. Eliot, *The Varieties of Metaphysical Poetry*, ed.Ronald Schuchard (New York: Harcourt Brace, 1993), 258.
24. *Pseudo-Martyr*, 13.

CHAPTER 5

Donne's Poetics of Obstruction

Kimberly Johnson

The best introduction to John Donne's idiosyncratic poetics may come from eavesdropping briefly on an exchange between two of his contemporaries. William Drummond of Hawthornden kept surprisingly careful notes from a series of conversations he had with Ben Jonson, who traveled to Scotland in late 1618 and paid a visit to the literary laird. Drummond records Jonson's pronouncements on a number of his fellow poets including Donne, about whom Jonson opines "That Done, for not keeping of accent, deserved hanging." To this judgment, Jonson added "That Done himself, for not being understood, would perish."[1]

Jonson's comments not only reflect his high-minded, not to say persnickety, sense of his own authoritative position in English letters, but they also signal his own absorption in the aesthetic currents of his day. Jonson is a product of a culture that sought to adopt classical literary and rhetorical values, and to give those values new expression in the English tongue, thus aligning the literature of England with the grand legacies of the ancient world. The earliest works of what we might call English literary criticism in the sixteenth century enumerated in detail the qualities of good writing, urging quite particular considerations of both style and content. The gentlemen who authored these texts were careful to demarcate the parameters of what was, as George Gascoigne says, "lawfull" in verse. George Puttenham makes his regulatory goals explicit: "our intent is to make this Art vulgar for all English mens vse, & therefore are of necessitie to set downe the principal rules therein to be obserued."[2] In pursuit of such a legitimated art, Gascoigne advises that the writer cultivate a smooth and inviting poetic method, and avoid techniques that might alienate or discompose the reader: "frame your stile to *perspicuity* and to be sensible: for the haughty obscure verse doth not much delight."[3] Thomas Wilson, whose *Arte of Rhetorique* preceded and influenced the poetic theories of both Gascoigne and Puttenham, stipulated that an author must construct his text such "that the hearers maie well knowe what he meaneth, and understande him wholly, the whiche he shall with ease do, if he utter his mind in plain wordes, suche as are usually received, and tell it orderly, without goyng about the busshe."[4] And though George Chapman, writing (like Donne) some years after these manuals were published, denies "that Poesy should be as peruiall [i.e. transparent] as Oratorie" and argues that poets "must lymn" their expression to make it artful, he nevertheless inveighs against "Obscuritie in affection of words, & indigested concets" as "pedanticall and childish," not "utterd with fitnes" to its content.[5] Such characterizations of what is "lawfull" in poetry reaffirm the position inherited from Horace that poetry ought to be "dulci" and "utile," sweet and profitable, a formulation that makes the instructive utility of a work of art contingent upon the ease of its interpretive assimilation.[6]

Such stipulations of propriety in style – that is, of literary *decorum* – in which disorder and ostentation are abjured and perspicuity is most valued, ramify into all aspects of poetic practice, from metaphor to meter to matter. Puttenham allows that insofar as figurative language and conceits may dispose a reader "to mirth and sollace by pleasant conueyance and efficacy of speach, they are not in truth to be accompted vices but for vertues in the poetical science very commendable"; however, he warns, "such trespasses in speach (whereof there be many) as geue dolour and disliking to the eare & minde, by any foule indecencie or disproportion of sound, situation, or sence, they be called and not without cause the vicious parts or rather heresies of language."[7] Such watchfulness against the heresies of disproportion must also govern the nonsymbolic features of poetry, as Puttenham explains. Rhyme, which he calls by the suggestive term "concorde," should be judiciously and consistently handled, to preserve a sense of poetic proportion: "bycause your concordes contain the chief part of Musicke in your meetre, their distaunces may not be too wide or farre a sunder, lest th'eare should loose the tune, and be defrauded of his delight."[8] Moreover, rhymes should be "true, cleare, and audible . . . & not darke or wrenched." Meter, likewise, is subject to its own taxonomies of decorum: "the cadence which falleth vpon the last sillable of a verse is sweetest and most commendable; that vpon the penultima more light, and not so pleasant; but falling vpon the ante-penultima is most vnpleasant of all, because they make your meeter too light and triuial."[9] As the wide-ranging fastidiousness of Puttenham's primer suggests, this concern with propriety and decorousness is not just about conforming to rules. The many rhetorical manuals and style guides that emerged from Renaissance humanism understood writing as an ethical as well as an aesthetic activity – a notion that Philip Sidney articulates unambiguously when, in perhaps the period's best known treatise on decorum in poetry, he explains that "Poetrie euer setteth vertue so out in her best cullours," and endorses the moral effects of poetic propriety: "words set in delightfull proportion, either accompanied with, or prepared for, the well-inchaunting skill of Musicke ... doth intende the winning of the mind from wickednesse to vertue."[10] A well-regulated literature, Sidney argues, both bespeaks the well-regulated character of the mind that produces it and inspires the well-regulated subjecthood of the reader who digests it.

Implicit in Puttenham's and Sidney's shared insistence upon propriety and proportion is the argument that the poem is a means to an end, whether that end is conceived as the cultivation of virtue or the communication of ideas. Even independent of the kinds of social improvement programs that Sidney claims for good verses, sixteenth-century treatises on poetry agree that the content of a poem supersedes its style: "grounde it upon some fine invention," Gascoigne advises, and "that being founde, pleasant words will follow well inough and fast inough."[11] Both Sidney and Puttenham elevate to pre-eminence the "invention," the "*Idea* or fore-conceite of the work," and they each spend much ink categorizing poetic texts by subject matter and identifying the most appropriate form in its turn, admonishing for each theme a "stile conformable to his subiect."[12] Each of these formulations places the aesthetic priority on the subject matter of a poem to which poetic style is an accessory. It is content to which a poem's style must proportion itself, and the fit conforming of manner to matter defines a poem's decorum.

Recognizing this ethical dimension of late-sixteenth-century poetic theory helps to illuminate the undercurrent of outrage in Jonson's declarations about Donne. Donne's verse enthusiastically traffics in indecorum, defying those classical virtues of perspicuity and fitness so valued by Puttenham and his fellow handbookers. When Jonson complains about Donne's "not keeping of accent," it is the elastic relationship between metrical expectation and rhetorical emphasis, between form and content, in Donne's lines that provokes him. In part because of the expressive patterning of stress in Donne's lines, and in part because of Donne's many nonce verse forms, the temporal correspondences between rhyming words are unpredictable – their "distaunces" in flux, to borrow terms from Puttenham, causing the ear to "loose the tune." These sonic uncertainties combine with Donne's often ambiguous grammar and his predilection for conceits that are elaborated beyond clarity to produce poetry that is resistant and opaque rather than pellucid and easily digestible. Donne's poetics gives the impression not of decorous invitation and smooth delight but of interpretive obstruction and difficulty. In so doing, it offers an alternative aesthetic paradigm to the one championed by his recent pre-decessors, one in which the work of art functions as an end in itself rather than a self-effacing vehicle toward some external good. And against the insistence that style must ever be in the service of substance, Donne's verse answers that style *is* substance.

One need only read a few lines of Donne aloud to recognize that his metrical practice does not adhere to the classical ideal prescribed by Puttenham, in which lines flow "by slipper words and sillables, such as the toung easily vtters, and the eare with pleasure receiueth ... by the smooth and delicate running of their feete."[13] Guilty as Jonson charges, Donne does not keep accent but rather patterns his rhythms upon the cadences of speech even as he relies upon the expectations of meter to undergird his lines. Donne's expressive dynamism here bears many of the hallmarks of dramatic blank verse, hewing to iambic pentameter but only as a ghost, a phantom structure that throws into relief the poet's operatic departures from it. Think of the notorious Holy Sonnet 10 whose first lines deliver their hyperbolic demands in a cadence that might be described best (if not most technically) as *loud*:

> Batter my heart, three-personed God; for You
> As yet but knock, breathe, shine, and seek to mend;
> That I may rise and stand, o'erthrow me,'and bend
> Your force, to break, blow, burn, and make me new. (1–4)

If these lines are voiced with the bravura that their content suggests, they contain an unusually high proportion of stressed syllables for their five metrical feet (scansion is admittedly a subjective enterprise; nevertheless, my own ear counts seven stressed syllables in the first line, six in the second, seven in the third, and seven in the fourth). The words that demand to be stressed despite their unstressed positions ("breathe" in line 2 and "blow" in line 4 being the most obvious examples) are all the more clarion for their disrupting the sonnet's shadow of iambic pentameter. We become aware of the meter in its breaching: as Donne hammers his forceful monosyllables, the poem's meter registers in the ear as a site of transgression, of subversion.

The erratic nature of Donne's prosody is augmented by his flexible line, particularly in the *Songs and Sonnets*. These lyrics dispense with inherited formal structures, devising a remarkable variety of idiosyncratic stanzaic patterns whose internal consistency belies the poems' innovative unsettling of formal expectation. As Donne's lines whipsaw between long and short, as his stanzas depart from and return to rhyme, the irregularities compound, as in the opening stanza to "Farewell to Love":

> Whil'st yet to prove,
> I thought there was some deity in love,
>   So did I reverence, and gave
> Worship, as atheists at their dying hour
> Call what they cannot name an unknown power,
>   As ignorantly did I crave;
>   Thus when
> Things not yet known are coveted by men,
>   Our desires give them fashion, and so
> As they wax lesser, fall, as they size, grow.   (1–10)

I don't wish to diagram the patterns of rhyme and scansion here so much as I wish to register the structural tangle on offer: the first short line unevenly mated with its longer rhyming line; the initial gesture toward coupleted rhymes abandoned in the second pair; the uncertain elisions and jolting caesuras; the syntactic puzzle of line 10; and what Arnold Stein calls Donne's characteristic "stress-shift," as when the final stressed syllable of a line abuts the stressed syllable that begins the next one, a practice that privileges grammatical pauses over linear ones and suppresses the rhyme.[14] These features frustrate the ear's attempts to determine the arrangement of iambs and rhymes even as the ostentatiously visual stanza invites such a determination. This poem flaunts its patterns, in other words, only to have those patterns subverted by its plastic and irregular arrangement of stresses and line-breaks. The effect is that the medium of language becomes thick and substantial and disorientingly persistent. We cannot easily read through this poem's style as if it were either merely ornamental or assistive to its "fine invention," because the poem's every technical tool interposes itself, asserting its disruptions. Instead, we must grapple with the poem's linguistic surface for its own sake.

   This same obstructionist tendency informs Donne's figural practice. His use of outlandish conceits, metaphors extended until they become unfamiliar and unsettling, is perhaps his signature poetic trait. Whether he is comparing sexual intercourse to a bug-bite, as in "The Flea," or the search for Christ's church to an orgy, as in Holy Sonnet 18, Donne's figures perplex the correspondence between the metaphoric term and the idea to which it refers. It's not so much that Donne's metaphors defy understanding – indeed, many of his conceits turn upon perfectly familiar figures, as when in Holy Sonnet 18 he adopts the figure of the church as the Bride of Christ. This metaphor appears throughout the text of the

Bible, and was a cultural commonplace for Donne's contemporary readership. But in Donne's hands that conventional trope is elaborated until it reveals the strangeness it contains, as he describes the desire of the devout soul to seek out and unite with that bridal church:

> Betray, kind husband, Thy Spouse to our sights,
> And let mine amorous soul court Thy mild dove,
> Who is most true and pleasing to Thee then
> When she'is embraced and open to most men. (11–14)

As Donne probes the terms of the familiar marriage trope, its embedded implications render it unfamiliar, discomfiting. In this poetic expansion, God's marriage culminates ideally in an adulterous debauch, since this spouse is "most pleasing" when she is most sexually profligate and makes herself available to any suitor while God kindly procures his own cuckolding. Though critics have attempted to offer theologically safe readings aimed at neutralizing the disturbing turn at this poem's conclusion, Donne's elaboration of the church-as-Bride figure remains preposterous, and resists rationalization. Emphasizing its own transgressivities, Donne's conceit keeps interpretive focus on the details of the metaphor itself, even as its purported tenor, the quest for true religion, fades into referential obscurity. What persists about this poem is its audacious conceit, not its spiritual argument. Just as Donne's treatment of rhyme and rhythm halts interpretation at the prosodic surface, so the extremity of his conceits arrests referentiality, and disrupts transparency.

Donne's poetics, then, tend toward interpretive obstruction. His strategies of ornament and poetic style do not resolve into Horatian sweet utility but rather announce themselves, hijacking the smooth transmission of content and supplanting the "fore-conceite" with a style that is substantial and consequential. Here is no subordination of manner beneath matter, no privileging of "*Idea*" with the assumption that fit words will follow "well inough." In Donne's verses, the verbal surface disregards perspicuity, and rather courts refractoriness in both sound and trope. When Jonson worries that Donne would be forgotten "for not being understood," it is this quality in Donne's writing that provokes his concern: by employing opaque metaphors and a prosodic method that flouts the measure of numbers and the concord of the ear, Donne's poetry rejects the aesthetic of poetic instrumentality dictated by Elizabethan norms of decorum. Donne does not seek a "stile conformable to his subiect" but instead makes style a subject in its own right. Rather than imagining language as ever in service to the matter of content, he redirects interpretive attention to the *matter* of language. In other words, Donne's obstructive poetics asserts that the idea of the poem is finally indistinguishable from its ornament.

This focus on surfaces, which performs disruption and resistance and uncertainty as interpretive ends themselves, constitutes a departure from the aesthetic principles laid out by the sixteenth-century humanists. Moreover, it suggests a corresponding shift in the ethics of poetic production. As Donne's verse emphasizes its own interpretive resistance, it refocuses attention on the text as such, on the poem as an artifact worthy of contemplation in its own right. Despite the evident difficulties such a set of priorities presents for the conception of poetry as an instrument of virtue, the aesthetic shift we see in Donne's work should not be understood as somehow indifferent to its own ethical implications. For Donne's verbal innovations arise out of a cultural context that was increasingly skeptical about the stability of linguistic meaning. Especially in the wake of the Reformation, whose revolutions were so driven by interpretive disputation, literary texts reflect the challenge of having faith in words, of understanding language as a reliable referential system. As the essayist and scientist Francis Bacon recognized in his discussion of the "Idols of the Marketplace" in *Novum Organum*, words do not render things to the experience so much as they invite interpretation, and meaning tends to become less rather than more clear in the course of verbal communication.[15] Bacon's own strategy is to push toward the experiential knowledge of empiricism, to rely on the objective reality of the material as a foundation for meaning. We might consider Donne's obstructionist poetics a literary cognate to this scientific approach: displacing the edifying certainties of the humanist program with a set of techniques that assert poetic surfaces, Donne's lyrics offer up poems as objects to be confronted and grappled with not for the way they might illuminate virtue or curate decorum but for their own sake, as literary artifacts that enact relation and association and surprise and subversion through their verbal materials. This ethic prioritizes the experience itself over whatever might be gained from it, and emphasizes the activity of interpretation over its ends. Donne's hanging crime, finally, lies in a breach of poetic propriety that encompasses a critique of classical values. If the principle of decorum assumes that there is such a thing as fit correspondence and absolute order, Donne's poetics reflects a creeping suspicion that such absolutes are untenable, and throws its lot instead with uncertainty. Donne's poetic practice replicates the disorienting era in which he lived, fraught with revolutions of the mind and of the spirit; but he offers the experience of the thing itself as a mooring line. His substantial – or perhaps *substantiating* – style suggests that rather than doggedly chasing ideals and deferring meaningfulness to some ever-retreating end, we should attend to that which is present to our apprehension, and find meaning in what's at hand.

Notes

1. *Ben Jonson's Conversations with William Drummond of Hawthornden*, ed. R. F. Patterson (London: Blackie and Son Limited, 1923), 5, 18.
2. George Puttenham, *The Arte of English Poesie* (London, 1589), 19.
3. George Gascoigne, "Certayne Notes of Instruction Concerning the Making of Verse or Ryme in English," in *The Posies of George Gascoigne Esquire* (London, 1575), sig. 291r–295v.
4. Thomas Wilson, *The Arte of Rhetorique* (London, 1585), 14.
5. George Chapman, from the dedicatory epistle "To the Truly Learned, and my Worthy Friende, Ma. Mathew Royden," in *Ovids Banquet of Sence: A Coronet for his Mistresse Philosophie, and his Amorous Zodiacke* (London, 1595), sig. A2r.
6. Horace's proverbial perspective comes from *Ars Poetica*, lines 343–44.
7. Puttenham, *Arte*, 129, 63.
8. Puttenham, *Arte*, 68.
9. Puttenham, *Arte*, 66.
10. Philip Sidney, *An Apologie for Poetrie* (London, 1595), sig. E2v, E4v.
11. Gascoigne, "Certayne," sig. 291r–291v.
12. Sidney, *Apologie*, sig. C2r; Puttenham, *Arte*, 35.
13. Puttenham, *Arte*, 64.
14. Arnold Stein's suite of essays on structure in Donne remain the most attentive, though he does not always recognize how flexible Donne's practice is. See Arnold Stein's "Donne and the Couplet," *PMLA* 57.3 (1942), 676–96; "Donne's Prosody," *PMLA* 59.2 (1944), 373–97; "Meter and Meaning in Donne's Verse," *The Sewanee Review* 52.2 (1944), 288–301; and "Structures of Sound in Donne's Verse," *The Kenyon Review* 13.1 (1951), 20–36.
15. Francis Bacon, *The New Organon*, eds. Lisa Jardine and Michael Silverthorne (Cambridge University Press, 2000), 41–41, 48–49.

CHAPTER 6

Elegies and Satires

Melissa E. Sanchez

Rosalie Colie has aptly observed that Donne's elegies are not only "rarely elegiac" but also "often indistinguishable from his satires."[1] To be sure, the elegies rarely are poems of mourning and lamentation in the classical sense. They are witty, angry, spiteful, obscene, and salacious – the affects typical of satire – far more often than they are sad. But Donne's verse does not so much dissolve the generic boundaries between elegy and satire as insist on their interplay. If we ask what Donne's elegies lament and what his satires ridicule, the answer is surprisingly the same: the realization that the world of matter is also that of appearance and convention and therefore cannot give us access to the world of mind or spirit in any predictable or consistent way. In struggling to understand the relationship between appearance and reality, body and soul, Donne draws on the vocabularies of Renaissance courtiership, Platonic philosophy, and Petrarchan courtship, discursive and philosophical traditions that scholars have long agreed provide significant contexts for understanding Donne's writing. While these traditions differ in important ways, they share a belief in the analogical relationship between matter and spirit. In his elegies and satires, Donne does not so much reject the insights of courtiership, Platonism, and Petrarchism as illuminate the complexity within them.

The bitterness and disillusionment that pervade many of Donne's elegies and satires respond, on the most obvious level, to the values conventionally associated with Renaissance courtiership. Baldesar Castiglione's *The Book of the Courtier* was the most influential of the conduct, or "courtesy," books that explained how to become the perfect courtier. In offering to teach readers the "grace" that is the courtier's cardinal virtue, *The Courtier* introduces a number of ethical and ontological problems. The perfect courtier must, in effect, pretend that he has not consulted a conduct manual like *The Courtier*, so that being and seeming, truth and performance, become inseparable. *Sprezzatura*, which Thomas Hoby's sixteenth-century translation rendered as "Recklessness" and which most modern editions translate as "nonchalance," was at least as important as grace. The courtier must learn, Castiglione's Count Ludovico explains, "to cover art withal, and seeme whatsoever he doth and sayeth to do it without pain and (as it were) not myndyng it . . . Therefore that may be said to be a very art that appeereth not to be an art, neyther ought a man to put more diligence in anything then in covering it."[2] In effacing the distinction between outer appearance and inner reality, *sprezzatura* not only disguises the effort required to achieve grace, a word which itself treats this quality as a divine gift. *Sprezzatura* also conceals the primary motive for cultivating personal grace, which is to win the Prince's grace, or favor, and the social and economic rewards that come with it. Because princely favor is a finite resource, its pursuit provokes both the desire to unmask others as ingratiating rather than authentic and the anxiety that one's own grace will be similarly exposed. As the ready availability of puns on the term grace illustrates, the court as presented by Castiglione is a realm of unstable meaning which begets suspicion and insecurity. Accordingly, Federico Fregoso warns in Castiglione's dialogue, "it behoveth oure Courtyre in all his doings to be charie and hedefull" lest his grace be exposed as an act.[3]

In England, satires became fashionable in what Patrick Collinson has dubbed "the nasty nineties,"[4] that final decade of Elizabeth I's reign when, many believed, principled royal servants were displaced by self-serving flatterers. It was a commonplace that, as Donne puts it in "Satire V," Castiglione's precepts "being understood, / May make good courtiers, but who courtiers good?" (3–4). Drawing on models provided by Juvenal, Horace, and Persius, Donne's satires condemn a world where "all are players" ("Satire IV," 185). In a context in which self-promotion is everyone's central aim, lawyers are "more shameless far / Than carted whores" in their greed and mendacity ("Satire II," 72–73); in matters of faith men "more choose men's unjust / Power from God claimed, than God Himself to trust" ("Satire III," 109–10); and royal "officers / Are the devouring stomach, and suitors / The excrements which they void" ("Satire V," 17–19). Even the seemingly private relations of friendship and love fail to provide a refuge from the superficiality and insincerity of the court. Seeming friends may desert one another in favor of "some more spruce companion" ("Satire I," 16), and love, as Donne's elegies obsessively lament, may be mere "sophistry" ("Nature's Lay Idiot," 2), lovers' "oaths and tears" producing nothing but "empty blisses" ("The Expostulation," 15, 18).

Satire as a genre resists such superficial values, choosing the "coarse attire" of truth – manifested formally in irregular meter and rhyme – over the nonchalant grace exhibited by "Every fine silken painted fool" ("Satire I," 47,

72). Yet as Donne is well aware, such resistance itself rests on appearance and convention and therefore is always imitable and unreliable as a sign of truth. "Satire IV" exemplifies this dilemma, for it registers the speaker's difficulty in proving – to himself or others – that he is any different from the courtiers he scorns without resorting to the courtly tactics he deplores.

In this poem's narrative, the speaker goes to court, gets stuck talking with a tedious gossip, leaves, regrets not having rebuffed the gossip more bluntly, and returns to observe (again) the pride and pretension of the court. The opening lines promise to describe a harrowing experience that has absolved the speaker of the sins he confesses:

> Well, I may now receive and die. My sin
> Indeed is great, but I have been in
> A purgatory, such as feared hell is
> A recreation and scant map of this.   (1–4)

We can paraphrase Donne's opening lines as "I'm ready to die now that I have absolved my sin [of going to court] through penance [of talking with a courtier]." This sanctimonious horror contrasts markedly with the urbane irony of Donne's model, Horace's "Satire 1.9," which we can paraphrase as "please just kill me now instead of slowly boring me to death":

> Dispatch thou me, so it must be:
> for many yeres a gone,
> *Sabella,* (I a very chylde)
> did reede, my drerye fate,
> In folowynge forme, with tendre hande,
> pressed vpon my pate.
> Not poyson keene, nor emnies sworde,
> this babe away shall draw,
> Not stitch or coughe, or knobbyng gowte,
> that makes the patiente slaw,
> A prater shall becom his death,
> therfore, let him alwayes
> If he be wyse shun iangling iacks,
> after his youthefull dayes.   (59–72)[5]

Unlike the Horatian speaker, who hyperbolically casts the "prater" as more lethal than poisons, swords, or disease, Donne's speaker is unable to laugh off the situation. The structure of "Satire IV" underscores the seriousness with which the satirist takes the threat of the courtier. For while the opening lines initially impress us as coming at the end of the story, the narrative of "Satire IV" in fact begins *in media res.* The line "Well, I may now receive and die" (1) comes between the end of the conversation with the courtier that takes up the speaker's first visit to court (which ends at line 150) and his second visit (175–244) when he promises to defend Mistress Truth against "th'huffing braggart, puffed nobility" (164) but instead simply watches the court in silent disgust. The contrast between "Satire IV"'s epic structure and the satirist's impotence reveals that his assumed role of heroic truth-teller is as much a pose as that of the courtiers he loathes.

It is not just, as Stanley Fish has argued, that the courtier who accosts the poet is also a satirist,[6] but that the poet himself is also a courtier – or at least passes as one, which in the courtly world of Donne and Castiglione amounts to the same thing. Indeed, the courtier who traps the speaker is not a fool who idealizes the court. He is a "player" (in both the early modern sense of actor and the modern colloquial sense of manipulator) who knows the intimate details of its ugly underbelly: he "names a price for every office paid," complains that "offices are entailed" and that "great officers / Do with the pirates share and Dunkirkers," and reveals "Who loves whores, who boys, and who goats" (121, 123, 125–26, 128). In contrast to the Horatian bore, Donne's courtier threatens the satirist not because he is dull, but because he is too interesting: "I, more amazed than Circe's prisoners when / They felt themselves turn beasts, felt myself then / Becoming traitor" (129–31). The satirist again reveals his failure to live up to the epic heroism he imagines for himself. Like Circe, the courtier does not much transform his target though the external force of magic but by offering him what he wants. He thereby reveals the boundary between court insider and outsider, like that between human and beast, to be porous and uncertain. For his part, the satirist is no Ulysses. Rather than openly reject or castigate the courtier, he first shows "All signs of loathing" (137) and, when the courtier does not take the hint, pays him to go away. Hardly a heroic defender of Mistress Truth, our satirist is as much "privileged spy" (119) as the courtier. He can gather informa-tion because he blends in with the "flocks" at court (178), but the more successful the disguise, the harder it is to distinguish it from his "real" self. This may be why at the end of "Satire IV" the speaker imagines that his cover has been blown and, "I shook like a spied spy" (237). Being discovered is more fantasy than fear, since the spy who is recognized as spy is one who has inadvertently revealed his "true" identity as the enemy of those he observes.

This fantasy of authenticity is decisively undermined by the satirist's final recourse to that key quality of the courtier, *sprezzatura*, which Harry Berger Jr. has described as "conspicuously false modesty."[7] In one breath the satirist proclaims humility and demands admiration:

> Though I, yet
> With Maccabee's modesty, the known merit
> Of my work lessen, yet some wise man shall,
> I hope, esteem my writs canonical.   (241–44)

This final sentence reveals the distance between what our satirist says and what he wants: he may "lessen" the "merit / Of [his] work," but in truth he hopes that his writing will be accorded status no lower than that of divine truth. He thus reveals the adage that virtue is its own reward to be, however heartfelt, itself a stock trope for conveying sincerity. Given that some print and manuscript copies read "men," whereas others read "man," in line 243, the final two lines may be seen as expressing either disinterested hopes for posthumous recognition or a bid for the same patronage that the courtier seeks – secured through the same appearance of *sprezzatura*.

Castiglione's *The Courtier*, in fact, justifies its project not by defending appearance as such, but by insisting that only the truly virtuous can achieve the grace of the perfect courtier. In its final section, Castiglione's Pietro Bembo argues that "beawtie commeth of God, and is like a circle, the goodnesse wheof is the Centre. And therefore, as there can be no circle without a centre, no more can beawty be without goodness." Because the body is "a marke of the soule," it offers a reliable index of inner worth by which we can navigate the external world and conceive of that which lies beyond it. Attraction to beauty is but the first step in a ladder by which the lover progresses from contemplation of one beautiful body to appreciation for the "universall" beauty "that decketh out all bodies"; to beholding "the beawty that is seen with the eyes of the minde" so that the soul "wexed blinde about earthlye matters, is made most quicke of sight about heaven-lye"; to leaving behind even this "particular understanding" of the individual mind in favor of an ecstatic "universall understanding" of "pure heavenlye beawtye."[8]

The view that the attraction to earthly beauty initiates the lover into a quest for divine wisdom also structured the most widely imitated – and parodied – poetic form of late-sixteenth-century England: the Petrarchan sonnet. Petrarch's *Canzoniere*, which spawned countless imitations, describes Petrarch's failed pursuit of Laura, whose flawless beauty inspired excruciating desire but whose incorruptible chastity (and, later, death) forbade satisfaction. Erotic frustration proves redemptive here because it leads the lover to "the clear awareness / that worldly joy is just a fleeting dream" (1.13–14).[9] Yet whereas *The Courtier* imagines a smooth progression up the ladder of love, Petrarch depicts a process of doubt and indirection. As Richard Strier puts it, Petrarch "at times seems to accept the perversion of his will, his inability to desire what he knows to be the highest good."[10] Because the "pure heavenlie beawtye" celebrated by *The Courtier* is inaccessible except through analogy with earthly beauty, the allure of the flesh may overtake that of the spirit – or become so confused with spiritual devotion that the individual is helpless to tell the difference.

It is this difficulty of discerning one's own true motives, much less those of others, that Donne's elegies examine. The satires reveal that because the pursuit of virtue is also the pursuit of recognition as virtuous, the satirist may be as much a "player" as the courtiers he condemns; the elegies portray the erotic consequences of this dilemma. A particularly concise example occurs in the shortest of the elegies, "His Picture," where the speaker gives his mistress a picture of himself as he leaves for war, then imagines her response when he returns deformed and crippled. In this attempt to envision a love immune to physical change, Donne explores the dizzying series of reversals to which even the most sincere Platonism is subject. "His Picture" begins with the Platonic truism that the body is but a shadow of the soul:

> Here take my picture, though I bid farewell;
> Thine in my heart, where my soul dwells, shall dwell.
> 'Tis like me now, but I dead, 'twill be more
> When we are shadows both, than 'twas before. (1–4)

Because the speaker's spirit currently animates his body, it is easy to think that it is more "like" him than the picture he leave with his mistress, but when he is dead, the likeness of these two physical "shadows" will be clear. Because bodies are insignificant, moreover, her own likeness will "dwell" in his heart, so this is not a true separation. The speaker of the "His Parting from Her" puts it more forcefully: "thou canst not divide / Our bodies soe, but that our soules are tied" (69–70).

The elegy "On His Mistress," however, casts doubt on this Platonic ideal of the union of souls, treating as "flattery" the belief "That absent Lovers one in th'other be" (25–26). "His Picture" is distinct from the other elegies and the valediction poems in that it is not concerned with the lovers' separation but with what will happen upon their reunion. Will love endure, he wonders,

When weather-beaten I come back – my hand,
Perhaps with rude oars torn or sunbeams tanned,
My face and breast of haircloth, and my head
With care's rash sudden hoariness o'erspread,
My body'a sack of bones broken within,
And powder's blue stains scattered on my skin.   (5–10)

Here, Donne adopts a Petrarchan form, the blazon, to explore the consequences of a Platonic ideal of mutual love. In the early modern period, the blazon was not only imitated in earnest but also widely mocked in poems like Shakespeare's Sonnet 130 ("My mistress' eyes are nothing like the sun") and, especially, the popular genre of the "ugliness" poem, of which Donne's elegies "The Anagram," "The Comparison," and "The Autumnal" provide ready examples. As feminist critics have observed, the blazon divides the mistress's body into a series of parts to be subjected to the poet's rhetorical mastery: rather than a whole person, she becomes an assemblage of snowy skin, rosy cheeks, starry eyes, and pearly teeth.[11] In "His Picture," Donne acknowledges the objectifying potential of this trope as he anatomizes his own body in much the way the Petrarchan blazon anatomized that of the mistress. He thereby demonstrates that because a Platonic ideal of love depends on mutual attraction, the roles of lover and beloved, subject and object, cannot be neatly assigned to those of male and female. Mutuality, however, does not necessarily mean equality: men may be as vulnerable to physical evaluation and objectification as women, and women are just as likely to be motivated by sexual as spiritual desire. The first consequence, that of male objectification, appears in the acceptance in "His Picture" of the conventional standards that Donne's speaker in "The Comparison" gleefully evokes in describing the "odious" mistress:

Like rough-barked elm boughs, or the russet skin
Of men late scourged for madness or for sin,
Like sun-parched quarters on the city gate,
Such is thy tanned skin's lamentable state.   (29–32)

With his "tanned," "torn," "weather-beaten" skin, the speaker of his picture will be no less repellant. Similarly, the speaker's description of his body as "a sack of bones, broken within" resembles that of the "winter faces, whose skin's slack, / Lank, as an unthrift's purse, but a soul's sack" from which the speaker of "The Autumnal" recoils (37–38). The speaker of

"His Picture" imagines being held to the same standards to which other of Donne's elegies hold women and mocked just as mercilessly when he no longer measures up.

This problem is compounded by the speaker's acknowledgment that his mistress's initial love may have been provoked not by her recognition of his inner virtue, but rather by his physical conformity to the standards of what Castiglione's Bembo calls the "universall" beauty "that decketh out all bodies":

> If rival fools tax thee to'have loved a man
> So foul and coarse as, O, I may seem then,
> This shall say what I was; and thou shalt say,
> Do his hurts reach me? Doth my worth decay?
> Or do they reach his judging mind that he
> Should now love less, what he did love to see? (11–16)

The speaker here reframes his self-description as "foule and coarse" as the superficial perspective of the "rival fools," who, like Donne's speakers in "The Comparison," "The Anagram," and "The Autumnall," are unable to look beyond physical ugliness. Yet even as the poet clings to the opening conceit that he is not his body and therefore will only "seeme" ugly, the agonized "Oh" betrays regret that his future self may have no choice but to deny the importance of beauty. He can imagine his mistress's love as sincere only if she makes in earnest the tongue-in-cheek argument of "The Anagram": "Love built on beauty, soone as beauty, dies" (27).

The very terms of this fantasy of the mistress's continued love suggests that to transcend the body is not only impossible, but also undesirable insofar as its ugliness is the only evidence that his mistress's love is more than skin deep:

> That which in him was fair or delicate
> Was but the milk which in love's childish state
> Did nurse it; who now is grown strong enough
> To feed on that which to'disusd tastes seems tough. (17–20)

These lines, as scholars have long noted, allude to the Pauline distinction between spiritual novices and initiates: "For everyone that useth milk is inexpert in the word of righteousness, for he is a babe, but strong meat belongeth to them that are of age" (Hebrews 5:13–14). In "His Picture," however, consumption is literal as well as spiritual. "Love," personified here, grammatically shifts from object of the verb "nurse" to subject of the verb "feed," signaling not only the mistress's increased agency and

autonomy, but also the carnal dimension of her love. As the speaker argues
in "Love's Progress,"

> Although we see celestial bodies move
> Above the earth, the earth we till and love;
> So we her airs contemplate, words, and heart,
> And virtues, but we love the centric part.   (33–36)

Indeed, if "Love must not be, but take a body too" ("Air and Angels," 10)
then the true, spiritual object of the mistress's desire can, paradoxically, be
manifested only by conspicuously feeding on a body that anyone else
would find "tough" to love.

Such a stance is not a reaction against Platonism, but a more careful
engagement with its logic than Donne's critics have noticed. For Plato's
Symposium, one of Castiglione's as well as Petrarch's key sources, concludes
not with the famous ladder of love celebrated in *The Courtier*, but with
a speech in which Alicibiades points out Socrates' ugliness and thereby
throws into crisis Bembo's simplistic assertion that "The foule therefore for
the most part be also yvell and the beawtifull, good."[12] As Marsilio Ficino's
commentary on the *Symposium*, a key text for early modern readers,
reminds us, Alcibiades' description of Socrates suggests the folly of expecting inner goodness to appear in conventional outer beauty:

> Consider now; recall to your soul that picture of love [described to Socrates
> by Diotima]. You will see in it Socrates pictured. Put the person of Socrates
> before your eyes. You will see him *thin, dry*, and *squalid*, that is, a man
> melancholy by nature, it is said, and hairy, thin from fasting, and filthy from
> neglect. In addition, *naked*, that is, covered with a simple and old cloak.
> *Walking without shoes.*[13]

Like the beautiful Athenian youths, Alcibiades among them, who demonstrate
their love of wisdom in their pursuit of the physically repulsive Socrates, the
mistress of "His Picture" will prove that her love is sincere rather than superficial through her continued desire for the poet now that he is "foul and
coarse." The poet's desire to prove himself innately loveable generates not the
trite Platonic fantasy of transcending the body, as in the poem's opening lines,
nor the romanticized sexuality associated with the Platonism of Leone Ebreo
and often cited as an influence on Donne. Instead, his fantasy that his
deformed body will be embraced instead of rejected reveals the uncertainty
of the Platonic relation between beauty and goodness. In *The Symposium* the
highest love is not for the gorgeous Agathon (whose very name is derived
agathos, or "the good") but for Socrates, who is compared to the notoriously
ugly Silenus and Marsyas the satyr.[14]

It is, of course, this fantasy that the lover and the satirist share: the hope that an ugly exterior will perform the work of distinguishing those who love the inner person from those attracted to external attributes of beauty, wealth, or power. "His Picture" thus registers with particular precision the conflicted self generated by the performance of courtly, Platonic, and Petrarchan contexts that inform the elegies and satires more generally. For if, as Donne memorably puts it in *Devotions upon Emergent Occasions*, "No man is an Island, entire of itself," then the difference between his satirists and lovers, on the one hand, and his courtier, on the other, may not be the degree of sincerity with which they say "Such services I offer as shall pay / Themselvues" ("O, Let Me Not Serve So," 8–9). It may be the degree to which they believe themselves sincere, a fine but significant distinction.

Notes

1. Rosalie Colie, *Paradoxia Epidemica: The Renaissance Tradition of Paradox* (Princeton University Press, 1966), 128.
2. Castiglione, *The Book of the Courtier, from the Italian of Count Baldassare Castiglione: Done into English by Sir Thomas Hoby* (New York: AMS Press, 1967), 59.
3. Castiglione, *Courtier*, 111.
4. Patrick Collinson, "Ecclesiastical Vitriol: Religious Satire in the 1590s and the Invention of Puritanism," in *The Reign of Elizabeth I: Court and Culture in the Last Decade*, ed. John Guy (Cambridge University Press, 1995), 170.
5. Horace, *A Medicinable Morall, that is, the Two Bookes of Horace His Satyres, Englished According to the Prescription of Saint Hierome*, trans. Thomas Drant (London, 1566).
6. Stanley Fish, "Masculine Persuasive Force: Donne and Verbal Power," in *Soliciting*, 240–41.
7. Harry Berger, Jr., *The Absence of Grace: Sprezzatura and Suspicion in Two Renaissance Courtesy Books* (Stanford University Press, 2002), 12.
8. Castiglione, *Courtier*, 350, 349, 358, 359, 360.
9. Petrarch, *The Canzoniere, or, Rerum Vulgarium Fragmenta*, trans. Mark Musa (Bloomington, IN: Indiana University Press, 1996).
10. Richard Strier, *The Unrepentant Renaissance: From Petrarch to Shakespeare to Milton* (University of Chicago Press, 2011), 62.
11. See Nancy J. Vickers, "Diana Described: Scattered Women and Scattered Rhyme," *Critical Inquiry* 8 (1981), 265–79.
12. Castiglione, *Courtier*, 349.
13. Marsilio Ficino, *Commentary on Plato's Symposium on Love*, trans. Sears Jayne (Dallas, TX: Spring Publications, 1985), 155–56.
14. Plato, *The Symposium*, trans. Walter Hamilton (Harmondsworth, UK: Penguin, 1951), 100.

CHAPTER 7

The Unity of the Songs and Sonnets

Richard Strier

Of course, my title is ironic. One of the most striking things about this spectacularly mistitled collection – which contains no sonnets and, at most, a handful of songs – is its astonishing variety and range of attitudes.[1] Each poem is a discrete lyric with its own title (probably not authorial), and there is no frame or implied narrative.[2] To say that the volume – or, better, collection – is a gathering of John Donne's love poems would itself be misleading, since many of the poems included therein could hardly be called "love poems" in any intelligible sense, although the most famous ones certainly bear out that rubric.[3] The collection is probably best thought of as something like "lyrics illustrating many varieties of erotic experiences and attitudes." Although there are only fifty-odd poems in the collection, it is almost impossible to sit and read through them in one sitting, since one is so bounced around from attitude to attitude from one poem to the next.[4] To take just the first three in the carefully edited 1635 edition, how does one understand going from "The Flea" – given pride of place there – to "The Good Morrow" to "Song" ("Go and catch a falling star")?

Helen Gardner's edition of the elegies and *Songs and Sonnets* reorganized the lyrics, and did so independently of any order that appears in any manuscript or early printed edition. Like William Empson, I have problems with Gardner's groupings.[5] And yet, like Empson, I feel that going back to the order (or lack thereof) in 1635 or any other edition that follows one of the manuscripts is "like having the lights go out."[6] One needs to group the poems in some way in order to make the reading experience bearable, but also, and this is clearly more important, to make it intelligible that all these lyrics were written by the same person. It could, no doubt, be said that to demand this sort of intelligibility is to fall into various Romantic, biographical, or other "fallacies," and that there is no reason

---

* I want to thank Ted Leinwand and Gordon Braden for extremely helpful comments on an earlier draft of this essay.

why a person cannot imagine (or have) one attitude one day and another on another. But it does not seem unreasonable to think that there are going to be some significant continuities. Even Montaigne – with whom Donne is often compared – thought that he and everyone else had *"une forme maistresse"* to his personality.[7] So my title is not simply ironic.

One of the striking things about the way in which Donne's erotic poems exist in the world is how few of them actually do.[8] Every general anthology of English poetry includes "The Good Morrow," "The Sun Rising," "The Canonization," and "A Valediction Forbidding Mourning." If one adds a handful of other lyrics – "Air and Angels," "The Ecstasy," "Love's Growth," and "The Flea" – one has practically all the widely anthologized Donne love lyrics. And the criticism mirrors this. For every 100 pages of critical commentary on "The Canonization," "The Ecstasy," or "A Valediction Forbidding Mourning," there is perhaps one page on "Love's Usury," "Love's Exchange," or "The Blossom." One might assert that the most widely anthologized and commented upon lyrics are the best of them. That might well be true (though I would want to follow Wilbur Sanders in distinguishing problematic poems like "The Canonization" and "The Ecstasy" from true masterpieces like "The Good Morrow" and "Forbidding Mourning").[9] But if we want to appreciate Donne as a writer of erotic lyrics, and not of simply either "love poems" – the category into which seven of these eight poems fall – or clever seduction poems like "The Flea" (of which there are very few), we need to find a way of appreciating the "cynical" poems as well as the rapturous and charmingly audacious ones, and – to take up the theme with which I began – be able to find some continuity of consciousness within the poems that we choose to group together, and even among the groups themselves.

My suggestion with regard to the "cynical" poems – which, given Donne's biography, are hard not to think of as "early," issuing, that is, from the same period as the satires and elegies – is to read them as dramatic monologues, as poems in which we are meant to judge the speaker, or at least be aware of his strategies, as well as to follow them. Young Donne was known to be a great frequenter of plays as well as a devotee of the ladies;[10] there is no anachronism in seeing the lyrics as dramatic monologues, even if their speakers are not named characters. Donne seems always to have had the ability to think about attitudes even as he was expressing them, to stand both inside and outside a particular attitude or state of mind. He was a trained logician and rhetorician, and he knew when he was using or misusing both. Pierre Legouis may or may not have been right that we are supposed to recognize the speaker of "The Ecstasy" for the hypocritical cad that he is, but Legouis was, I think, properly modeling how we are to read

many of the lyrics – as long as we do not forget the person behind the
"persona."[11]

Take, for instance, "Community," a poem that seems to be merely an
exercise in what Empson calls "boyish" cynicism. It is probably "early," but
it clearly comes from the period out of which the great "Satire III"
emerged, the period in which Donne had been ferociously reading the
arguments on both sides of the Reformation divide in order to determine
where (if anywhere) he stood, or wished to stand. He focuses on a key
concept for the Church of England, that of *adiaphora*: "Good we must
love, and must hate ill, / For ill is ill, and good, good still, / But there are
things indifferent" (1–3). Readers of this are surely meant to hear the
speaker's boredom with normal moral categories (good and evil or "ill"),
and what is normally said about them, and to feel that the new category
introduced offers a kind of opening or freedom. This is indeed something
like the Hookerian or "Anglican" position (to use the anachronistic term),
but we are getting to the point in the argument when we need to start
paying attention. The speaker tells us that "we may neither hate, nor love"
(4) things indifferent. But this is false. And we are meant to know it.
The theological point is not that we "may not" love or hate things indifferent, but that we do not have to do so; we are not under any inherent
obligation in respect to them (though we may be under a secondary obligation – which was the Church of England's position).[12] The speaker's point is
the sophistical one that we must be indifferent toward things indifferent.
And in case we were not paying attention, Donne makes it clear that
something has gone very wrong with what looked like a straightforward
argument when he finishes the stanza with the needed rhymes for "love" and
"indifferent." We are instructed that no principles whatever are to guide how
we "prove" (test out, experience) things indifferent, so that we can deal with
them entirely "As we shall find our fancy bent" (6).

At this point we know the speaker is a witty sophist, and are not
surprised (especially after "one, and then another prove") to find that the
"things" indifferent in question are women. The second stanza follows the
"logic" of the first in asserting that since women are things indifferent (and
made such by "wise nature," 7, the libertine's friend), we may not, if we are
being rational, either love or hate them – "Only this rests, all, all may use"
(12). The speaker now realizes (or pretends) that he has moved too fast, and
needs to offer an argument as to why women fall into the key category.
Again, he relies, as in the opening, on great moral commonplaces: goodness
is "visible" and obvious ("as visible as green," 14), and evil ultimately self-
destroying ("If they were bad, they could not last," 16). Since it is not

obvious that women are good, but it is obvious that they do "last," he has made his case: they are outside the moral realm ("they deserve nor blame, nor praise," 18). From this point, the poem proceeds logically – there are no rules as to how "we" (males) should use "them" (females): "they are ours as fruits are ours, / He that but tastes, he that devours, / And he that leaves all, doth as well" (19–21). This is true indifference – there is no moral difference between abstinence, finicky selectivity, and promiscuity. And there is a true ideal here – one of detachment, not caring one way or the other. But, despite the clear logic of this (given the dubious premise asserted in stanza one), and the admirable or shocking equanimity of this view, this is not where the poem ends. Following this lofty and calm stance of indifference, the poem ends by justifying and endorsing the devourer: "Changed loves are but changed sorts of meat, / And when he hath the kernel eat, / Who doth not fling away the shell?" (22–24). So is the ideal that of indifference or that of ferocious and non-repetitive (and repetitive) "use"? And is there an element of disgust in the very emphatic "meat," and in the surprisingly intense and transparently defensive final question, where the speaker seems to look up from his paper, so to speak, and challenge us to disagree with him?

This is the kind of complexity that one must recognize in even the "minor" poems in the *Songs and Sonnets*. The display of rhetorical mastery often leads to self-disgust. I believe, with Stanley Fish, that "rhetorical mastery" is highly problematic in the poems, but I do not believe – at least in the *Songs and Sonnets* (and the satires) – that Donne was unaware of the self-undermining qualities of rhetorical display. As Fish says, "the large question is, does Donne *know*."[13] "Woman's Constancy" helps us answer this. Like "Community," it is a poem that reeks of the study, or rather of the Inns of Court, where young lawyers were trained.[14] The body of the poem consists of a series of arguments the speaker postulates that the woman he is addressing is planning to address to him (as far as we know, she has as yet done nothing other than, it seems, express affection – "Now thou has loved me one whole day," 1). The hypothesized female speaker is both impressively fertile in devising excuses for inconstancy and clearly a sophist (the wonderfully fussy stress on "we are not *just* those persons" (5) tells the story; emphasis added). In the finale of the poem, the speaker claims to be able to win a disputation against each of the arguments that he has devised for her: "I could / Dispute, and conquer, if I would" (15–16). We believe this. But, in the final twist, when the speaker says that he "abstains" from doing so because "tomorrow" he "may think so too" (17), it is impossible to believe that this speaker could happily use arguments for which he has such obvious (and proper) contempt. What seemed like the set-up for a simple joke turns out to be more complicated. And why this set-up in the first place? Why imagine these arguments in the mouth of the other when all that seems to have happened is that the speaker and this other have spent a day together, apparently harmoniously? This helps us recognize the poem as a first or pre-emptive strike, a way of guaranteeing the non-continuance of the relationship under the guise of attributing this desire to the person with whom a relationship seems to be developing. Self-disgust connects the two poems we have analyzed, disgust at the rhetorical facility that is demonstrated. But the "cynical" poems can be seen to connect in another, perhaps deeper way. Defensiveness might be the term we need.

"The Indifferent" begins with the "indifference" theme – "I can love both fair and brown" (1) – but, like "Community," does not stick to this theme. It turns out (again) that the speaker is not indifferent at all. He has one very strict requirement – "I can love any, so she be not true" (9). But why should this be the case? The poem suddenly becomes very intense. In place of the calm assertions and balanced antitheses of the opening stanza, the second stanza is a series of quite overheated rhetorical questions – "Will no other vice content you?" (10) – and strong assertions – "Oh we are not, be not you so" (14) (again, "we" men versus "you" women). It ends with an intense but barely intelligible question: "Must I, who came to travail thorough you, / Grow your fixed subject, because you are true?" (17–18). What is the logic of this? Why should this speaker care that a woman might be "true" to him? And why should he fear that this situation might lead him to lose his status as a mobile and purposive "travailer" and turn into a helpless "fixed subject"? The only answer seems to be that the speaker feels that a woman making a commitment to him lays an unbearable implication of reciprocity on him. But the contentedly promiscuous speaker of the opening would not feel this. A woman who loved him would be just another woman (like "Her who believes," 5, etc.). The speaker revealed in the poem is much more vulnerable than this, even conscientious. It would be easy to think that fear of relationship is the issue, and that would not (as we will see) be entirely mistaken. Certainly there is fear at work here. But the third stanza reveals the fear to be of something else. The curse that Venus is imagined as putting on those who seek to establish "dangerous constancy" (25) – a wonderfully rich phrase – is that they be fated to be betrayed by someone they love. So the fear is not of being in a relationship *per se*, but of what being in a relationship might open the self to – the possibility of being betrayed. And that is what is completely unacceptable. Indifference seems a very happy state when compared to where, psychologically, this speaker is revealed to be.

To take another poem that would fall for both Gardner and Empson into "Group I," "Love's Usury" seems to find a way to combine the "ideals" of indifference and promiscuity. The poem involves another deity, the one named in "Love's Deity" and complexly non-covenanted with in "Love's Exchange." "Love" here means the emotion, the impulse that leads one to care and, as in "The Indifferent," to be vulnerable. "Love's Usury" is a high-spirited poem, happily imagining the life of a cad ("let / Me … snatch, plot, have, forget / Resume my last year's relict," 5–7). The speaker delights in imagining outrageous triumphs in seduction, but, interestingly, is very insistent not only that he "love[s] none," but also that he does not become compulsive, and find himself, Don Giovanni-like, loving "the sport" (13). He pretends to be fully engaged not only in body ("let my body reign," 5) but also in mind ("let report / My mind transport," 15–16). The speaker concludes by stating that if he is allowed such emotionless and detached promiscuity in his youth, he is willing, in old age, to endure being in love, even with "One that loves me" (24). The joke, to spell it out, is in imagining mutuality as a fate worse than death; but again, one has to ask why this would be so, what sort of creature one would have to be to actually mean this. Independence, absolute self-enclosure, would seem to be what "indifference" would provide.

"Love's Usury" deflects the threat of relationship onto old age, and hopes to escape even then ("*if* when I'am old," 17, emphasis added). Other poems, however, find the maintenance of non-commitment more difficult. "Love's Diet" has been analyzed by Barbara Hardy in a remarkable essay that sees Donne in his erotic poetry as having "a special sense of the exposure of human beings in their relationships." She views "Love's Diet" as showing the difficulty of keeping the erotic life manageable; value in the poem, and in the speaker's consciousness, "has existed," as she says, "and must be destroyed."[15] The "diet" that the speaker puts the emotion on is cynicism. This is the means used to keep it trim, to keep it from getting large and unmanageable ("a burdenous corpulence," 2). The speaker diminishes his emotion, his temptation to recognize and enter into a relationship of mutuality, by refusing to take the responses of the woman in question as meaning what they seem to (and almost certainly do). By telling his emotional self (his "love") that the apparently devoted and responsive woman with whom he could be involved is promiscuous and insincere, the speaker reclaims his "buzzard love" (25) and brings it under control of the will, "to fly / At what, and when, and how, and where I choose" (25–26). How triumphant those last two words are! But that is not where the poem ends. It develops the idea expressed in "let me love none, no, not the sport." Falconry, seduction – "the sport" – can become an obsession. True indifference would be indifference not just to the (superficial) differences between women but to the whole realm of the erotic. The speaker, now supposedly disencumbered of fatty response to "One that loves me," presents himself as "negligent of sports" (27), and not caring whether he succeeds in the hunt or not – "the game killed or lost, go talk, and sleep" (30). But it has taken a lot of effort to get to this lovely state of "negligence." And the loving woman still remains somewhere in the background of the picture.

The situation is even more complicated in "The Blossom," a poem that, even for Donne, goes through a remarkably complex number of twists and turns. William Hazlitt saw it as a case of "beautiful and impassioned reflections losing themselves in obscure and difficult applications."[16] It is the kind of poem that led Empson to argue that Gardner's two-part division of the erotic lyrics – cynical and unphilosophical before Donne's marriage; complex and philosophical (neoplatonic) after – was too simple. Empson argues that a category in between is needed, one that allows for both cynicism and overt complexity (and that can use complex stanza forms to express this complexity of attitude), so that there would be three groups, instead of two.[17] "The Blossom" begins with the speaker's sweetly condescending address to a "poor flower" that, like the Anacreontic grasshopper, "Little think'st" (1) that it will "freeze anon" (7) (this is what Hazlitt admired). The speaker then addresses his own emotion in what attempts to be the same vein – his poor heart "Little think'st" (in the same stanzaic position) that it will "tomorrow" have to leave a woman who is either "forbidden or forbidding" (12), and whom the heart thinks to win through constancy and persistence. It is (more or less) the Petrarchan situation, and the speaker rightly characterizes and addresses a consciousness of this sort as "Subtle to plague thyself" (18). But this part of the self, instead of meekly agreeing, is suddenly imagined as speaking up, and doing so in a remarkably vigorous and colloquial voice that refuses the intimacy of "thou" – "Alas, if you must go, what's that to me?" (19). The heart insists on staying with (that is, continuing to be focused on) the woman, and points out that the condescending speaker really doesn't want to have a "heart," since that speaker has a whole world of material, social, and sexual pleasures to indulge in:

> You go to friends, whose love and means present
> > Various content
> To your eyes, ears, and tongue, and every part.
> If then your body go, what need you'a heart?   (21–24)

The question is obviously a good one. The speaker who will be in every way taken care of by his wealthy and loving friends clearly has no need, or desire, for a capacity for self-lacerating devotion. The worldly voice concedes this – "Well then, stay here" (25) – but insists that his devoted part is mistaken about what women in general (and therefore the one in question) are capable of. After the concession, the worldly voice strongly asserts the key limitation: "but know," this voice says, "When thou hast stayed and done thy most, / A naked thinking heart, that makes no show, / Is to a woman but a kind of ghost" (25–28). "A naked thinking heart" – this is the kind of phrase that seems to validate Eliot's talk of a unified sensibility that feels its thought[18] – is a perfect description of the Petrarchan stance: at once vulnerable and analytical toward its own emotional vulnerability. In context, the phrase hovers somewhere between contempt and admiration; the worldly speaker's point is not the striking confluence of thought and feeling but what the second half of the line says – women are only capable of empirical perception, so that something deeply interior and hidden, and does not make an effort to appear, has at best only a shadowy reality to such creatures. The stanza ends coarsely, with its final couplet continuing the characterization of women as only capable of physical perception: "Practice may make her know some other part, / But take my word, she doth not know a heart" (31–32).

The poem ends with the worldly voice taking on a kind of bluff manliness; it accepts fully the characterization that the voice of feeling has offered of what the worldly voice desires and will find. With striking geographical specificity – this is the "real" world – the worldly voice continues to try to cajole his heart to give up its "long siege" (13): "Meet me at London, then" (33). What is promised is (as the other voice postulated) happy sociability (as in "go talk" at the end of "Love's Diet"); the worldly self will be "fresher, and more fat, by being with men" (35). And this voice offers a clear solution to the problem of the "forbidden or forbidding" woman: "I will give you / There to another friend whom we shall find / As glad to have my body as my mind" (38–40). But this is a "solution" to a different problem than the one that the poem is about. What the "naked thinking heart" wants, as the other speaker actually knows, is emotional, not sexual, responsiveness. If the woman in question were in fact glad to have the speaker's mind, this would be a different poem. That some other woman would be willing to have his body – or even, as the previous stanza suggested, that this woman would ("Practice may make her know some other part") – does not respond to the issue at hand. Donne knows this. He concludes his oration, which turned into a dialogue, with a spectacular non-sequitur.

The poem that can be seen as the culmination of Empson's "Group 2" – cynical, but complex in both expressed attitude and stanza form – is "Love's Alchemy." Gardner thinks that Donne did not discover Neoplatonism until the period of enforced retirement following his marriage, but this seems unlikely (as Empson says, "she wants the poet's head to be practically empty until he is converted to Neoplatonism"); Donne's interest in alchemy is present in the elegies.[19] Here, in two devilishly complex twelve-line stanzas that begin with a pentameter couplet, move through a couplet with a seven-syllable line and a pentameter to a pentameter line rhyming with the first couplet, then to rhyming trimeter and tetrameter lines that frame another pentameter–tetrameter couplet, and, before the final pentameter couplet, include a pentameter that rhymes with the framing trimeter–tetrameter, Donne's speaker directly confronts the mystification of love. But here the "solution" is not happy acceptance and encouragement of promiscuity and unfaithfulness, (supposedly) happy reveling in the pleasures of the body, or even anxious or hard-won indifference. Here, as in "The Blossom," but more explicitly, there is no solution. The problem is not only the (supposed) limitation of women, but also the limitation of the physical itself, specifically, of sex. The opening (normal) couplet is either a descriptive assertion or a challenge: "Some that have deeper digged Love's mine than I, / Say where his centric happiness doth lie" (1–2). Either some do claim this (where "centric" equals essential or spiritual) or the speaker is challenging them to do so. But in any case, his skepticism is clear. "Deeper digged" is not likely, in both sound and meaning, to produce something sublime, and it is impossible for a reader who knows Donne's elegies (which circulated widely in manuscript) not to recall the focal "centric part" of a woman's body in "Love's Progress."[20] The voice that is inquiring or neutral competes with one that is nasty and sneering. And possibly one is supposed to hear that "some . . . lie."

The speaker then baldly states his own view. Speaking as an experienced cad who has "loved, and got, and told" (3), he knows that there is no "hidden mystery" (5) in eros. The central short line of the stanza (its only trimeter) figures alchemy not as a quest for refinement but as a fraud – "O, 'tis imposture all" (6). The exclamation suggests, as it is meant to, impatience with "all" claims about something mysterious and valuable in the erotic, but the lines that describe what alchemists do are not quite what one would have expected:

> And as no chemic yet th'elixir got,
>   But glorifies his pregnant pot,
>   If by the way to him befall
> Some odoriferous thing, or medicinal.   (7–10)

The alchemist as fraud had disappeared. Instead, the alchemist is scorned for being proud of what he has accidentally produced. But the odd thing is that he has in fact produced something. Instead of finding nothing or something vile, he stumbles onto something either pleasant or useful. But, needless to say, it is not "th'elixir," the ultimate goal of the alchemist's quest, the philosopher's stone that produces the quintessence of gold and cures all diseases (it might merely be, for instance, penicillin).[21] We are confronted with a mental state in which not finding "all" amounts to finding nothing, in which if one doesn't succeed at the ultimate goal, no other successes matter. And in case we have somehow missed the oddness of this, Donne "clarifies" it for us by providing the tenor of the alchemical vehicle: "So, lovers dream a rich and long delight, / But get a winter-seeming summer's night" (11–12). A line of "golden" poetry ("So lovers dream") is rudely halted by "But get." The poem is about what lovers "get," but the strange thing here is the failure of the analogy. The lovers "get" nothing at all valuable; they "get" something cold and short. But what about "Some odoriferous thing, or medicinal"? That has fallen away – or rather, Donne wants us to see that to this speaker, the two sets of unintended results are the same.

The second stanza returns to "the centric part." It is about sex, and disdains it as something unworthy of a refined, aristocratic sensibility – "Ends love in this, that my man, / Can be as happy as I can; if he can / Endure the short scorn of a bridegroom's play?" (15–17). "Can" replaces "get" here. All that is needed to be "happy" is mechanical potency; anyone, even a servant ("my man"), who "can" can. Marriage merely licenses this disappointing outcome; one could hardly put more contempt onto a syllable than Donne puts onto "Ends love in *this*." The idea of a marriage of minds is mocked, with reference to a village wedding ceremony:

> That loving wretch that swears,
> 'Tis not the bodies marry, but the minds,
>   Which he in her angelic finds,
>   Would swear as justly, that he hears,
> In that day's rude hoarse minstrelsy, the spheres.   (18–22)

This speaker wants to hear the music of the spheres – something purely intellectual – and can see/hear/feel no connection between coarse physical music and that. On the other hand, a less unhappy Platonist, like Sir Thomas Browne, could in fact make such a connection.[22] The ending of the poem continues the demonstration of the speaker's demandingness. He turns to his (male) readers and issues an injunction: "Hope not for mind in women; at their best, / Sweetness and wit they'are, but mummy possessed" (23–24). We are back to the first part of the failed analogy. "Mummy" was highly valued by alchemists, and was indeed an "odoriferous thing" and medicinal.[23] "Sweetness and wit" certainly sound pleasant enough – but not for this speaker. What he wants is something greater. He wants "mind" – a woman who will be glad to have his, and, the impossible thing, has one of her own. Nothing else counts.[24]

We are now in a position to see how the cynical poems can lead to the great celebrations of mutual love and wonder. What if the consciousness dramatized in "Love's Alchemy" were to find "mind" in a woman, and to find his own appreciated, and not dulled but enlivened? It is at that point that we can get – given genius – a poem like "The Good Morrow." As I said earlier, I agree with Sanders that two of the most famous and much commented upon of the *Song and Sonnets*, "The Canonization" and "The Ecstasy," are not among the greatest achievements in the collection, and are "treacherous" pieces in their tonal and attitudinal instabilities (which is not to say that they are not fascinating poems that only Donne could have written). The greatest of the lyrics, those that celebrate what we take "love" to mean in its highest human sense (whether consummated or not), are fully assured, yet always have what Eliot called "wit" – "a recognition implicit in the expression of every experience, of other kinds of experience that are possible."[25] The speaker of "The Good Morrow" is just as experienced in the erotic as the speakers of "Love's Alchemy" or "Farewell to Love," but instead of disillusion, he finds himself experiencing "wonder." The sober, almost amazed joyousness of the poem is reflected in its very sober stanza form, which is a variant of traditional "rhyme royal," but instead of repeating the "b"-rhyme and ending with a couplet, it ends its seven-line stanza with a triple rhyme, of which the final one extends from the pentameter of the rest of the stanza to a very slow-moving Alexandrine.[26] Instead of speaking about "a woman" or "women," this poem actually addresses a particular person, and, unlike, say, "Woman's Constancy," does so non-aggressively. The speaker and his beloved are seen as equals; the opening question applies to both of them together (and separately): "I wonder by my troth, what thou and I / Did, till we loved"

(1–2). The time until the present of the relationship seems to the speaker entirely empty – the strong stress on "Did" is wonderfully expressive – but the time in question was not, in fact, empty; rather it was filled with the sort of experiences celebrated in some of the other poems and disdained in others, "country pleasures." These are seen not merely as childish but as infantile, almost (oddly) pre-sexual (or at least pre-genital) – they "sucked on country pleasures, childishly" (3). These activities are then demoted to pure unconsciousness in the next line, but the sleep in question is imagined as coarse rather than untroubled ("snorted we in the'seven sleepers' den," 4). In the triplet, the speaker affirms these strange characterizations ("'Twas so," 5) and then takes a Platonic route, an explanatory rather than merely descriptive one, a route in which lower pleasures anticipate or foreshadow higher ones: "but this, all pleasures fancies be. / If ever any beauty I did see, / Which I desired, and got, 'twas but a dream of thee" (5–7).

"And got" is clearly a brave move here. The speaker is acknowledging his own past as someone who has "loved, and got, and told." But the contrast between the sharpness of "and got" and the extreme smoothness of "a dream of thee" is perhaps too extreme – too much, perhaps, merely reversing the movement from dreaming to getting in "Love's Alchemy." It has the feeling of a pulled punch. But, as Sanders says, instead of worrying this further, the speaker "simply shakes clear of it" at the beginning of the next stanza, and returns dramatically to the present and to the recognition of shared experience.[27] He steps fully into the moment: "And now good morrow to our waking souls" (8). "Souls" is a striking word here, making it clear that what the poem celebrates is a matter of consciousnesses, not primarily or only bodies (I am not sure that there is a difference between minds and souls in this context). But the speaker is aware of "other forms of experience that are possible." The intense scrutiny that is postulated of the lovers could be a product of anxiety, the fear of betrayal that we have seen haunting so many of the (presumably) earlier poems. Part of the greatness of "The Good Morrow" is that this possibility (like "and got") is not ignored but acknowledged in it. The effort of the first stanza – to relate the present to the past – continues; Donne (or his speaker) remembers the fear, but notes that it is absent. Instead of the almost exuberant lyricism of line 8, the tone turns neutral, discursive; we are told not what the "waking souls" do but what they do not do: "Which watch not one another out of fear" (9).[28] And the next line turns explanatory; the speaker cannot simply note the phenomenon but has to try to understand and explain how such lack of "fear" can be – "For love, all love of other sights controls" (10).[29] This explains the steadiness of the lovers' focus, but still in the mode of producing a positive by discounting a negative. The next line turns from what love does not do, and what it prevents, to what it does: "And makes one little room an everywhere" (11). This is still explanatory in mode, and still in the realm of ordinary reality ("one little room"), but the poem opens up in an extraordinary way at "an everywhere." The triplet moves into full expansiveness. We return from the constative to the speech-act mode. But the speech-act represented is now even greater than that of greeting each other and the day. It is an act of lordly dismissal. The speaker indicates his grand indifference to the geographical and cosmological discoveries and speculations that repeatedly and consistently fired Donne's imagination. Instead of merely going to and returning from "new worlds" (12) and merely seeing "worlds on worlds" (13), the speaker's current aim is to "possess one world" – which he is careful to note is created by mutuality, not by merging: "Let us possess one world, each hath one, and is one" (14). Each of the lovers is a world in him/her self, and is a world to the other. This is a poem that values distinctness as well as togetherness. Loss of ego is not required by this relationship.[30]

The opening of the final stanza moves even closer to the beloved and to the scene in the "little room." It shows, in the simplest possible language and syntax – after the conceptual density of "hath . . . and is" – what the relation between individuality and mutuality in the relationship actually is. A physical reality is described: "My face in thine eye, thine in mine appears" (15). But the point of this is not the physical reality (stressed, for instance, in "The Ecstasy") but what the physical reality reveals: the candor, vulnerability, and serenity of the lovers' self-presentation to the other. Each sees reflected in the other's eyes what the other sees: "true plain hearts do in the faces rest" (16). We recall that love, for Donne, involves not only "a special sense of the exposure of human beings in their relation-ships," a naked heart, but also a "naked *thinking* heart." Intellectuality and awareness of the wider world, and of geography, re-enter the poem. Moving into surprisingly technical language, the speaker finds the "hemi-spheres" of the lovers' eyes at least as good as those of planet earth (17) before asserting that they are better ("Without sharp North, without declining West," 18). Both of these phenomena suggest imperfection and death. But at this point, in thinking about balance, the speaker recalls an actual metaphysical principle. It enters the poem seemingly from nowhere, since nothing like it has occurred in the poem before, and yet even as it jolts one to a higher level of abstraction, it feels as if it somehow follows from what has already been said and shown. It's an extraordinary moment, and the only self-contained line in the poem: "Whatever dies was not mixed equally" (19). It's a moment when thought arises, as if spontaneously, from feeling. The principle is that whatever (in the physical world) is perfectly balanced is indissoluble ("*Non enim invenitur corruptio nisi ubi invenitur contrarietas*").[31] The speaker has had a recognition of something amazing, of the possibility of indefinite extension in time, of the possibility that the quality of the present might guarantee the quality of the future. The last two lines, retreating from the excitement of the metaphysical recognition, explicate it, slowly and carefully – as if wanting to make sure that its calculations are correct: "If our two loves be one, or thou and I / Love so alike, that none do slacken, none can die" (20–21).[32] The last three words have the sense of amazed recognition of how the "equation" has come out. The speaker can barely believe what he has recognized. As in the earlier versions of the lines, what cannot die are the feelings (the "loves") the lovers share, though I think this discovery also gives the speaker a sense of personal immortality. But I do not think that there is "an element of doubt" here.[33] In those three final words, we move, I think – in feeling and rhetoric, if not in syntax and logic – from the world of hypotheticals to the world of full assertion.[34] The deep "fear of separation" that Ramie Targoff sees in the love poetry needs to be balanced by a recognition of the deep desire for continuity. Donne's poetics of love is not simply a "poetics of taking leave."[35]

What Donne achieved in "The Good Morrow" is extended and developed in the other great love poems – actual love poems – in the collection. Once he recognized, in "Love's Alchemy," what it was that he truly wanted, and celebrated finding that in "The Good Morrow," then poems like "The Sun Rising," "A Lecture upon the Shadow," "The Anniversary," and "Love's Growth" were made possible – given, again, his extraordinary talent. Some material from the "cynical" poems remains – vulnerability, the awareness of the possibility of betrayal, the desire for equability, the valuing of autonomy – but these become deepening, not inhibiting factors. Sex is present but not an issue in these poems, the key thing is to be, as in "A Valediction Forbidding Mourning," "Inter-assurèd of the mind" (19). With that in place, two remarkable possibilities open up for an erotic relationship: faithfulness and futurity.

Finally, it may be asked, "How do I know that the poems were composed in the order in which I have treated them (or anything close)?" The answer is that I don't (any more than Gardner or Empson do), but I would claim that the way of reading the erotic poems that I have suggested and tried to enact allows us to imagine an intelligible human being behind the collection. And I am prepared to believe, with Arnold

Stein, that all true lyric poets "stand naked behind their enabling fictions."[36]

Notes

1. The printer's title for the erotic lyrics in 1635 is surely meant to recall the ground-breaking Elizabethan lyric collection, Tottel's "Miscellany": *Songes and Sonettes Written by the Ryght Honorable Lord Henry Howard, Late Earle of Surrey, Thomas Wyatt the Elder and Others* (London, 1557).

2. See Helen Gardner, "The Titles of Donne's Poems," in *Friendship's Garland: Essays Presented to Mario Praz*, ed. Vittorio I. Gabrieli, 2 vols. (Rome: Storia & Letteratura, 1966), 1:189–207; and John T. Shawcross, "But is it Donne's? The Problem of Titles on His Poems," *JDJ* 7 (1988), 141–49.

3. There is no manuscript volume or collection corresponding to the 1635 *Songs and Sonnets*, but the erotic lyrics do seem to have circulated in groups rather than as individual lyrics. See Alan MacColl, "The Circulation of Donne's Poems in Manuscript," *John Donne: Essays in Celebration*, ed. A. J. Smith (London: Methuen, 1972), 28–46.

4. C. S. Lewis observes that "When we re-read the Songs and Sonnets they always seem to be fewer than we had remembered," from *English Literature in the Sixteenth Century, Excluding Drama* (Oxford: Clarendon, 1954), 549.

5. See *John Donne, The Elegies and The Songs and Sonnets*, ed. Helen Gardner (Oxford: Clarendon, 1965), xxv–xxx. For William Empson's critique, see "Donne in the New Edition," in *Essays on Renaissance Literature*, ed. John Haffenden, 2 vols. (Cambridge University Press, 1993), 1:129–58.

6. William Empson, "Rescuing Donne," in Empson, *Essays*, 1:185.

7. The quoted phrase is from *Du Repentir* (*Essais* III:2).

8. This is part of C. S. Lewis's point in "Donne and Love Poetry in the Seventeenth Century" in *Seventeenth Century Studies presented to Sir Herbert Grierson* (Oxford University Press, 1938), 64–84.

9. Wilbur Sanders, *John Donne's Poetry* (Cambridge University Press, 1971), 50–57.

10. See Bald, *Life*, 72.

11. See Pierre Legouis, *Donne the Craftsman* (Paris: H. Didier, 1928), 47ff, 69.

12. For the controversy over "things indifferent," see John S. Coolidge, *The Pauline Renaissance in England: Puritanism and the Bible* (Oxford: Clarendon, 1970), chapter 2.

13. Stanley Fish, "Masculine Persuasive Force: Donne and Verbal Power," in *Soliciting*, 245.

14. On the importance of the Inns of Court for Donne, see Marotti, *Coterie*, chapter 1.

15. Barbara Hardy, "Thinking and Feeling in the *Songs and Sonnets* of John Donne," *The Advantage of Lyric: Essays on Feeling in Poetry* (Bloomington, IN: Indiana University Press, 1977), 19, 24.

16. Quoted in Clay Hunt, *Donne's Poetry: Essays in Literary Analysis* (New Haven, CT: Yale University Press, 1954), 223n.65.

17. See Empson, "New Edition," 1:155 and "Rescuing," 1:197; see also Gardner, *Elegies*, liv–lvii.

18. T. S. Eliot, "The Metaphysical Poets," in *Selected Essays* (New York: Harcourt, Brace, 1932), 247.

19. Empson, "New Edition," 1:149; for alchemy in the elegies, poems which almost everyone dates in the early- to mid-1590s, see the lines in "The Comparison" about the "chemic's masculine equal fire" (35–38).

20. This elegy was not included in an edition of Donne's *Poems* until 1669, but did circulate in manuscript (38 full or partial copies) though not as widely as the most popular elegies (69 mss of "The Anagram" and 67 of "Going to Bed"). See *The Variorum Edition of the Poetry of John Donne*, gen. ed. Gary A. Stringer (Bloomington, IN: Indiana University Press, 2000), 2:304, lxi.

21. The discovery of penicillin, completely by accident, is one of the great stories in medical history. The chemist who found it ruining his staph culture did indeed "glorif[y] his pregnant pot." See Kevin Brown, *Penicillin Man: Alexander Fleming and the Antibiotic Revolution* (Stroud, UK: Sutton, 2004).

22. See Thomas Browne, for whom even "vulgar and Taverne Musicke" leads to "a profound contemplation of the first Composer." *Religio Medici, Selected Writings*, ed. Sir Geoffrey Keynes (University of Chicago Press, 1968), 80. On the unhappy Platonism of this speaker, see Hunt, *Donne's Poetry*, 39, who also makes the contrast with Browne.

23. For the Paracelsian theory of using serums from a dead body ("mummy") for a cure – based on the theory of the "natural balsam" – see J. A. Mazzeo, "Notes on John Donne's Alchemical Imagery," *Isis* 48 (1957), 103–23.

24. In the companion piece to "Love's Alchemy," "Farewell to Love," the organ that the speaker finds "dulled" by sexual activity is "the mind" (20).

25. Eliot, "Andrew Marvell," *Selected Essays*, 262.

26. Rhyme royal was the normal meter of serious late medieval narrative poems (like Chaucer's *Troilus and Crysede*), and was used for similar purposes in many Elizabethan poems.

27. See Sanders, *Donne's Poetry*, 65.

28. I owe to Gordon Braden a sense of what he calls the "pivotal" status of this line to the poem and to my argument (personal communication).

29. In line 10, "controls" must be read in the strong sense of *prevents*, rather than its modern, weaker sense. See "control, v.," 4b, *OED Online*.

30. As Ted Leinwand notes, "the speaker gets to have his cake (love) and eat it too (no threat to ego)." Personal communication.

31. Quoted from Aquinas in *The Poems of John Donne*, ed. Herbert J. C. Grierson, 2 vols. (Oxford: Clarendon, 1912), 2:11.

32. There is a textual issue regarding these lines. The version given here is that of 1633. The 1635 edition has "If our two loves be one, both thou and I / Love just alike in all, none of these loves can die." There are other variants in some of

2 RICHARD STRIER

the manuscripts. For a discussion, see Gardner, *Elegies*, 197–98. Her conclusion – that the 1633 version represents a revision (and improvement) by Donne – seems highly plausible.

33. Gardner, *Elegies*, 199.
34. I do not find Ilona Bell's sexual reading of these lines convincing. See "The Role of the Lady in Donne's Songs and Sonets," *SEL* 23 (1983), 123.
35. Ramie Targoff, *John Donne, Body and Soul* (University of Chicago Press, 2008), 50.
36. Arnold Stein, *George Herbert's Lyrics* (Baltimore, MD: Johns Hopkins Press, 1968), 210.

CHAPTER 8

Divine Poems

David Marno

How would John Donne have responded to Anne Locke's 1560 sonnet sequence *Meditation of a Penitent Sinner?* The question is hypothetical as we have no evidence of Donne knowing Locke's poems or even their author. Indeed, between the two poets there was not only more than half a century but an immense cultural divide as well: a Puritan woman and Marian exile on the one hand, and a Catholic-born courtier eventually ordained in the Jacobean Church of England on the other. What makes this an intriguing question nevertheless is that in using poetry as a medium of devotion, the two authors weaved themselves into a number of shared contexts. Juxtaposing the ways in which Locke's and Donne's poems respond to these contexts highlights the differences between their poetics, and offers, I suggest, a perspective on what is unique in Donne's religious verse.[1]

Discussions of Donne's religious verse often focus on Donne's turn to the sonnet and the sonnet sequence in his religious poetry. The stakes of this turn go far beyond the use of a particular lyric genre. The sonnet was the signature form of Petrarchism, the premier lyric tradition in late medieval and early modern Europe. Toward the end of the sixteenth century, when Donne began to write and circulate his love poetry, such was the influence of Petrarchism that Donne could seek poetic distinction by writing love poems that appeared, at least on their surface, *not* Petrarchist. The eroticism in Donne's elegies is not only an homage to Ovid, but a deliberate challenge to the Petrarchist monopoly on love. The poems of the *Songs and Sonnets* mock and subvert Petrarchan tropes while they conspicuously avoid the sonnet form. For much of Donne's love poetry, Petrarchism is the foil against which his originality can sparkle more brightly. When Donne began using the sonnet and the sonnet sequence in his religious poetry, first in *La Corona* and later in the Holy Sonnets, the gesture was as meaningful as its opposite in the love poetry. It is a gesture of "sacred parody": a deliberate attempt to convert the sonnet as a symbol of Petrarchist love and idolatry. Yet by the time Donne began writing devotional verse, there had been a significant tradition of devotional sonnet sequences.[2] While on the continent this tradition went back to some of the earliest "spiritual" imitators of Petrarch, in England the first religious sonnet sequence was authored by a Puritan woman, Anne Locke.[3]

Since Locke's sonnets had no influence on later sonnet sequences, her chronological precedence might seem an antiquarian point, were it not for the fact that Locke and Donne also shared a vision about poetry's potential for religion. They both saw in verse a medium for religious *practice*. The view that Donne's religious poems should be seen in the context of early modern meditations was first advanced in the 1950s by Helen Gardner and Louis Martz. When Gardner, in her 1952 edition of Donne's religious poems, suggested that Donne's poems should be seen as "poetry whose subject is not the doctrines of religion, but man worshipping or man at prayer," she distinguished Donne's work from other kinds of religious verse, such as mystical or prophetic poetry, in effect clarifying the meaning of "devotional poetry."[4] Two years later Martz argued that the affinity between the late-sixteenth- and early-seventeenth-century religious poets was due to their debt to Catholic and Counter-Reformation meditations and spiritual exercises. Martz suggested that both the Holy Sonnets and the *Anniversaries* might be from a period in Donne's life when he was already contemplating the option of taking holy orders, and that they "may be seen as part of the spiritual exercises which Donne was performing in the effort to determine his problem of 'election.'"[5]

Martz's argument had some obvious flaws. Of his three main poets, only Robert Southwell wrote unequivocally Catholic poetry, while Donne's and George Herbert's poems are interlaced with references to Protestant liturgy and doctrine. Chief among these are references to the Calvinist doctrine of election. Yet Martz addresses Calvinism only in one chapter, in which he suggests that until Marvell, Milton, and Bunyan, Protestantism did not have literary achievements comparable to Catholic and Anglican poets; and he argues that this was because of the incompatibility between Catholic spiritual exercises and the Calvinist doctrine of grace. This view received a major challenge in Barbara Lewalski's *Protestant Poetics*, which suggested that "the major seventeenth-century religious lyrists owe more to contemporary, English, and Protestant influences than to Counter Reformation, continental, and medieval Catholic resources."[6] These influences, Lewalski argues, were primarily biblical and inflected by a Calvinist interpretation of the biblical materials. Thus, for Lewalski, seventeenth-century poetry shows affinity not with Catholic meditations but with Protestant biblical paraphrases, psalm translations, and sermon literature. When the poems do appear meditative, Lewalski suggests they tend to be occasional rather than monastic. Most importantly for Lewalski, seventeenth-century poetry expresses the predominantly Calvinist theological milieu of the period in England.

At the time of working on *Protestant Poetics*, Lewalski would not have known Anne Locke as a poet.[7] It is a testament to the genius of her argument that virtually every aspect of it is borne out in Locke's *Meditations*. First published in 1560, Locke's sonnet sequence appeared as an appendix to her translation of five sermons by Calvin. The connection between the sermons and the sonnets is in part formal: they both cite and elaborate on specific biblical passages. Indeed, in describing the sequence as a "Paraphrase upon the 51 Psalme of David," Locke associates the poems not only with psalm translations but more generally with biblical paraphrases. But there is also a deeper, theological and devotional affinity between the two parts of the volume. As Locke explains, "I have added this meditation followyng unto the ende of this boke, not as parcell of maister Calvines worke, but for that it well agreeth with the same argument."[8] The argument of Calvin's sermon turns doctrine into a religious ethic: it stresses the imperative of acknowledging all afflictions as just punishments for sinfulness, and seeing any good exclusively as a result of divine mercy. If Calvin's sermons are already about applying doctrine to life, Locke's sonnets take this agenda one step further by using the sonnets as an exercise in habituation. While in Petrarchism the sonnet sequence is an opportunity of story-telling, in Locke's hands it becomes a framework in which the reader can repeat time and again the back-and-forth movement between the "heinous gylt of my forsaken ghost" and the "cry for mercy to releve my woes."[9] Each sonnet functions as a *machina memorialis*; for instance, "my place," "my case," "face" are all phrases that invoke "grace" as their rhyme with a regularity that makes the association almost automatic. Locke's sonnet sequence is a meditation in the specific sense of affective exercise: in merging Calvinist doctrine and the voice of the Psalmist, Locke creates a poetics that is in the service of internalizing doctrine as a habit of mind.

This raises the question: does Donne's poetry similarly fit seamlessly into the pattern of Protestant poetics? Looking at Donne's religious verse from the perspective of Locke's Calvinist poetics, it is easy to see that while Donne is not quite a Jesuit poet, he isn't as Protestant as Lewalski depicts him either. Donne's "The Lamentations of Jeremy" comes closest to the Protestant exemplars of biblical paraphrases, though Donne's verse translation builds mainly on the Jewish-Italian Immanuel Tremellius' Latin version. Affinity with the psalms in tone and content pervades Donne's devotional poems. In the Holy Sonnets and in the hymns, the speakers perform the kind of intimate yet inhabitable personae that we associate with the psalmist; and Donne's poem on the Sidney psalter testifies to his investment in psalm transla- tions and public devotion. Yet none of Donne's devotional poems seem intended for public worship, and it is remarkable that Donne, virtually alone among the great religious poets of the English Renaissance, never tried his hand at translating psalms.[10] Lewalski's model of Protestant "occasional" meditations also proves elusive in Donne's case. The majority of the Holy Sonnets, Donne's most explicitly meditative poems, are not occasional. When Donne's speakers meditate on spe- cific occasions, they do so by reflecting on an event of personal significance ("A Hymn to Christ" and "Hymn to God my God") or a Christian festival ("Goodfriday, 1613"). None of Donne's meditative poems focus on the kind of regular events of nature or life that one sees in the specifically Protestant meditative tradition from Bishop Hall to Robert Boyle.

But the most idiosyncratic aspects of Donne's devotional poetry emerge if we compare Donne's treatment of what Lewalski calls "the Protestant paradigm of salvation" with Locke's. Here the Holy Sonnets offer a test case, not only because these poems have traditionally been considered "the pulsing heart of all Donne's religious verse," but because they are the poems in which critics have most often found Donne engage with Calvinist doctrine.[11] One poem in particular proves helpful because, strik- ingly, it has been cited as paradigmatic by both sides: Holy Sonnet 3 appears in Martz as a typical example of Donne's spiritual exercises, while Lewalski cites it as proof that Donne's poems dramatize "justification and regeneration in language often remarkably precise."[12] Both critics are right: the sonnet begins as a Catholic spiritual exercise but ends by reciting Protestant doctrine. The first quatrain supports Martz's argument; here, Donne's speaker performs an exercise that closely resembles the Jesuit *compositio loci*, the systematic imagination of a soteriologically significant scene:

> This is my play's last scene, here heavens appoint
> My pilgrimage's last mile; and my race
> Idly, yet quickly run, hath this last pace,
> My span's last inch, my minute's latest point.   (1–4)

The abrupt, immediate beginning familiar from Donne's love lyrics here turns into an exercise in devotional deixis. The problem is that in Martz's Catholic model, a meditation should now continue to the next two stages: first, to the intellect that seeks to understand the meaning of the images provided in the *compositio loci*, and then to the will that is supposed to respond affectively. Indeed, the poem ends with what Martz calls an affective petition to God. But the petition is set in conspicuously Protestant language: "Impute me righteous, thus purged of evil, / For thus I leave the world, the flesh, Devil" (13–14). In invoking the Book of Common Prayer, the poem's last line is itself a direct quotation from a Protestant document. The penultimate line's "Impute me righteous" is even more striking. Its language evokes the distinctly Protestant doctrine of justification only by grace, which is further emphasized by the strained temporality that the word "thus" creates: even after the penitential work that the poem has ostensibly performed, sin remains, and it can only be removed by God.

How are we to read a poem that begins by performing Catholic spiritual exercises but ends with a Protestant prayer? Commenting on the discrepancy, Richard Strier argues that the final lines' "Reformation vocabulary does not correspond to the vision presented; the matter will not take this print," and adds that in general we see in the Holy Sonnets "Donne's deep inability to accept the paradoxical conception of a regenerate Christian."[13] But this judgment is based on the assumption that there is no reason within the poem to conclude on the note of Calvinist petition. Yet such a reason does exist – indeed it is developed in a characteristically Donnean fashion insofar as it emerges out of the forgettings, distractions, and errors of the poem. Let us look at the two middle quatrains:

> And gluttonous death will instantly unjoint
> My body'and soul, and I shall sleep a space,
> But my'ever-waking part shall see that face
> Whose fear already shakes my every joint;
> Then, as my soul to'heaven, her first seat, takes flight,
> And earth-born body in the earth shall dwell;
> So fall my sins, that all may have their right,
> To where they'are bred, and would press me, to hell. (5–12)

While the purpose of meditation is to focus one's attention on a single image, here the speaker leaves behind the first quatrain's focus on death and moves beyond to imagine what happens *after* death. He does so by creating images of separation. The second quatrain focuses on death as separation of body and soul. The speaker's scholastic hesitation about the state of the soul after death indicates that this is already a boldly speculative gesture in a poem that was supposed to meditate on dying rather than on the afterlife. The transgression continues in the third quatrain, where the systematic character of the meditation is taken to such an extreme that it becomes its own absurd reflection. Separations now multiply, and the moment of judgment is depicted as a physical and mechanical process where soul, body, and sin duly return to their "right" places.

The path leading out of the derailed imaginative exercise and to the concluding couplet's prayer emerges with the recognition of what the speaker has forgotten during the first three quatrains. The poem's prosodic structure offers useful hints here. The final rhyming couplet is prefigured by the first two quatrains: in the embrace of the first and last lines of each quatrain, the two middle lines constitute an enclosed rhyming couplet. If we turn to these middle lines, we notice that their rhyming ends speak of an absence. "Race," "pace," "space," and "face" are all words early modern poets were fond of rhyming with the ever-present word "grace." As if silenced by the imprisonment of the sonnet, however, the language does not arrive at "grace": amidst all the soteriological fantasies, the very condition of salvation remains absent. That is, it remains absent until the final couplet where, escaped from the embrace of the first two quatrains, it is finally evoked in the form of the couplet's prayer. As if it has just occurred to the speaker that during all his thinking about salvation he has forgotten the one thing necessary for it, he now asks for grace: "Impute me righteous." But if the final petition is literally a recollection of grace from within the poem's body, it is also a recollection of a scattered self from the previous quatrains. In the whirlwind of salvation that the third quatrain depicts, the self remains unaccounted for. It is this absence of the self that pulls the speaker back from the speculative imaginations of the two middle quatrains into the "this," the now of the poem. This absence motivates the speaker to abandon the imaginative exercises and turn to an altogether different speech act, a petitionary prayer: "Impute *me* righteous, thus purged of evil" (emphasis mine).

We are now in a position to see some of the fundamental differences between Locke's and Donne's poetics of meditation. In Locke's sonnet sequence, the function of poetry is to engrave doctrine into the mind of the poems' reader. The two aspects of Calvinist doctrine are already *given*, literally so in the sermons that precede the poems in the 1560 volume. The "self" that speaks and reads must recognize in herself the cause of her afflictions; and simultaneously she must recognize God as the sole source of salvation. The poems are designed to turn these imperatives into automatisms of the mind, and they do so by using them as automatisms of the verse. This is why in Locke's sonnets the "I" of the speaker and the grace of God are never let out of sight: there is virtually no line without a mention of at least one of them (or their synonyms), and there is virtually no noun that does not belong either to God or to the self.

In Donne's poem, in contrast, the "I" of the speaker and the grace of God are precisely the two entities that remain forgotten until the very end of the poem. Rather than reliable substances, they are elusive objects of the poem's quest that become all the more elusive in the course of this quest. Similarly, doctrine in Donne's poem is not given, the way it is in Locke's, but rather emerges out of the poem's paradoxical movements. But this is not to suggest that in Donne's poem the speaker in some way merits grace: though the petition for mercy could not appear in the closing couplet without the wanderings in the previous twelve lines, it emerges not because, but in spite of, these lines. Between the Catholic opening and the Protestant closing, Donne creates an experimental poetics that affords the reader occasional revelations through the cracks and crevices of language.

As one of England's most famous converts in the period, Donne had a bewildering range of opinions in religious matters. His early love poetry is interlaced with references to Catholic themes. The sermons of his later years display, on the other hand, commitment to the Church of England. The devotional poems stand somewhere in the middle: confessional and doctrinal inconsistency appears throughout, indeed oftentimes within, the fluctuations of each individual poem. Yet these poems do not yet advocate a moderate, Church of England religiosity – the *via media* – but instead bounce back and forth between the extremes of Christianity. To make sense of their movement, we need to think of their speakers as Protestant thinkers but Catholic actors: individuals who seek to discover the possibilities of devotional action. In this sense, it is precisely by being a unique combination of the modalities of the period that Donne's poetic experiments with devotion are paradigmatic of an entire era's conflicts between thought and action, grace and human agency, the Catholic past and the Protestant present.

Let me conclude here on a note about contextualization itself. While in the aftermath of Lewalski's book the scholarship on Herbert has had a particularly productive period, Donne's religious poetry has still not seen a book-length study. The sheer range and diversity of the poems is certainly a reason for this; but it is also that Donne's devotional poems seem to have yielded less easily to historicist and new historicist methods of inquiry than Shakespeare's, Milton's, or even Herbert's work. In *Common Prayer*, for instance, Ramie Targoff discusses Donne's sermons and his dedicatory poem to the Sidney psalms as documents of the early seventeenth-century English interest in public forms of devotion; but she sets aside the Holy Sonnets as idiosyncratic poems not representative of the period's devotional poetry.[14] When Targoff later returns to the Holy Sonnets, she considers them in the context of the poet's lifelong concern with body, soul, and the relationship between the two.[15] Donne appears here as a *sui generis* poet who must be considered on his own terms; and the Holy Sonnets as unique poems that must be interpreted in the context of their author's life. As I have tried to show in this chapter, this view has merit: Donne's devotional poems seem indeed idiosyncratic when seen in their contexts. The question is whether we should therefore give up on them as relevant historical sources – or on the contrary, we should find new paradigms that make literary uniqueness not a threat but a valuable asset to historical inquiry.

Notes

1. For a comparison between Donne and Locke, see P. M. Oliver, *Donne's Religious Writings: A Discourse of Feigned Devotion*, 2nd edn (London: Routledge, 2014), 142–43. In addition, I would like to thank Kirsten Stirling for sharing her unpublished essay "Anne Locke and John Donne: The Sonnet Sequence and Salvation; *or* One Damned Thing After Another."
2. Including Henry Constable's *Spirituall Sonnettes* (1594), Barnabe Barnes' *A Divine Centurie* (1595), and Henry Lok's *Sundry Christian Passions* (1593).
3. In fact, since Petrarch's English translators and imitators did not begin writing sonnet sequences until the 1570s, Locke's sonnets constitute the first sonnet sequence of any kind in English.
4. John Donne, *The Divine Poems*, ed. Helen Gardner (Oxford: Clarendon, 1952), xv.
5. Louis Martz, *The Poetry of Meditation* (New Haven, CT: Yale University Press, 1954), 219.
6. Barbara Lewalski, *Protestant Poetics and the Seventeenth-Century Religious Lyric* (Princeton University Press, 1979), ix.
7. *Meditations of a Penitent Sinner* was published unsigned, and Locke introduced it by saying it "was delivered me by my friend with whom I knew I might be so bolde to use & publishe it as pleased me." *The Collected Works of Anne Vaughan Locke*, eds. Anne Prowse and Susan Felch (Tempe, AZ: Arizona Center for Medieval and Renaissance Studies, 1999), 62.
8. *Locke*, 62.
9. *Locke*, 63.

10. The 1633 *Poems by J. D.* includes a psalm translation that is now attributed to Francis Davison. See Francis Davison, *The Poetical Rhapsody*, ed. Harris Nicholas, 2 vols. (London, 1826), 2:321–23.

11. Lewalski, *Protestant*, 219.

12. Lewalski, *Protestant*, 25.

13. Richard Strier, "John Donne Awry and Squint: The 'Holy Sonnets,' 1608–1610," *Modern Philology* 86 (1989), 373–74.

14. Ramie Targoff, *Common Prayer* (The University of Chicago Press, 2001), 92.

15. Ramie Targoff, *John Donne: Body and Soul* (The University of Chicago Press, 2008).

CHAPTER 9

Letters

James Daybell

More scholarly ink has arguably been spilt over the letters of John Donne than on any other early modern English letter-writer, and his prose letters are the subject of a long-awaited Oxford University Press edition, begun by I. A. Shapiro and continued by a distinguished scholarly team headed by Dennis Flynn.[1] More letters survive for Donne than for any other Jacobean writer, with the exception of Sir Francis Bacon. The majority of the critical studies, however, have been largely concerned with analysing Donne as an epistolary stylist, mining surviving correspondence for biographical purposes to put flesh on the chronological bones of his life, studying clusters of letters to shed light on relationships and friendships, and helping reconstruct Donne's inner life as well as his outer self-representation.[2] John Carey maintains that the apparent "dullness" of Donne's "newsless letters" was intentional, "a highly specialized and functional sort of dullness, based on imaginative theories which tie in closely with his poems."[3] Annabel Patterson reads Donne's "personal letters" as a means of understanding and re-evaluating his "disingenuous" character and reputation.[4] Arthur Marotti notes "a high degree of self-consciousness about the genre," while Lynne Magnusson remarks on the "performative virtuosity" of his letters.[5] In a series of articles and essays Margaret Maurer has explored various aspects of Donne's prose letters, paying attention to language, structure, style, and content; she has related the nine letters printed in the 1633 edition of his *Poems* to verse in the volume, and studied his epistolary output in relation to the genre of Renaissance letter-writing, looking at the survival of his letters, potential models, and tropes of secrecy and anxiety with the insecurity of the epistolary medium. Maurer has also written on Donne's verse letters (which this essay does not address) and a strong component of her scholarship is the relationship between Donne's prose and verse.[6] Ramie Targoff has argued

[*] I am grateful to Andrew Gordon and Alan Stewart for helpful comments on earlier drafts of this essay.

for the metaphysical nature of Donne's letters.[7] And lastly, Donne's correspondence has formed the basis for a wide-ranging and important series of articles and essays by Dennis Flynn on Donne's letters, life, and friendships.[8]

Despite this veritable industry of scholarship on Donne's letters, critics have used them as clues to other things, namely what they tell us about the man, and their relationship to his other writings, especially his poetry. The latest work by Flynn and Maurer, however, has been influenced by recent developments in the field of Renaissance letter-writing.[9] Scholarship influenced by the 'material', 'archival', and 'linguistic' turns has emphasised the complexity of letters as socio-cultural texts, and the range of interpretative methodologies that need to be deployed in order to read, situate, and understand fully early modern correspondence. This essay interprets Donne's letters in the context of the cultural and social practices of early modern epistolarity, re-evaluating Donne and his corpus as one of the most significant correspondents of the period. It focuses on the materiality of Donne's letters – defined both in terms of the physical features of texts as well as the social conditions of their production, reception, and archiving – arguing that material forms (such as seals, paper use, and manuscript spacing) were imbued with social significance, and worked in tandem with rhetorical and textual tropes to generate meaning. The essay concentrates on Donne's manuscript letters, but also studies printed letters for what they tell us about the cultural practices of letter-writing. Donne is an artfully self-conscious correspondent, who spends an awful lot of time discussing letters: the nature and style of the epistolary forms and conventions, anxieties associated with postal delays, and the protocols of reciprocal exchange.

To date, the corpus of John Donne's prose letters has not been established with the publication of any authoritative critical edition, with debate over both his authorship of certain letters and the identity of particular addressees. The most comprehensive current (and surprisingly rarely cited) critical edition of the correspondence is William Davies's 1992 PhD study, which provides texts of 241 prose letters 'attributed' to Donne, including letters in print and manuscript by Donne, letters written for others, and letters 'possibly' by Donne; Davies provides context and new dating for some of the letters.[10] Of the extant letters, 159 were collected by John Donne the younger, and printed in Donne's *Letters to Severall Persons of Honour* (1651; reissued 1654) and *A Collection of Letters Made by Sr Tobie Mathews K^t* (1660; reprinted 1692), which includes seventeen letters written to Donne.[11] Several of these texts had previously been published in the 1633 and 1635 editions of Donne's *Poems*. Two of his letters addressed to George Villiers, Duke of Buckingham, were printed in successive editions of the

Cabala (1654) alongside 'secret' letters of state and government, and four appeared in Izaak Walton's *Life of Mr George Herbert* (1670).[12] In addition to these printed letters, Peter Beal has identified thirty-eight original prose letters in scattered archives that survive in manuscript in Donne's hand, two of which were printed by the younger John Donne (letters to Sir Edward Herbert and Lady Kingsmill).[13] Scribal copies of a further thirty-two letters attributed to Donne survive in the Burley MS now at Leicestershire Record Office (including three love letters that Ilona Bell conjectures were from Donne to Ann More), but the integrity of these authorial identifications is far from certain.[14] Included within the body of surviving letters are three texts that he wrote in a secretarial capacity for Sir Robert and Lady Drury, a letter penned for Sir Henry Goodyer in Latin, another for Goodyer to the Earl of Salisbury, and there is a strong case for also including a copy in his hand of a widely circulated letter from Robert Carr, Viscount Rochester, to Henry Howard, Earl of Northampton.[15] Donne was also secretary to Thomas Egerton, although Steven May argues that his 'secretarial duties for Egerton remain unknown' and Andrew Gordon has argued while 'it is possible that Donne played some junior role in managing Egerton's correspondence networks ... there is no manuscript evidence of Donne's hand in the correspondence of Egerton'.[16] Nevertheless, letters penned in a secretarial capacity should clearly be incorporated into the Donne corpus in the manner of Zurcher and Burlinson's edition of Spenser's correspondence, although we lack any equivalent material evidence of Donne's secretarial involvement.[17] Furthermore, any definition of an individual's correspondence for the early modern period must include not only those letters he or she penned, but also those received, read, endorsed, or archived (as in the case of the edition of Bess of Hardwick's correspondence), which includes for Donne a letter he received from John Allsop dated September 26, 1602, letters from Henry Wotton, and letters from other letter-writers printed in Tobie Matthew's *Collection of Letters*.[18] This is in contrast to the current editorial policy of the Oxford edition, which rather defines the 'entire canon of Donne's Letters (228 at present)' as those 'from Donne'.[19] Their interest is thus in Donne as author, rather than as correspondent, or as someone deeply engaged in the cultures of correspondence.

Donne was a prolific and regular letter-writer – he wrote, for example, weekly to Sir Henry Goodyer – but only a small proportion of his epistolary output is extant, largely due to the publication of many of his letters during the seventeenth century. Very few of his autograph letters survive among the state papers in the manner of Bacon's correspondence, but instead remain among the papers of recipients or passed into the hands of Donne's son and Henry Wotton, the latter preserving many of Donne's letters with his own replies. Robert Ker also looked after Donne's papers while he was abroad.[20] What tends to survive is Donne's side of the correspondence, making it hard to reconstruct epistolary exchanges except through textual inference. Donne appears to have archived and kept copies or drafts of his own correspondence, which can be gleaned from a letter to Goodyer, in which he informed his friend 'This morning I spend in surveying and emptying my Cabinet of Letters'.[21] A 1658 inventory of papers of the Drury family tantalisingly records '25 old Letters sowed together of Mr. Jo. Donne', letters that were later removed from Redgrave Hall and subsequently lost.[22] While the majority of Donne's correspondence has not survived, some perhaps remains still to be discovered by painstaking trawls of local archives.[23]

In addition to printed and original holograph letters, Donne's letters also survive as scribal copies, but they did not circulate in manuscript in the way that the letters of Francis Bacon or Philip Sidney did (or indeed as did Donne's verse), although a copy of a letter to Lucy Russell, Countess of Bedford (printed in the 1633 edition of Donne's *Poems*) survives in eleven distinct copies.[24] Thus the corpus is extremely complex textually, incorporating letters that survive solely in print, autograph originals, scribal copies of originals, as well as those written by Donne acting in a secretarial capacity. Donne's letter of October 26, 1624 to Lady Kingsmill survives in holograph, as well as in printed versions in Donne's *Letters to Severall Persons of Honour*, Walton's 'Life of Donne', and Matthew's *Collection of Letters*. This rare multiple survival of a Donne letter illustrates the instability of the letter (since the four versions are different), in contrast to the aims of many editions. Given the marked variations between this holograph example and its printed descendants, there is a strong sense that printed editions of Donne's letters, such as *Letters to Severall Persons of Honour*, were highlighted edited volumes concerned with Donne's posthumous literary reputation. Beyond issues of collation, the textual afterlife of this letter is interesting in terms of its reception. Clearly the initial framing of the letter and the context in which it was first read in manuscript form differed from its later reapplications in printed editions when grouped among other texts, and intended for wider public consumption.

The textual status and archival traces of Donne's letters are therefore fundamental in framing how we read, decode, and indeed edit them. In many ways then these are questions at the heart of a modern critical edition of Donne's letters. What survives is a highly complex assortment of letters, and the re-arrangement chronologically of letters in some ways removes them from the contexts of their reception. Indeed, some surviving letters were meant to be read by a wider audience as a corpus of printed letters or alongside poems or other texts, while manuscript originals were intended to be read by the recipient. Several letters were intended as presentation letters, which accompanied volumes or texts, and survive either as manuscript separates, were inscribed in volumes themselves, or tipped in to manuscript works. For example, a letter to Sir Edward Herbert accompanied a presentation manuscript of Donne's tract on suicide, *Biathanatos*, which appeared opposite the title-page; another accompanied a copy of *Biathanatos* to Sir Robert Ker;[25] while a letter to his former patron Sir Thomas Egerton accompanied a presentation volume of *Pseudo-Martyr*, and is fixed to a blank leaf at the end of the presentation copy.[26] Donne's letters often functioned as gift texts in this manner, accompanying textual enclosures, such as sermons, poems, books, other letters, translations, and material goods. Letters to Sir Thomas Roe, Susan, Countess of Montgomery, Goodyer, and Elizabeth Queen of Bohemia all enclosed sermons.[27] A letter to Lady Magdalen Herbert contained a sonnet, and Donne enclosed a translation for the Countess of Bedford in a letter to Sir Henry Goodyer.[28] Sir Robert Cotton received a letter from Donne accompanied by a copy of *Pseudo-Martyr*, which was 'almost certainly' intended for the Earl of Northampton.[29] Fundamentally then the letter acted as a kind of textual or cultural portmanteau, facilitating the broader transmission of other manuscript texts (prose, verse, libels, and recipes) as well as in the wider dissemination of news, information, scientific knowledge, and ideas. More mundanely, a letter to his brother-in-law Robert More accompanied parcels and a horse.[30] Furthermore, letter bearers often acted as corporeal extensions of the letter. Indeed, as Donne expounded to Goodyer, the bearer was sometimes quite literally figured as the letter, which imparts an extra textual, oral quality: "You husband my time thriftily, when you command me to write by such a messenger, as can tell you more then I can write, for so he doth not onely carry the Letter, but is the Letter."[31] Donne's letters were thus not isolated texts, but rather multi-agent forms involving letter-writer, recipient, and bearer, and they must be interpreted within the context of a broader textual exchange.

In addition to their textual and scribal complexity, Donne's letters that survive in print and manuscript are incredibly varied generically, extending from the virtuosi epistles, rhetorically clever and sophisticated, many of which were printed, to the more simple practical letters that transacted business, which tend to survive solely in manuscript. There is perhaps thus a division between the prosaic and the pragmatic. The letter was to Donne a rather porous form which suited a range of uses, often functioning as a textual vehicle that carried paradoxes and problems. Scholars have registered the thematic parallels between Donne's letters and verse, and his correspondence also echoed his sermons in a rather studied, self-conscious way. Donne wrote to Sir Robert Ker, 'Sir I took up this Paper to write a Letter; but my imagination were full of a Sermon before, for I write but a few hours before I am to Preach, and so instead of a Letter, I send you a Homily'; while he informed Goodyer 'I must not give you a Homily for a letter', and in another missive wrote, 'I am beyond my purpose; I meant to write a letter, and I am fallen in to a discourse'.[32] In contrast to the elaborate linguistic dexterity of some of Donne's letters, others simply take the form of requests. Those addressed to Sir Nicholas Carew are perfunctory, such as requests for a buck or that his man be allowed to run his horse in his park.[33] It is unsurprising that such modest missives were not chosen for print publication but survive in manuscript.

Another strand of Donne's epistolary output, which has perhaps been overlooked, is the letter catering to troubled consciences, a form of correspondence suited to his later clerical career. Describing the contents of Donne's study, Izaak Walton referred to 'Copies of divers Letters and cases of Conscience that had concerned his friends, with his observations and solutions of them; and divers other businesses of importance; all particularly and methodically digested by himself'.[34] Few letters of this nature are extant, nor were they collected to be published in the 'godly and comfortable' tradition, as Edward Dering's were.[35] The closest to this kind of religious letter-writing are the letters of consolation, such as that to Anne Cockayne on the death of her son.[36] Overall, there is a discernible variation across Donne's prose letters that reflects his changing contemporary literary interests and circumstances. Early letters before 1603 are generally more 'satirical and cynical', replaced later 'by a belief in the importance of virtue and displaying goodness through action in the world'. His letters between 1612 and 1614 when he accompanied Sir Robert Drury to France reflect his changed situation, containing more news and less elaborate and less frequent discussions of friendship, while those post 1615, after Donne took orders, tend to reflect his new profession.[37]

Evidence within the letters themselves permits a partial reconstruction of the material conditions of Donne's letter-writing activities, his habits and patterns of corresponding, where, when, and how frequently he wrote, as well as details about conveyance and delivery, all of which structured his correspondence. The writing of letters was for Donne a routine, quotidian activity. By his own admission, he wrote weekly to Sir Henry Goodyer between about 1604 and 1625 – his 'continuall tribute of Letters' – claiming in one letter 'I would have intermitted this week without writing, if I had not found the name of my Lady *Huntington* in your Letter'.[38] Donne appears to have written with similar regularity to Magdalen Herbert whom he addressed with rhetorical exuberance: 'in my resolution of writing almost daily to you, I would have no link of the Chain broke by me, both because my Letters interpret one another, and because only their number can give them weight'.[39] For Donne the writing and reciprocal exchange of letters was an intimate part of friendship, and he expended considerable rhetorical energies in cloaking his missives in elaborate conceits of friendship (here the protocols of letter-writing are central to understanding Donne's discourses of friendship). 'I send not my Letters', he wrote to Goodyer,

> as tribute, nor interest, nor recompense, nor for commerce, nor as testimonials of my love, nor provokers of yours, not to justifie my custome of writing, nor for a vent and utterance of my meditations; for my letters are either above or under all such offices; yet I write very affectionately, and I chide and accuse my self of diminishing that affection which send them, when I ask my self why: onely I am sure that I desire that you might have in your hands Letters of mine of all kindes, as conveyances and deliverers of me to you, whether you accept me as a friend, or as a patient, or as a penitent, or as a beadsman, for I decline no jurisdiction, or refuse any tenure.[40]

Famously Donne represented letter-writing an 'extasie', a fundamental part of friendship:

> I make account that this writing of letters, when it is with any seriousness, is a kind of extasie, and a departure and secession and suspension of the soul, which doth then communicate itself to two bodies: And, as I would every day provide for my souls last convoy, though I know not when I shall die, and perchance I shall never die, so for these extasies in letters, I oftentimes deliver my self over in writing when I know not when those letters shall be sent to you, and many times they never are, for I have little satisfaction in seeing a letter written to you upon my table, though I meet no opportunity of sending it.[41]

Friendship for Donne was one that could be sustained intellectually through the sharing of news, knowledge, and ideas – a philosophy at the heart of the Republic of Letters; and central to the dynamics of epistolary friendship was the mutual exchange of correspondence. 'Sir, The messenger who brought me your Letter', he informed Goodyer, 'presented me a just excuse, for I received them so late upon *Thursday* night, that I should have dispatched before I could begin; yet I have obeyed you drowsily, and coldly, as the night and my indisposition commanded'.[42] Detailed discussions of the practicalities of receipt in this manner abound in Donne's correspondence, and reflect a social practice charged with anxieties – not wanting to be in 'debt' of a letter – and dictated by protocols that demanded timely response.

Beyond the regularity of correspondence, it is possible to infer from the contents of the letters the spatial sites of Donne's letter-writing, within the household or abroad, solitary or in company. On one occasion he informed Goodyer that he wrote 'in my bed, and with much pain'; another was penned 'from the fire side in my Parler, and in the noise of three gamesome children; and by the side of her, whom because I have transplanted into a wretched fortune, I must labour to disguise that from her by all such honest devices, as giving her my company, and discourse, therefore I steal from her, all the time I give this Letter'.[43] He wrote a letter to Sir Robert Ker while at the Red Lion Inn.[44] Letter-writing was thus often conducted within the household, within communal places, rather than closeted in a private study or library. The concept of spatial privacy as it relates to the writing, reading, and storing of letters is thus not necessarily singular or solitary, but one that involved being alone in chosen company, a definition of privacy that was familial rather than individual. The physicality of the writing process is a marked feature of Donne's letters, mingled with discussions of illness or well-being that frequently punctuate his letter-writing. He excused himself to Goodyer that 'I have been travelled with a pain, in my right wrist, so like the Gout, as makes me unable to write'.[45] A letter to George Garrard contained an apology for closing too abruptly:

> It is a better office from me to you, that I goe to bed, then that I write a longer letter. For if I doe mine eyes a little more injurie, I shall lose the honour of seeing you at Michaelmas; for by my troth I am almost blinde: you may be content, to beleeve that I am always disposed to your service, without exception of any time, since just at midnight, when it is both day, and night, and neither.[46]

Here a discourse of friendship is bound up with the apologetics of dispatch expressed through bodily incapacities and the late hour of writing.

The nature of early modern postal conditions further influenced the patterns of Donne's letter-writing. His letters were delivered by various private means since he wrote before the 1635 postal reforms of Charles I, which opened up the Royal Post to delivery of private letters. Instead, Donne's letters were conveyed in a more haphazard manner by carriers, merchants, personal servants, and acquaintances.[47] His corresponding was thus often shaped by the rhythms of the carrier networks, or delayed or hastened by the absence or departure of a bearer. Indeed, his weekly letter to Goodyer was ordinarily written on a Tuesday to coincide with the Tamworth and Polesworth carrier whose London base was the Rose at Smithfield, and who conveyed letters to Goodyer at Polesworth Hall in Warwickshire.[48] His correspondence is full of the exigencies of dispatch, often revealing anxieties about the delivery and lateness of letters, and they exhibit a rich apologetics of 'silence or slacknes in writing', and fear of interception and loss.[49] During periods abroad Donne had to make ad hoc arrangements for delivery and receipt of his letters. While travelling in Europe, he used Lady Bartlett's lodging as a mailing address; he wrote to Goodyer when in Paris: 'If you write this way any more, chuse no other means, then by Mr *Bruer*, at the Queens Arms, a Mercer in *Cheapside*: he shall alwaies know where we are'; and Donne had his letters directed to him on several occasions by the newsletter writer John Pory.[50] Donne himself functioned as an important postal conduit, regularly receiving and forwarding letters for Goodyer to his correspondents.[51] In the case of highly sensitive or presentation letters, Donne carefully selected the bearer in order to attempt an effective reception. Goodyer was employed to forward Donne's letters to the Countess of Bedford, and Donne's first letter to George More after his unauthorized marriage to his daughter was carried by his powerful and influential friend Henry Percy, ninth Earl of Northumberland (although it was not successful).[52] Again, the mechanics of delivery are key to understanding the reception of Donne's letters, and his selection of bespoke bearers tailored to particular social situations speaks of his facility with the epistolary medium in its broadest sense.

Donne's reputation as a 'textual specialist' has recently been highlighted in an important piece by Andrew Gordon, who has argued for him as a pragmatic trafficker in texts, tentatively exploring Donne as a member of the secretariat of Lord Keeper Egerton that devised a famous letter from Egerton to Robert Devereux, Earl of Essex.[53] Donne's textual skills are clearly evident in his letters: his correspondence with Sir Robert Cotton shows that he borrowed manuscripts from Cotton's library, 'I send yo^w back by this bearer the letters wch I borrowed of yo^w', asking if he could 'spare some of the french negotiacons, yo^w shall haue them as faythfully kept and as orderly returnd as these'.[54] Another letter to Cotton digested Valdesius's *De dignitate Regum regnorumque Hispaniae* (Madrid, 1600), which defended Spanish precedence; the letter survives bound into the book, and Bald claims that Cotton had consulted Donne for his opinion; and a further letter accompanied a copy of his *Pseudo-Martyr*, which he wished Cotton to deliver 'to my L[ord]', which is 'almost certainly' the Earl of Northampton.[55] Such a reading of Donne's textual skills provides a useful framework for interpreting the materiality of Donne's letters. These textual skills were at the heart of Donne's usefulness as a secretary in which capacity he was employed by Egerton and later by the Drurys. Egerton spoke of his usefulness as a secretary, copies of letters drafted for the Drurys survive in Donne's hand, and he was also involved in the scribal copying of notorious letters that circulated widely in manuscript (Robert Carr, Viscount Rochester, to Henry Howard, Earl of Northampton).[56] More evidence of his secretarial skills is seen in a letter to Sir William Trumbull, one of the clerks of the council, promising to forward to him letters for the courtier Grey Bridges, fifth Baron Chandos: 'Sr, Not vpon my strength, but vpon my L: chandos hys Interest, I ame bolde accordinge to hys direction to addresse as many letters, as come to my hands for hym, to yo^{rs}'.[57] Henry Goodyer asked Donne to write letters for him in the pursuit of a grant or court appointment: 'The good Countesse [of Bedford] spake somewhat of your desire of letters; but I am afraid, she is not a proper Mediatrix to those persons, but I counsail in the dark'; this request suggests that Donne was known for his ability to analyse court politics and counsel his friend in terms of strategy.[58] Donne was therefore useful not only for his writing skills, but also as a political strategist. Cumulatively then, Donne was skilled in a series of textual and manuscript forms, many of which were directly linked to his skill as a letter-writer.

Donne's letter-writing is soaked with what Alan Stewart would describe as a 'grammar of the letter', or in other words 'a vocabulary and set of images that originate in the material practices of letter-writing culture of early modern England'.[59] Indeed, Donne displays a marked awareness of the physical features of different components of the letter – such as handwriting, paper, seals, and postscripts. In a letter to Sir Robert Ker he excuses his 'short Letter', which he describes as a 'ragge of Paper', part of a mannered and conventional deferential rhetoric widely employed by letter-writers of the period.[60] The size and quality of paper becomes an honorific trope, weighing social distinctions between correspondents, but also as a way of expressing friendship. In another to George Garrard he pleads that 'there is not size of paper in the Palace, large enough to tell you how much I esteeme my selfe honoured in your remembrances; nor strong enough to wrap up my heart so ful of good affections towards you, as mine is'.[61] To Sir Robert Harley he writes, 'Sr as I was wyllinge to make this paper a little bigger than a physicians Receit'.[62] In a letter to Martha Garrard, Donne writes that he will 'come thither to you; which I do, by wrapping up in this paper, the heart of *Your most affectionate servant* J. Donne', the letter effectively functioning as a corporeal embodiment of Donne himself – figuratively the wrapper of an enclosed heart.[63] The materiality of the letter thus becomes part of Donne's linguistic repertoire.

Moreover, significant meanings were attached to distinct physical characteristics and attributes of letters – for example, manuscript layout and seals – social signs, codes and cues inscribed materially within the form, which would have been readily understood during the early modern period by those conversant with epistolary cultures. Throughout the period, the use of deferential blank space in the placing of signatures and salutations on the manuscript page was particularly prevalent in letters of petition alongside a rhetoric of humility, where the sender sought to convey a sense of their own social inferiority or obeisance in relation to the recipient. In 1602 Donne, in writing to his estranged father-in-law Sir George More, employed deferential tropes in seeking a rapprochement after his clandestine marriage to More's daughter Anne: 'I humbly beseeche yow', he wrote in one letter, 'so to deale in yt, as the persuasions of Nature, reason, wisdome, and Christianity shall informe yow; And to accept the vowes, of one whom yow may now rayse or scatter'.[64] He sought to underline his contrition in this series of letters by signing his name in the extreme bottom right hand corner of the letter, a sign of contrition which was a departure from his normal signing practice.[65] He likewise subscribed the beseeching letters he wrote to Egerton after his dismissal from the Lord Keeper's service, and subsequent imprisonment in the Fleet.[66] A similar rhetorics of humility was employed in a letter to the Marquess of Buckingham for preference, in which he 'All y^t I meane in vsinge thys boldnes, of puttinge myselfe into yor lops presence by thys ragge of paper, ys, to tell yor Lp: that I ly in a corner, as a clodd of clay attendinge what kinde of vessell yt shall please yo^w to make', signing his name at the bottom right-hand corner of the page.[67]

Finally, the sealing of letters, bound up as it was with authentication, identity, and privacy, was also fraught with its own distinct set of material considerations with seals themselves conveying significant meaning. Donne used at least three different personal seals, all of which had a symbolic potency: a sheaf of snakes, a wolf rampant surrounded by a sheaf of snakes, and after his ordination in 1615, a seal

of Christ crucified on an anchor ('the Emblem of hope'), which, according to Walton, not long before his death Donne had set in gold and 'sent
to many of his dearest friends to be used as *Seals*, or *Rings*, and kept as
memorials of him, and of his affection'; a fourth seal of a heraldic
antelope passant crined, which appears on a letter written from the
house of his friend Sir John Danvers, may have been borrowed simply
for the purpose of sealing.[68] His new seal after ordination appears on
a letter to Sir Edward Herbert, in which he refers to receiving 'a new
character'.[69] Several of John Donne's letters display seals on the outside
of the letter, which had been attached on top of a separate tongue of
paper that had itself been secured onto what appears to be a cross of wax
applied to the outside of the letter in its folded rectangular form and on
the opposite side to the address leaf.[70] The practicalities of sealing were
tied up with issues of privacy, access to knowledge, and reading practices
that inflected the nature of the letter. He informed Goodyer that his
letter was sealed in the presence of Lady Bartlett.[71] Other letters were
sent unsealed to be passed around, read by those other than the addressee. Writing to George Garrard, Donne apologises for sealing up a letter
to his sister (Martha Garrard) and reminds Garrard that he had her
permission '*to open it again*'.[72]

Donne's letters need to be read and understood within the context
of the culture and social practices of early modern letter-writing, as
well as with an awareness of their biographical and literary aspects, in
order that they might fully be decoded. As a corpus, his prose letters
represent an extremely complex set of texts, which survive in printed
form as well as in manuscript originals and scribal copies, and reveal
a real range generically. Likewise, Donne's letter-writing activities show
him to have been a talented textual and epistolary specialist, who
conducted regular correspondence with a wide range of individuals,
was employed in a secretarial capacity, and involved in the scribal
circulation of infamous letters. The letter form was an extremely
flexible vehicle for Donne, with stylistic echoes of his other writings
(namely his verse and sermons), which could be employed for a wide
variety of purposes, to maintain close and meaningful intellectual
friendships, to impart news and conduct business, and to console and
advise in a spiritual capacity. Above all, his letters are immersed with
a self-conscious awareness of letter-writing as a practice, which not
only informs the rhetoric of his writing, but also permits
a reconstruction of the material conditions, patterns, and habits of
Donne's letter-writing.

Notes

1. Information about *The Oxford Edition of the Letters of John Donne* can be found at: http://donneletters.english.tamu.edu/ [accessed 17 December 2018].
2. Edmund Gosse, *The Life and Letters of John Donne, Dean of St Paul's*, 2 vols. (London: Heinemann, 1899).
3. John Carey, "John Donne's Newsless Letters," *Essays and Studies* 34 (1981), 45.
4. Annabel Patterson, "Misinterpretable Donne: The Testimony of the Letters," *JDJ* 1 (1982), 39–53.
5. Arthur Marotti, "The Social Context and Nature of Donne's Writing: Occasional Verse and Letters," in *CCJD*, 40; Lynne Magnusson, "Donne's Language: The Conditions of Communication," in *CCJD*, 189.
6. Margaret Maurer, "The Poetical Familiarity of John Donne's Letters," *Genre* 15 (1982), 183–202; and "The Verse Letter, Chicago:" in *OHJD*, 348–61.
7. Ramie Targoff, *John Donne, Body and Soul* (University of Chicago Press, 2008), 25–48.
8. Dennis Flynn, "Donne, Henry Wotton, and the Earl of Essex," *JDJ* 14 (1995), 185–218; "Familiar Letters: Donne and Pietro Aretino," *Renaissance Papers* (2002), 27–43; and "John Donne in the Ellesmere Manuscripts," *Huntington Library Quarterly* 46.4 (1983), 333–36. See also M. T. Hester, "Introduction" in *Letters To Severall Persons of Honour (1651): A Facsimile Reproduction* (Delmar, NY: Scholars' Facsimiles & Reprints, 1977), v–xxii; R. J. Corthell, "'Frendships Sacraments': John Donne's Familiar Letters," *Studies in Philology* 78 (1981), 409–25; E. M. Simpson, *A Study of the Prose Works of John Donne* (Oxford: Oxford University Press, 1948), chapter 12; A. C. Partridge, "The Prose Letters," in *John Donne: Language and Style* (Oxford: Blackwell, 1978), chapter 7; E. W. Sullivan II, "The Problem of Text in Familiar Letters," *Papers of the Bibliographical Society of America* 75 (1981), 115–26; E. Roth-Schwartz, "Colon and Semicolon in Donne's Prose Letters: Practice and Principle," *Early Modern Literary Studies* 3 (1997), 37; N. Barker, "Donne's 'Letter to the Lady Carey and Mrs. Essex Riche': Text and Facsimile," *Book Collector* 22 (1973), 487–93; R. J. Bauer, "Donne's Letter to Herbert Re-Examined," *New Essays on Donne*, ed. G. A. Stringer (Salzburg: Institut für Englische Sprache und Literatur, 1977), 60–73; C. Summers and T. L. Pebworth, "Donne's Correspondence with Wotton," *JDJ* 10 (1991), 1–36; M. L. Westerman, "John Donne and the Art of Letter-Writing: A Study of the Verse Letters" (PhD diss., Yale University, 1974); J. Hennekam, "The Role of Utterance: Speech and Text in the Letters and Sermons of John Donne: 'It is a Desperate State, to Be Speechlesse'" (PhD diss., University of Toronto, 1994).
9. See *John Donne's Marriage Letters in The Folger Shakespeare Library*, eds. M. Thomas Hester, Robert Parker Sorlien, and Dennis Flynn (Washington, DC: Folger Shakespeare Library, 2005), and Margaret Maurer, "The Prose Letter," in *OHJD*, 348–61.
10. William A. Davies, "The Prose Letters of John Donne" (PhD diss., University of Alberta, 1992), prints critical texts of 226 Donne letters, including 38

holographs, and a further 15 letters with extracts in appendices. An Oxford University Press edition of the complete correspondence is also underway, which establishes a corpus of 228 letters at present. See also, G. Keynes, *A Bibliography of Dr John Donne, Dean of St Paul's*, 4th edn (Oxford: Clarendon Press, 1973), 133–59; Gosse, *Life and Letters; Letters; Donne, Selected Letters*, ed. P. M. Oliver (New York: Routledge, 2002).

11. J. P. Feil, "Sir Tobie Matthew and his Collection of Letters" (PhD diss., University of Chicago, 1962), 276–77.

12. *Cabala, Sive, Scrinia Sacra Mysteries of State & Government* (London, 1654), 314–15.

13. Peter Beal, *Catalogue of English Literary Manuscripts, 1450–1700*, www.celm-ms.org.uk/authors/donnejohn.html.

14. Leicestershire Record Office, MS Finch DG.7, Lit. 2; Ilona Bell, "'Under ye Rage of a Hott Sonn & Yr Eyes': John Donne's Love Letters to Ann More," in *The Eagle and the Dove: Reassessing John Donne*, eds. C. Summers and Ted-Larry Pebworth (Columbia, MO: University of Missouri Press 1986), 25–52.

15. Joseph P. Regenstein Library, University of Chicago, Bacon MSS of Redgrave Hall, 4199, 4199v, 4202, 4203, 1611–1612; *Letters from Redgrave Hall: The Bacon Family, 1340–1714*, ed. Diarmaid MacCulloch, Suffolk Records Society, vol. 50 (Woodbridge, UK: The Boydell Press, 2007), 90–91, 93–95; R. E. Bennett, "Donne's Letters from the Continent in 1611–12," *Philological Quarterly* 19 (1940), 66–78; Davies, "Prose Letters," Appendix 2; R. C. Bald, *Donne and the Drurys* (Cambridge University Press, 1959), 100–11.

16. L. A. Knafla, "Mr Secretary Donne: The Years with Sir Thomas Egerton," in *John Donne's Professional Lives*, ed. David Colclough (Cambridge: D. S. Brewer, 2003), 48; Andrew Gordon, "Donne and Late Elizabethan Court Politics," in *OHJD*, 465, 467.

17. *Selected Letters and Other Papers*, eds. C. Burlinson and A. Zurcher (Oxford: Oxford University Press, 2009).

18. Bodleian Library, Tanner MS 76, fol. 162r-63v.

19. E. W. Sullivan II, "Modern Scholarly Editions of the Prose of John Donne," in *OHJD*, 79.

20. David Stevenson, "Ker, Robert, First Earl of Ancram (1578–1654)," in *Oxford Dictionary of National Biography*, www.oxforddnd.com.

21. *Letters*, 193.

22. Bald, *Drurys*, 3.

23. Dennis Flynn, "Donne Manuscripts in Cheshire," *English Manuscript Studies* 8 (2000), 280–92.

24. Bodleian Library, Additional MS, 25707, fol. 64b; Lara M. Crowley, "Archival Research," in *OHJD*, 36; Davies, "Prose Letters," 368–69; Beal, *Catalogue*; Peter Beal, "Philip Sidney's *Letter to Queen Elizabeth* and that 'False Knave' Alexander Dicsone," *English Manuscript Studies* 11 (2002), 1–51; Andrew Gordon, "'A fortune of Paper Walls': The Letters of Francis Bacon and the Earl of Essex," *ELR* 37:3 (2007), 319–36.

25. Bodleian Library, MS e. Mus 131, p. x. Beal, No. 21.
26. Owned by Robert S. Pirie, Hamilton, Massachusetts; Sotheby's Sale Catalogue, 19 March 1951, Lot 109; Davies, "Prose Letters," 227; Beal, *Catalogue*.
27. The National Archives, SP 12/134/59: 1 December 1622; *Letters*, 21–23, 172–73; *A Collection of Letters, Made by Sr Tobie Mathew* (London, 1660), 304.
28. Walton, *Lives*, 32–34; *Letters*, 179–80.
29. Bodleian Library, Cotton MS, Julius C.III, fol.154, January 24, 1610. Bald, *Life*, 221 n.3.
30. Folger Library, b.539.
31. *Letters*, 71–72.
32. Mathew, *Collection*, 305; Donne, *Poems* (London, 1633), 356–58, 370–72.
33. Bodleian Library, Add. MS, 29598, fols. 13, 15; Pforzheimer Library, MS 130; Huntington, HM 7281; Harvard MS Eng 1290.
34. Walton, *Lives*, 68.
35. Edward Dering, *Certaine Godly and Comfortable Letters, Full of Christian Consolation* (Middelburg, 1590).
36. Mathew, *Collection*, 349.
37. Davies, "Prose Letters," xviii–xx.
38. *Letters*, 179, 159.
39. Izaak Walton, *The Life of Mr George Herbert* (London, 1670), 144.
40. *Letters*, 94.
41. *Letters*, 10.
42. *Letters*, 166.
43. *Letters*, 27, 118–19.
44. *Letters*, 255.
45. *Letters*, 133.
46. *Letters*, 239.
47. Mathew, *Collection*, 172.
48. Alan Stewart, *Shakespeare's Letters* (Oxford University Press, 2008), 127–28.
49. The National Archives, SP 14/134.59: Dec. 1, 1622.
50. *Letters*, 114–15; Folger, L.b. 535; Bennett, "Donne's"; Davies, "Prose Letters," 292; William S. Powell, *John Pory, 1572–1636: The Life and Letters of a Man of Many Parts* (Chapel Hill, NC: University of North Carolina Press, 1977), 6.
51. Davies, "Prose Letters," 335.
52. *Letters*, 81–83; Folger MS, L.b. 526; Bald, *Life*, 133.
53. Andrew Gordon, "Donne and Late Elizabethan Court Politics," in *OHJD*, 465.
54. Bodleian Library, Cotton MS, Julius C.III, fol.153: Feb. 20, 1602.
55. Bodleian Library, Cotton MS, Cleopatra F.VII, fol. 293; Bald, *Life*, 202, 221 n.3; Bodleian Library, Cotton MS, Julius C.III, fol. 154: Jan. 24, 1610.
56. Bald, *Life*, 93; Joseph P. Regenstein Library, University of Chicago, Bacon MSS of Redgrave Hall, 4199, 4199v, 4202, 4203, 1611–1612; Davies, "Prose Letters," Appendix 2; Bald, *Drurys*, 100–11.
57. Bodleian Library, Trumbull MS, Sept. 10, 1614.

58. *Letters*, 167.
59. Stewart, *Shakespeare's*, 5.
60. *Letters*, 257.
61. *Letters*, 218.
62. Bodleian Library, Loan MS 29/202, fol.131, April 7, 1613.
63. *Letters*, 36.
64. Folger, L.b.526, Feb. 2, 1602.
65. Folger, L.b.526, L.b.527, L.b.529, L.b.532. Cf. L.b.542, June 22, 1629. *Donne's Marriage Letters*, 17.
66. Folger, L.b.528, L.b.530, L.b.534, L.b.533.
67. Bodleian, Additional MS, D 111, fols. 133–34: August 8, 1621.
68. *Donne's Marriage Letters*, 33; Walton, *Lives*, 63.
69. The National Archives, PRO 30/53/7/8, fol. 15: January 23, 1615.
70. Folger, L.b.528, L.b.533, L.b.534: Feb. 12, 1602, March 1, 1602, c. Feb. 15, 1602.
71. *Letters*, 155–57.
72. *Letters*, 214.

CHAPTER 10

Orality and Performance

Ilona Bell

In the twenty-first century when written words are omnipresent, when a single digital reader can hold over a thousand books, and the complete collection of early modern books is available online, it is easy to forget that writing was itself a major technological revolution that drastically altered the structure of the human mind. The very words sign, text, and literature (from *literae*, the letters of the alphabet) presume writing. Around 1600 when John Donne was composing his poems, England was also undergoing a dramatic technological revolution, from orality and handwriting to print. But earlier technologies don't simply expire or disappear. Just as many people today continue to buy books they can hold in their hands, in Donne's day poets continued to write lyrics that were performed or circulated in handwritten copies, and only later, perhaps, ending up in print.

Donne published three long philosophical, encomiastic poems, *The First* and *Second Anniversaries* and "Elegy on Prince Henry," but regretted doing so. "[T]he fault that I acknowledge in my self, is to have descended to print any thing in verse," Donne wrote to a friend. "I confesse I wonder how I declined to it, and do not pardon my self."[1] Widespread manuscript circulation is a form of publication since it endows poems with a life apart from their author, their meanings proliferating as readers impart their own points of view; however, Donne's lyrics only began to circulate widely in the second decade of the seventeenth century, more than a decade after they were probably written.[2] His collected poems were not published until 1633, two years after his death. Since speech and song disappeared as soon as they were uttered, how can we recuperate the vitality of Donne's poems in performance, before they were "published"?

In Donne's day, reading was still generally vocalized, whether for the reader's own pleasure and edification or for listening family and friends including some, especially if they were women, who could not read. Hence, a person reading a poem would have *heard* the words, whether spoken to himself or performed for others. When circumstances prevented Donne from reciting poems to his friends, he wrote them letters – the only way to have a long-distance conversation. Donne envisioned his verse epistles as a form of speech: "Sir, more than kisses, letters mingle souls, / For, thus friends absent speak" ("To Mr Henry Wotton," 1–2). He expected them to be read aloud.

Like many of his peers from Sir Philip Sidney to Lady Mary Wroth, Donne wrote songs with shorter lines, simpler diction, and more readily comprehensible syntax that could be sung and enjoyed with musical accompaniment. Indeed, the word *lyric* originally meant "of or pertaining to the lyre; adapted to the lyre, meant to be sung; pertaining to or characteristic of song"[3] – a meaning still used for song lyrics. By the 1580s and 90s "lyric" had also come to refer to any short poem divided into stanzas. The word "sonnet" could also describe any short poem. Donne wrote nineteen Holy Sonnets in a conventional Petrarchan rhyme scheme, but his collection of lyrics, known as the *Songs and Sonnets*, contains no fourteen-line sonnets.

Most of Donne's *Songs and Sonnets* sound less like songs and more like spoken English, as his dramatic opening lines and "rough," or metrically irregular lines attest: "For God's sake hold your tongue, and let me love" ("The Canonization," 1); or "I wonder by my troth, what thou and I / Did, till we loved" ("The Good Morrow," 1–2). Of course, Donne's poems are not spontaneous outpourings of powerful feeling. Rather they are carefully crafted works of art, written with the expectation that they would be performed for an audience known to the poet.

Performance and poetics are closely allied because performance is, by definition, artful speech rather than unpremeditated utterance. Performance provides a frame that invites reflection and critique, which is what Donne's poems do: "Stand still, and I will read to thee / A lecture, love, in love's philosophy" ("A Lecture upon the Shadow," 1–2). During Donne's day, when live performance was the only form of entertainment available, poetry readings were enormously popular. Just as Shakespeare's text provides modern-day actors with all the clues they need to construct a gripping performance, Donne's poems contain performance cues – what anthropologists who study oral cultures call contextualization cues – that can still enhance our understanding and enjoyment.

"The Indifferent" is a performance piece, designed for a social gathering, at a friend's house or perhaps at York House, the London mansion of Donne's employer, Sir Thomas Egerton, where Donne worked and socialized during the years when he was most actively writing and performing his lyrics. Like an epic bard, "The Indifferent" begins *in medias res*, addressing an audience that was expecting a lively, lusty performance:

> I can love both fair and brown,
> Her whom abundance melts, and her whom want betrays,
> Her who loves loneness best, and her who masques and plays,
> Her whom the country formed, and whom the town . . .
> I can love her and her, and you and you,
> I can love any, so she be not true.   (1–4, 8–9)

The flirtatious tone and charismatic self-possession were calculated to charm and entertain a roomful of women, with a variety of attributes and inclinations. Donne was also performing for the men in the audience who would have been amused by his hyperbolic promiscuity. And yet, the tug of intimacy that emerges in the second stanza – "Must I, which came to travail thorough you, / Grow your fixed subject, because you are true?" (17–18) – hint that there was one woman in the audience who had reason to think he would become her "fixed subject." Was Donne buttressing his reputation as a staunch bachelor in order to conceal the fact that he was secretly wooing Anne More who had come to live at York House with her aunt? Very likely. By adopting a variety of tones as the poem unfolded, Donne invited the various members of his audience to hear whichever of the poem's conflicting messages they wished.

Performance dramatizes poetry the way an actor interprets and enacts a script. It can be a communal experience involving a social group as in "The Indifferent" or a private dialogue as in "The Sun Rising." Either way, performance is an interactive experience. A poet writing for someone he knows could use the poem to elicit a desired response as in "The Good Morrow," or to rebut an undesired one as in "The Canonization." The poet has all the resources of rhetoric at his command, but there are limits to his persuasive power since the audience can ironize, alter, rebut, or misconstrue his words.

Oral performance relies on body language – gestures, posture, facial expressions, and, most important, tones of voice – to convey and delimit meaning. Although before audiovisual recording these non-verbal cues were as evanescent as the speaking voice, Donne's language often includes the lyric equivalent of stage directions. In "The Good Morrow," the all-important, non-verbal means of communication enact the lovers' intimacy and interdependency: "My face in thine eye, thine in mine appears, / And true plain hearts do in the faces rest" (15–16). In "A Valediction of my Name in the Window" the drowsy tone that emerges at the end – "this

I murmur in my sleep" (64) – indicates a strikingly private performative context.

Oral literature typically follows an additive or cumulative structure rather than a logical or analytic one. Along with "The Indifferent," the numerous Donne poems that follow this form include "The Curse," which directs a barrage of vituperative maledictions at "Whoever guesses, thinks, or dreams he knows / Who is my mistress," (1–2), and "Woman's Constancy," which compiles excuses that the lover might make when she leaves him, or he leaves her, the following morning. In aggregative poems like these, the forward momentum comes less from a carefully structured argument than from the variety and ingenuity of the examples.

Yet, proliferation by itself is not sufficiently dazzling or daring to satisfy Donne. The true brilliance of his aggregative poems emerges at the end when a final stroke of wit overturns the audience's carefully cultivated expectations, replacing reiteration with antithesis, another characteristic feature of oral literature. "Woman's Constancy" illustrates the pattern. After setting up a series of "scapes," or excuses which "I could / Dispute, and conquer, if I would" (14–15), the speaker suddenly shifts direction: "Which I abstain to do, / For by tomorrow, I may think so too" (16–17). To an audience of irreverent young men about town, this would have sounded like another instance of Donne's audacious libertinism. In this performative scenario, the speaker's reluctance to be tied down to one woman comprises a synecdoche for the poet's refusal to be limited to any single rhetorical strategy, the sheer exuberance of the language epitomizing Donne's willingness to say almost anything to showcase his wit and entertain his male coterie.[4]

The ending sounds very different, however, if we heed the contextualization cues of the opening lines: "Now thou hast loved me one whole day, / Tomorrow when thou leav'st, what wilt thou say?" (1–2). If the poet conceived these excuses while waiting for his beloved to give herself to him, and if he then performed the poem as they were about to spend their first night together, the obsessive attempt to imagine and preempt any excuse she might make would have been a way of controlling his fear that their relationship would not last. The final claim that he "may think so too" is a defensive gesture, making him seem less vulnerable while producing a twinge of jealousy that would remind her not to take his love for granted.

"Woman's Constancy" becomes a far more intriguingly multilayered poem when we consider the interaction between performer and interlocutor. Remarkably, there is nothing in the language to indicate whether the speaker is male or female. If Donne gave his lover a copy of the poem and asked her to read it to him, her inflection and bearing would have conveyed her response. Because "Woman's Constancy" could be spoken either by a man or a woman, the conditionality of the ending, "For by tomorrow, I *may* think so too" (my emphasis), captures the anxieties and uncertainties facing any new lover, whether male or female. Like the cross-dressing heroines in Shakespeare's comedies, the gender-bending possibilities of "Woman's Constancy" destabilize conventional sex roles, challenge the double standard, and repudiate antifeminist stereotypes about woman's inconstancy.

Classicists who study ancient epics and anthropologists who study oral cultures have identified common features of orality that persist across continents and centuries, features that are particularly prevalent in Renaissance England where rhetoric, from the Latin word *rhetor* meaning public speaker, constituted the core of the educational curriculum. Rhetoric pervades all types of writing and performance, from poetry to sermons; therefore, it helps solve "the problem of linking the artful speaking of performance to other modes of language use so that performance analysis does not fall into the trap of segregating poetics from other ways of speaking."[5]

"The Sun Rising" is one of Donne's most audaciously performative poems, and, appropriately, it has an unusually concrete dramatic context: "Why dost thou thus, / Through windows and through curtains call on us?" (2–3). The sun's appearance is a wake-up call, reminding the speaker that he needs to leave before some busybody, some "Busy old fool" (1), discovers him in bed with his lover. Like classic mock-heroic verse, "The Sun Rising" parodies literary conventions it simultaneously exalts. The apostrophe to the sun begins with mock epic epithets: "Busy old fool, unruly Sun ... Saucy pedantic wretch" (1, 5). The ensuing imperatives – "go chide / Late schoolboys and sour prentices, / Go tell court-huntsmen that the King will ride, / Call country ants to harvest offices" (5–8) – deploy, even as they derive humor from the rhetorical figure of *copia*, repetition and variation on a theme, which was recommended to increase fluency. The couplet that brings stanza 1 to a resounding conclusion – "Love, all alike, no season knows, nor clime, / Nor hours, days, months, which are the rags of time" (9–10) – mimics the apothegms, or familiar sayings, that pervade oral literature.

"The Sun Rising" fuses the defiant antagonism and encomiastic praise that are the two most common stances of oral literature. The vaunting challenge that begins stanza 2 sounds like an epic hero preparing for battle, magnifying his own strength by exalting and then defeating his adversary's renowned power:

> Thy beams, so reverend and strong,
> Why should'st thou think?
> I could eclipse and cloud them with a wink,
> But that I would not lose her sight so long:
> If her eyes have not blinded thine . . .   (11–15)

The primary lyric audience is Donne's lady, and her reaction is critical. The apostrophe to the sun enables the speaker to impress her with his bold audacity, amuse her with his wit, and flatter her by flamboyantly praising her luminous eyes. If Donne later performed the poem for a wider lyric audience, envisioning him in bed with his lover would have produced an added frisson of pleasure.

"The Sun Rising" humorously plays with the formal structure of microcosm and macrocosm recommended by rhetoric manuals to enhance memory and magnify the scope and import of a speech. After commanding the sun to illuminate all of English society, from country laborers to city apprentices to court and king, Donne sends the sun off to circle the world ("Look, and tomorrow late, tell me / Whether both the Indias of spice and mine / Be where thou left'st them, or lie here with me," 16–18) before inviting it into their bed: "Thine age asks ease . . . Shine here to us, and thou art everywhere; / This bed thy centre is, these walls, thy sphere" (27, 29–30). "The Sun Rising" shows how forms of play "provide settings in which speech and society can be criticized and transformed."[6] Just as "The Good Morrow" "makes one little room an everywhere" (11), "The Sun Rising" makes the lovers' bedroom into the model for a brave new world: "She's all states, and all princes I, / Nothing else is. / Princes do but play us; compared to this, / All honour's mimic, all wealth alchemy" (21–24). By using humor to defy and deride the social, political, and economic forces that threaten to separate the lovers, "The Sun Rising" confronts "the perennial micro-macro problem of how to relate the situated use of language to larger social structures, particularly the structures of power and value that constitute the political economy of a society."[7]

"The Sun Rising" is not only a mock-heroic, miniature epic, it is also a mock-valediction. Donne's especial fondness for the valediction – a subgenre derived from the Latin verb *valedicere* meaning to bid farewell – shows just how deeply his lyrics are rooted in distinct dramatic contexts. The opening of "A Valediction of Weeping" is about as performative as a poem can be: "Let me pour forth / My tears before thy face, whil'st I stay here, / For thy face coins them, and thy stamp they bear" (1–3). These tears are slow and deliberate, each tear comprising a reflection of the lover's face and a reflection upon their love. Paradoxically, the speaker's tears are all the more laden with meaning precisely because they are premeditated and staged. By making such a concerted effort to confront her sadness and avert her anxiety, Donne demonstrates just how much he cares. At the end of the first stanza, a tear crashes, exposing the inadequacy of his metaphor and the limits of his rhetorical power: "When a tear falls, that thou falls which it bore, / So thou and I are nothing then, when on a diverse shore" (8–9). Eager to "quickly make that, which was nothing, all" (13), he transforms the tear into a globe, but that also fails to console. By the end of the second stanza the lovers are wrapped in each other's arms, weeping uncontrollably: "Till thy tears mixed with mine do overflow" (17). The poem draws to an end by begging her to stop crying for his sake, lest she destroy him with her grief: "Draw not up seas to drown me in thy sphere, / Weep me not dead in thine arms, but forbear / To teach the sea what it may do too soon" (20–21). As verbal language merges with body language, the fluidity of the tears symbolizes the ways in which performance anticipates, incorporates, and adapts to the audience's reactions.

"Song" ("Sweetest love, I do not go") also sets out to dispel the sadness of an impending departure:

> Sweetest love, I do not go
>   For weariness of thee,
> Nor in hope the world can show
>   A fitter love for me,
>   But since that I
> Must die at last, 'tis best
> To use myself in jest,
>   Thus by feigned deaths to die.　　　　(1–8)

The jocular puns on "go" and "die," Renaissance circumlocutions for making love and reaching sexual climax, invoke the lovers' shared pleasure in sexual and verbal play. But why does Donne feel compelled to explain that he is not leaving her to seek "A fitter love"? Presumably, because they are clandestine lovers, bound together not by law and society but by a freely chosen love that could easily be destroyed, should they waver in their resolve. Their imminent separation catalyzes the social pressures and ideological forces, both external and internal, that threaten to drive them asunder.

"A Valediction of My Name in the Window" draws on the Latin root of valediction, *dicere*, meaning to say, speak, or name. Donne inscribes his name on the window of his lover's chamber in the hope that it will speak for him in his absence: "As much more loving, as more sad, / 'Twill make thee" (40–41). The repeated puns on "more" – "'Tis much that glass should be / As all-confessing, and through-shine as I; / 'Tis more, that it shows thee to thee" (7–9) – identifies his clandestine lover and future wife, Anne More, as the poem's original lyric audience. At the climax of the poem, in stanzas VIII–X, Donne imagines that seeing his name in the window will prevent Anne from marrying a rival suitor. The poem ends by apologizing for this fit of jealousy: "And this I murmur in my sleep; / Impute this idle talk to that I go, / For dying men talk often so" (64–66). Once again, the erotic double entendres of "go" and "dying" derive consolation and strength from their sexual and verbal intimacy.

"A Valediction of My Name in the Window" expresses a deep fear that their enforced separation will become permanent. Contextualization cues abound, indicating that the poem was written before the lovers were married, when Anne's name was still More and "When love and grief their exaltation had" (38) – most likely when Anne's father, Sir George More, upon discovering their affair, forced her to leave York House and return to the country. Donne hoped that the "exaltation," or rapturous passion, of their lovemaking would transform their "grief" into a sublime revelation of their abiding commitment to each other. Yet anxieties and uncertainties persist. In order to stay together, John Donne and Anne More were ultimately forced to elope. When Donne later wrote to inform her father that "We adventured equally,"[8] he was not exaggerating; their marriage, like their clandestine love affair, required extraordinary courage and commitment on her part as well as his. Sir George was so furious that he had Donne imprisoned and fired (Donne's boss, the Lord Keeper, Sir Thomas Egerton, was More's brother-in-law). Donne waged a successful lawsuit to have the marriage declared legal but was unable to salvage his promising career as a civil servant.

Donne's valedictions are persuasion poems that seek to prevent an impending separation from becoming permanent. Yet the tone and situation vary dramatically. The tender intimacy of "Song" is clearly meant for Donne's lover, but the poem omits any identifying characteristics so that it could have been sung to a wider lyric audience without compromising Anne More's reputation or endangering their relationship. By contrast, "A Valediction of My Name in the Window" is a gravely serious poem, addressed expressly to Anne and intended for her eyes and ears alone. It could not have been performed for a wider lyric audience, at least not while her father was actively trying to separate them, without undermining the poem's primary rhetorical purpose: to ensure their future together.

Donne's valedictions run the gamut, from the most intimate of lovers' dialogues to a meditation on what it would take to transform their private conversation into a book, appropriate for a wider public readership. "Valediction of the Book" is a farewell to private dialogue between lovers and a meditation on what would be required for the next step, publication. Here as in all the valedictions, Donne begins by speaking directly to his lover: "I'll tell thee now, dear love, what thou shalt do" (1). What distinguishes this poem is the directive to transform their private correspondence into a book: "Study our manuscripts, those myriads / Of letters which have passed 'twixt thee and me, / Thence write our annals" (10–12). To begin with, there is the all-important question of audience. As we have seen, Donne was accustomed to writing poems that could mean different things to different members of his audience. Nonetheless, a published book of poems would need to satisfy an ever greater range of readers, from Neo-Platonic idealists and clandestine lovers – "Whether abstract spiritual love they like" or "they choose / Something which they may see and use" (30, 33–34) – to religious dissidents, skeptical lawyers, and overweening statesmen "Whose weakness none doth, or dares, tell" (52).

The interactive nature of oral performance includes persuasion, critique, and counter-response. By contrast, printed texts cannot defend themselves against the objections they provoke. Hence, publication often involves a kind of self-censorship – especially in Donne's day when the authorities regularly prohibited publication on ethical and political grounds. Indeed, Donne's most erotic elegies were excluded from the posthumous first edition of his poems. Donne knew that his private lovers' dialogue would have to be encoded, expurgated, obfuscated, and rewritten, turned into an "all-gravèd tome / In cipher writ, or new-made idiom" (20–21), in order be published. No wonder Ben Jonson, Donne's friend and fellow poet, thought Donne's poems would perish for not being understood.

Yet, despite Jonson's fears, we are still reading and discussing Donne's poetry. As it turns out, his dazzling performance pieces are also brilliant texts that continue to accrue meanings long after their original context has disappeared. "Much of what we do" as scholars "amounts to the decontextualization and recontextualization of other's discourse." By exploring what "the recontextualized text brings with it from its original context,"[9] we can recuperate the multifold layers of meaning that are all too easily occluded when poetic performances become a "book, as long-lived as the elements" ("Valediction of the Book," 19).

Notes

1. *Letters*, 206.
2. As H. R. Woudhuysen explains in *Sir Philip Sidney and the Circulation of Manuscripts, 1558–1640* (Oxford: Clarendon Press, 1996), 154, "once a poet's work began to circulate in manuscript, it tended to continue to do so."
3. "lyric, adj. and n.," *OED Online*.
4. See Marotti, *Manuscript*.
5. Richard Bauman and Charles L. Briggs, "Poetics and Performance as Critical Perspectives on Language and Social Life," *Annual Review of Anthropology* 19 (1990), 79.
6. Bauman and Briggs, "Poetics," 63.
7. Bauman and Briggs, "Poetics," 79.
8. "To Sir George More," in *The Life and Letters of John Donne*, ed. Edmund Gosse, 2 vols. (New York: Dodd, Mead, and co., 1899), 1:101.
9. Bauman and Briggs, "Poetics," 78, 75.

CHAPTER II

Reading and Interpretation

Katrin Ettenhuber

Recent scholarly approaches to the history of reading can be summed up in one iconic image: the book wheel invented by the Italian engineer Agostino Ramelli, first presented in his illustrated book *Le Diverse et Artificiose Machine* (Paris, 1588). Based on the design of a water wheel, Ramelli's device allowed the reader to consult up to a dozen books in one location; the wheel rotated vertically and enabled its user to access all the volumes at exactly the same angle. While the wheel moved vertically, however, its prime intellectual design was to facilitate lateral thinking: rather than embarking on the in-depth study of a single work, the reader was able to compare and collate various opinions on a single topic or theme. Sections of a page most pertinent to the inquiry were often marked or annotated in various ways; once this process was completed, information could be excerpted and arranged in a notebook or commonplace book, either with a view to longer-term storage, or as an intermediate stage towards the creation of a new text. Examining these material aspects of the reading process gives us an insight into early modern information technology, as it were (with the book wheel as a multi-tabbed browser of sorts): the means by which readers managed written knowledge in an age that saw a huge increase in the output of written books, and eventually converted that knowledge into new forms of cultural production.

Yet a chapter on Donne's reading must begin with the somewhat discouraging acknowledgement that the material traces of his engagement with texts are largely lost: he did not leave any reading notes or common-place books, and the occasional examples of faint underlinings and pencil marks in his library reveal almost nothing about his reading practices, or about the intellectual assumptions they may have reflected. There are, however, other substantial forms of evidence available to us: Donne's explicit pronouncements on habits of reading and interpretation – good and bad – in his prose works, and scenes of reading depicted in his poems, for instance. Most importantly (and voluminously), quotations from other authors embedded in Donne's writing have a great deal to tell us about his priorities as a user of texts, and also offer an opportunity to observe the workings of readerly principles in practice. It is crucial to note from the start that textual transactions are very rarely a simple matter of scholarly or technical procedure. From his earliest days at Lincoln's Inn, Donne describes reading as an intimate process: "Satire I" situates its speaker in cramped lodgings, "Consorted with these few books," and couches legal study in the provocative language of "lie[ing]" and "die[ing]" (3–4); in the *Songs and Sonnets*, meanwhile, the moves that readers make on texts are cast as a potent analogy for romantic relationships – for the ways in which lovers accept, or resist, invitations to self-disclosure, and the questions of trust and commitment raised by this process. In the prose works, inter-pretation is equally implicated in problems of knowledge and revelation, though the contextual parameters are radically different. Protestant theo-logians maintained that the true character of Christ's church could only be known through a reformation of its texts and interpretive traditions; in the highly pressurised environment of controversial debate, therefore, habits of reading were also markers of spiritual and doctrinal identity.

If Donne ever had occasion to use a book wheel, the most likely setting for such activity was the period of his association with the king's chief polemicist, Thomas Morton (Dean of Gloucester, 1607), in the first decade of the seventeenth century. During this time, Donne undertook sustained research into legal, theological, and political issues raised by the Oath of Allegiance controversy, which centred on the question of whether Catholic English subjects owed their chief loyalty to the monarch or to the pope. Donne's own contribution to the debate, *Pseudo-Martyr* (1610), draws on hundreds of sources, ranging from Roman law and the Bible to the most recent polemical exchanges between Morton and his principal adversary, the Jesuit Robert Parsons. Donne's "Advertisement to the Reader" com-ments both on his own scholarly approach to the work and on the response he expected from its recipients. He discards the criticism of those who have argued against his position "having only seene the Heads and Grounds handled in this Booke" (i.e. the brief chapter summaries that often accom-panied the Table of Contents in early modern treatises); announces that no user of his text could "well and properly be called a Reader, till he were come to the end of the Booke"; and gives reassurance about his own credentials: he has read thoroughly to avoid misrepresentation, and has "no where made any Author, speake more or lesse, in sense, then hee intended, to that purpose, for which I cite him."[1] The ramifying qualifica-tions of this last quotation remind us that the rhetoric of Donne's

"Advertisement" is part of a polemical strategy, designed to deflect attacks
and shore up the Protestant case; a straightforward assertion that Donne
had "no where made any Author, speake more or lesse ... then hee
intended" may have initially inspired confidence, but could also be refuted
far more easily further down the line.

Nevertheless, the key aspects of Donne's reflections on the reading
process in *Pseudo-Martyr* – the distinction between genuine readers and
self-serving consumers of texts, and the insistence on the dangers of
piecemeal, selective reading – are restated consistently in his prose writings
and in his preaching. The sermons most frequently address these issues as
part of an interconnected argument about textual and spiritual integrity, in
which direct exposure to the writings of the early church was thought to
furnish proof for the doctrinal and spiritual authenticity of Reformed
religion. The leading Protestant controversialist Daniel Tossanus maintained that Catholicism would not survive when confronted with the
collective and authentic evidence of ancient Christianity: "they dare not
stand to the decision of the sacred Scriptures, nor of the Fathers themselves, except they bee mutilated, and altered according to their will, and
deformed with many supposititious books."[2] Thomas James, the first
librarian of the Bodleian Library in Oxford, reported that there was
a secret vault in the Vatican set up for the mass production of patristic
forgeries to perpetuate Catholic irreligion, and Donne similarly claimed
that once the authentic texts were established, the early church would
speak firmly on the Protestant side:

> at the beginning, ... because most of those men who laboured in that
> Reformation ... had never read the body of the Fathers at large; but only
> such ragges and fragments of those Fathers, as were patcht together in their
> [the Catholics'] Decretat's, and Decretals, and other such Common placers,
> for their purpose, and to serve their turne, therefore they were loath at
> first ... to try controversies by the Fathers. But as soon as our men that
> imbraced the Reformation, had had time to read the Fathers, they were
> ready enough to joyne with the Adversarie in that issue.[3]

The image of Catholicism as a patchwork religion, stitched together from
textual fragments that have lost their true meaning and spirit, meets
a powerful counter model in the humanist return to the sources of
Christianity. Concepts of textuality and reading are once again imbued
with moral and ideological significance: the "Common placers" – thematic
or doctrinal compilations of excerpts from the Fathers and church coun-
cils – are always already instrumentalised ("to serve their turn"); only the

complete and genuine text can reveal theological meaning in the fullest sense, and thus connect its readers with the truths of Christianity in their original form.

This fiction of textual, readerly, and religious integrity dominates Donne's scholarly practice in his sermons. In his Lincoln's Inn preaching, for instance, he cites freely and overtly from the Fathers, but suppresses any debt to mediating authors such as Aquinas, even when his recourse to Thomistic sources is sustained and profound. The nature and use of his patristic references suggests that, with the exception of Augustine and Tertullian, Donne had little direct exposure to the source texts, yet even the most recondite allusion to St Gregory of Damascus is presented as an original discovery. Some of these manoeuvres can doubtless be attributed to Donne's desire to display his learning and knowledge, but it is clear that Donne's vision of the Protestant church is contingent, at least to some extent, on the textual and hermeneutic image projected by its clergy. A medieval pedant like Aquinas, hide-bound by authority and locked in the procedural labyrinth of scholastic disputation, was hardly a suitably companion for a church trying to bypass the Middle Ages and find its way back to an earlier tradition of Christianity. By contrast, a preacher visibly engaged in the arts of textual archaeology, reading judiciously and with a solicitous eye on the spirit of the text, served as a far more fitting guide to the sources of the Protestant faith. At Lincoln's Inn, where students attempted to master the complex arts of legal reasoning through a haphazard combination of oral instruction and unsupervised study, Donne's advice on the importance of readerly judgement was especially apposite. In "Satire II" he explicitly targets the lawyers' love for taking intellectual short-cuts, in the form of "Common placers," abridgements, and cribs:

> But he is worst who (beggarly) doth chaw
> Others' wits' fruits, and in his ravenous maw
> Rankly digested, doth those things out-spew
> As his own things; and they'are his own, 'tis true,
> For if one eat my meat, though it be known
> The meat was mine, th'excrement is his own.   (25–30)

The term "beggarly" arrests our attention through its parenthetical place-ment and offers a withering indictment of the legal digest and its con-sumers. It defines the latter as intellectually "poverty-stricken," while casting the process of absorbing pre-filtered knowledge as both "sordid" and "destitute of meaning or intrinsic value";[4] such material cannot be

properly assimilated and yields waste rather than new matter (or food) for
thought. At the risk of inspecting Donne's gastro-intestinal analogy too
closely, the etymology of the word "excrement" – from the Latin *excremen-
tum*, "that which is sifted out" – invites us to think across to another text that
meditates extensively on the moral and practical ramifications of the reading
process. *Biathanatos*, Donne's hugely intricate, mock-scholastic examination
of whether suicide should always be considered a mortal sin, opens (perhaps
unsurprisingly) with an appeal to the good judgement of its audience. This is
delivered through a taxonomy of readerly types, in which issues of sifting and
retention are once again paramount. Donne's classification includes
"Spunges which attract all without distinguishing; Howre-glasses which
receive and power out as faste; Bagges, which retaine onely the dregges of
the Spices, and let the Wine escape; And Sives which retaine the best onely".[5]
It is those "of the last sort" that are best suited to the intellectual and ethical
contortions of Donne's argument. But what might it mean to read like
a sieve? Yet again, the near-absurd literalism of Donne's analogy conceals
a crucial philosophical point. A sieve strains, divides, or separates different
kinds of matter, and this is precisely the methodological conceit around
which *Biathanatos'* entire hypothesis revolves. Donne argues that it is
impossible to adjudicate the moral status of suicide by using a general
precept or prohibition; such questions need to be decided on a case-by-
case basis, and this in turn requires sifting out the different elements of an
act: if suicide is a gesture of self-sacrifice for the greater good, for instance –
and Donne provocatively allows for the possibility that Christ's death may
have been an example of this – the moral complexion of the act changes
dramatically. Donne, as the preface to his satirical poem *Metempsychosis*
asserts, "will have no such readers as I can teach" (20–21); the idea of teaching
refers to instruction through doctrine or general rule, and if there is one
general rule we can reliably extract from Donne's writing, it is that circumstances will always alter the case.

   The act of critical sifting or straining may involve an element of con-
structive readerly opposition or resistance, as is illustrated by Donne's
comments on his *Paradoxes and Problems* (1633). This is a series of short
treatises or essays attempting to persuade their readers of hypotheses that
seem specious or at least highly idiosyncratic, couched in the abstract and
general terms we have been taught to distrust – "Why haue Bastards best
Fortunes?" or "Why is there more Variety of Greene, than of any other
Colour?" In a famous passage from a letter to the diplomat Sir Henry
Wotton from 1600, Donne describes these texts as exercises in productive
sophistry:

They were made rather to deceive time and her daughter truth, although they have been written in an age when anything is strong enough to overthrow her. If they make you find better reasons against them they do their office, for they are but swaggerers: quiet enough if you resist them. . . . They are rather alarums to truth to arm her than enemies.[6]

The notion of having to "find better reasons" against a text has obvious applications in a well-established genre like the formal paradox, which early modern readers would have approached with a firm and secure set of expectations. *Biathanatos*, an infinitely more complex work, makes proportionately greater demands on its audience, and Donne's post-ordination correspondence reveals a profound anxiety about its reception. Even in the library of a friend such as Sir Edward Herbert, to which a copy of the manuscript treatise was eventually committed, Donne dreads the censorious gaze of fellow authors: "If any of them grudge this book a room, and suspect it of new or dangerous doctrine, you who know us all, can best moderate".[7]

The fear that Donne's writing might simply pose too much of a challenge for the reader found its most pithy formulation in Ben Jonson's remark to Drummond of Hawthornden that "Donne for not being understood would perish."[8] Jonson's concern was with the author's afterlife in print, a question to which he had himself devoted an inordinate amount of time, labour, and energy. Jonson published no fewer than thirty-one books during his lifetime, including nineteen plays carefully revised to manage the transition from performance to reading, as well as the massive Folio edition of *The Workes of Beniamin Jonson* (1616), modelled on the collected works of classical writers and shepherded through the production process by the author. Donne, of course, largely eschewed print during his lifetime, and in the 1635 edition of his *Poems*, the "Printer" appealed not to mere readers but to "Vnderstanders," pleading the extraordinary nature of the collection as an excuse for this form of address: "this time I must speake onely to you: at another, *Readers* may perchance save my turne[.] . . . I should say it were the best in this kinde, that ever this Kingdome hath yet seen; he that would doubt of it, must goe out of the Kingdome to informe himselfe, for the best judgements, within it, take it for granted."[9]

Scholars have argued that manuscript circulation preserves the fiction of a "residual orality,"[10] and thus allows us to imagine a closer connection between author and reader. In a manuscript letter to Susan de Vere, the Countess of Montgomery, accompanying the copy of a sermon he had preached before her in February 1619, Donne seems to appeal to a cognate idea, observing "what dead carkasses things written are, in respect of things spoken";[11] however, he also proposes an elegant remedy for this dilemma. In the case of a sermon, the depletion of meaning that occurs during the writing process can be compensated for by a higher authorial power: "The Spirit of God that ... is present in his [the preacher's] tongue or hand, meets himself again ... in the eies and eares and hearts of the hearers and readers: and that Spirit, which is ever the same to an equall devotion, makes a writing and a speaking equall means to edification."[12] On a less exalted plane, Donne is equally keen to establish an equivalence of devotion between the spoken and written version of his sermon: "that that your Ladiship heard in a hoarse voyce then, you read in a course hand now: but in thankfulnesse I shall lift up my hands ..., and a voyce as clear as his spirit shall be pleased to tune in my prayers for your Ladiship in all places of the world."[13] In this instance, the text functions as a form of mnemonic, which extracts the sermon from its particular occasion of delivery and converts it into a universal signifier of loyalty, as the prayer Donne would have delivered at the beginning of his discourse is extended, metaphorically, into "all places of the world."[14] Donne's intentions remain legible in his handwriting, which cannot fully communicate the physical impact of prayerful gesture and voice, but invites the recipient to complete the transaction through a commensurate investment of good will.

Donne's epistle to the Countess frames its argument about the material dimension of communication in the recognisable language of patronage and social obligation. But the idea that processes of reading and interpretation can articulate the anxieties attendant upon more intimate relationships is also deeply relevant to his poetry. In "The Good Morrow", for instance, Donne unfolds a fantasy of perfectly mutual love, which comes to rest on the idea that inward motions – and consequently moral intent – are readily available through external signs, and do not require further processes of inference and interpretation. If the internal life is displayed on the body's surface, "devotion" can remain forever "equall":

> My face in thine eye, thine in mine appears,
> And true plain hearts do in the faces rest;
> Where can we find two better hemispheres
> Without sharp North, without declining West?
> Whatever dies was not mixed equally;
> If our two loves be one, or thou and I
> Love so alike, that none do slacken, none can die.   (15–21)

In Donne's letter to his patron, the Holy Spirit working in the preacher "meets himself again (as we meet our selves in a glass) in the eies and eares and hearts of the hearers and readers"; in "The Good Morrow", the interior life is figured in similarly unproblematic terms, as Donne reworks a conventional trope – that the eyes are mirrors of the soul – into a multi-layered vision of fidelity. The intrusion of the conditional mood in the penultimate line disrupts the speaker's declarative confidence, however, and introduces an element of suspicion that is made more overt in other poems. The pathologically jealous lover of "Twickenham Garden," for instance, presents a counter-argument to the hopeful epistemology of "The Good Morrow." After a series of experiments designed to test his mistress' constancy, he finds the results far from encouraging:

> Hither with crystal vials, lovers come,
>   And take my tears, which are love's wine,
>   And try your mistress' tears at home,
> For all are false that taste not just like mine;
>   Alas, hearts do not in eyes shine,
> Nor can you more judge woman's thoughts by tears,
>   Than by her shadow what she wears. (19–25)

It is crucial to note that these final lines are not simply a denunciation of female treachery; the speaker's condemnation of love is inflected by his own emotional disposition, and he enters the titular garden in full awareness of his self-destructive impulses: "And that this place may thoroughly be thought / True paradise, I have the serpent brought" (8–9). Interiority is rendered threateningly opaque, and appears in the poem as a wholly private process of reflection, equally resistant to disclosure and intervention. These forms of psychological occlusion, as the breakdown of Donne's visual metaphor suggests, may conceal the critical fracture points of a relationship; once such "treason" manifests as "an overt act" ("A Valediction of My Name in the Window", 55–56), it is usually too late to intervene.

Yet although it emphatically discounts the visual evidence of lovers' "eyes," "Twickenham Garden" clings to the idea that transparent objects can acquire probative value and thus facilitate psychological legibility. The crystal vial – believed in folklore to be imbued with magical properties to detect infidelity – is invoked to test the sincerity of the female lover's tears (another translucent body). The mode of experiment chosen in this instance, through ingestion rather than inspection, suggests the escalation of an epistemological crisis, as well as a state of emotional degeneration. In "A Valediction of My Name in the Window," the fear of the illegible female heart is addressed through the fantasy of complete authorial control, and of a text that influences its female reader in a bizarrely literal sense

by directing responses at every turn. Like "The Good Morrow,"
"Valediction" begins with a conventional enough image – a departing
lover engraving his name with a diamond in his mistresses' window as
a reminder of his devotion:

> 'Tis much that glass should be
> As all-confessing, and through-shine as I;
>   'Tis more, that it shows thee to thee,
>   And clear reflects thee to thine eye.
> But all such rules love's magic can undo,
> Here you see me, and I am you.　　　　　(7–12)

Donne's poetic scenario positions the female lover as a reader, not simply
because the engraved name in the window is a text of sorts, but because she will,
in due course, be the recipient of a love letter from a rival, delivered (punningly)
by a "page" who has seduced her maid and persuaded her to leave a message on
her mistress's pillow (49–51). The implication is that by immersing herself in an
alternative text, his lover's affection might change, and that the absent partner
will be powerless to halt this process of emotional detachment. Loss of physical
contact, in other words, eventually leads to infidelity because it entails a loss of
control and supervision. In this sense, Donne's conceit also applies to the
process of reading his poem: the acts of interpretation and writing depicted in
the text not only speak to the emotional dangers of separation, but also
illustrate the predicament of the author, who absents himself from his work
once it is complete and is therefore forced to confront his own kind of
separation anxiety, as agency shifts to the (only intermittently present) reader.

    The vision of love developed in the opening stanzas of the "Valediction"
resembles the base conceit of "The Good Morrow" in some ways: there is the
idea of reflecting devotion, but now Donne's speaker emphasises his own
clarity of commitment while reminding his mistress that the windowpane will
act, for better or worse, as a mirror and revelation of her own character. In the
final stanzas of the poem, however, the speaker's prophecy forecasts a more
invasive form of surveillance. Under the influence of astrological forces, he
argues – continuing the poem's preoccupation with "love's magic" – the
engraved name on the window pane will come to life and take pre-emptive
action on its errant reader:

> So, since this name was cut
> When love and grief their exaltation had,
>   No door 'gainst this name's influence shut . . .
>
>   And when thy melted maid,
> Corrupted by thy lover's gold and page,

His letter at thy pillow'hath laid,
   Disputed it, and tamed thy rage,
And thou begin'st to thaw towards him, for this,
   May my name step in, and hide his.

   And if this treason go
To'an overt act, and that thou write again,
   In superscribing, this name flow
   Into thy fancy from the pane.
So, in forgetting thou rememb'rest right,
   And unaware to me shalt write.   (37–39, 49–60)

Donne's conceit transforms the initial proffer of transparency into a disturbing scene of transgressive incursion: under the invasive gaze of the lover's name, there is no question of keeping the "door . . . shut" on private thoughts. Authorial influence is re-imagined as a form of dark magic that can guard against deviant readings – those threatening to displace the speaker-author's spirit or "genius" (48) – both through constant supervision and through active manipulation: "May my name step in, and hide his". The act of tampering with the "superscription" or address is designed as a fail-safe should thought turn into action, and the language of treason and usurpation ("superscription" also signifies a piece of text inscribed above something else) illustrates the cost of protecting "an equall devotion". Donne's poem ends with a jokey retraction – "Impute this idle talk to that I go, / For dying men talk often so" (65–66) – but it's worth pausing to consider this radical response to threatened masculinity in its wider context. The *Songs and Sonnets*, and the valediction poems in particular, repeatedly stage a search for palpable evidence of affection and constancy, while dramatizing the speaker's inability to obtain such evidence: the pseudo-mathematical analogy of "A Valediction Forbidding Mourning" is at once the most touching and the most painful attempt to address this dilemma. The hyperbolically extended fantasy of knowledge depicted in "A Valediction of My Name in the Window" projects the desire for a female "text" that gives the reader total access to its soul, spirit, essence, and intent; at the same time, this intent can be directed, obscurities clarified, lacunae filled in – and the text's ending rewritten so that it remains desirable and chaste forever. Constancy and change thus become conditions of legibility in a poetics of love that figures relationships as a form of idealised soul-commerce, but also evokes, occasionally, the spectre of something more disturbing: the idea of female infidelity as a kind of thought crime, and the conceit of the writer's controlling gaze as a safeguard against male insecurity.

Notes

1. *Pseudo-Martyr*, ed. Anthony Raspa (Montreal: McGill-Queen's University Press, 1993), 8, 10.
2. Daniel Tossanus, *A Synopsis or Compendium of the Fathers* (London, 1635), sig. A3r.
3. *Sermons*, 6:56.
4. "beggarly, adj.," 1, 3, 2 *OED Online*.
5. Donne, *Biathanatos* (London, 1646), sig. C3v.
6. Qtd. in *John Donne: A Critical Edition of the Major Works*, ed. John Carey (Oxford University Press, 1992), 64.
7. *Letters*, 18.
8. *The Works of William Drummond of Hawthornden* (Edinburgh, 1711), 225.
9. Donne, *Poems* (London, 1635), sig. A2r–A2v.
10. Richard Wollman, "The 'Press and Fire': Print and Manuscript Culture in Donne's Circle," *SEL* 33 (1993), 89.
11. *Sermons*, 2:179.
12. *Sermons*, 2:179.
13. *Sermons*, 2:179.
14. *Sermons*, 2:179.

CHAPTER 12

Education

Andrew Wallace

The little that is known about the earliest and most formal stages of John Donne's education can be stated quite bluntly. Born in 1572, as a boy he was privately educated by teachers whose names will not be recovered with anything approaching certainty. He matriculated at Hart Hall, Oxford, in Michaelmas term 1584. He left Oxford, we do not know when, without taking a degree. In May 1592 he was admitted to Lincoln's Inn, one of the law schools that made up the network of London's Inns of Court. His admission documents constitute our evidence that the entry to Lincoln's had been preceded by a period of study, presumably a year, at Thavie's Inn, an Inn of Chancery designed to prepare students for the transition to the Inns of Court. Donne drifts from the records of Lincoln's Inn in 1594. He never formally practiced the law.

* * * *

This educational *cursus* is silently organized by what might be called "the fact of Rome." Indeed, Donne's Catholicism would have been the decisive factor in determining the trajectory of his private education. Among other considerably greater threats to a young boy and his recusant family, private education would have kept Donne beyond the reach of the casual but energetic anti-Catholicism that could permeate standard curriculum texts in the grammar schools of the late sixteenth century. In the *Colloquiorum Scholasticorum Libri Quatuor* of Maturin Cordier, for example, a hugely popular collection of dialogues designed to enable schoolboys to speak and write in Latin on any respectable subject, a boy named Stephanio describes his recent travels to Rome. Hungry to ask whether Stephanio managed to catch a glimpse of the pope, his friend Phrygio lends vivid form to the question: "Did you see that great beast?" Rome, we are told, was once called the head of the world but is now the source and origin of all abominations.[1] The distinction focuses on the gap that has opened up between ancient Rome, source of the Latin texts that were central to grammar school education, and modern Rome, seat of the papacy. Private education in a family such as Donne's would have seen him immersed all at once in versions of Rome that post-Reformation education insisted on severing.

Donne's family had close and deep ties to the Jesuits. His maternal uncles, Ellis and Jasper Heywood, were received into the Society of Jesus in 1566 and 1562 respectively. Jasper Heywood returned to England from exile in 1581 and remained there (with time spent incarcerated in the Tower of London) until his deportation in January 1585. Whether or not Donne was educated by Roman Catholic missionary priests, as Dennis Flynn has argued, it is reasonable to suppose that the elite private education his uncles had received at the court of Henry VIII, and Jasper Heywood's own long immersion in the world of Jesuit schooling, would have informed family attitudes and provisions for their nephew's early education.[2] In any case, Jesuit pedagogical rhetoric echoes much of the practice of advanced humanist pedagogical theorists in placing ancient Latin (and to a much more limited extent Greek) texts at the heart of the reading programs of schoolboys. Because of this, the matter of Rome was one of the great fault lines running through elementary education during the period. Henry VIII's 1542 proclamation that the two parts of "Lily's Grammar" would be the sole authorized Latin grammar in England had worked to bring earlier versions of that text's composite image of Rome (its ancient Latin authors, its Roman church) under the power of the royal supremacy's efforts to secure educational and religious conformity. For since the time of the earliest layers of the work that would come to circulate under William Lily's name – initiated many years before the Reformation by John Colet in his Latin accidence the *Aeditio*, and by Lily himself in his syntax the *Rudimenta Grammatices* – the goal of grammar school education had been to offer instruction in Christian principles as well as in the skills necessary to digest ancient Roman authors.

Private education helped ensure that Donne's schooldays could unroll, by design, away from prying eyes. Even so, private education could pose a danger for the boy and his family. His case thus differs from, for example, those of Sir Philip Sidney (Shrewsbury School), John Lyly (King's School Canterbury), and Edmund Spenser (Merchant Taylors' School), for whom surviving information concerning curricula and methods of instruction enables us to reconstruct with considerable confidence the methods by which they were instructed as boys. Without such institutional evidence on which to draw, what we can see most clearly are latent traces of readings likely first encountered by Donne before 1584 and then nurtured over many years: the evident hunger for the license of Ovid's voice, for the subtle poses of Horace, and for the writing of epigrams (a feature of his work that Flynn persuasively connects to Jesuit pedagogical practices).[3] Later, during and after Donne's time at Lincoln's Inn, legal terms weave their way in and out of his poems and prose, helping us to see that the business of education was in some sense the business of mastering new vocabularies and pressing them into unexpected contexts. Beyond such residues of training, Izaak Walton's "Life of Dr. John Donne" advances several claims about Donne's educational attainments. Walton asserts, for example, that Donne had obtained "a good command both of the French and Latine Tongue" in his youth.[4] He would certainly have had the latter, and the former is a safe inference from Donne's obvious interest in French lyric poetry.

Almost nothing new in the way of firm and direct knowledge of the course of Donne's education becomes accessible with his move to Oxford, where his early matriculation was a response to several pressing considerations. Under ordinary circumstances matriculation at an Oxford Hall or College at the age of twelve would have ensured that a young Catholic scholar could pursue a course of study without having to subscribe to the Thirty-Nine Articles and the Oath of Supremacy. This subscription was required of all Oxford scholars at the age of sixteen, but Dennis Flynn reports that in the early 1580s twelve-year-old Oxford scholars were newly at risk of being called upon to subscribe to the terms of the Elizabethan settlement.[5] Accordingly, the family played fast and loose with the ages of Donne and his younger brother Henry when they joined Hart Hall, which was commonly regarded as a point of relative safety for boys from recusant families during the second half of the sixteenth century. Donne was already twelve at the time but was listed as eleven; Henry was eleven but listed as ten. Once again, it is not known when the boys left Oxford, but their Catholicism would leave them vulnerable, even at the scene of instruction, for years to come, as the fate of Henry Donne makes clear. In 1593 he was caught sheltering a Catholic priest in his rooms at Thavie's Inn. He died under horrific conditions at Newgate prison a month later.

* * * *

To step farther beyond the reach of facts that can be documented is to become almost wholly dependent upon Walton's biography, wherein Donne's life is depicted as a sequence of scenes in which education becomes a condition of existence for the young man. Walton asserts that Donne's time at Oxford was curtailed, "About the fourteenth year of his age," by a period of study at Cambridge whose duration Walton does not

set.[6] Cambridge records are silent on this point. There was no matriculation statute there, and Donne and his brother need not have matriculated
or joined a college at all in order to study at Cambridge. These lacunae –
indeed, the basic, inescapable fact that the desire to know precisely how
Donne was educated continues to be frustrated – tantalize because Donne,
the great poet and preacher of immoderate desire, would in his later years
speak of himself as "*imbracing*" in his youth "*the worst voluptuousness*, an
hydroptique immoderate desire of humane learning and languages."[7]
These remarks cast the hunger for learning as an appetite that sickens
and weakens; that threatens the health even as it demands to be satisfied;
that enthralls the student instead of liberating him. Donne offers this
account of himself in a letter recalling his turn away from the study of
the law. In its original context (printed in Walton's biography) the statement is part of Donne's effort to depict his immoderate desire for learning
as part of an extended process by which he unmade himself: "*and there
I stumbled, and fell too: and now I am become so little, or such a nothing, that
I am not a subject good enough for one of my own letters.*"[8]

It is clear that these remarks need to be situated within the broader
context of the career disappointments that followed his marriage. Even so,
they speak powerfully to Donne's tendency to depict himself as having
pursued his appetite for learning to extremes that set him at odds with
himself and the society into which he was born. This helps explain why
regimens of private and self-guided study are so prominent in Walton's
biography: Walton asserts that "a private Tutor had the care of him, until
the tenth year of his age"; he writes that at Oxford Donne had "Tutors of
several Sciences to attend and instruct him"; at Cambridge "he was a most
laborious Student, often changing his studies." While at Lincoln's Inn, says
Walton,

> His Mother and those to whose care he was committed, were watchful to
> improve his knowledge, and to that end appointed him Tutors both in the
> *Mathematicks*, and in all the other *Liberal Sciences*, to attend him. But with
> these Arts they were advised to instil into him particular Principles of the
> *Romish Church*; of which those Tutors profest (though secretly) themselves
> to be members.[9]

Walton goes on to assert that "About the nineteenth year of his age" Donne
was motivated to "lay aside all study of the Law: and, of all the other
Sciences that might give him a denomination; and begun seriously to
survey, and consider the Body of Divinity, as it was then controverted
betwixt the *Reformed* and the *Roman Church*."[10] Walton claims this new

program of study was carried out via a close engagement with the works of Cardinal Bellarmine; these were soon "marked with many weighty observations under his own hand" as though designed to constitute conclusive evidence of the depths of his engagements. Donne's "Learning, Languages, and other Abilities," says Walton, led to his employment by Thomas Egerton.[11] The disappointments that follow these years and Donne's hunger for a career are followed by further self-study, now in "the *Civil* and *Canon Laws*," a prelude to "a constant study of some points of Controversie betwixt the *English* and *Roman Church*; and especially those of *Supremacy* and *Allegiance*."[12] Walton says that Donne's decision to enter sacred orders was formalized by means of application "to an incessant study of Textual Divinity, and to the attainment of a greater perfection in the learned Languages, *Greek* and *Hebrew*."[13] Such scenes of self-initiated and autonomous study explain Walton's clear desire to represent Donne's life as a continuous series of educations and reformations, both when the young Donne was under the thumb of family-appointed tutors and also when, as an adult, he was working to make himself fit first to speak publicly on matters of faith and obedience in *Pseudo-Martyr* and, later, from the pulpit.

As always, the matter of Rome sits at the center of this educational trajectory, governing both the particular rhythms of his own educational career and also his negotiations with the discourses and even the possibility of education. Powerful testimony to this dynamic comes in the "Advertisement to the Reader" that opens *Pseudo-Martyr* (1610), where Donne gathers his entire family and its history into a scene of instruction and suffering. The sequence of reflections on view here begins by acknowledging with some irritation what Donne regards as overly hasty expressions of disappointment among Catholics. It then moves, as though inexorably, to an effort to describe for the benefit of readers the conditions under which Donne and his family were educated:

> And for my selfe, (because I have already received some light, that some of the Romane profession, having onely seene the Heads and Grounds handled in this Booke, have traduced me, as an impious and profane under-valewer of Martyrdome,) I most humbly beseech him, (till the reading of the Booke, may guide his Reason) to beleeve, that I have a just and Christianly estimation, and reverence, of that devout and acceptable Sacrifice of our lifes, for the glory of our blessed Saviour. For, as my fortune hath never been so flattering nor abundant, as should make this present life sweet and precious to me, as I am a Moral man: so, as I am a Christian, I have beene ever kept awake in a meditation of Martyrdome, by being derived from such

> a stocke and race, as, I beleeve, no family, (which is not of farre larger extent, and greater brances,) hath endured and suffered more in their persons and fortunes, for obeying the Teachers of Romane Doctrine, then it hath done. I did not therefore enter into this, as a carnall or over-indulgent favourer of this life, but of such reasons, as may arise to his knowledge, who shall be pleased to read the whole worke.[14]

Donne is at pains here to emphasize, first, that he was no recalcitrant student of the men who taught him, no "under-valuer" of an idealized vision of martyrdom that must have been held before his eyes for emulation during the course of his early education. After all, the spectacle of martyrdom was, for this descendent of Sir Thomas More, the spectacle of his own family's history. "Teachers of Romane Doctrine" are likely to have made up the entirety of his early educational experience, and it is necessary to recognize that Donne is in effect shoring up his reputation as a student in the first half of this passage, emphasizing that he was no instinctive scorner of lessons set before his eyes as a boy. Even word of Catholic disappointments with his work come wrapped in a conventional educational trope as he asserts that he has "received some light" concerning the reactions of the unborn book's critics. It is well to note in this context that the language of teaching recurs almost ceaselessly in *Pseudo-Martyr*, with matters of doctrine (appropriately enough given that word's etymology) treated as matters of teaching. Such passages see Donne depicting his entire life as a series of scenes of teaching that pitted him against himself as frequently as they pitted him against the world of Elizabethan and Stuart England.

This notion that an educational *cursus* pursued to a powerful extent under the name of Rome could be a mark of self-division is still being extended and explored later in Donne's career at a key moment in *A Sermon Preched at the Spittle upon Easter Monday, 1622*. There, Donne speaks of the duty of preaching and insists that many members of his audience will be deeply and inescapably at odds with themselves:

> preaching is in season to them who are willing to hear; but though they be not, though they had rather the Laws would permit them to be absent, or that preaching were given over; yet I must preach. And in that sense, I may use the words of the Apostle, *As much as in me is, I am ready to preach the Gospel to them also that are at Rome*: at *Rome* in their hearts; at *Rome*, that is, of *Rome*, reconciled to *Rome*.[15]

That phrase "at *Rome* in their hearts" means something more here than a simple assertion that his targets are crypto-Catholics in the pews, since the rest of the passage goes on to generalize the lesson by emphasizing that preaching "can make a Moral Man, a Christian; and a Superstitious Christian, a sincere Christian; a Papist, a Protestant; and a dissolute Protestant, a holy man."[16] Donne's Rome is a condition in which one finds oneself, and there is a sense in which his conviction that his audience will include many who are "at *Rome* in their hearts" must mean that he finds their hearts organized by the world, by its preoccupations and teachings, rather than by the word of God. The point is further developed later in the sermon, where Donne proposes that when Christians are gathered to God

> Then and there, we shall have an abundant satisfaction and accomplish-ment, of all St. *Augustines* three Wishes: He wish'd to have seen *Rome* in her glory, to have heard St. *Paul* preach, and to have seen Christ in the flesh. We shall have all: we shall see such a *Jerusalem*, as that *Rome*, if that were literally true, which is hyperbolically said of *Rome, in Urbe, in Orbe*, that City is the whole world, yet *Rome*, that *Rome*, were but a Village to this *Jerusalem*.[17]

Rome, the name, provides a lesson in the powers of synecdoche and a means of measuring (as Augustine himself does in *De Civitate Dei*) the extent to which our passions are organized in terms set by that name.

* * * *

I propose that these problems and texts explain why the language of teaching so frequently attaches itself to scenes of self-division in Donne's prose and poetry. Consider as a single conclusive example the famous penultimate line of Donne's "To His Mistress Going to Bed" – "To teach thee I am naked first" (47) – where it is hardly possible to determine whether recourse to pedagogical diction is to be regarded as having empowered or disabled the speaker. Away from the eyes of an educational culture bent on simultaneously fostering and ferreting-out different forms of devotion to Rome, Donne was educated out of the possibility of comfortably regarding his training-up as a process of coming into his own.

Notes

1. Translated from Maturin Cordier, *Colloquiorum Scholasticorum Libri Quatuor* (London, 1608), sig. I3r, contractions expanded. Cordier's colloquies were first printed decades earlier at Geneva and Lyon in 1564, thereafter circulating widely in Northern European and English grammar schools.

2. Dennis Flynn, "Donne's Education," in *OHJD*, 408–423.
3. On Ovid and license see especially Heather James, "Ovid and the Question of Politics in Early Modern England," *ELH* 70 (2003), 347–73. On epigrams see Flynn, "Donne's Education," 419.
4. Walton, *Lives*, 23.
5. Flynn, "Donne's Education," 411.
6. Walton, *Lives*, 24.
7. Walton, *Lives*, 37 (original emphasis for all extracts from *Lives*).
8. Walton, *Lives*, 37.
9. Walton, *Lives*, 23–24.
10. Walton, *Lives*, 25.
11. Walton, *Lives*, 26–27.
12. Walton, *Lives*, 35, 38.
13. Walton, Lives, 46.
14. *Pseudo-Martyr*, 8.
15. *Sermons*, 4:109–10. I owe particular thanks to Jeanne Shami for this reference.
16. *Sermons*, 4:110.
17. *Sermons*, 4:129.

CHAPTER 13

Law

Gregory Kneidel

Reflecting on the growing controversies about the structure and practices of the official Elizabethan church, Richard Hooker wrote in 1593 that if his puritan opponents "had been willing to learn how many Laws their actions in this life are subject unto, and what the true force of each Law is, all these controversies might have died the very day they were first brought forth." To illustrate, Hooker considers the act of eating: like other animals, humans learn from the law of nature what we can eat; the law of reason tells us how much to eat (not too much!); divine law tells us when we must fast or prepare special meals; and, lastly, every "civil society" has any number of laws, from written regulations to informal customs, that dictate what, how, when, and where its residents eat.[1] Hooker's simple example hardly approaches the anthropological sophistication of Levi-Strauss's *The Raw and the Cooked* (1964). But his basic point is that to measure "all the Actions of Men" by "any one kind of Law" – he means, in this context, the laws for church government that the puritans found exclusively in Holy Scripture – is "to confound the admirable Order, wherein God hath disposed all Laws."[2]

Even if we focus narrowly on the laws that make up "civil society," Hooker's point is worth remembering. There were in early modern England many kinds of law claiming concurrent jurisdiction over the actions of its citizens. The three broad kinds of law considered here – English common law, Roman-derived civil and canon law, and equity – coexisted and regularly cooperated with each other. But they were also jealous of each other and competed for power, prestige, and profit. So, for example, in 1607, the civilian lawyer Thomas Ridley complained about a particular legal fiction whereby foreign cities such as Amsterdam or Antwerp were "pled" to be actually located in "the Parish of St. Mary le Bow in the Ward of Cheapside" (i.e., in the financial center of London). This blatant ploy brought contracts between English and foreign merchants, which were typically enforced under civilian procedures in the courts of admiralty, within the purview of the English common law courts: "if this were graunted," Ridley predicted, "then matter enough would be offered to one Jurisdiction to devour up the other, and the Law" which "hath set either of them their bounds and limits ... would bee easily eluded."[3] While Hooker believed that God Himself ordered "all lawes," Ridley feared for the viability of a sort of "Law" of laws, one that prevents each law from devouring the others. Ridley's fears proved to be well founded. Over the next centuries, the common law slowly devoured its rivals (the High Court of Admiralty lasted until 1875) and absorbed their competencies into its own, though newly emergent jurisdictions (e.g., international congresses, military tribunals) continue to remind us that the common law's triumph is not yet final.

Donne lived at the *beginning* of the common law's rise. The "Oracle" of the common law, Edward Coke, for example, was a generation older than Donne but died a year after him; the first volume of Coke's *Reports*, the oldest collection of case law still regularly cited, was published in 1600 when Donne was 29 and employed by Coke's professional rival, Thomas Egerton. Legal historians have attributed the common law's success in part to its ability to centralize its operation in and around the three royal courts in Westminster Hall: the King's Bench for criminal cases, Common Pleas for civil cases, and Exchequer for cases involving government revenue. Already in 1582, the civilian lawyer Thomas Smith, in his perceptive survey of England's legal institutions, wondered "how all Englande (being so long and so large, and hauing so many shyres and provinces therein) can be answered of justice in one place."[4] From that one place – and with the aid of itinerant courts (the Assizes and Quarter Sessions) that brought royal justice out to the people – these royal courts supervised and slowly supplanted the many minor courts that filled England's "shyres and provinces."

An elegy on Donne's death by a certain "R.B." captures something of the common law's centralizing impulse and shows how easily it could be combined with two of the common law's other key ambitions: to rationalize and formalize the law. Upset by puritanical criticism of Donne's preaching, R.B. imagines summoning a jury to settle the case:

> No, no, had Donne need to be judged or tried,
> A jury I would summon on his side,
> That had no sides, nor factions, past the touch
> Of all exceptions, freed from passion, such
> As nor to fear nor flatter, e'er were bred;
> These would I bring, though called from the dead:

Southampton, Hambleton, Pembroke, Dorset's earls,
Huntingdon, Bedford's Countesses (the pearls
Once of each sex). If these suffice not, I
Ten *decem tales* have of standers by,
All which, for Donne, would such a verdict give,
As can belong to none that now doth live.

("In Memory of Doctor Donne," 65–76)

In a different elegy, Thomas Carew praises Donne for committing "holy
rapes upon our will" and ruling the "*universal monarchy of wit*" ("Elegy,"
17, 96). But here he is brought to trial and put before a jury. Significantly,
this jury initially consists of noblemen and noblewomen from across
England – from Southampton to Hambleton – who knew and admired
Donne. But, if that jury "suffice not," R.B. suggests another jury composed
simply of ten "decem tales," i.e., replacements who, according to English
common law procedure, must be found by the sheriff to replace any juror
deemed to be "not indifferent" to one party.[5] Just as the central common
law courts had to arrogate to themselves the authority of many lesser
regional courts, here England's nobility, identified by their geographic
titles, yield the jury box to the anonymous but uniform "decem tales."
And while the nobles may never be "freed from passion," the ten "decem
tales" would have "no sides" and form no "factions," just as juries evolved
historically from self-informing (they were effective because, as local residents, they already knew something about the case) to fact-weighing (they
were effective because they were rational and impartial). R.B. also carefully
follows form, citing procedural rules (e.g., the summons, the appeal) and
using correct, if inelegant, terminology (e.g., the painfully reduplicative
"Ten *decem tales*"). One can't help but think that Donne himself would
have preferred the first jury of England's Peers to the second jury of his
supposed peers.

A core principle of the common law was that no matter who comprised
the jury and no matter who presided over the court, the justice they
delivered was the king's. How the king projected his presence throughout
the realm, and even claimed some kind of mystical identity with it, is the
great subject of political theology. But under common law, that principle
was rooted in the land, specifically in the feudal system of tenures that
divided the land-holding population into lords and tenants. The king
alone was always a lord and never a tenant. Everyone else was a tenant at
least to him and likely to any number of intermediary (mesne) lords.
Tenants held their land for varying lengths of time and received their
lord's (or lords') protection in exchange for varying kinds of feudal service,

from homage and knight service to mere rent payment. The treatise that codified this labyrinthine system, Thomas Littleton's *Tenures* (1481), was so venerated that, as one lawyer put it in 1600, "*Littleton* is not now the name of a Lawyer, but of the Law it selfe."[6] But, a Londoner by birth and inclination, Donne had little nostalgia for England's manorial customs. His medievalism was scholastic, not feudal. And he recognized early on that this feudal system of land holding had been thoroughly fiscalized. That is, the Crown fully expected feudal services to be paid off with fines, so homage and knight service and the rest were just quaint names for taxes, many of them crippling. Then as now, great legal energy was put into avoiding these obligations through trusts, conveyances, and other dodges; equal legal effort was put into enforcing them. As Donne well knew, this brand of fiscal feudalism was especially suited to fleecing the ancient nobility of their estates and enriching not just the Crown but also the increasingly prosperous ranks of common lawyers.

Even as the major courts of Westminster became the focal point of the common law's centralized jurisdiction, neighboring London and its surrounding Liberties offered some relief from it. London had various borough rights that exempted its residents from the common law's reach. More importantly, in metropolitan London Donne would have ample exposure to the major external threat to the common law's dominance: Roman-based civil and canon law, sibling traditions that together formed what is called (somewhat unhelpfully) the *jus commune*, the law that was common to all of Western Christendom. Civilian lawyers took their authority from a broadly European and more academic tradition that dated back to the eleventh-century rediscovery of the *Corpus Juris Civilis* (529–34), the famous compilation of Roman laws commissioned by the emperor Justinian. In an analogous way, canon lawyers were trained in a tradition that originated with Gratian's *Decretals* (c. 1140) that had accrued its own exhaustive set of glosses and commentaries, and that, unlike the more settled civil tradition, continued to add new legislation issued on papal authority; these texts constituted the *Corpus Juris Canonici*. In early modern England, the most profitable competency for civilian lawyers was, as we have seen, international maritime trade. For their part, canon lawyers had historically claimed jurisdiction over a wider range of lucrative issues: marriage and divorce, last wills and testaments, defamation, tithes and benefices (the transaction of land in marriage settlements and wills especially aroused the jealousy of common lawyers). Following Henry VIII's break with Rome, proposals were made to replace the *Corpus Juris Canonici* with a different body of church law. But, like similar proposals to modernize or replace the civilian *Corpus*, these never materialized. Instead, Roman canon law was shorn of its most objectionable papalist provisions and bound up together with civilian training so that, as had long been the practice, the most accomplished members of the *jus commune* were still doctors "of both laws." The judge who ruled on the validity of Donne's clandestine marriage, for example, was Richard Swale, L.L.D. (*Legum Doctor* or Doctor of Laws). In the absence of papal jurisdiction, new courts, still closely allied with the episcopacy, were created to administer England's state-supervised church law. As Dean of St. Paul's Cathedral, Donne sat on the most powerful of these, the Court of High Commission. The Court's unusual blending of secular and sacred authority was recognized at the time. Its judges, called commissioners, were "not properly tearmed Spirituall Judges" since the court was created by statute in Parliament (1 Eliz. I, c. 1) and its judges "proceede by virtue of the Kings Commission."[7] It was abolished just a decade after Donne's death.

Despite his long-standing personal and professional association with the common lawyers of Lincoln's Inn, Donne was more attracted to the *jus commune* tradition. Some of the more manifest differences between the two traditions help to explain why. Common lawyers issued formulaic writs and recorded decisions in law French, a readily-parodied mongrel Latin that was touted by its proponents as a specialized, professional argot "so apt and significant to express the true sense of the law" that it was impossible to change one without changing the other.[8] Civilians and canonists, by contrast, wrote in crisp, unadorned Latin. In most private and criminal matters, the common law claimed to enforce practices that had existed "time out of mind," customary law no less venerable for being unwritten. The *jus commune* was a professional *lex scripta*, a written law no less authoritative for being at times impracticable. English common law was aggressively nationalistic, even insular, and claimed solidarity with other vernacular systems of law in resisting the universalizing claims of the *jus commune*. The *jus commune*, for its part, proudly transcended national boundaries and sectarian divisions. Its leading figures during Donne's lifetime, for example, included the Spanish Jesuit Francisco Suárez (1548–1617), Alberico Gentili (1552–1608), an Italian Protestant exile who taught at Oxford, and the Dutch jurist Hugo Grotius (1583–1645). The most influential books in the common law tradition tended to be practical or procedural (e.g., manuals on correct forms of pleading, collections of statutes, pedagogical tracts, dictionaries). The more theoretical *jus commune* tradition produced learned scholarly treatises on specific transactions (e.g., marriages, contracts, wills), crimes (e.g., robbery, murder, libel), or jurisprudence (e.g., standards of proof), as well as on broader legal issues emerging from contemporary international politics (e.g., diplomacy, piracy and conquest, war and peace). Donne's two major controversial tracts, *Biathanatos* (written in 1608 but not published until 1646) and *Pseudo-Martyr* (1610), clearly fall within the *jus commune* tradition. *Biathanatos*, as its title page announces, "diligently survey[s]" the "Nature, and the extent of all those Lawes, which seeme to be violated" by self-homicide, a prospectus that betrays a methodological link between it and *jus commune* legal writing, and to the earlier penitential and casuistic traditions, which typically sought to untangle knotty legal and moral problems by using basic definitions, first principles, and increasingly fine-grained distinctions. Likewise, even though *Pseudo-Martyr* takes up a specific Jacobean controversy over the Oath of Allegiance, Donne seasons his arguments with references to dozens of jurists from across Europe who had parsed out before him the conflicting demands of temporal and spiritual authorities.

Though distinct in theory, these legal traditions could be difficult to untangle in practice. For example, in a 1622 sermon to the assembled members of the Virginia Company, Donne explains the legal claim that the English colonists had on New World territories: "In the Law of *Nature* and *Nations*, A Land never inhabited, by any, or utterly derelicted and immemorially abandoned by the former Inhabitants, becomes theirs that wil possesse it. So also is it, if the inhabitants doe not in some measure fill the Land, so as the Land bring foorth her increase for the use of men."[9] The kernel thought here concerning the right to occupy derelict property is derived from Roman law (cf. *Digest* Bk. 41). But it had been filtered through scholastic natural-rights theory ("Law of *Nature*"), brought into the arena of international law ("Law of . . . *Nations*"), and given a hint of scriptural imperative (the idea of "fill the Land" harkens back to Genesis's "Be fruitful and multiply"). What is more, the core principle from the civil tradition had long since been "received" or adopted into English common law, so that common law judges could cite versions of it in their decisions. Moreover, perhaps in order to imply a desired distinction between English colonialism and a more authoritarian Spanish imperialism, Donne identifies it as a maxim of "Municipall Law" that had "passed through" "all particular states" to "the whole world" – in other words, a local custom that had through use accrued the force of universal law. Like Hooker, Donne implies that these multiple laws all work in harmony to legitimate both the Virginia Company's commercial enterprise and its Christian mission. But modern critics at least have noted that they jar in ways that might seem to jeopardize the whole English colonial enterprise. For example, if the law of dereliction in the *jus commune* applied in the case of the native inhabitants of Virginia, does that not imply that they *were* a civil society and not, as the more virulent colonial ideology had it, merely animals in a state of nature foraging off the land?

But when Donne implores the members of the Virginia Company to "enamour" the Native Americans "with your *Justice*," he implies that such legal claims are not in and of themselves identical to the claims of justice. There is, in other words, a gap between what is legal and what is just. This gap was measured and notionally bridged by equity, a wide-ranging concept whose origins were traced back to ancient philosophy. Aristotle recognized that laws, as general statements, can never anticipate the immense variety of human life (*Nicomachean Ethics* V.x.4). Moreover, experience shows that there will be times when the law, when pursued to its extreme or followed to the letter, will produce unjust or immoral results. So equity supplied justice where the law was absent or deficient or manifestly unfair. Its duty, located chiefly in ancient times in the office of the Roman Praetor and in England in the office of the Lord Chancellor, was to moderate the law's extremity, temper its rigor, and sweeten its strictness with mercy (barely beneath the surface of these antitheses are the more prejudicial dichotomies between the Old and the New Testament, Judaism and Christianity). In practice, courts of equity were to resolve cases of fraud and breach of trust, protect those with little access to the law such as widows and orphans, and, conversely, hold accountable those with too much access to it, such as local magnates and even legal professionals.

But was equity "before, behind, between, above, [or] below"[10] the common law? Opinions varied and controversies flared, along much the same lines as they did in theological debates about grace and works, or political controversies between the Crown and the Parliament. It is important to remember that at the time equity had its own institutional presence: the Chancery, which was also physically located in Westminster Hall, heard private suits and the Star Chamber heard criminal causes, so that these two courts of equity effectively mirrored the common law courts of Common Pleas and King's Bench, respectively. Both the Chancery and Star Chamber were presided over by the Lord Chancellor, who had traditionally been a cleric but whose office was being secularized so that it could be obtained even by common lawyers trained at the Inns of Court, men such as Egerton and, decades before him, Donne's famous ancestor, Thomas More. Operating alongside the common law, the courts of equity claimed that, even though they ruled after the common law courts, they

did not overturn the common law courts' judgments since equity did not
rule on the actual legal issue (*in rem*) but rather on the persons involved (*in
personem*). Put differently, while the law ruled in the external forum of the
court, equity governed the internal forum of conscience and bound individuals to disregard a lawful but unconscionable judgment. And this was
more than just good spiritual advice since the Chancellor was said to keep
the king's or queen's conscience clear of blame as well.

To the champions of the common law, however, this meant that equity
was not parallel to but above the law, and that equity could prohibit their
proceedings, overturn their decisions, and supervise their courts. They
claimed that the flexibility offered by equity was already baked into the
common law itself. They were especially keen on recognizing the "equity of
a statute" (something like the spirit of law or the legislators' intention) that
allowed judges the flexibility to interpret statutes so as to avoid Aristotle's
problem of the general rule and to make sure similar cases brought similar
verdicts. As for remedying the abuse of law too rigidly executed, the
common law had its own formal means of appeal (e.g., the writ of error).
Moreover, proponents of the common law complained that the Chancery's
jurisdiction, with its less formal, more inquisitorial proceedings and its
scant record-keeping, was either foreign in origin (a major theme in the
seminal writings of More's anti-papal nemesis, Christopher St. Germain)
or arbitrary in execution (a charge leveled by parliamentarians in the years
leading up to the civil war) or both. Unsurprisingly, advocates for royal
authority also felt that the Chancery and Star Chamber were in effect above
the law, but for them, that was proper since the extraordinary power of
these courts flowed directly from the Crown itself. This was the position
outlined by James I in a famous 1616 speech to Parliament in which, in the
course of surveying the entire English legal system, he settled a long-
simmering feud between Egerton's Chancery and Coke's King Bench.
"Keepe ... your owne limits towards the King, towards other Courts,
and toward other Lawes," James warned Coke and the other common law
judges who had impugned the legitimacy of the equity courts. "I must say
with CHRIST," he continued, easily slipping into the role of divine
mediator amid many rival laws, "Away with the new polygamie, and
maintaine the ancient Law pure and undefiled, as it was before."[11]

What Ridley had characterized as the common law's voracious appetite,
James here casts as its promiscuous desire: unwilling to respect the supposedly sacred bond between other courts and their core competencies, the
common law claimed the brides of all other laws as its own. In describing
this as a "new polygamie," James may be cleverly mimicking the common

law's own backwards-looking rhetoric, so that England's current pluralistic division of judicial labor was cast as "ancient," "pure," "undefiled," and simply what was "before." Certainly James won this battle – Coke was ousted from the King's Bench – though his son, Charles I, would lose the jurisdictional war (among others). Thus, it may be that James was not mimicking Coke but rather ceding ground to him: James was, after all, arguing in good common law fashion for the superiority of any practice or policy that could be labeled "as it was before."

A few years before James's speech, in a well-known letter to Henry Goodyer, Donne confessed that as a young man he had been "diverted" from his study of "our Law" – that is, of the common law at Lincoln's Inn – "by the worst voluptuousnes, which is an Hydroptique immode-rate desire of humane learning and languages."[12] Few critics have ever believed that Donne really wanted to be a barrister. Moreover, like the puritans Hooker complained about, critics have tended to assume that his diversion from one kind of law amounted to a rejection of all law. But that diversion from the common law only steered him toward the civil-canon *jus commune* and toward the administration of equity. And it was various rivalries between those three kinds of law – between many laws and one centralized, rational, and formal law; between the secular and the spiritual; between the general rule and the particular exception – that helped to the shape Donne's literary imagination and professional career.

Notes

1. Richard Hooker, *The Works of that Learned and Judicious Divine, Mr. Richard Hooker* (London, 1676), 102.
2. Hooker, *Works*, 103.
3. Thomas Ridley, *A View of the Civile and Ecclesiastical Law* (London, 1607), 120.
4. Thomas Smith, *De Republica Anglorum* (London, 1583), 52.
5. John Cowell, *The Interpreter* (London, 1607), *s.v. Tales*.
6. William Fulbecke, *A Direction or Preparative to the Study of the Law* (London, 1600), sig. 27v.
7. Thomas Egerton, "Some Notes, and Remembrances, Concerning Prohibitions," in Louis A. Knafla, *Law and Politics in Jacobean England: The Tracts of Lord Chancellor Ellesmere* (Cambridge University Press, 1977), 295.
8. Edward Coke, *The First Part of the Institutes of the Laws of England, or, A Commentary upon Littleton*, 16th edn (Philadelphia, PA: Johnson and Warner, and Samuel Fisher, 1812), xxxvii. See also Richard Helgerson, *Forms of Nationhood* (University of Chicago Press, 1992), 63–105.

9. *Sermons*, 4:274. All subsequent quotations are from this same page.
10. "To His Mistress Going to Bed," 26.
11. King James VI and I, *Political Writings*, ed. Johann P. Sommerville (Cambridge University Press, 1994), 217.
12. *Letters*, 44.

CHAPTER 14

Donne's Prisons

Molly Murray

In early February of 1602, John Donne found himself in the Fleet prison, after the discovery of his clandestine marriage to Anne More, the young ward of his employer, the Lord Keeper Sir Thomas Egerton. Two friends who had assisted the elopement, Christopher and Samuel Brooke, would be held in the Marshalsea and Newgate prisons for some weeks, but Donne himself remained in the Fleet for mere days. By February 13 he was under house arrest in London, and wrote to his new father-in-law, George More, to thank him for "this mild change of Imprisonment"; several days later, he asked Egerton "so much more to slacken my fetters" as to "graunt me Liberty to take the Ayre, about this Town" – assuring Egerton that "[t]he whole world ys a streight Imprisonment to me, whilst I ame barrd your Lordships sight."[1] Donne's physical freedom would soon be restored entirely, but his loss of position would be permanent, and he would never re-enter Egerton's service.

Donne's description of his world as a "streight Imprisonment" may have been a hyperbolic (and vain) attempt to regain Egerton's favor, but the actual prison was in fact a constant feature of Donne's life, even beyond his own brief experience of confinement. As the scion of a Catholic family in a time when avowed Catholicism amounted to treason, Donne grew up aware of his blood relation to the martyr Thomas More, and witnessed many of his relatives and friends held captive for the old faith. Donne's Jesuit uncle Jasper Heywood followed More's footsteps into the Tower in 1584, where he was regularly visited over the next several months by one of his sisters, possibly Donne's mother Elizabeth; Donne's later mention, in *Pseudo-Martyr*, of having observed "a Consultation of *Jesuites* in the *Tower* in the late Queenes time" may indicate that he accompanied his mother on her prison visits.[2] A little less than ten years later, as Donne was reconsidering his allegiance to his family's faith, his younger brother Henry died of plague in Newgate prison after his arrest for harboring a fugitive priest (William Harrington, who was executed after torture). Even after his own conversion to Protestantism, Donne remained close to a number of men who were imprisoned for the old religion. The Earl of Northumberland, who had brought George More news of his daughter's marriage on Donne's behalf, was sent to the Tower in 1605 under suspicion of complicity with the Gunpowder Plot, and remained there until 1621. Donne's associates Ben Jonson and Sir Tobie Matthew were each briefly imprisoned after their respective Catholic conversions; in his autobiography, Matthew recalls that Donne was among the "very many friends who . . . came to visit me very often" in the Fleet, and was "very full of kindness to me at that time."[3]

If Donne's links to Catholicism brought him into close contact with the prison and its denizens, so did his attempts at advancement in the secular spheres of politics and courtly preferment. In 1596, Donne joined the military expeditions led by Essex and Ralegh. After joining Egerton's service upon his return, Donne witnessed the fall of one of his erstwhile heroes at close hand, as the Lord Keeper held the disgraced rebel Essex under arrest at York House for six months in 1599 (as Lord Chancellor, and after Donne had left his employment, Egerton would later preside over Ralegh's confinement in the Tower and his eventual execution for treason). Through his marriage, Donne was related to Elizabeth Throckmorton Ralegh (whose own illicit marriage to Sir Walter resulted in their first imprisonment in 1592, and who later returned to the Tower to live with her husband during his second imprisonment). Donne's father-in-law, George More, served as Lieutenant of the Tower from 1615–18, where he had custody of both Ralegh and Northumberland – as well as Robert Carr, Earl of Somerset, the former royal favorite and Donne's erstwhile patron, imprisoned for murder in 1615 along with his wife, Lady Frances Howard. In addition to his association with such elevated inmates, we also find evidence that Donne's personal and professional life brought him into some contact with more common prisoners. In 1600, while in Egerton's service, Donne offered his assistance to a prisoner identified only as "G. H.," alluding to such logistical matters as the bureaucratic delays involved in prison correspondence.[4] Decades later, Donne would pay a "trifling" amount to liberate the son of his friend Henry Goodyer, briefly imprisoned for debt in the Counter. In this endeavor, Donne had the help of the lawyer and antiquary John Selden, who himself had been briefly imprisoned the prior year for asserting the legal rights of Parliament.[5]

Throughout his life, Donne experienced imprisonment in a variety of venues (in the Tower, the Fleet, the Counters, York House, and his own house) and from a variety of vantage points (as visitor, correspondent, inmate, officer, commentator). The frequency, and the variety, of these prison experiences should not be understood as unique, or even unusual in the period. Indeed, over the sixteenth and seventeenth centuries, the prison became an increasingly prominent feature of English cultural life, affecting all aspects of society to an unprecedented degree. The period's combination of population growth, restive politics, religious reformation, and economic instability resulted in the imprisonment of more and more men and women for offences ranging from debt to recusancy to treason. The absence of legal procedures governing imprisonment (the *Habeas Corpus Act* was not passed until 1679) meant that people could be taken into custody without sentence or trial, often not knowing the grounds of their imprisonments – and peremptory imprisonments often ended in equally peremptory pardons or releases. Imprisonment for debt, meanwhile, could be as unregulated as the nascent credit economy itself, placing prisoners at the mercy of either rapacious creditors or munificent friends or associates (as in the case of Goodyer's son). While individual instances of imprisonment could be inscrutable, the phenomenon of imprisonment *per se* gained ever greater visibility in the English cultural landscape, and, indeed, in its *actual* landscape: in London alone, prisoners were held in Newgate, Ludgate, Bridewell, the Poultry, Breadstreet and Woodstreet Counters, the White Lion, the Fleet and the Marshalsea, the King's Bench, the Clink, the Westminster Gatehouse, and of course the Tower of London. In the opening lines of *The Prayse and Vertue of a Jayle and Jaylers* (1623), John Taylor offers a less conservative estimate, announcing that "in London and within a mile I weene / There are of jailes or prisons full eighteene."[6]

These varied early modern prisons were also various within their walls. Differing dramatically from the material standardization of later prisons (most famously the Benthamite "panopticon"), the architecture of the early modern prison was for the most part ad hoc and unsystematic. This, coupled with the for-profit basis of prison administration, meant that inmates in the same prison could be held in radically disparate conditions, from crowded "common wards" to luxurious apartments, depending on the fees they were willing or able to pay. Furthermore, belying our modern sense of the prison as a place of invariably straitened or solitary confinement, early modern prisons also allowed or enabled various kinds of communication and congregation both within and beyond their physical boundaries. In this world, religious prisoners like Jasper Heywood and Tobie Matthew would receive frequent visits from proselytizing reformers, as well as their friends and family. Political prisoners like Ralegh and Northumberland could keep up vigorous correspondence with the world at large, and maintain active roles in it; in Ralegh's case, this involved briefly being furloughed to lead an expedition to Guiana while still nominally an inmate of the Tower. Common prisoners, such as criminals and debtors, were also frequently moved from prison to prison according to available space, as well as claims of jurisdiction (Henry Donne, for example, was moved from the Clink to Newgate in the short period before his untimely death), and could often congregate in ways that were either permitted or enabled by the irregular nature of prison administration.

Rather than an idealized space of heroic suffering or solitary contemplation and transcendence, the early modern prison was a site of fraught encounter, a scene of political and social conflict (and sometimes collaboration), and, above all, a world marked by a radical contingency and permeability. This is the prison that Donne knew, and this is the prison that he evokes, metaphorically and literally, throughout his writings. In a late sermon, Donne reminds his listeners that St. Paul was a prisoner whose circumstances depended on the whims of those who had him in their power: so, he was "emprisoned at Jerusalem; from thence sent bound to Caesarea; practiced upon to be killed by the way; forced to appeal to Caesar; upon that Appeal sent Prisoner to Rome; ship-wracked upon the way at Malta; emprisoned under guard, though not close prisoner two years after his coming thither, and though dismissed, and so enabled to visit some Churches. Yet laid hold upon again by Nero, and executed."[7] In the figure of Paul, and his constantly changing captivities, Donne offers an exaggerated version of the mutable and unfixed imprisonments familiar to many of his contemporaries. Elsewhere, remarking upon the admirable "vehemency" of "those epistles which Saint Paul writ in prison," and noting that "a sentence written with a cole upon a wall by a close prisoner, affects us when we come to read it," Donne offers a deeply cynical account of prison writing: "ordinarily a prisoner is the lesse to be beleeved for his being in prison and in fetters, if he speak such things as conduce to his discharge … it is likely enough that a prisoner will lye for such an advantage" (3:336). Perhaps, in this moment, Donne was recalling the obsequious letters he once wrote to More and Egerton from the Fleet. In any case, his allusion to prison writing here evokes the voluminous petitions and pleas drafted by inmates, writings born out of expediency and presumptive of an audience, and thus very different from the romantic image of the "close prisoner" finding stoic consolation by writing on his walls "with a cole."

The cynicism that colors Donne's reference to prison writings extends to – and intensifies in – his references to the authorities that govern imprisonment. Preaching at Lincoln's Inn, Donne reminds his listeners of the parable in which "the master forgave his servant ten thousand talents ... and that servant took his fellow by the throat and cast him into prison, because he did not presently pay an hundred pence, perhaps fifty shillings" (3:158); this allegory of hypocrisy sharpens its point on the contemporary culture of credit, in which men – like Henry Goodyer's son – found themselves imprisoned for small sums owed. Elsewhere, Donne rehearses Seneca's Lear-esque maxim that "the judge condemns a man for that which himself is farre more guilty of, then the prisoner" (2:117), and emphasizes the unpredictability, and possible reversibility, of imprisonment in a later sermon, asking "can any glory in any thing of this world be any thing other than vain-glory? What Title of Honour hath any man had in any state, in Court, that some prison in that State hath not had men of that Title in it?" (3:223). Donne's allusion to noble prisoners would have resonated with an audience aware of the high stakes of Stuart politics, and of the imprisonment of prominent figures from Ralegh to Somerset. Indeed, the passage contains a proleptic irony, as Donne's friend John Selden, the renowned jurist and author of the treatise *Titles of Honor*, would himself be imprisoned in the Tower in late 1621, several months after Donne preached these words.

In a 1622 sermon preached to his old associate Northumberland, Donne suggests that any man "in his own imprisonment, can see Christ in the grave, and in his own enlargement, Christ in his resurrection" (4:175). Quite apart from its ad hominem allegory (Northumberland had been released from the Tower several months prior to this sermon, after nearly two decades), Donne's commentary on captivity and enlargement falls in line with his general tendency to use the prison as an illustration of confinement that is provisional and temporary, governed by unpredictable forces. In a sermon preached at Whitehall in November 1617, Donne elaborates on a line from Psalm 55:19: "because they have no changes, therefore they fear not God." He begins by inviting his listeners to imagine "a prison, where men wither'd in a close and perpetual imprisonment" (1:223). Despite the word "perpetual," the prison functions in the sermon not an example of changelessness, but rather the precise opposite: a site of incipience, "where any change that could come, would put them in a better state, then they were before." In a sermon on Psalm 38, Donne ponders the principle of "*titulus clavis*" – that the title of the psalm is the key to its interpretation: "Being locked up in a close prison, of multiplied calamities, this turns the key, this opens the door, this restores him to liberty" (2:74). In restoring the word *"clavis"* to its literal meaning, this paradoxical metaphor once again invokes the prison as a "close" space that can nevertheless be opened. Similarly, in his frequent evocations of "the prison of our mother's womb," Donne imagines confinements that are brief by definition. "What is our birth," Donne asks, using one of his favorite comparisons, "but a breaking of prison?" (4:52). Following this train of thought to a somewhat unnerving conclusion, Donne elsewhere imagines "so putrid a prison, as the wombe would be to us, if we stayed in it beyond our time" (10:232). Such an exit, however, is fraught with its own difficulties, as Donne acknowledges when he likens the baby's umbilical connection to the mother to the state of "prisoners discharged of actions [who] lye for fees ... we cannot go thence, nor stay there" (10:233). Alluding to the fact that many former prisoners – those technically no longer in custody – could not leave the prison until they had discharged their sizable imprisonment debts, Donne here uses the prison to evoke a liminal state, one that confounds an absolute distinction between in- and outside, and further confuses the categories of free and unfree.

Similar images recur with some frequency in Donne's poetry, where the prison also seems to conjure material and existential uncertainty, rather than strictly regulated enclosure. At times this takes the form of casual references to details of carceral corruption and procedural injustice. "The Storm," for instance, addressed to the same Christopher Brooke who would be (or had been) imprisoned for helping Donne's illicit marriage, describes an idling ship's crew as "Withering like prisoners which lie but for fees" (18), again alluding to the complex logistics of prison release. In "Satire II," Donne refers to "prisoners, which whole months will swear / That only suretyship hath brought them there" (67–68), alluding to the legal process by which men who had merely provided "surety" for an unpaid debt could be imprisoned for it, confounding any clear association of imprisonment and guilt. Donne makes a similar point in a letter to the Countess of Bedford ("T'have written then"), where the commonplace image of the body as the soul's prison acquires a tinge of social satire: "As men to'our prisons, new souls to'us are sent, / Which learn vice there and come in innocent" (59–60) – in other words, a prisoner's criminality might be a *result* of his imprisonment, rather than its cause. This notion of the corrupt, corrupting nature of the prison reappears in "Satire IV," where the speaker describes departing "with such or more haste than one / Who fears more actions doth haste from prison" (153–54). Here, the freed prisoner's "haste" reflects his fear of further "actions," or lawsuits that might return him to captivity, regardless of his innocence.

Elsewhere in the poetry, Donne invokes the prison as a space of ambiguous and mutable power relations, where the positions of captor and captive refuse to remain stably opposed, and where the prison is itself the object of profound ambivalence. The speaker of "Love's War" celebrates a mutual erotic subjection, as his lover's "arms imprison me, and mine arms thee" (31), an image which, despite its paradoxical charge, also conjures the confusions of agency and authority so common in the early modern prison (where, for example, Bess Ralegh could live in the Tower with her husband, while related by marriage to the lieutenant in charge of their captivity). At other moments, Donne heightens the violence implicit in the Boethian conceit of liberty-in-constraint, as in Holy Sonnet 10, where the speaker beseeches God to "Take me to You, imprison me, for I, / Except you'enthral me, never shall be free" (12–13), demanding an "enthrallment" that seems anything but isolating or secure. In Holy Sonnet 2, the speaker imagines himself *in extremis*, facing death; at this moment, his soul quails

> like a thief, which till death's doom be read,
> Wisheth himself delivered from prison,
> But damned and haled to execution,
> Wisheth that still he might be'imprisoned.   (5–8)

With this image, Donne inverts and parodies the figure of the pious prisoner embracing his captivity in order to find inner tranquility and resignation to God; the prisoner in Donne clings to his cell not out of a desire to transcend bare earthly life, but out of a desperate attachment to that life. The prison functions here, again, less as an implacable constraint than as a contingent one, which can be entered or exited, loved or loathed.

Finally, Donne's devotional poetry makes frequent use of the same body-prison analogy we have already encountered in the sermons, using the prison to convey the idea that the soul is only temporarily held by the physical bonds of flesh, which are themselves unstable. In *The Second Anniversary*, the speaker invites his addressee to recall birth as release from captivity: "in how poor a prison thou did'st lie / After, enabled but to suck, and cry" (173–74). And *La Corona* addresses the Virgin Mary, recalling how Jesus "yields Himself to lie / In prison in thy womb" (19–20), and eventually "leaves His well-beloved imprisonment" to join humanity on earth (30). The most dramatic elaboration of this point, of course, is *Metempsychosis*, a long fable describing the fate of the soul found in the

Edenic apple. In this picaresque tale of the "progress of a deathless soul" (1) through various "Prisons of flesh" (67), Donne again modifies the conventional notion of the physical body as the soul's prison, by transforming enclosure into mutability. As the soul moves from sparrow to mouse to elephant to ape to human, each new confinement seems further to underscore the radical unfastness of confinement itself; when the ensouled fish is swallowed by a swan, Donne exclaims that "now swam a prison in a prison put" (241), an image that at once redoubles the bonds of imprisonment and reveals their arbitrariness.

Such moments of imaginative bravura suggest that the early modern English prison – with all its material and existential ambiguities – offered Donne a fruitful source of metaphor. In turn, this prison might also offer us a fruitful metaphor for Donne's poetry more generally. In "The Canonization," Donne's famous reference to the "pretty rooms" (32) of the stanza might seem to invite a reading of his poetry in terms of the enclosures it seems constantly to describe: not only rooms, but wombs, tombs, and of course well-wrought urns, all seemingly hermetic spaces that seal the world out, and the speaker in. But Donne's prisons – and his poems – are not such spaces. Instead, both metaphorically and structurally, they often draw attention to the contingency in any constraint, and the potential impermanence of any "close" captivity. Indeed, Donne's poetry, restive and reticent, solitary and populous, enclosed and iconoclastic, provides the early modern prison world with an aesthetic corollary.

Notes

1. *John Donne's Marriage Letters in the Folger Shakespeare Library*, eds. M. Thomas Hester, Robert Parker Sorlien, and Dennis Flynn (Washington, DC: The Folger Shakespeare Library, 2005), 40, 42.
2. Donne, *Pseudo-martyr* (London, 1610), 43.
3. Toby Matthew, *A True Historical Relation of the Conversion of Sir Tobie Matthew*, ed. A. H. Matthew (London: Burns & Oates, 1904), 85, 86.
4. *Letters*, 178–79.
5. *Letters*, 198.
6. The 1633 edition of John Stow's *Survey of London* contains descriptions and short histories of most of the major prisons, as does another early modern urban chorography. See D. Lupton's *London and the Countrey Carbonadoed and Quartred* (London, 1632).
7. *Sermons*, 8:170. Subsequent references to the sermons will give volume and page number in text.

CHAPTER 15

Donne and the Natural World

Rebecca Bushnell

When we think of Donne and his world, nature rarely comes to mind. In contrast, for example, with Shakespeare's plays and poems, filled with evocations of forests and gardens, Donne's work relies mostly on images of people and their made world: the body, bone, window, bed, street, map, compass, ship. The satires, epistles, songs, and sonnets are set mostly in urban, court, or domestic settings, not pastoral landscapes. As a result, many critics have concluded that Donne was just not that interested in nature.[1] And for most of his life he did indeed live in the city. Although for nearly a decade his home was in the country, he was hardly content to stay there. Robert Watson concludes crisply, "Donne's references to pastoral and georgic are persistently negative, and he never practices the nature-loving genres himself; socially and financially embarrassed by his lack of land, he strives to subordinate landscape to mindscape."[2]

But the natural world, as we think of it, was still very much Donne's world, both in his lived experience and in his thinking. In early modern England people lived in close proximity to other living creatures, whether in the city or country, and they were much more acutely aware of their dependence on them to sustain life. It was not, however, a sentimental association; people knew they could not survive without what nature provided. Animals supplied meat, labor, and transportation, and plants were the source not only of food but also of medicine. The sea and the forest were both to be feared and to be mined for profit.

Several conflicting yet interrelated narratives dominated the view of humanity's relationship to nature in Donne's time. Keith Thomas lays out one forcefully in *Man and the Natural World*, where he describes the profoundly and even brutally anthropocentric culture of the sixteenth and seventeenth centuries, which saw human beings as uniquely rational, superior, and created to dominate all other things in nature.[3] In this view, the natural world existed to serve people: beasts for food and labor, plants for consumption, medicine, and pleasure, and the forests and wasteland for men to tame and master. Multitudes of cattle were slaughtered to sate the English appetite for beef, and the woodlands were dangerously depleted to supply the demand for fuel and building. Cities were choked with smoke from burning fuel and the urban rivers with human and animal waste.

Reinforcing the human exploitation of nature was a traditional ideology of a universal natural order, in which creation was imagined to exist in a hierarchy, all aspiring upward, with human beings subject only to God and his angels. This view was perhaps most succinctly expressed in the early sixteenth century by Thomas Elyot in *The Boke Named the Governor*, where, to bolster his broader argument about good governance, Elyot asked his reader to "behold also the order that God hath put generally in all His creatures, beginning at the most inferior or base, and ascending upward," where "every kind of trees, herbs, birds, beasts, and fishes, beside their diversity of forms, have ... a peculiar disposition appropered unto them by God their creator: so that in everything is order, and without order may be nothing stable or permanent; and it may not be called order, except it do contain in it degrees, high and base, according to the merit or estimation of the thing that is ordered."[4] Much recent early modern scholarship has undermined the argument of E. M. W. Tillyard and other earlier scholars that claimed everyone at the time sincerely believed this. It was certainly more official doctrine than an everyday habit of thought, and hardly adequate to describe the real state of the world, human or natural. By Donne's time new discoveries in natural philosophy from the cosmic to the microscopic level had begun to challenge all traditional views of how things worked on earth and in heaven. But for all that, it was one important framework for describing man's place in creation, which we see reflected in imaginative as well as political and religious writing.

Profoundly complicating that traditional vision of cosmic order was a belief in the deep *connectedness* of the natural and human worlds. As Tillyard himself observed, while vertically structured, the "Elizabethan World Picture" of order also drew innumerable horizontal links of analogy and attraction, called correspondences and sympathies, among all things on earth, including humanity.[5] This layering, with its mixing of the concrete and abstract, brought Tillyard to call the Elizabethan period "a very queer age."[6] In *The Order of Things*, Michel Foucault emphasized that this period was less an age of order and more one of "resemblance": "The universe was folded in upon itself: the earth echoing the sky, faces seeing themselves reflected in the stars, and plants holding within their stems the secrets that were of use to man."[7] While it may still have been a world in which man (and in this case truly man, not woman) was at the center, everything in creation touched and reflected others: in Foucault's words, "in the vast syntax of the world, the different beings adjust themselves to one another; the plant communicates with the animal, the earth with the sea, man with everything around him," as man is a microcosm of the universe, containing all within him.[8] It is this kind of interconnectedness that has led Gabriel Egan to partially vindicate Tillyard's "Elizabeth World Picture" from an ecocritical perspective: one could, he observes, argue that "a macrocosm/microcosm correspondence need not of itself run counter to the particularities of life as it is lived on Earth and events in the wider universe," insofar as it implies all things on earth are in some sense alive and interdependent.[9] The doctrine of correspondences and sympathies also appears to anticipate actor-network theory as developed by Bruno Latour and others, whereby both human and non-human, subject and object, are understood to have agency and to interact in a network of exchange and mutual influence. This is the recognition of the dejected speaker of Donne's "Nocturnal on St Lucy's Day," that all creation, "plants, yea stones, detest, / And love; all, all some properties invest" (33–34): all are in motion, and all in touch with each other.

The duality of human interaction with the natural world in the period is perhaps best exemplified in the flourishing practice of gardening and husbandry, and writing about it in both handbooks and literary texts. On the one hand, the increasing investment of people at every rank in improvement of the land and their own status, whether in a small plot or a grand country estate, imprinted culture on the land and extracted profit from it. On the other hand, writers both low and high conveyed the delight and wisdom that comes from the contemplation of nature.[10] In his *Herbal*, John Gerard asked "what greater delight is there than to behold the earth appareled with plants, as with a robe of embroidered work, set with orient pearls and garnished with great diversity of rare and costly jewels," where "the principal delight is in the mind, singularly enriched with the knowledge of these visible things, setting forth to us the invisible wisdom and admirable workmanship of the almighty God."[11] For Reverend Samuel Gilbert, every plant in the garden was a means to access the divine, as "Each plant's engravened with [God's] heavenly name / Like the hyacinthea stamped with Ajax['s] name."[12] The natural world is both subject to the human will and a divine, mysterious, and powerful text.

The implicit conflicts between the imposition of human art and the inherent value of nature, between hierarchy and connectedness, between

dominance and likeness, are all amply illustrated in the complexity of
Donne's engagement with contemporary ideas of the natural world.
Commentators generally see him as being relentlessly anthropocentric,
where the man at that center is Donne himself, fundamentally antagonistic
to nature. This negative view can be traced back as far as Samuel Johnson,
who condemned the metaphysical poets for being profoundly "unnatural":
"If the father of criticism has rightly denominated poetry . . . an imitative
art, these writers will, without great wrong, lose their right to the name of
poets; for they cannot be said to have imitated anything: they neither
copied nature nor life; neither painted the forms of matter nor represented
the operations of intellect. . . . Their thoughts are often new, but seldom
natural."[13] Robert N. Watson locates Donne's work in the tradition of
a "Protestant poetics" that values words over things, and celebrates man's
power to control and remake nature, where Donne's "vivid narcissism
manifests itself partly as a belief that his poetic restructurings of the
universe can alter its reality: mind over matter."[14] In "The Bait," the
speaker indeed celebrates the power of the poet and lover to transcend
the ordinary world – that of the vulgar fisher and slimy nests of fish – in
order to walk on golden sands and in crystal brooks, the nature of art. In his
epistle "To Sir Edward Herbert, at Juliers," the poet recognizes that man is
a thing of nature, "a lump where all beasts kneaded be"(l), yet he praises
any man who can extirpate those bestial and even vegetative parts of him:
"How happy'is he which hath due place assigned / To'his beasts, and
disaforested his mind! / Impaled himself to keep them out, not in"
(9–11). At the same time, as Laura Ralph has noted, in his persistent
questioning mode, "Donne's philosophically inclined mode of thought
[enables] him to interrogate the order of being."[15] So he begins Holy
Sonnet 8 (XII) ("Why are we by all creatures") by asking the hard question:
"Why are we by all creatures waited on?" (1), if other creatures are purer or
more powerful than man? The sonnet both implies Donne's recognition of
human dominance of all others and undermines it, for the purposes of his
mediation on the wonderful mystery of Christ's sacrifice.

   If Donne's work reflects that endemic imposition of the human self on
nature, it also evokes the notion that the same self participates equally in all
creation. In her work on the effects of the "new science" on seventeenth-
century poetry, Marjorie Hope Nicolson foregrounds the lack of distinction between human and nature inherent in the imagined network of
correspondences and sympathies, where "Man was so involved in Nature
that no separation was possible – nor would an Elizabethan have understood such separation."[16] This involvement could be understood as both

symbolic and radically real, for example, as when developed most extensively in the work of Paracelsus, who "believed man *was* the elements; he was minerals and metals; he was fruit and trees, vegetables and flowers. He was also wind and storms and tempests."[17] Nicolson sees Donne writing "in the Paracelsian strain" when he writes of man as a little world or a microcosm, as in the *Devotions*, where the shaking and torments of the heavens and earth are felt within his real body, with earthquakes and sudden shakings: "these lightenings, sudden flashes; these thunders, sudden noises; these eclipses, sudden offuscations, and darkening of his senses; these Blazing Stars, sudden fiery exhalations; these Rivers of Blood, sudden red waters."[18] Sometimes it is a case of human beings acting in analogy and even harmony with things in nature. For example, in "A Letter Written by Sir H.G. and J.D. *alternis vicibus*," the speaker asserts that human emotions should burgeon with the growth of trees: "Since ev'ry tree begins to blossom now, / Perfuming and enamelling each bow, / Hearts should as well as they some fruits allow" (1–3). But the correspondences swell far beyond that in Donne's conceits of the body of the lover or the beloved, or the two together, both at the center of the world and analogous to it. The most extraordinary use of the conceit is, of course, in *The First Anniversary*, a poem of praise and lament for Elizabeth Drury, "She to whom this world must itself refer, / As suburbs, or the microcosm of her" (235–36).

Thus, while the metaphysical poets may have been "unnatural" in the sense that they did not "imitate life," they reveled in the interconnectedness of the human and natural world through correspondences and sympathies. Samuel Johnson himself noted that their poetry depends on "a combination of dissimilar images or discovery of occult resemblances in things apparently unlike," where "nature and art are ransacked for illustrations, comparisons, and allusions." Their art, that is, is "analytical," engaged with nature but not representative of it. Johnson complained that such a poet "could no more represent, by their slender conceits and laboured particularities, the prospects of nature, or the scenes of life, than he who dissects a sunbeam with a prism can exhibit the wide effulgence of a summer noon."[19] If for Johnson the true poet was a painter of "prospects of nature," one could argue that the metaphysicals, and Donne among them, were like the physicians and natural philosophers of their time, undoing the stuff of nature in order to understand its sympathies and mysteries, and to make it into something new. In some cases, Donne's object of examination may be a single natural thing, for example, the flower in "The Blossom" which the speaker has "watched six or seven days" (2). The image stands in the poem as a fact on its own, to demonstrate the effects of time and cold, in the context of a broader argument about the cold hearts of women. In "The Primrose," the primrose hill that the speaker walks serves as the counterpart to the sky, as the constellation of flowers, "their form, and their infinity / Make a terrestrial galaxy, / As the small stars do in the sky" (5–7). The primrose itself is dissected as a symbol of true love, as the poet contemplates the number of its petals, and arrives at the perfect number by a mathematical calculation.

Even more than in our own time, the natural world in Donne's was always framed through a human lens. People looked to the garden, the forest, the sea, and the sky, both for what they could produce from them, and to see both themselves and God in them. For Donne, the relationship was just one at its most extreme. In Donne's most extended meditation on nature, "Twickenham Garden," the speaker enters into this garden as a disappointed lover and imagines that his sorrow transforms it:

> Blasted with sighs, and surrounded with tears,
> Hither I come to seek the spring,
> And at mine eyes, and at mine ears,
> Receive such balms, as else cure everything;
> But, O, self traitor, I do bring
> The spider love, which transubstantiates all,
> And can convert manna to gall. (1–6)

While early modern gardens were often conceptualized as paradise begun anew,[20] the speaker acknowledges that while "this place may thoroughly be thought / True paradise, I have the serpent brought" (8–9). He looks to find his correspondence in the garden, but not finding it there, he begs to be transformed into part of it, first as a mandrake and then as a stone fountain, "weeping out my year" (18). Watson criticizes "Twickenham Garden" insofar that it "subordinates the country-estate garden to a state of mind."[21] But Renaissance gardens were always place of culture, or "a state of mind," as much they were states of nature. The speaker's imagining himself as a weeping fountain, both stone and alive, clearly marks the idea that at the garden's core is a work of art: it is a made thing.

Twickenham Garden was indeed a real garden, designed by Lucy, Countess of Bedford. Like many other great Jacobean gardens, it was set out in an elaborate geometric design of circles set in a square defined by severe hedges of quickthorn, "trees cut into beastes," rosemary, and fruit trees. Roy Strong interprets the plan as a microcosm of the order of the pre-Copernican universe, "the circle in the center being Earth followed by

Luna, Mercury and Venus (made of birch), Sol and Mars (lime trees), Jove (fruit trees) and Saturn (beyond)."[22] Thus the garden itself, while made of living things, was itself also an *emblem* or representation of nature, ordered after an anthropocentric conception of the cosmos. In this sense, Donne's early modern "natural world" as represented in Twickenham Garden was already a construct, both vibrantly alive and imprinted by the mind of its human makers.

Notes

1. See Laura Ralph, "'Why are we by all creatures waited on?': Situating John Donne and George Herbert in Early Modern Ecological Discourse," *Early English Studies* 3 (2010), www.uta.edu/english/ees/fulltext/ralph3.html.
2. Robert N. Watson, *Back to Nature: The Green and the Real in the Late Renaissance* (Philadelphia, PA: University of Pennsylvania Press, 2006), 148.
3. Keith Thomas, *Man and the Natural World: Changing Attitudes in England, 1500–1800* (Oxford University Press, 1983).
4. Thomas Elyot, *The Boke Named the Governor*, ed. S. E. Lehmberg (London: Everyman's Library, 1962), Book 1.1, 4.
5. E. M. W. Tillyard, *The Elizabethan World Picture* (New York: Vintage, 1960), 83.
6. Tillyard, *Elizabethan*, 108.
7. Michel Foucault, *The Order of Things: An Archaeology of the Human Sciences* (New York: Random House, 1970), 17.
8. Foucault, *Order*, 18.
9. Gabriel Egan, *Green Shakespeare: From Ecopolitics to Ecocriticism* (London: Routledge, 2006), 25.
10. See Rebecca Bushnell, *Green Desire: Imagining Early Modern Gardens* (Ithaca, NY: Cornell University Press, 2003), 12–48.
11. John Gerard, *The Herball or Generall Historie of Plants* (London, 1597), sig. A2r.
12. Samuel Gilbert, *The Florist's Vade-Mecum* (London, 1683), "Epistle to the Reader."
13. Samuel Johnson, "The Life of Cowley," in *Lives of the Poets: A Selection*, eds. Roger Lonsdale and John Mullan (Oxford University Press, 2006), 15.
14. Watson, *Back*, 138.
15. Ralph, "'Why.'"
16. Marjorie Hope Nicolson, *The Breaking of the Circle: Studies in the Effect of the "New Science" upon Seventeenth-Century Poetry* (New York: Columbia University Press, 1960), 128.
17. Nicolson, *Breaking*, 23.
18. John Donne, "Meditation 1," in *Devotions upon Emergent Occasions* (Ann Arbor, MI: University of Michigan Press, 1959), 8.
19. Johnson, "Life," 16.

20. See John M. Prest, *The Garden of Eden: The Botanic Garden and the Recreation of Paradise* (New Haven, CT: Yale University Press, 1981).
21. Watson, *Back*, 146.
22. Roy Strong, *The Renaissance Garden in England* (New York: Thames and Hudson, 1998), 121–22.

CHAPTER 16

Money

David Landreth

Like many of the "contexts" addressed by this volume, money is a text within Donne's production as much as it is a context for that production. I mean "text" here in a number of senses: as an object developed by his poetic attention, an element that arises frequently in his texts; as a model for the operation of his poetics, a pattern for its texture; and as a "text" in the most typical early modern usage, the Biblical verse that an individual sermon uses as its occasion. Donne's earliest published sermon takes as its text a paradoxically monetized verse of Isaiah (52:3), "Ye have sold your-selves for nought, and ye shall be redeemed without money," and he returns often to Scripture's complex negations of exchange value through-out his preacherly career.[1] But I want also to argue that attending to the manifest textual presence of money in Donne's corpus offers only an incomplete account of how the forms of money mediated his authorship; and that the partiality of such an account manifests a formal distinction between coined and credit monies. Donne prefers coined gold to all the other forms of money that competed with gold for use in his era's fiscal transactions. He presents gold coins again and again as the definitive instances of his masterful, autonomous poetics, yet that monetized mastery itself arises in a context of resentful dependence on the judgment of creditors. In demanding to be read so directly, as texts, Donne's coins occlude the humiliating constraints of credit relations, which are left to be read resistantly, as context.

John Carey has delineated the searching philosophical activity enacted as witty play in Donne's "loved contemplation of coins," and I will begin by addressing his comprehensive analysis.[2] Carey demonstrates that the primary axis along which that contemplation operates in Donne's poems and sermons is Aristotle's metaphysical distinction between form and matter within the being of material objects. Matter, for Aristotle, is merely the substrate of being, an inert potentiality meaningless without form: form is being's realization, its diachronic dynamism, and its meaningful

165

purpose or *telos*. Although form and matter are indivisible in all existing objects and substances, Aristotle uses the metaphor of molten wax impressed with a seal to articulate his distinction between inchoate matter and shaping, meaning-giving form.[3] The maneuver in which Donne's wit delights is to substitute the golden coin for the waxen seal in this philosophical paradigm, and to demonstrate how changing the metaphor redefines the metaphysics. The relation between form and matter is the same in each metaphoric instance: the form is a flat circle with a signifying type (of image and/or word) in relief, imposed upon the matter by pressure from another object. But the absolute dichotomy between meaningful type and meaningless wax is destabilized by adducing a matter, gold, that has its own kind of meaning:

> I, when I value gold, may think upon
> The ductileness, the application,
> The wholesomeness, the ingenuity,
> From rust, from soil, from fire ever free.
> But if I love it, 'tis because 'tis made
> By our new nature (use) the soul of trade.   (11–16)

The speaker of "Love's Progress" here professes that there are two qualitatively different ways in which gold may claim his interest, attention, and affection. One is through the metal's unique natural properties: its power to maintain its integrity even when "to airy thinness beat,"[4] its ability to coat other surfaces, its resistance to corruption or decay, and its benign influence on the human body according to early modern medicine. The second, competing mode of appreciation – which the speaker calls not "value" but "love" – attends to the conventional and extra-natural role that gold has been assigned to play within human society, as money.

The work that "our new nature" "use" (here meaning habit, but playing upon the etymon of "usury") performs upon gold in making it money is at once epiphenomenal and all-important: it makes all the difference, without making any material difference, as the speaker's queasy formulation of the coin as an immaterial "soul" for the most material of practices, "trade," suggests. In the precious currency that Donne knew, nearly all of the value represented by a coin in circulation – its face value – came from its metal content, the price that the bullion contained in the coin would fetch in the international market for precious metals. This is the "intrinsic value" of the coin. But it is necessary in a precious currency that the face value be at least a small amount greater than the intrinsic value; otherwise a spike in the bullion market might cause the coin to be worth more as bullion than as money, which in turn would cause the coin to be melted down. This buffer between the absolute price represented by the face value of the coin and the contingent fluctuations of its intrinsic value was the "extrinsic value." Extrinsic value was understood to inhere in the monarch's stamp upon the coin: it was one of the aspects of what made money to be itself, as the difference between money and uncoined gold.

The minting stamp performed several simultaneous functions. It measured the bullion content of the coin, assuring everyone who encountered the coin that its metal was of a specified fineness and weight. The stamp announced the coin's face value, and authorized its use to represent that value in any monetized transaction. It produced the extrinsic value separating the coin's quantity as bullion from its price as money, and kept the difference as a profit for the sovereign in operating the mint. And the stamp represented the monarch: not only by name and titles, but also by images both emblematic and mimetic, and by a motto in some way germane to the minting authority. The stamp represented the monarch *as* the minting authority, the figure responsible for the coin's measurement and for its currency, and reciprocally represented that authority as an aspect of sovereignty. Extrinsic value was a price paid *by* the common-wealth at large for the integrity of the coinage – its currency, its reliability, its continuing to exist – *to* the sovereign, who in accepting that payment extended both his own faith and credit, and his prerogative, across all transactions in which money was used at its face value.

Current money is simple and banal in its use, at least for those of us who've been habituated to that "use" as second "nature." But Donne's attention to the complexity of the production which precedes that use opens up a gap between the everyday experience of the coin as a thing in the world, its *physis*, and the preconditions of its being that thing – its metaphysics. As we've seen, the being of money is a different thing from the being of uncoined gold, even though the difference between the two is a formal rather than a material difference. So far Donne accords with Aristotle. But the matter that gold provides to the coin is not an arbitrary substrate for its form. Gold is remarkable in many ways, and is suitable to many forms and ends, of which the coin is only one; realizing its potenti-ality to be money excludes its use to any of those other unique ends, for example as gold leaf or as medicine. And the quantitative value of the coin in circulation is supplied almost entirely by the gold, not by the stamp. The stamp does its own qualitative work in turning intrinsic, commodity value into a different and more stable kind of quantity, the face value, but it does so by adding an additional quantity, the extrinsic value, which is only compensatory and not-quite negligible with respect to the intrinsic value. The new kind of meaning produced by the stamp in the coin would not be worth anyone's attention were it not for the intrinsic value of the gold being stamped. The already complex character of the matter in question is the precondition for the meaning of the stamp, and in some ways constrains its meaning. And, as I've suggested, the forming impression of the stamp upon the coin realizes multiple functions upon the coin simultaneously: its *telos* is not unitary but multifarious, a mutually dependent complex or texture of purposes.

The plunge I'm charting in Donne's coins, from a depthless lived banality into a fathomless conceptual complexity opening up beneath that surface of habit, is the leap Donne's metaphysical wit loves to take. It is no wonder that, once having conceived of the coin in this set of problematics, he returns to it again and again. Donne puts his coins to a wide variety of uses across his long career, uses that diverge as different speakerly personae address them to different occasions. But they are consistently couched in terms of the metaphysical relation of matter to form, as Carey demonstrates; and they address that relation in order to organize and assess, from different viewpoints and along different conceptual axes, the competition among different accounts of value. Converging in a coin at any moment of Donne's "loved contemplation" are at least two of the following vectors of valuation: the natural qualities of gold; gold's intrinsic value as a traded commodity; gold's status as matter created and sustained in being, like all matter, *ex nihilo* by God; gold's alchemical status as the perfection of metal, what all metals aspire to become in time; the stamp's synechdochic substitution for the sovereign's person; the analogy between the relation of metal to stamp and that of body to soul in all human persons; the ownership exercised by the sovereign upon the coin in the stamp; the puns that join the names of coins, such as "noble" or "angel," to the non-monetary things that share those names; the force of the stamp as the force of sovereign prerogative; the relation of human conventions to natural qualities and divine signatures; the relation of human sovereignty to divine sovereignty. Different texts follow different threads into the knot of values that Donne locates in the gold coin.

As the material object to which Donne's poetics most frequently attends, the gold coin seems paradigmatic of the object world in that poetics. Indeed, it seems paradigmatic of the relation of his poetics to individual objects, and to the universal conditions of materiality through which individual objects exist. In a 1623 sermon, Donne remakes the turn at the end of Psalm 6 from the listing of David's wants and grievances to a short, yet powerful, expression of thanksgiving, and explains:

> therefore *David* might be later and shorter here, in expressing that duty of thanks ... because being reserved to the end, and close of the Psalme, it leaves the best impression on the memory. And therefore it is easie to observe, that in all Metricall compositions, of which kind the book of Psalmes is, the force of the whole piece, is for the most part left to the shutting up; the whole frame of the Poem is a beating out of a piece of gold, but the last clause is as the impression of the stamp, and that is it that makes it currant.[5]

Like other objects, poetic texts have a metaphysics. The theoretical pre-conditions of a poem's present existence may be articulated as a theory of composition, a poetics, and that poetics may reciprocally be articulated as the ontology of another paradigmatic object, the gold coin. The poetics first selects, circumscribes, and develops a body of matter to serve as the body of the poem, but the crucial stroke is the last. The "last clause" gives both closure ("shutting up") and currency to the poem: it defines the poem's form, and that final form endows the whole of the poem with telos, sending the poem out from the writer's desk into the world to be read – and read in a relatively determined fashion, as Donne imagines the whole experience of the poem to be controlled in memory by the final and "best impression." Value accretes throughout the lines of the poem, as it conveys the "gold" of the poem's matter towards its final impression, but the "last clause" redefines everything that has come before, its own conditions of possibility, into its own terms. That single, definitive stroke imposes itself at once upon the poem's prior being, its prehistory of composition, and upon its futurity of circulation, reading, and interpretation: it is an "impression" both upon "the whole frame of the Poem" and upon the reader's "memory." And that duple orientation of the "last clause" as the poem's telic form is its *currency*, the new and qualitatively different value imparted upon already-precious matter by the sovereign stamp.

To define the poetics of the Psalms in the terms of minting is peculiarly apropos: David was both poet and sovereign. But the poetics Donne asserts here is not unique to David's Psalms. It is true of "all Metricall compositions," of which the Psalms are a generically consistent instance, and Donne allows his audience to infer that he is extrapolating from his own compositional expertise to David's. By construing poetics in these meta-physical terms, as the coordination of divergent values upon matter in the unifying and propulsive masterstroke that endows the poem with form and purpose, Donne effectively assigns to the poet the same role in the production of text that is played in the production of coins by the sovereign. What the coin offers Donne in the last instance, and across all the many instances of its appearance in his writings, is *mastery*: a demonstration of wit's mastery at once of abstruse philosophy and of the banal stuff of everyday living; a theory of mastery in which poetics models its metaphysical interactions with matter and value upon those of the sovereign; and a fantastic usurpation of mastery, an autonomous poetic field in which political sovereignty is merely redundant and may be dismissed. Donne's monetized poetics is one in which the king gives way to the poet.

* * * *

As I've remarked, the extrinsic value afforded to the coin by the sovereign stamp is at once an assertion of mastery over contingent material conditions – the fluctuating price of gold bullion in the market – and a compensation for those material conditions, which are themselves beyond the sovereign's control. I'd like to argue now that Donne's monetized poetics is at least as compensatory as it is masterful, and I will demonstrate that claim by pointing to the ways in which Donne's apparent immersion in the material conditions of early modern value is in fact quite limited. Attending as deeply and repeatedly as he does to the gold coin, over which he is poetically masterful, serves to exclude from Donne's "loved contemplation" the manifold value relations of his society that do not offer him the same opportunity for mastery, and to which he remains painfully subject.

Donne's poetry and his sermons pay elaborate and searching attention to the metaphysics and the poetics of coined gold, as we've seen. Donne seems, like Marlowe's Barabas and Shakespeare's Bassanio, to have no patience for silver; and that effective dismissal is itself telling, since silver made up more than 90% of the circulating medium by mass in the period, and was the medium of most everyday transactions requiring the use of coin.[6] Silver is more prevalent than gold as a monetary medium, but less fraught with meaning or value as a substance. The fact that silver is excluded from Donne's "loved contemplation of coins" immediately suggests that what preoccupies Donne is the work of reconciling different versions of value in the matter and form of the coin, and not the work performed by coins in the context of their circulation – that is, that the contemplation concerns the manufacturing of a particular object, whose form and character as money is important as the final cause or telos anticipated in its manufacture, rather than concerning itself with the activity of the money form once manufactured and distributed.

Indeed, the money of Donne's period materialized itself in a bewilderingly diverse variety of forms: not only as coins, but as entries in accounting ledgers, as formal credit instruments, as informal promises both written and oral, as the proliferation of interest over time, as over-valued "commodities" exchanged to launder the taking of interest, as chalk on a tavern wall, as the clicking of beads on an abacus, or the tapping of knuckles on a hand. The gold and silver currency minted by the Crown was the normative form of money to Donne's mind, and to the minds of most of his contemporaries. But coinage was by no means the most prevalent form of money among Donne's generation. Eric Ketteredge calculates that the average testator in the period left behind at least nine times as much wealth in itemized debts as he did in coin.[7] We might better think of the precious coin's circulation as an occasional condensation of early modern money into its most solid form, precipitating momentarily out of the flows of credit.

Craig Muldrew has thoroughly documented the everyday practices of credit in early modern England, and has argued convincingly for the ideological significance of their pervasiveness.[8] According to Muldrew, the monetized and ethical senses of "credit" were continuous in Donne's culture. There was no institutionalized distinction, as there is in modern credit culture, between an individual's fiscal history and expectations (the stuff of a modern bank's credit report) and the other dimensions of his reputation and self-presentation. Credit relations were a matter of indivi-duals' judgments of other individuals' trustworthiness. But those judg-ments referred themselves to communal norms of accreditation and consensual opinions about the prospective borrower. Most lending took place among members of the same communities, neighbors or relatives, and both the borrower and the lender relied on the communitarian imperatives of intimacy and trust – the borrower to advance the claim of credit upon the lender, and the lender to enforce the claim of debt upon the borrower. Credit relations worked through the medium of other social relations, and worked to affirm and deepen them, or to snap them where they failed. Not only the maintenance of particular credit relations, but the projection of creditworthiness to the world at large, were the constant concerns of all early modern English people who bore any fiscal responsi-bility. The man conscious of his credit was a man submitting himself at all times to the judgmental attention of an unblinking communal eye. Donne was accepting of, though anxious about, such unremitting scrutiny on the part of God. He seems deeply to have resented it in his peers and patrons.

For Donne had discredited himself spectacularly in his scandalous elopement with Anne More. He had lost not only the direct pecuniary benefit of Egerton's employment, but also the far-reaching effect of Egerton's "countenance" – the medium through which his great patron's credit sustained his own. Better never to have had it than to be known so to have lost it: Donne was essentially unemployable after his marriage in government and law, the professions for which he had trained. Donne's poetry had been a relatively minor feature of the ethos he presented to the accrediting world, as an ingenious and omni-capable young man on the rise. After his marriage, poetry became a direct channel for what countenance that world might still consider extending to him, one of the only sites of creditworthiness left standing among the wreckage of his "ruined fortune."[9]

Donne's patrons in the years between his marriage and his investiture were not directly enmeshed with Egerton's and More's circles. And clearly Donne's position as unreclaimed prodigal itself appealed to the Countess of Bedford, since it is the ethos from which his epistles so often address her. What she valued in patronizing Donne was wholly different from what Egerton had valued: a dashing, yet abjected genius paying her court served to enhance the eccentric glamour of her own countenance. But the mode of calculating credit in that relationship was the same, as we may see from the way in which Donne let Lady Bedford's patronage slip away.

> First I confess I have to others lent
>   Your stock and over prodigally spent
> Your treasure, for since I had never known
>   Virtue or beauty but as they are grown
> In you, I should not think or say they shine
>   (So as I have) in any other mine.   (11–16)

These lines occur in the 1612 fragment "To the Countess of Bedford, Begun in France but never perfected," in which Donne sought to palliate a crisis in his patronage relation to the Countess – a crisis which we may understand in Muldrew's terms as a credit crunch. Seeking to widen his patronage circles to encompass first the Drurys, and then their acquaintance in Amiens, Donne had spread his hyperboles too thin. Here he acknowledges that the praises that had been the currency of Lady Bedford's patronage were now being retailed to multiple women of lower standing and undistinguished (even chequered) reputation.[10] The *desunt caetera* with which the verses break off marks a permanent retrenchment in Donne's patronage relations. Though he continued to pursue new patrons with the ingenious idolatries that had been the Countess's "stock" and "treasure," they seem to have won him nothing like the credit with which the Countess had once countenanced them. Indeed, the poems of 1613–14 with which he courted such potential patrons as the Earl of Somerset and his sister-in-law the Countess of Salisbury seem woefully self-conscious of their squandered credit. The epithalamion on Somerset's already scandal-ridden marriage to Frances Howard exacerbates the awkwardness of its occasion by both apologizing for, and attempting to justify, the poem's belatedness to that occasion, while the Salisbury verse-letter spends most of its lines explicating, albeit wittily, why this Countess should take for herself praises that are manifestly the hand-me-downs of Lady Bedford.

Nor does Donne seem to have attempted to win Lady Bedford herself back to that courtly vein – at least, no apparently later pane-gyric to her survives. Instead, his last bid to regain credit with her is "Obsequies upon the Lord Harrington, the Last that Died," an elegy on the death of her brother, which ends by declaring that "my muse ... hath spoke her last" (256, 258) – offering itself to Lady Bedford as Donne's last work as a poet. With this poem Donne solicited Lady Bedford's patronage to enter the church, and to leave his old identity as courtly poet – and her old identity as patron of his courtliness – behind. He was only partly successful. In a querulous letter to Goodyer, Donne complains that, although the immediate impact of the elegy on the Countess was so forceful as "to move her to so much compassion heretofore, as to offer to pay my debts," his attempts to follow up on the promise found her with second thoughts:

> she was somewhat more startling, then I looked for from her: she had more suspicion of my calling, a better memory of my past life, then I had thought her nobility could have admitted ... my greater wants now, and for so good a purpose, as to come disengaged into that profession [i.e., the priesthood], being plainly laid open to her, [worked] no farther but that she sent me £30, which in good faith she excused with that, which is in both parts true, that her present debts were burdensome, and that I could not doubt of her inclination, upon all future emergent occasions, to assist me. I confess to you, her former fashion towards me, had given a better confidence; and this diminution in her makes me see, that I must use more friends, then I thought I should have needed. ... I am afraid out of a Contemplation of mine own unworthinesse, and fortune, that the example of this Lady, should work upon the Lady where you are [the Countess of Huntingdon].[11]

Donne's complaint well exemplifies the multiple dimensions of early modern credit. The "diminution" of Lady Bedford's bounty, from the whole of Donne's debts in promise to £30 in practice, discredits *her* in his anxious mind: it serves to belittle both "her nobility" – the magnanimous spirit that ought to be able to overlook such petty concerns as Donne's "past life" – and his "confidence." But her pulling back from the initial promise of course indicates new reservations in her judgment of Donne, reservations simultaneously ethical and fiscal. The debts of Donne's that she had offered to pay turned out to be "greater" than she'd imagined (or been led to believe), and that fiscal shortfall apparently put her in mind of the old shortcomings of his private life – his rakish reputation, his privateering marriage, the very courtly flirtatiousness which she had patronized in him – which might compromise his credit as a candidate for holy orders. The outcome of the Countess's calculation of the relations among Donne's "wants," his liabilities, her "inclination ... to assist [him]," her obligation to her recent promise, her past commitments to him, and her own "present debts" – that is, her own situation in credit relations that must have been by far more complex than Donne's – is the gift of thirty pounds and the new promise of ongoing goodwill. And Donne is not only disappointed by the gift, but justifiably concerned that a smaller-than-expected gift from his most prominent patron will diminish his credit in the eyes of other potential patrons. Lady Bedford's countenance is an asset too complex and fluid to be quantifiable, but as it waxes and wanes so do all the other relational assets upon which Donne's credit also depends.

Attending to the multiple forms of early modern money, both as coin object and as credit relation, shows Donne's textual production to be poised between the autonomous mastery he locates through his "loved contemplation of coins" within his texts and the context of dependence upon credit relations in which those texts arise. Yet, though Donne habitually counterposes the values of a sovereign, materialized, objectified autonomy to those of a judgmental, ungenerous, relational community, he cannot forget that these two sets of values are themselves entirely fungible manifestations of a continuous money form:

> For God's sake hold your tongue, and let me love,
>   Or chide my palsy, or my gout,
> My five gray hairs, or ruined fortune flout,
>   With wealth your state, your mind with arts improve,
>   Take you a course, get you a place,
>   Observe his honour, or his grace,
> Or the King's real, or his stamped face

Contemplate, what you will, approve,
So you will let me love. ("The Canonization," 1–9)

Countenance and coin blur together in the equivocation between "the King's real, or his stamped face": "real" or "ryal" is the name of a gold coin, so the offered alternative collapses into hendiadys. The "ruined fortune" of this speaker leaves cash and credit equally unavailable to him. The firm situatedness of his expostulation, as much as its force, invites us to identify the speaker's sense of his position in the community of which he is a not very willing part with Donne's own: as universally and unsympathetically judged, as wholly discredited even among his friends – one of whom, as the interlocuting "you" of the poem, voices the judgment of the community at large in counseling him to find some way of redressing that judgment to restore his credit. Such ostensibly friendly advice, the speaker intimates, is no real friendship, but only a disguised version of the interlocutor's self-interest – the interlocutor's desire to inoculate himself from an association potentially contagious to his own credit by stabilizing the speaker's credit. And so the speaker turns the advice back on the interlocutor with hyperbolic disdain, while professing his "love" to be at once the cause of his ruin and the object of the interlocutor's envy. He develops that erotic relation in the verses that follow into a new and "mysterious" version of autonomous communion that is to project itself, in the last stanza, out upon that world at large, to substitute a self-generated (and manifestly paradoxical) "pattern" of communal desire for the worldly-wise values of communally arbitrated credit.

The speaker is not Donne. But he is an ethos that we are invited to identify as an ethos of Donne's; and he is an ethos that is not only conscious of his interpellation by the ideology of credit, but actively resentful of it. Poetics offers the speaker an autonomous exteriority whose value is self-contained, self-determined, and self-generated, an Archimedean point from which he may redefine the values of the world that disdains him into his own (and his beloved's) image. The conceit of the last stanza of "Canonization" is an optical one, but its "shutting up" is nevertheless characteristic of Donne's monetized poetics.

Notes

1. *A Sermon Preached at Greenwich, Aprill 30. 1615*, in *Sermons*, 1:1.
2. John Carey, "Donne and Coins," in *English Renaissance Studies Presented to Dame Helen Gardner*, ed. John Carey (Oxford: Clarendon, 1980), 151.

3. Aristotle, *De Anima*, Book 2, chapter 1, in *Basic Works of Aristotle*, ed. Richard McKeon (New York: Random House, 1941), 535–60.

4. "A Valediction Forbidding Mourning," 24.

5. *Sermons*, 6:3.

6. According to C. E. Challis in *The Tudor Coinage* (Manchester University Press, 1978), 232, gold comprised less than 3 percent of the volume of sixteenth-century mint output by weight.

7. Eric Ketteredge, *Trade and Banking in Early Modern England* (Manchester University Press, 1988), 98–99.

8. Craig Muldrew, *The Economy of Obligation: The Culture of Credit and Social Relations in Early Modern England* (New York: St. Martin's, 1998); and "'Hard Food for Midas': Cash and Its Social Value in Early Modern England," *Past and Present* 170 (2001), 78–120.

9. "The Canonization," 3.

10. John Stubbes, *Donne: The Reformed Soul* (New York: Viking, 2006), 277–82.

11. *Letters*, 189–90.

CHAPTER 17

Sexuality

Catherine Bates

Donne's poetry took some time to come into fashion. For a long while it was greeted, albeit with varying degrees of enthusiasm, as all but incomprehensible: at best, a poetry that was open to misunderstanding and accessible to only a few elite and elect "understanders."[1] His contemporaries were at a loss to say what his love poetry in particular was doing, except that it was not doing what it might have been expected to do or what had been done before – Petrarchan lyric – and it did not even conform to what, by that time, had already become well recognized as that venerable tradition's counter-discourses. As his fellow poet Thomas Carew observed, Donne's love poetry banished outright the timeless conceits of Petrarchanism – its classical mythology, ageless metaphors, and claims to immortal fame – filling the scene instead with the frangible objects of everyday life: clothes, clocks, crucibles, coins. Above all, Donne's poetry sounded different, doing away with the decorous measures that had long been practiced in and expected of lyric, and replacing them with the accentual rhythms of everyday speech, as if the sounds of the street and of ordinary conversation had invaded the otherwise airless confines of the bedroom. For Ben Jonson this constituted a hangable offence, and for many years Donne's "rough" measures were smoothed away, regularized, much as Wyatt's had been, or simply put aside and not read at all.

It was because it contemporized experience, situating it within the familiar sights and local sounds that surrounded them, that Donne's love poetry seemed to his contemporaries alien and strange. With some notable exceptions (Coleridge being one), it would take another three centuries – by which time those sights and sounds were well and truly antiquated – before that poetry's break with tradition was heard to chime with a revolution in poetic idiom and an alteration of metric – "a new appeal to the ear," as T. S. Eliot called it – and began to look modern, to sound contemporary, for the first time.[2] Donne's verse seemed to match the poetry of the present moment, a poetry that must of necessity be *"difficult"* and, in responding to a massively varied and complex civilization, be "more and more comprehensive, more allusive, more indirect."[3] Of course, Donne's poetry is still greeted with varying degrees of enthusiasm, and his best critics are no less wary of claims to comprehend it than his earliest: "[c]omprehension is precisely what Donne studies have always been forced to defer."[4] But his decisive reintroduction into the canon in the first half of the twentieth century as the master of ambiguity and indirection was consolidated in subsequent decades, when a certain putting of sex into discourse, the rise of the "heterosexual imaginary," the sentimental tradition, and a sexual revolution resulted in Donne's poetry being increasingly recognized, appreciated, embraced, and, in some quarters, canonized for love.

In such a context, it seems entirely self-evident that a chapter on sexuality should be included in a collection of essays on Donne. With its faintly medicalized air and hints of dispositions, orientations, and identities to be pinpointed, measured, and ascertained, "sexuality" is not, naturally, a Donnean locution. The poet has plenty of words for what we might call sexual activity: "amorous delicacies," "dalliance," "fruition," "joys," "lust," "passions," "sport," even, arguably, "sex" itself. But the word he uses for what we would call sexuality – one that, along with its cognates, is within his English poetry the most commonly used word by quite some margin – is "love," a word of suitably ancient origin whose multiple linguistic forms and meanings, deriving from an Indo-European base, have extended across worlds of time and space to include notions of inclination, piety, hope, agreeableness, affection, friendship, libido, and confusion (all aspects that Donne's love poetry might be said to feature in spades).[5]

With this focus on "love" coming into fashion, however, came a certain amount of fashioning. In particular, there has been a tendency in Donne criticism to mould the poet into the image he appeared to reflect and, in so doing, to extrapolate from his signature effects a continuous, self-identical, sovereign subject – most often hypostasized as a living breathing historicized human person – as if the centripetal pull of biography and its shaping narrative of chronological sequence and development were ultimately irresistible, even in those places where such "life-writing" tendencies were deplored.[6] Which is not to level any bland charges of naïveté: persona and poet have, of course, long been scrupulously distinguished in Donne studies, as "Jack" and "Dr. Donne" have been treated as transparent self-fictions among an already extensive repertoire of dramatic roles, and much work done on the poet's multiple ventriloquisms and the construction of his poetic "voice."[7] But whether critics love Donne or (in equal measure, since it amounts to much the same thing) love to hate him, the effect is often the same, and that, by and large, is to impute behind the performance a controlling mind – an actor or author, a writing or speaking subject – whether that subject is understood as speaking from the heart, as knowingly fashioning a "self" for some ulterior purpose, or as peddling social or sexual fantasy.[8] Not infrequently, this creature hardens into a distinct figure, "John Donne" or Donne "the man" – "man" in such cases often being the operative word – as critics set about fashioning a figure with whom, depending on their theoretical or political position, they may either identify ("Donne" as the first great poet of mutual love, for example) or, in loudly abominating, assert their own, quite different affiliations ("Donne" as the rampant misogynist, and so on).

This is not so much Renaissance self-fashioning as other-fashioning: the presenting of a Renaissance writer in such a way as to reflect back the critic's own image (generally an idealized one) or, failing that, to damn him for looking different. Stanley Fish identifies a series of "critical romances" in which, over the years, Donne has been cast as hero (ahead of his time, master of authenticity, consummate craftsman, political radical, and so forth), but his own position – a very public purging of Donne ("Donne is sick … Donne is bulimic")[9] – is no less symptomatic, although it might more accurately be said to characterize what Ben Saunders has seen as the most typical and intense kind of critical romance that finds itself attaching to Donne: the "classic 'love-hate relationship.'"[10] A performance in its own right – indeed, something of a tour de force – Fish's essay excoriates the poet for his showmanship, for the sheer staginess with which he enacts a "dislodgement of the centered self" and parades like "one who is without a center," leaving the reader "wondering if there is or could be anything real – anything other than artifice – in his performance."[11] For the critic, evidently, this is the ultimate horror. Donne is lambasted for being "able to say anything or many things as he combines and recombines words and letters into whatever figurative, and momentarily real, pattern he desires," as if this were not the act axiomatic of poiesis itself and as fine a description as any of poetry or, indeed, of any literary art.[12] Fish's Donne, in other words, is condemned for not reflecting back the critic's image of himself: centered, meaningful, professional, "real," with something substantial, concrete, and useful to say, as opposed to simply "made up." Perhaps Donne has always been a poet for poets rather than for critics.

This may seem a roundabout way of considering the question of sexuality in relation to Donne, but it brings to the fore two issues that, if not addressed, are set to perpetuate a certain amount of repetition and circularity. In the first place, accounts of "sexuality" as it might find itself represented in "Donne" cannot be dissociated from critical responses and interventions that, highly invested, could indeed be said to constitute so many romances, love affairs, or love-hate relationships in themselves. In the second place (and no doubt precisely to keep the above association *in situ*), there remains a stubborn determination to keep a certain "Donne" in play – namely, a continuous, self-identical, historicized, preferably embodied, by default gendered, but at bottom essentially humanist subject – as is nowhere more evident than in the denial and panic that ensues where that subject is felt to be absent. These two issues, intimately related as they are, require a little further probing.

One of the motifs to appear most constantly in Donne's poetry, and particularly in those poems that are most frequently identified as celebrating fully shared and requited love, is the specular narcissism that all such relations entail. Poem after poem details the way in which the lovers' mutual gaze does not show other to other but rather reflects self back to self: "My face in thine eye, thine in mine appears," a reflection that in this case also extends to the "true plain hearts" that are manifest in each face ("The Good Morrow," 15, 16); lovers are to be praised by future generations for making "the glasses of your eyes" into "mirrors" ("The Canonization," 41, 42); if not the eyes themselves, then their issue, teardrops, will reflect back the other's face to themselves, "Let me pour forth / My tears before thy face ... For thy face coins them, and thy stamp they bear" ("A Valediction of Weeping," 1–3); "I fix mine eye on thine, and there / Pity my picture burning in thine eye, / My picture drowned in a transparent tear" ("Witchcraft by a Picture," 1–3); at its very best, the mutual gaze replicates an infinite series of miniature "I"s, "pictures in our eyes to get / Was all our propagation" ("The Ecstasy," 11–12). In his magisterial book on Shakespeare's sonnets, Joel Fineman notes the specular narcissism that is entailed in any love relation that is commemorated by a poetry of praise – where an idealized object reflects back an idealized subject – but the logical next step is to apply this insight to the relation between critic and poet: not with a view to denying that relation but rather to acknowledging it and giving it its due.[13] The critic who pores admiringly over Donne's poetry, then, might be seen to behave much like the lover who reads the word "Donne" engraved on a window pane only to see their own face reflected back in it: "it shows thee to thee, / And clear reflects thee to thine eye" ("A Valediction of My Name in the Window," 9–10). It is not to shatter but better understand the satisfactions and investments entailed in such writing and reading – such looking and seeing – that what might be called a kind of "quantum criticism" should be applied to all such operations in the future, a criticism that accepts the fact that observation itself has a material bearing on the results and that the picture of Donne that ensues (or of love or "sexuality" for that matter) is in large part a product of that relation.

Occasional examples notwithstanding, such good practice can prove difficult to sustain and – if only as a way of making sense of the sheer variety of "sexualities" that appear in Donne's poems – there is all too often a tendency to revert to an assumed biographical entity as that which stands behind these many masquerades, or at least to flesh out his various speakers as if they, too, constituted similarly bodied, gendered beings ("voice" being understood to emanate from such supposedly stable entities and not the other way round). Variety, of course, is presented as a "sexuality" in its own right – the "so much loved variety" of the Ovidian omnivore ("Variety," 2), free to sample any number of whores, not to mention boys or goats, available on London's riotous and libertine streets (see also "Satire IV," 128; "Satire I," 40; and "The Juggler"). In addition, there are the "heterosexual" poems, understood as being addressed for the most part by a male voice – alternately promiscuous or "monogamous" – to female ears (or sometimes to other female parts), although a few of these have also been attributed to female speakers who are assumed to be addressing men (such as "Break of Day," "Confined Love," "Self Love," and "Woman's Constancy"). Then there are verse letters addressed by a presumed male speaker to named male friends or patrons that might be described as "homosocial" or even "homoerotic"; elegies and lyrics in which the relations of a presumptively male speaker with a sado-masochistic Cupid might be similarly described; and indeed religious poems in which the same speaker's relations with God could be seen to amount to much the same. Even where this bewildering array of positions or orientations is seen as so many performances – with nods in the direction of gender and sexuality being always "performatively enacted" rather than innate – there can remain a tendency to posit, behind the performance, a voluntarist subject, a human agent, an actor and author who assumes a gender or sexuality of choice for purposes of, for example, experimentation or display.[14] A good case here is the critical response to the overtly lesbian love epistle, "Sapho to Philaenis," which (once admitted into the canon at all) has, in the main, been interpreted – whether sympathetically or otherwise – as a piece of play-acting: an "entering-into," impersonation, or brief exhilarating foray into other-speak that is nevertheless always framed, ultimately, by the architectonic mind of the (male – that is always assumed) maker.

One of the reasons why this subject-position so often resurfaces in readings of Donne is that, for good or ill, there remains a certain professional investment in it – in the assumption that, behind it all, there must always be a "subject-who-knows" – as Stanley Fish's vigorous defense makes plain. But the costs of assuming that position are plain too: not only the wholesale rejection of poiesis *per se* (a loss large enough in itself) but, more locally for the purposes of this essay, the sense that to project that centered self onto "Donne" or his various speakers is to miss what is genuinely radical about his poetry, which is precisely that it ritually and reiteratively performs sexuality and gender without the assumption of any such "center" at all. In order to appreciate the extent to which critics have made sense of the "variety" in Donne's poetry by filling that gap with various characters and personae whose narratives, positions, orientations, and views have already been assumed in advance, it can be an instructive exercise to read his "heterosexual" poems as "homosexual" or his "male-voiced" poems as "female-voiced" (and, of course, vice versa). For in the alienating and disorientating effects that follow, it becomes more difficult to deny that, as Saunders (who performs just such an exercise) puts it, "the gender of a representation is no more 'inherent' or self-declaring than any other aspect of its meaning" and, as a consequence, that "gender is itself always already a form of representation and therefore something that is recognized and produced in the interactive process of interpretation."[15]

Once narratives ascribed to "Donne" or to his speakers are put aside (life-stories that, it has to be said, can seem somewhat caricatured or wish-fulfilling in the behavior they impute to the rakish youth, the loving husband, the "strong" woman, and so on), sexuality and gender emerge in all their fluidity, variability, changeability, and contingency. To this extent, Stanley Fish is exactly right: attempts on the part of the poet to "confirm to himself that he is a self, someone who exceeds the theatrical production of signs and shows" in order to demonstrate that "behind the words ... stands a self-possessed being" are indeed what fail.[16] But for readers to fashion such a "self" and either to screen it onto Donne and his speakers or to mourn its absence there, is to miss the point that any such entity – and any identity, gender, or sexuality that might attach to it – is never anything more than a production, a fragile holding together and public reiteration of such "words" (never, one might say, anything other than poetry). To admit such a thing might not come without costs itself – it might entail on the part of the critic an avowal of radical instability, for one thing ("the horror, the horror" is Fish's comment at such a prospect),[17] not to mention a public renunciation of any supposed impartiality – but the gain, arguably, might be a closer appreciation of Donne as a poet and a proximity to those whom his earliest printer addressed as the "UNDERSTANDERS," as opposed to mere "*Readers*," of his poetry.[18]

A number of Donne's traditionally best-loved poems appear to offer instructions as to how they should be read and to envisage future readers who will find in them a model – "A pattern" ("The Canonization," 45) or "Rule and example" ("Valediction of the Book," 14) – of love. Readings that have done so – and there are many – may be said to have followed these instructions to the letter. Yet the texts offered up for such interpretation remain provisional: anticipated, imagined, but not yet realized. The famous "verse," "sonnets," and "hymns" of "The Canonization" (30, 32, 35), like the "annals," "records," and "all-gravèd tome" of the "Valediction of the Book" (12, 18, 20), remain to be written. And the prospective readers of such poems are no more substantial either but equally notional and speculative, like the shadowy eavesdropper of "The Ecstasy" who virtually disappears into the conditional tense: "If any ... That ... souls' language understood ... Within convenient distance stood," he might depart "purer then he came" (21, 22, 24, 28), "if some lover ... Have heard this dialogue of one, / Let him still mark us" (73, 74–75; *has* any such reader stood, understood, heard, and marked?). "The Relic," likewise, would ideally address the putative readers of a newly idolatrous age (in Reformation England a suitably distant if not fantastical prospect): "I would have that age by this paper taught / What miracles we harmless lovers wrought" (21–22). In the suppositional space they open up between the not-yet readers of not-yet texts, such examples propose a greater degree of circumspection in approaching the poetry of Donne than has sometimes been apparent, and a willingness to allow for interpretations that put all positions – insofar as they hold out the promise of stability on the matter of sexuality, gender, or anything else – into play.

Notes

1. From the unsigned address from "The Printer to the Understanders" in *Poems*, 1633, ctd. in *Critical Heritage*, 84.
2. T. S. Eliot, *Selected Prose of T. S. Eliot*, ed. Frank Kermode (London: Faber and Faber, 1975), 272. From an essay on Milton originally published in 1947.
3. T. S. Eliot, "The Metaphysical Poets," *Selected Prose*, 65.

4. William Kerrigan, "What Was Donne Doing?," *South Central Review* 4.2 (1987), 2–3.
5. See "love, n^1.," *OED Online*.
6. See Thomas Docherty, *John Donne, Undone* (London: Methuen, 1986).
7. Elizabeth D. Harvey, *Ventriloquized Voices: Feminist Theory and English Renaissance Texts* (London: Routledge, 1992); and Ronald Corthell, *Ideology and Desire in Renaissance Poetry: The Subject of Donne* (Detroit, MI: Wayne State University Press, 1997).
8. For representative examples of these three positions, see: Ilona Bell, "Gender Matters: The Women in Donne's Poems," in *CCJD*, 201–16; Marotti, *Coterie*; and Antony Easthope, *Poetry and Phantasy* (Cambridge University Press, 1989).
9. Stanley Fish, "Masculine Persuasive Force: Donne and Verbal Power," in *Soliciting*, 250, 223.
10. Ben Saunders, *Desiring Donne: Poetry, Sexuality, Interpretation* (Cambridge, MA: Harvard University Press, 2006), 20.
11. Fish, "Masculine," 231, 235, 241.
12. Fish, "Masculine," 225.
13. Joel Fineman, *Shakespeare's Perjured Eye: The Invention of Poetic Subjectivity in the Sonnets* (Berkeley, CA: University of California Press, 1986).
14. Judith Butler, *Gender Trouble: Feminism and the Subversion of Identity* (New York: Routledge, 1990), 33.
15. Saunders, *Desiring*, 137.
16. Fish, "Masculine," 247.
17. Fish, "Masculine," 247.
18. *Critical Heritage*, 84.

CHAPTER 18

Donne and the Passions

Christopher Tilmouth

Donne is commonly described as a passionate poet, and with reason. Fear, for example, is powerfully evoked in his "Elegy on the Lady Markham" where death's touch is an encroaching sea that doth "roar, and gnaw" (5) and "breaks our banks when ere it takes a friend" (6). "The Storm's" description of wretched anxiety in face of shipwreck prompts the same feeling:

> as sin-burdened souls from graves will creep
> At the last day, some forth their cabins peep,
> And tremblingly'ask, what news, and do hear so,
> As jealous husbands, what they would not know.   (47–50)

Donne can invoke emotion more directly too; witness "Satire III's" challenge to readers to gauge true religion's magnitude: "O, if thou dar'st, fear this; / This fear great courage and high valour is" (15–16). In contrast to terror, the corporeal turn Donne gives to Neoplatonism's traditionally chaste conception of love promises another kind of passion. "The Ecstasy" describes love as a mutual comprehension of souls, in that respect reproducing the idealism of Plato's *Symposium* and its Florentine imitators (Ficino, Castiglione). However, for Donne, unlike Plato, this passionate state also encompasses a physical dimension, bodily contact being the medium by which psychic union assumes everyday life's emotional and sensory qualities (hence, "souls descend / T'affections and to faculties / Which sense may . . . apprehend," 65–67). The ramifications of that ideal are evident elsewhere, for instance in "To the Countess of Bedford ('You have refined me')," where Donne admires Countess Bedford as the soul of virtue and beauty yet permits himself to worship her as "virtue's temple, not as she" (44), adoring "eyes, hands, bosom . . . not as consecrate, but merely'as fair" (46, 49). Emotion here derives equally from spiritual and corporeal stimuli, each edifying the other. Bodily ties are not always temperate though. Another affective Donne is the lyricist who, understanding that passionate experiences are physiologically grounded, registers their deleterious effect on the body. This Donne follows the *Greek Anthology* 5.78 in lamenting that kiss which literally "sucks [forth] two souls, and vapours both away" ("The Expiration," 2), and regrets, likewise, that, "Since thou and I sigh one another's breath" ("A Valediction of Weeping," 26), "When thou sigh'st, thou ... sigh'st my soul away" ("Song ['Sweetest love, I do not go'']," 25–26).

However, the descriptive or preaching Donne of my opening examples here is a rarity; "The Ecstasy," struggling to give phenomenological content to the ideal it articulates, cannot escape its abstractions; and poetry is never more clichéd than when dissolving in Petrarchan sighs and tears. Ultimately, the *vitality* of Donne's encounter with the passions derives not from these topoi but from the interpersonal cast of his writing, which sees his subjectivity locked always in frictional encounters with another party. His poetry typically presents not introspective emotions (long brooded upon, or subjected to careful ethical assessment) but passions of the moment, feelings activated, impromptu, by the fact of engagement with another. We witness an extemporary voice thrown out – for "Man is but a voice," Donne says, "a groaning ... a Trumpet ... a thunderclap"[1] – a voice not speaking to itself but reaching, intersubjectively, towards someone else, and exuding, discovering, generating passion in the tension of that transactional gesture.

Two contexts influence Donne's interest in the spontaneous affectivity of verbal exchanges. One is Augustine's ethics. Donne's fascination with Augustine is well documented, and *De Civitate Dei* had a particular bearing on early modern understandings of the passions. Book XIV of *De Civitate* contends that man's moral worth should be measured by the orientation, the directedness, of his will as manifested in everyday emotions. A will dedicated to charity will express itself through its love of God and His creations, thus directing itself outwards. Augustine emphasizes that the secondary passions derived from such love will be spiritually valuable. A will which, by contrast, defines itself through self-love – its own, not God's, measures of value – and which thus directs its impulses inwards, can only produce those passions condemned by St. Paul as carnal. Donne, who surely had this distinction in mind when he asked Bedford, "What hate can hurt our bodies like our love?" ("To the Countess of Bedford ['T'have written then']," 53), recalled Augustine's doctrine repeatedly in his sermons. In 1617, for example, he preached, "the first thing that the will ... does, is to affect, to choose, to love something."[2] He then warned against self-love (the misdirection of this impulse), but he also reassured his audience that a soul "transported upon any particular worldly pleasure," once turned to God, could find "just occasion to exercise the same affection piously ... which had before so sinfully ... possest it."[3] In 1623 he made the theme of Christ's tears a synecdoche for the claim that Jesus experienced all human passions, yet experienced them as "sanctified in the roote"[4] – as spiritual, because born of self-sacrificing charity and not self-love. Other sermons reflected similarly on sanctified joy and fear, underlining their all-absorbing quality: "he that fears the Lord, fears him with all his fear ... God takes no half affections."[5] Donne's poems do not mirror these sermons' moralizing cast, but they do capture Augustine's emphasis on passion's capacity to preoccupy the soul by giving it a particular *directedness*.

My second context is rhetorical. Rhetoric training was a given of Elizabethan education, and Donne would have found in Cicero's *De Oratore* and Quintilian's *Institutio Oratoria* instruction in the simulation of passions. *De Oratore* II.189's argument that auto-arousal on the rhetorician's part is an essential prerequisite in moving others was endlessly cited in contemporary sources, witness Wright: "*Cicero* expressly teacheth that it is ... impossible for an Orator to stirre vp a Passion in his auditors, except he bee first affected with the same passion himselfe ... & therefore *Horace* obserued, that he which will make me weepe must first weepe himselfe."[6] Cicero himself offered scant instruction in how to achieve this auto-arousal, but Quintilian was more forthcoming with *Institutio* IX detailing various "figures of thought" best suited to evoking strong emotions, namely: *interrogatio* (rhetorical questions), *dubitatio* (contrived hesitation), *ecphonesis* (exclamation), *communicatio* (simulated discussion with another), prosopopoeia, apostrophe, *hypotyposis* (vivid description appealing to sight), insinuation, and aposiopesis. Brian Vickers has demonstrated that Renaissance rhetoricians accorded growing emphasis to the moving of the passions such that Quintilian's *figurae sententiae* assumed center-stage in textbooks.[7] Hence, Peacham's 1593 *Garden of Eloquence* identifies its "second order" of figures – exclamation, *interrogatio*, and other figures of consultation all of which directly button-hole the auditor – as "verie sharpe and vehement, by which the sundrie ... passions ... are properly ... vttered."[8] For Peacham, the first and third orders (which play upon word repetition, word omission, amplification, and structuring) are but pleasantly diverting by contrast. In his poetry, Donne, I suggest, mirrors and develops this prioritizing of emotional button-holing, privileging *figurae sententiae* over those figures of merely verbal dexterity favored by such earlier poets as Sir Philip Sidney and, incidentally, by Donne the prose preacher.

Poet-Donne thus produces the reality-effect of high passion, first, by over-emphasizing the vocative directedness of his lyrics. "The Apparition" punctuates its address to a treacherous lover with the invocations, "O murd'ress" (1), "feigned vestal" (5), and "poor aspen wretch" (11). "Woman's Constancy" announces its accusatory "thou" four times in three lines and then directs six questions (implicit charges) at her/him. *Interrogatio* thus becomes Quintilian's *communicatio*, the performance of an imagined discussion, but one where the speaker, by purporting merely to ventriloquize the other's excuses, condemns the latter the more. Meantime, Holy Sonnet 18 takes aim at Christ, subjecting him to ten urgent questions. *Interrogatio* exerts an emotive effect here, as also in "The Sun Rising," which opens vocatively ("Busy old fool, unruly Sun," 1), then loads its addressee with clipped interrogations: "Why dost thou thus" (2), "Why should'st thou think?" (12). Here, though, Donne betters the rhetoricians' example, interleaving Quinitilian's questioning with insistent imperatives, his own contribution to the *figurae sententiae*: "go chide / Late schoolboys" (5–6), "Go tell court-huntsmen" (7), etc. Imperatives are Donne's default mode, indicative of a will that characteristically experiences each passion as sharply directed towards another and that (in the Holy Sonnets) *demands* God's prevenient grace in order to initiate repentance. "Satire I" thus begins with an arresting combination of command and vocative address: "Away thou fondling motley humorist" (1). "His Picture," "The Anagram," and "To His Mistress Going to Bed" likewise commence with imperatives. In "The Prohibition" identical commands initiate and conclude each verse. The poet who urges God to "Batter my heart" (Holy Sonnet 10) opens Holy Sonnet 7 (XI) ("Spit in my face, you Jews") with a catalogue of imperatives ordering his own personal Passion. Here, the sinner-persona demands that penitential suffering be imposed on him as proof that he is in receipt of grace – proof, because such suffering attests that he is now expiating his guilt, has been "counted *worthy* to suffer rebuke for the name of Christ," and so "finds [Christ's] seale printed upon" him.[9] Elsewhere, however, imperatives reveal more ambivalent emotional states. The phrasing in "Love's Usury" and "Twickenham Garden" betrays a lack of self-command even as Donne's speakers strive to be assertive: "Love, *let* my body reign, and *let* / Me travel," "Only *let* me love none" ("Love's Usury," 5–6, 13; emphasis added); "Love *let* me / Some senseless piece of this place be" ("Twickenham Garden," 15–16; emphasis added). Likewise, whilst Holy Sonnet 4 begins with an octave of three imperatives inviting Armageddon, this is balanced against a sestet of three more revoking brash confidence, imploring instead a suspension of time, and instructing God, "Teach me how to repent" (13).

Turbulence is preeminently apparent in "The Canonization." Here, the opening stanza's imperatives defying criticism of Donne's love-devotion ("For God's sake hold your tongue," 1) are followed by rhetorical questions ("Who says my tears have overflowed his ground?" 12) collectively excluding the world from the idealized sphere of Donne's canonized lovers. The shift to a calmly indicative mood in subsequent verses, where the couple "build in sonnets pretty rooms" (32), is made possible by the exorcising effect of the initial imperatives and *interrogatio*; yet that shift has its fault-lines. For instance, latterly, in a rare use of prosopopoeia, Donne's speaker ventriloquizes future lovers praying for his and his equally sanctified beloved's intercessionary efforts (the poem thus utilizes vocative phrases but, unusually for Donne, these are directed inwards, towards the persona himself). Absurdly though, the terms in which devotees are imagined invoking the canonized pair – "You, to whom love was peace" (39) – hardly fit this lyric's opening combativeness. Furthermore, whilst Group II and III manuscripts frame the canonized lovers' future imitators as commanding their saints to "beg from above," on their behalf, "A pattern of *your* love" (44, 45, emphasis added), some Group I texts instead read "beg from above / A Pattern of *our* love!" In context, the latter is nonsensical since it introduces, as the later lovers' imperative to their saints, phrasing that only makes sense as an instruction from the saints to those later lovers; yet that inconsistency proves telling if understood as a moment when the persona's prosopopoeiac voicing of others slips, exposing that ventriloquizing voice as, really, the persona's own. Arguably, an imperative ("beg") first lent to a third party is instinctively, even unwittingly, reclaimed by the first-person speaker in a re-imposition of the lyric's opening, passionately self-assertive dynamic. Whatever the case though, Donne's exaggerated use of questions and imperatives throughout his poems clearly puts these forms' implied addressees on the defensive, under pressure. Suggestions of challenge and assertion, even when ambivalent, evoke an immediate emotional charge.

Donne elicits this emotional charge (the reality-effect of passion) by other means too, means which again exceed the precepts of rhetoric and his poetic predecessors' practice. The starkness of interrogatory and imperative relations is matched, as Magnusson shows, by an equally pressurizing use of pronouns, for example in "The Legacy":

> I heard me say, tell her anon
> That myself (that's you, not I),
> Did kill me, 'and when I felt me die,
> I bid me send my heart, when I was gone.   (9–12).[10]

Different kinds of focal effect also give Donne's verse its unique dynamism. Sometimes focal movement is linear, moving rapidly from macroscopic to microscopic scale. Thus, "A Nocturnal upon St Lucy's Day, Being the Shortest Day" begins, "'Tis the year's midnight, and it is the day's" (1), and Holy Sonnet 3 turns from "last scene" (1) to "last mile" (2) to "last pace, / My span's last inch, my minute's latest point" (3–4), its lens magnification increasing with the acceleration towards death. Elsewhere, focal effects arise from rhetorical symmetry. Donne creates lines the scope of which first expands, then contracts, in a feat of chiasmus, each dilation bookended by pronouns or verbs which manifest their power in opposition to that expansion. Such is the effect of "The Sun Rising's" "She's all states, and all princes I" (21). Conversely, the focal point may fall at a line's center. This is best exemplified in Holy Sonnet 13 – "Repair me now, for now mine end doth haste; / I run to death, and death meets me as fast" (2–3) – where the celerity of the motions in play is enacted by the compressed reiteration of "now" and "death," both words literally coming forward, as if personified, to meet the speaker. To these indices of urgent passion we may add, finally, the live force that Donne derives from his writing's improvisatory quality. Poems such as "The Comparison" or "Lovers' Infiniteness" have an improvised air, fired by associationist logic. Where that movement is paratactic (such as every challenge in "Woman's Constancy" being introduced by another "Or … "), the absence of grammatical subordination (and therefore modulation of pace) creates a crescendo of fervor. Donne's inventiveness becomes most charged, though, when actions are implied in the interstices between stanzas. The wit of "The Flea's" protagonist stems from our impression that the woman's threatened, then actual, squashing of the creature in the stanzaic interstices fuels rather than silences the argument; indeed, that the lover is relying on her so to act to clinch his case. *La Corona* likewise exploits the break between its fifth and sixth sonnets to deliver a brilliant touch of antanaclasis. The former ends with the imperative to Christ, "*Moist with one drop of Thy blood my dry soul*" (70); the latter begins adjectivally, "*Moist with one drop of Thy blood, my dry soul* / Shall … be / Freed" (71–74), Donne daring to imagine that grace sought might indeed be conferred, but making the mystery of conferral invisible by staging it between poems.

Donne, then, adopts various devices – innovative variations on the means of auto-arousal prescribed by his rhetorical context – to convey the charge and dynamism of poetic encounters that always have a passionate directedness about them. Nevertheless, C. S. Lewis and Barbara Hardy drew opposite conclusions about his love lyrics, the one thinking them preoccupied with the froth of transitory feelings, oblivious to deeper, more permanent emotions, the other supposing they anatomized precisely how passions manifest themselves.[11] Subsequently, Carey and Marotti divined real, heartfelt emotion in the poems but only by countering their stated sense, reading into Donne's professed insouciance and other-worldly idealism coded protests against real-world marginalization.[12] The religious verse has elicited similarly polarized reactions, Oliver thinking the sonnets' displays of feeling contrived and strategically performative, Stachniewski insisting that their struggle with Calvinist despair bespeaks emotional conviction.[13] Such divergences are possible because, impassioned though these works are, they are framed in the moment, as products of frictional but (in narrative terms) isolated encounters. One may juxtapose individual poems to create a narrative, but this is only ever a fabrication: it remains impossible to verify how absolute or deep-seated a charge each poem really bears. This is the more true because, whilst other contemporaries – Spenser, Chapman, Jonson – explored the passions with a demonstrably ethical intent, instructive purpose (which might promise some decisiveness) is absent here. Donne's investment in performative rhetoric renders his writings' tone and commitment ambiguous. We are offered only voices, captured at moments of interaction; sketches of impassioned feeling, but without the certainty of whether those feelings flow from composed experience, are the caprice (or calculation) of an instant, or are indeed affects generated by linguistic *jouissance* itself – since, as Montaigne grasped, "An Orator ... in the *play* of his pleading, shall be mooued" (increasingly so, minute by minute) simply "at the sound of his owne voice."[14] How often do Donne's poems constitute exactly that last, factitious kind of auto-arousal?

Evasiveness pervades Donne's writings. In "A Valediction Forbidding Mourning," for instance, the geometer's imagery might seem to epitomize heartfelt attachment because, whilst one compass arm can only "lean" forlornly "after" (31) the other as a radius is established, it nonetheless anticipates eventual reunion when the pair of dividers, currently open, will be re-closed. Donne, however, thwarts this expectation in his final stanza, twisting his metaphor to emphasize only the drawing of a circle. The assurance, "Thy firmness makes my circle just, / And makes me end where I begun" (35–36), is mathematically beautiful, but it implies that, on completing his circuit, this lover will be as distant as ever from his pivotal beloved; hence, that the pose of passionate confession is less than might appear.

Three factors explain such evasiveness. First, a suspicion of passionate involvement *per se*: Marotti put forward this case in analyzing Donne's libertine poetry,[15] and both "Witchcraft by a Picture" and "A Valediction of Weeping" suggest as much. The "witchcraft" here is a beloved's capacity to exert the kind of intersubjective pressure widely seen in Renaissance literature, a bond which compels Donne's lover to confront his own emotional vulnerability, hence: "I fix mine eye on thine, and there / Pity my picture burning in thine eye" (1–2). The speaker deals with this exposure by kissing away the beloved's reflective tears and proclaiming, "My picture vanished, vanish fears / That I can be endamaged by that art" (10–11); but it is telling that (as in *La Corona*) the moment of physical contact goes unspoken, being merely implied between the stanzas as if, again, emotional involvement were being evaded. The alternative to evasion is "Weeping's" global inundation: there, the tears the lover finds himself shedding for his beloved become, themselves, drowned by her tears, her waters overflowing his world in a tide of passion.

A second explanation for the qualified, provisional nature of the poems' engagement with affect lies in the fact of distraction. Donne famously said,

> I am not all here, I am here now preaching upon this text, and I am at home in my Library considering . . . *S. Hierome* . . . I am speaking to you, and yet I consider . . . in the same instant, what . . . you will say to one another, when I have done. You are not all here neither; you are here now, hearing me, and yet you are thinking that you have heard a better Sermon somewhere else . . . You are here, and you remember . . . that now you think of it, this had been the fittest time, now, when every body else is at Church to have made such and such a private visit; and because you would bee there, you are there.[16]

Elsewhere, reflecting on his efforts at fervent prayer, Donne acknowledges that, though he might "talke on, in the . . . posture of praying," his mind wanders at "the noise of a Flie, . . . the ratling of a Coach, . . . the whining of a doore; . . . a memory of yesterdays pleasures, a feare of tomorrow's dangers."[17] No passion is, for Donne, a pure, concentrated mental state, whatever the continuity of outward speech – of a voice in transaction – might suggest. He tells even Christ, with an obvious pun on his name, "When Thou hast done, Thou hast not done" ("A Hymn to God the Father," 5); the same applies to his lyrics.

Third, the poems indicate more neurotic sources of self-evasion, another explanation for their emotional reserve. Holy Sonnet 2 contains the perplexing simile, "Thou art like a pilgrim which abroad hath done / Treason, and durst not turn to whence he's fled" (2–3). "Pilgrim," "abroad," "Treason," "fled": all are problematic words for an apostate Catholic once encouraged to consider Rome as home. My focus, though, is on the lines' final, paradoxical clause. Following Robbins's gloss of the near-identical verses in *Metempsychosis* stanza 10,[18] one might take this to mean "dares not (re)turn to that (good) place from which he's fled" (the place perhaps being Paradise; the flight, original sin). An alternative would be: "dares not turn to that place where [reading 'whence' as where-hence] he in truth already is, his bolt-hole." Either way, the idea is of a conscience refusing to confront itself, and that notion fascinated Donne. His epistle "To Mr Henry Wotton ('Sir, more than kisses')" avows that if ever men "Durst look for themselves and themselves retrieve" – an improbable event – "They would like strangers greet themselves" (44–45). Another epistle, "To Mr Rowland Woodward ('Like one who'in her third widowhood')," imagines the benefit that might follow "if we into ourselves will turn" (22). Again, "Goodfriday, 1613" revolves around the conceit of turning one's back on the Passion, only to find its events "present yet unto ... memory, / For that looks [eternally] towards them" (34–35), and thus to feel Christ's accusing gaze. Donne, then, knew what it was to evade introspection and manifests as much in his impassioned yet slippery poems.

That Donne mistrusted the emotions' invasive power is clear. "The Calm" revealingly describes "hope of gain," "the queasy pain / Of being beloved and loving," and "thirst / Of honour" as forces which threaten to "out [push] me," dispossessing man of his own agency (39–42). Donne's oft-declared project in his letters is, instead, precisely to "out push" his passions. Epistles being the means by which he "ideates" things (forms an idea of them, by objectifying them on the page; "To Mr Henry Wotton ['Sir, more than kisses']," 4), they thereby become the vehicle not just for conveying his "soul" or "affections" to another in an "extasie,"[19] but also, implicitly, for stabilizing those same affections and disburdening himself of them. "The Triple Fool" reveals how easily that strategy may backfire. Its speaker hopes to "allay" his "pains" by drawing them "Through rhyme's vexation, ... / Grief brought to numbers" (8–10). However, in practice "when I have done so" (12) – the pun on Donne's name lends "have" a momentarily stabilizing force – another soon "Doth set and sing my pain" (14), and through that act of voicing unleashes the passion anew. Donne may therefore dream of a pure, fluid, Stoic self, untouched by the remora of worldly emotions: such is the fantasy idealized in those fishes that "glide" through life, "leaving no print where they pass" ("To Mr Henry Wotton ['Sir, more than kisses']," 56), which Wotton is enjoined to emulate. But the poet cannot hold to that dream, even as he articulates it: the same passage here also likens the autarkic Stoic, less flatteringly, to a gastropod, wryly urging Wotton: "Follow (for he is easy paced) this snail" (51). Ultimately, Donne is too much the poet of transactions, of charged encounters and feelings "out pushed" upon others (however ambiguously), to keep faith with any ataractic ideal. If anything, what I have called his impassioned voice's directed quality testifies to one of the great vocabulary shifts of the seventeenth and eighteenth centuries: the gradual abandonment of the word "passion," with its suggestions of passive suffering and exposure to powers invading the soul from without, in favor of "emotion," a word implying, rather, an outward moving force, something exuded by an agent – a will – who is embedded, interactively, within his world. Donne was, in this new sense, an "emotional" poet *par excellence*.

Notes

1. *Sermons*, 9:61–62.
2. *Sermons*, 1:242.
3. *Sermons*, 1:236.
4. *Sermons*, 4:328.
5. *Sermons*, 6:109.
6. Thomas Wright, *The Passions of the Minde in Generall* (London, 1604), 172.
7. Brian Vickers, *In Defence of Rhetoric* (Oxford: Clarendon Press, 1988), 276.
8. Henry Peacham, *The Garden of Eloquence* (London, 1593), 91–92.
9. *Sermons*, 3:343.
10. See Lynne Magnusson, "Donne's Language: The Conditions of Communication," in *CCJD*, 183–200.
11. C. S. Lewis, "Donne and Love Poetry in the Seventeenth Century," in *Selected Literary Essays*, ed. Walter Hooper (Cambridge University Press, 1969), 106–25; Barbara Hardy, "Thinking and Feeling in the *Songs and Sonnets*," in *John Donne: Essays in Celebration*, ed. A. J. Smith (London: Methuen, 1972), 73–88.
12. Carey, *Mind*; Marotti, *Coterie*.
13. P. M. Oliver, *Donne's Religious Writing: A Discourse of Feigned Devotion* (London: Longman, 1997); John Stachniewki, *The Persecutory Imagination: English Puritanism and the Literature of Religious Despair* (Oxford: Clarendon Press, 1991).
14. Michel de Montaigne, *The Essayes*, trans. John Florio (London, 1603), 503.
15. Marotti, *Coterie*, 74–78.

16. *Sermons*, 3:110.
17. *Sermons*, 7:264–65.
18. John Donne, *The Complete Poems of John Donne*, ed. Robin Robbins (New York: Longman, 2010), 434.
19. *Letters*, 20, 10.

CHAPTER 19

Pain

Joseph Campana

What's pain to the poetry of John Donne – punishment or poetics, salve or salvation? Pain is equal parts fact and fiction, mind and body, nature and culture. To say that pain is a context seems to strip it of its insistent corporeality and intransigent mystery. And yet as Esther Cohen argues, "No pain stands naked without a context."[1] Cultural attitudes towards the brute facticity of the body impact how pain is experienced – where we locate it and how we value it, whether it is destructive or transformative, provides remedies or seeks a cure. Much has been said, or perhaps assumed, about the scurrilous Jack Donne – his barbed wit and zeal for pleasure. And perhaps even more can be said about a certain enthusiasm for illness, weakness, and even the anticipation of death. Without pain what would the poetry of John Donne be?

In spite of elaborate attention to Donne's attachment to sickness and death, surprisingly little work approaches directly his entanglement in what C. S. Lewis famously called *The Problem of Pain* (1940). To a large extent, this is a function of an only emerging field of inquiry. The story of pain in the Renaissance is yet to be written; no comprehensive history such as Cohen's yet exists for the era, though of late some scholars have attempted to make sure the pain of early modernity will not stand "naked without a context." Most, indeed, still have recourse to Rosaline Rey's 1993 *The History of Pain*, which attempts to grasp many centuries of suffering, from antiquity to the mid-twentieth century. "If instinct prompts people and animals alike to repel pain with all their energy," she argues, "then from an historian's point of view, the most pressing question might be to attempt to understand and trace man's long struggle with pain."[2] Traces are to be found, she argues, not in the usual provinces of history but in search of "an evasive subject with a dual nature at the crossroads between biology and cultural or social convention." Such an account might be transformative. Rey asks, "Isn't an in-depth analysis of pain also a means of probing the relationship between mind and body, and of examining the dualism that somehow underlies our various ways of thinking?"[3]

To a great extent, to speak for pain and for the history of pain is to resist the powerful sway of Elaine Scarry's influential *The Body in Pain*, which conceives of pain as aversive, privative, and destructive; suffering provokes a "pre-language of cries and groans" and thus results in a loss of the capacity to project "the facts of sentience into speech."[4] The suffering body is rendered an object, becomes victim to a "corporeal engulfment" resulting from the "sheer material factualness" of pain.[5] "Pain's triumph," she argues, is "temptation to invoke analogies to remote cosmologies" in order to apprehend the pain of others; pain "achieves its aversiveness ... by bringing about, even within the radius of several feet, this absolute split between one's sense of one's own reality and the reality of other persons."[6] Whereas Scarry would consider pain a form of experience with world- and language-obliterating properties, Rey, although she too sees pain as essentially aversive, sees pain producing language and idiom rather than false analogies. "Pain," Rey argues, "always has a specific language, whether it is a cry, a sob, or a tensing of the features, and it is a language in and of itself."[7] No doubt this is what Cohen refers to as well when she argues that pain is "a multivalent sign."[8]

But Cohen also considers pain to be "a tool," something neither to be avoided nor merely expressed. Indeed, as Cohen argues, a central paradox in medieval attitudes towards pain is evident in a "tension between the natural human recoiling from one's own pain and the preachers' ubiquitous message that pain was morally beneficial for human virtue."[9] In the complex cultures of medieval devotion, pain was clearly put to work in the service of virtue and godliness. The question of pain's utility becomes central to understanding how early modernity inherits but also revises a certain medieval Christian compact with suffering. Rey's account of the history of pain exhibits less interest in such matters, concerning itself instead with the rise of the Renaissance individual, the Reformation (which she argues "freed the body from the grip of the Church"), the revival of anatomy, and the development of medical procedures, such as surgery, and procedures that conceived of pain as "the supreme ill of the human condition" as pain becomes more and more "the sole province of the physician or surgeon."[10] In essence, Rey's account is one in which the Renaissance witnesses the slow but steady march away from religion and toward Enlightenment, an era of an ever-greater scientific, or knowledge-oriented, approach to pain and its treatment.

And yet, as Jan Frans van Dijkhuizen argues in *Pain and Compassion in Early Modern English Literature and Culture* – a study that both corrects and extends Rey's account of a Renaissance chapter in the history of pain – medical models of suffering were perhaps not primary. "In early modern society," he argues, "the cultural work of attaching meaning to pain was done first and foremost outside the realm of medicine, and ... to a significant extent inside the domain of religion ... during the sixteenth and seventeenth centuries, medicine not only had a limited ability to alleviate pain, but also a limited *conceptual* interest in it."[11] Indeed van Dijkhuizen suggests that the dominant medical paradigm, Galenic theory, "did not see pain as a distinct medical phenomenon with its own specific mechanisms and logic."[12] As a consequence, "The conviction that pain was caused by humoral imbalance also meant that Galenic pain remedies were usually aimed at restoring that balance rather than directly alleviating the pain itself."[13] Galenism was not alone in its seeming indifference to pain. In spite of advancements in surgical practice, "surgery, like theoretical medicine, offered little in the way of an analytical perspective on pain that went beyond the immediate practicalities of pain management through trial and error."[14] Indeed, as Michael Schoenfeldt has argued, in spite of the fact that "the significant cultural productions of early modern Europe ... were deeply invested in the cultivation and articulation of pain," the medical tradition of the era placed only "sporadic emphasis on the deliberate amelioration of suffering."[15] Thus "significant cultural productions" that dealt with suffering, such as literary works, may have especially proved valuable for their "anesthetic effects" in an era without analgesics.[16] Stephen Pender similarly argues for this profound interpenetration of pain and aesthetics when he argues that the Renaissance witnesses a massive sea change "from the dominant conception of pain as a sensation related to touch to various interventions that suggest pain is a threat to vitality itself."[17]

Of course, to suggest the centrality of religious, as opposed to medical, contexts for pain is not to suggest one model of salvific or virtuous pain seized hold of Donne's England, which is far from true. The Reformation smashed more than idols, and its controversies extended from disagreement about sacraments to deep ambivalence about that touchstone of late medieval devotional adoration, the figure of the suffering Christ. As Deborah Shuger argues, "The figure of the crucified Jesus slips to the margins of English Protestantism, which favored dogmatic theology and devotional introspection over retelling the story of Christ's suffering and death – the pervasive focus of late medieval and Tridentine Catholicism."[18]

Ernst B. Gilman identifies ambivalence about the suffering Christ with a broader iconoclastic disdain: "Few people are likely to have envisioned an 'image' – certainly in its most narrowly proscribed form as a representation of the Trinity, of Christ or his cross, of the Virgin or the saints – without at the same time, perhaps for a fleeting instant charged with horror or glee, envisioning that image destroyed."[19] And as van Dijkhuizen argues, "the Protestant Reformation, in its preoccupation with the theological role of the human body, and of the physical world in general, did much to forge what was in some respects a radical revision of the Catholic concepts of bodily anguish, while the Catholic Reformation was in part an attempt to reassert some of the Catholic attitudes toward pain that reformers were at pains to discredit."[20] And yet in spite of Protestant rejection of pre-Reformation devotional cultures, attachment lingered. As I have suggested elsewhere, even the often-virulently anti-Catholic Edmund Spenser still longed for the ethical and affective touchstone of the suffering Christ.[21] If this was true for Spenser, what attachments might have lingered for Donne? According to van Dijkhuizen, Donne was intrigued and troubled by the possibility of identifying with the suffering of Christ, and the speakers of his poems "both record their desire to partake in the Passion and acknowledge their inability to do so. . . . [T]hey are troubled by a sense that their identification with Christ can only be merely linguistic, always at one remove from genuine participation – both emotional and physical – in the Passion."[22]

What begins to be apparent, quite quickly, is a kind of war for the soul of pain: which context is supreme? Which modalities were available and which was most critical? It seems two primary contexts or modalities competing for preeminence would be *medical* and *religious*, which both Rey and van Dijkhuizen see pulling in opposite directions as they highlight the importance of the *aesthetic* context for pain. And yet some might argue that, in fact, medical and religious contexts significantly intersect. Indeed, Stephen Pender's study of "medical semiotics" locates John Donne, and particularly his prose work *Devotions*, as the very point of intersection.[23] Pender suggests that the pain of a "living, sick body" is central to the interweaving of medical and devotional languages. Just as Donne's works have been insufficiently "examined for Donne's attitudes toward medical thought," so too has "recent critical attention paid to Donne's fascination with anatomy (that is with *dead* bodies) . . . led to a relative neglect of the role of the living body, and thus medical semiotics, in Donne's thought."[24]

More recently, John R. Yamamoto-Wilson's *Pain, Pleasure, and Perversity* considers an "ongoing debate" about suffering in the seventeenth-century.[25]

Yamamoto-Wilson notes not only a struggle between Stoic and Epicurean
ideals, a struggle won in the later part of the century with the Epicurean
endorsement of pleasure, but also an intensification of the eroticization of
both suffering and cruelty. In part, Yamamoto-Wilson investigates this
debate in the context of a series of tensions between Protestant and
Catholic practices, including traditions of hagiography. In so doing he
emphasizes a religious context, one that explores Stoic and Epicurean ideals
and introduces an *ethical* context that attends to how an individual responds
to his or her own pain and the pain of others.[26] In as much as perverse and
eroticized forms of cruelty, directed towards the self or towards others, come
to the fore, Yamamoto-Wilson also explores how a *sexual* context for pain,
one attendant to the eroticization of purportedly aversive experience, is
critical to our understanding of it; indeed, his study is, at least in part,
a genealogy of sadism and masochism as expressions of a perverse pleasure in
pain later codified in sexology and psychoanalysis.

Thus far a series of overlapping, sometimes contradictory, and sometimes nearly indistinguishable, contexts for pain in the Renaissance and in
the works of Donne has emerged – medical, religious, aesthetic, ethical,
sexual. What is a context if not an incitement to conversation rather than
the final answer to a question? As valuable as have been a certain cultural
poetics of pain that dwells upon myriad contexts, colliding anatomy and
surgery with devotional verse, I want to propose that a core concern
emerges when we consider how an *aesthetics of pain* enfolds these concerns
under a more apt rubric.

Esther Cohen tells us "No pain stands naked without a context." And
yet the fantasy of arriving at "the thing itself" has made so many scholars
erstwhile Lears seeking bare and unaccommodated essence: pain without
reference to context or expression. When discussing pain, Scarry remains
more than a little wary of poets, not only when she invokes the "temptation
to invoke analogies to remote cosmologies," but also when she warns
against the danger of finding more seductive and interesting a poet's
expression of pain than instances of real suffering. More recent studies
committed to speaking broadly of human pain, such as Harold Schweizer's
Suffering and the Remedy of Art and David Morris's *The Culture of Pain*,
remain deeply influenced by Scarry's insistence on the silent and unshared
nature of pain. Schweizer claims that "[w]hile suffering is a universal
human predicament, it also remains the most unsharable, incommunicable
mystery, the very epitome of secrecy and particularity."[27] Similarly, in
The Culture of Pain, while David Morris resists the medicalization of
pain and its consequent mechanization of the body, he too affirms the

silence of pain. "The writers who give voice to an otherwise often inarticulate discourse about pain," he argues, "also create a body of error and misrepresentation along with their knowledge. Pain passes much of its time in utter inhuman silence, and writers who describe something so inherently resistant to language must inevitably shape and possibly falsify the experience they describe."[28] And yet Donne's poetry suggests an alternative to this view of pain as what destroys language, consciousness, and world, which I will formulate in two propositions with instances from his poems.

First, pain *generates* languages and contexts. It is fundamentally entangled with the imagination, and literary works are not merely modes of its representation or conduits of its expression but its engines of generation. Take, for instance, Donne's "The Triple Fool":

> Then, as th'earth's inward narrow crooked lanes
> Do purge seawater's fretful salt away,
>   I thought, if I could draw my pains
> Through rhyme's vexation, I should them allay;
> Grief brought to numbers cannot be so fierce,
> For he tames it, that fetters it in verse.
>
>   But when I have done so,
> Some man, his art and voice to show,
>   Doth set and sing my pain,
> And by delighting many, frees again
> Grief, which verse did restrain.   (6–16)

It seems that pain and poetry are rivals, with the function of the latter to tame the former. Yet Donne imagines that the poem performs a series of operations with respect to pain that are cast in a number of metaphorical registers, all of which are ultimately tied to the mechanics of poetry. It purges, draws, brings to number, and tames – or at least it does so in the fantasy of the speaker, who later must admit the very literary operations that bind pain – setting it in meter and rhyme or to song – in fact repeat the source of grief and reopen the wound. In essence, not only is pain fundamentally aesthetic – tied to sensation and imagination – but it is also tied to a series of literary operations not reducible to the extractable content of a literary representation, even if that content represents an assertion – theological or medical – about the nature of pain. As Virginia Woolf noted long ago, in the absence of a "readymade" language for suffering, the sufferer "is forced to coin words himself, and, taking his pain in one hand, and a lump of pure sound in the other (as perhaps the people of Babel did in the beginning), so to crush them together that a brand new word drops out."[29] Woolf continues, "it is not only a new language that we need, more primitive, more sensual, more obscene; love must be deposed in favor of a temperature of 104; jealousy give place to the pangs of sciatica; sleeplessness play the part of a villain, and the hero become a white liquid with a sweet taste."[30] An aesthetics of pain would attend closely to the way we, in fact, suffer language, which is to say we undergo or bear up under its intensities and specificities. A cultural poetics of pain, on the other hand, might too quickly reduce such experiences of literary texture to mere context.

Second, pain, however unbearable it may be in its most extreme instances, is not merely destructive. It is, rather, constitutive and even world-building. Take Donne's "The Cross," which teases out the implications of what he refers to in "Goodfriday, 1613" as "That spectacle of too much weight" (16). The crucified Christ not only, as we noted, posed such problems for theology in post-Reformation England, but was also the site of renewed controversy in the age of Donne as Puritans militated for the elimination of crosses in English churches. "Since Christ embraced the cross itself," the speaker asks, "dare I / His image, th'image of His cross deny?" (1–2). Whereas "Goodfriday, 1613" witnesses the speaker who rides away from the world-breaking spectacle so as not to "see God die" (18), this speaker embraces the often-derogated broken body of God. Suddenly, Donne is not only committed to his *imitatio Christi* ("Who can deny me power and liberty / To stretch mine arms and mine own cross to be?," 18–19) but he also sees the whole cosmos as a fractal composition of cruciform structures:

> Look down, thou spiest out crosses in small things;
> Look up, thou see'st birds raised on crossed wings;
> All the globe's frame, and spheres, is nothing else
> But the meridians crossing parallels.   (21–24)

If everywhere there are crosses, and if the body is itself a living cross, pain is the fabric out of which all things are woven as well as the shape of what is made.

Notes

1. Esther Cohen, *The Modulated Scream: Pain in Late Medieval Culture* (University of Chicago Press, 2009), 7.
2. Rosaline Rey, *The History of Pain*, trans. Louise Elliott Wallace, J. A. Cadden, and S. W. Cadden (Cambridge, MA: Harvard University Press, 1995), 1.
3. Rey, *History*, 2

4. Elaine Scarry, *The Body in Pain* (Oxford University Press, 1987), 6.
5. Scarry, *Body*, 167, 14.
6. Scarry, *Body*, 3, 4.
7. Rey, *History*, 4.
8. Cohen, *Modulated*, 6.
9. Cohen, *Modulated*, 4.
10. Rey, *History*, 54, 68, 70.
11. Jan Frans van Dijkhuizen, *Pain and Compassion in Early Modern English Literature and Culture* (Cambridge: D. S. Brewer, 2012), 9.
12. van Dijkhuizen, *Pain*, 10.
13. van Dijkhuizen, *Pain*, 11.
14. van Dijkhuizen, *Pain*, 14.
15. Michael Schoenfeldt, "Aesthetics and Anaesthetics: The Art of Pain Management in Early Modern England," in *The Sense of Suffering: Constructions of Physical Pain in Early Modern Culture*, eds. Jan Frans van Dijkhuizen and Karl A. E. Enenkel (Leiden: Brill, 2009), 19, 25.
16. Schoenfeldt, "Aesthetics," 32.
17. Stephen Pender, "Seeing, Feeling, Judging: Pain in the Early Modern Imagination," in *Sense*, eds. van Dijkhuizen and Enenkel, 470.
18. Deborah Shuger, *The Renaissance Bible* (Berkeley, CA: University of California Press, 1994), 89.
19. Ernst B. Gilman, *Iconoclasm and Poetry in the English Reformation: Down Went Dagon* (University of Chicago Press, 1986), 11.
20. Jan Frans van Dijkhuizen, "Religious Meanings of Pain in Early Modern England," in *Sense*, 190.
21. See Joseph Campana, *The Pain of Reformation* (New York: Fordham University Press, 2012), especially chapter one, "Reading Bleeding Trees: The Poetics of Other People's Pain."
22. van Dijkhuizen, *Pain*, 28.
23. Stephen Pender, "Essaying the Body: Donne, Affliction, and Medicine" in *John Donne's Professional Lives* (London: D. S. Brewer, 2003), 219.
24. Pender, "Essaying," 220, 217, 219.
25. John R. Yamamoto-Wilson, *Pain, Pleasure and Perversity: Discourses of Suffering in Seventeenth-Century England* (Burlington, VT: Ashgate, 2013), 3.
26. On the centrality of sympathy, compassion, and pity for considerations of pain in the Renaissance see Campana and van Dijkhuizen.
27. Harold Schweizer, *Suffering and the Remedy of Art* (Albany, NY: State University of New York Press, 1997), 1.
28. David B. Morris, *The Culture of Pain* (Berkeley, CA: University of California Press, 1991), 3.
29. Virginia Woolf, *On Being Ill* (New York: Paris Press, 2002), 7.
30. Woolf, *On Being*, 7–8.

CHAPTER 20

Medicine

Stephen Pender

For Donne's acquaintance Edward Herbert, Baron of Cherbery, a young gentleman's *paideia* should include not only logic and arithmetic, geometry, and geography, but medicine. Begin with Petrus Severinus' *Idea medicinae philosophicae* (1571), he advises, then read Francesco Patrizi, likely *Nova de universis philosophia* (1591), and finish with Bernadino Telesio on physiology – "all which may be perform'd in one year." He should read widely in the "Pharmacopeia's or Antidotaries" of several countries; study Jean Fernel and Daniel Sennert, both famous physicians; know a variety of temperaments, especially those susceptible to cure by phlebotomy; manufacture remedies, since apothecaries are mendacious; and be able to remedy all "inward" and "outward hurts." Offering "some few directions to my posterity," Herbert settles on Johann Freitag's *Aurora medicorum Galeno-chymicorum* (1630) as "almost all that is necessary to be known for curing of Diseases, Wounds, &c."[1]

Herbert's counsel is eclectic, but decidedly current: he mentions Hippocrates and Galen, and lauds Freitag, but many of his authorities are followers of Paracelsus or sharp critics of Aristotle, still the doyen of early modern science. While some neoterics claimed that, were they alive, Hippocrates and Galen would "imbrace the new," that chemical physicians merely "inrich and adorne" the ancients with "newe inventions,"[2] most agreed with Donne: not only did new philosophy court innovation, perhaps a medical revolution was underway. As Donne avers in a 1609 letter, all sciences change, medicine most acutely. At its inception, doctors considered only "plain curing" without method; later, epitomised by Hippocrates' thought, practitioners merely contemplated remedial canons and rules, and the world slumbered for hundreds of years. Then, in "*Galens* time," dissatisfaction with tradition spurred a search after the causes of disease and the efficacy of cure. Galen proposed elements, humours, and qualities as keys to medical thought and intervention, but physicians gradually abandoned "these beggerly and impotent properties" for neo-

Aristotelian "specific forms," modes of attraction and antipathy. Now, Donne concludes, "we see the world hath turned upon new principles which are attributed to *Paracelsus*, but (indeed) too much to his honour."[3] Although Donne's attitude toward history varies, he often contrasts its mutability with the constancy that underwrites moral rectitude. Here, he uses his intricate knowledge of the history of medicine to impugn the art itself. While some of its rules are "certain," physic fails in application, and medical fashions change. As he put it in a 1622 letter to Henry Wotton, "Every distemper of the body now, is complicated with the spleen, and when we were young men we scarce ever heard of the spleen."[4]

Donne is not only conversant with medical history. The letters, for example, are replete with medical thought, from exquisitely detailed discussions of his own illnesses (including those he "cannot name or describe"), physicians from whom he seeks counsel, and the passions that accompany distemper in a brief treatise on emotional health, to mentioning specific remedies, such as *mumia*, dried human flesh.[5] While he did not study medicine formally, Donne's medical learning surpasses Herbert's counsel. He is "medically precise."[6] Since Jonathan Sawday's groundbreaking *The Body Emblazoned* (1995), Donne's precision has been amply demonstrated: he retails his knowledge of anatomy theatres, imagines post-mortem dissections, essays the "subtle knots" between bodies and souls, writes of vesical calculi and the perforated cordial septum, and explores the larders, cellars, and conduits of the viscera. While we may take this engagement with anatomy as evidence that "medical dissection is an unconscious preoccupation in his own mind,"[7] a more likely explanation is that Donne, like others in the period, treated medicine as a repository of supple, vivid metaphors for a range of inquiry. For instance, "solution of continuity," a surgical term meaning "a Dissolution of the Unity and Continuity of the Parts: as in Wounds, Ulcers, Fractures, &c,"[8] becomes for Donne a rich metaphor for ecclesiastical dissensus: "the Church is wounded by schisms, which make *solutionem continui*, (as Chirurgians speak)." Politic bodies, like natural bodies, do not suffer "solution or division" without lasting wounds, visible cicatrices.[9] Little wonder, then, that Donne's first biographer claims that he knew "the grounds and use of Physick."[10]

In this chapter, I offer a sketch of medical thought during a period roughly equivalent with Donne's lifetime. Medical thought is a broad church, and includes not only physicians and surgeons, but philosophers, theologians, and popularisers concerned with regimen and therapy, physiology and anatomy. Its eclecticism and pan-European scope are now

proverbial. As the period unfolds, its "grounds" became increasingly philosophical, evidenced by efforts to embrace new ways of understanding
vitality, founded on atomism, mechanism, and chemistry, the spread of
medical humanism, and the effects of both on university curricula.
At universities, beginning earlier but in full bloom by the late fifteenth
century, candidates intent on medical careers studied natural philosophy as
a prolegomenon to medicine, after thorough training in the "liberal arts,"
in *bonae litterae*. They read widely in philosophy, ethics and rhetoric, logic
and method, in Latin translations of Greek and Arabic medical texts; there
were strong efforts to "reconcile" philosophy and medicine, the
Aristotelian, Arabic, and the Hippocratic-Galenic traditions, in medical
instruction. Of course, what aspiring physicians read at grammar schools
and universities before studying medicine is well known: Virgil and Ovid,
Seneca and Horace, Cicero and Quintilian. This education in letters served
physicians well, as William Harvey's use of Terence attests. Even unortho-
dox physicians, eager to establish authority, confirmed that the "man
which intends the practice of Physick, must be qualified with good
Litterature," a "Philosophical foundation" necessary for reasoning about
causation.[11]

Although medical curricula were conservative, outside of universities
medical thought was responsive to the ferment of philosophical inquiry.
Some figures advocated a distinctly Epicurean programme, while skepticism, revived in the mid-sixteenth century, contributed significantly to the
development of medical semiotics. Available largely through Galen and
Cicero, stoicism underwrote the adequacy of sense perception, and offered
pneuma as solution to various problems of vitality and soul-body union; its
influences were everywhere felt in early modern treatments of the passions,
even though many rejected its strongest tenets. The influence of chemical
medicine is now well known.

Still, even if it was unevenly acknowledged, medical theory relied on
various forms of Aristotelianism, including its Paduan animadversions.
By the turn of the seventeenth century, philosophers and physicians of
most denominations, schools, and sects exhibit a confected mix of ancient
thought and Christian learning, scholasticism and the "new philosophy."
In 1618, Sennert, for example, compares Epicureanism with Augustine and
academic skepticism in his examination of the sensorium.[12] This eclecticism would have suited Donne, who was well aware, like others in his
period, that learned medicine was a vexed, uncertain body of interven-
tionist inquiry, often disparaged as poor philosophy and worse practice,
"the lowest of Professions."[13] Above all, this "low science" relied on

experience, on conjecture rather than *scientia*, for, as Donne notes, citing Paracelsus, "*Medicorum theoria experientia est*," physicians conclude "out of events."[14]

Medicine's "use" is equally complex. The cure of wounds, fractures, and trauma was the province of barbers and surgeons. For example, in 1631 Sir Gilbert Gerard sought the help of a "good chyrurgion" for his lameness, and was delighted with his care: the surgeon "hath taken so much paines with mee and care of mee during my lamenes that I must entreat you to give her thanks for it."[15] The "her" might surprise, but recent scholarship has established that women practised several types of healing in addition to midwifery.[16] For illnesses that did not require amputation, bone-setting, or surgery, a sufferer could seek manifold remedies, therapies, and cures. Various practitioners – local, often familial, lay healers, priests and parsons, apothecaries, barber-surgeons, physicians – vied for patients, who often sought several forms of therapy, occasionally changing practitioners in the course of an illness. Some even sought remedy by post. London in this period has been called a "medical marketplace," a controversial term meant to describe the availability of a range of treatments, competition between healers, as well as attempts at limited regulation by those, like the College of Physicians, who sought to legitimise certain practices while actively impugning others, at court and in print. The term fails to capture healing that occurred outside cash economies, and takes too little account of religious influence, but it does emphasise at least one aspect common to all medical exchange: *caveat emptor*.[17]

The boisterousness of the medical marketplace rarely distracts Donne, although he does deploy metaphors drawn from the apothecary's shop, comparing "simples" and compound medicines, for example, their curative efficacy marked by the "art of the Administrer."[18] His main concern is learned medicine, traditionally divided into several areas of inquiry and intervention, all of which possess theoretical and practical elements: physiology, including anatomy and the study of vitality; pathology, or the symptoms, etiologies, and nosologies of disease; hygiene, "the curative part," which is largely prophylactic and preservative, with a focus on dietetics, regimen, sometimes surgery; therapeutics, encompassing the *materia medica* and other forms of remediation; and semiotics, the interpretation of pathognomonic signs of disease. Even as its authority was challenged, Galenism remained sovereign well into the eighteenth century. Its basic principles are few, but remarkably adaptable: in addition to the other "naturals" – elements, temperaments, parts, faculties, actions, spirits[19] – the body contained four humours, corresponding to the elements earth, air, water, and fire (as well as radical moisture and innate heat, their interaction determining longevity). The humours were "essential to the physiological functioning of the organism" to which "largely hyopthetical origins, sites, and functions were ascribed." Concocted from ingested food into an amorphous matter ("chyle") by the stomach, blood, phlegm, yellow bile, and black bile were "cooked" in the liver, and distributed throughout the body via the veins. Humours fulfilled multiple functions: nutrition and growth, vitality and generation (semen was thought to be refined from blood). But they also conditioned "character," one's temperament or complexion, itself a mixture of qualities – warmth, moisture in the blood; cold, moisture in phlegm; warmth, dryness in choler or yellow bile; and cold, dryness in melancholy or black bile – that conditioned inclinations and dispositions, both mental and physical, in what has been called "psychological materialism."[20]

In this system, to which most "healers and sufferers" subscribed,[21] disease arises from the body's inability to rid itself of excess or peccant humours, and thus the practitioner's work is largely devoted to restoring putative balance by purgation, emetics, and phlebotomy, none of which escaped controversy in the period, and by applying remedies (herbs, minerals, chemicals) that occasioned qualities opposite to those in superabundance (cooling drugs for fevers, for example). Healing is "the translation of the *disease* into *health*. Which *affects* being contrary to each other, of necessity the transmutation of the one into the other must be performed by contraries."[22] Insofar as possible, treatment was moulded to individuals, and physicians accounted for season, age, circumstance, place, and *historiae*, patients' medical histories, as well as vocation and region.[23] A seventeenth-century "student of physick" translates Galen: "as to an exact administration of *Contraries*, it is expedient first to know the nature and temperament of the Body that is to Cured," and not only from books but "also from the age, and whole bygone life, which consists in the order of diet and exercise, beside the Region, the season of the Year, the season of the Weather, and the course of life." Neither should habit be neglected.[24] Thus, in sickbed conversations, patients disclosed "when and how the complaint had started, what events had precipitated it, the characteristic pains and symptoms, its periodicity," describing "key lifestyle features," like "eating and sleeping habits, . . . recent emotional traumas, and so forth."[25] As one sixteenth-century doctor insists, a physician is a "finder out of occasion."[26] Intervention was focussed on assisting patients in regulating, via contraries, "air" or environment, exercise and rest, food and drink, excretion and retention, sleeping and waking, and the passions of the soul – the "six non-naturals." The most frequently attested means of prophylaxis and cure was diet, but all six non-naturals received generous attention in medical and moral philosophical thought.

With this "weak materialism" in mind, learned practitioners revived ancient concern with healing *soma* and *psyche*, the senses, imagination, and passions, insomuch as they occasion, or are conditioned by, "bad complexion" or physical distress. Over-consumption or eating bad food, food inappropriate to season or temperament, made for rotten thinking, rotten feeling; again and again, physicians recommended adjusting and disciplining habits of eating, sleeping, and exercise, and, in those who followed Hippocrates closely, frequency of sexual congress.[27] Intimate connections between higher, sensory or rational functions and bodily disposition, turning on potential damage from lax regimen or injury, focus early modern inquiry into the "animal economy," a term used to denote not only physiological processes but perception and cognition, external and internal senses. Examining the body, "the mortal part," leads "far into the recesses where the material and the immaterial meet."[28]

Donne agreed. To properly constitute a man, "there must be a body, as well as a soule," he writes at Easter 1623; paraphrasing Tertullian, he continues, "All that the soul does, it does in, and with, and by the body," since its "naturall state" is union with the body.[29] This union, the "subtle knot," between bodies and souls so interests Donne that he devotes a section of a 1619 sermon to *spiritus*, a medical concept denoting an "ayry substance subtyll," divided into natural, "whiche taketh i[t]s beginninge in the lyver," vital, "whiche proceedeth from the harte, and by the arteries or pulses is sente into all the body," and "Anymalle, whyche is ingendred in the brayne, and is sente by the synewes [nerves] throughout the body, and maketh sence or felynge."[30] In a popular 1611 text the German physician Daniel Sennert presents *spiritus* in terms similar to those expressed throughout early modern Europe. Spirits are "the bond by which the body and soul are united, . . . and being wrought in the principal parts of the body are conveyed through channels [nerves] into the whole body . . . that they may help the powers and faculties perform their actions." Although animal spirits "perform internal and external senses," Sennert carefully insists that the soul is itself the faculty, that it alone acts and that the spirits are merely its instruments.[31] For a diverse audience in Germany, Donne uses this concept to explain how the Holy Spirit unites regenerate bodies and souls in ways similar to the function of animal spirits, which blood "labours to beget" ("The Ecstasy," 61): the union of body and soul "makes us man" (64). The "spirits in a man . . . are the thin and active part of the blood, and so are of a kind of middle nature, between soul and body"; they "doe the office, to unite and apply the faculties of the soul to the organs of the body, and so there is a man."[32] As "hand-maidens of the soule," its "chiefe attendants" spirits join matter and form, capacity and activity; human beings are hylomorphic.[33] While the spiritual body, the *soma penumatikon* of 1 Corinthians 15, merits special care, bodies themselves, just "so much *bone*,"[34] should not be defiled. Donne articulates Pauline doctrine in sophisticated medical terms, enlisting signs and spirits, faculties and sense, as keys to understanding, and husbanding, the soul. Far from "committed to an intellectuality that obviates emphasis on the senses,"[35] for Donne somatic experience is heuristic, insofar as the soul is "effigitated" in the body.[36] The ligatures between bodies and souls constitute "the fundamental problem of Donne's life, early, middle, and late."[37]

This "problem" informs Donne's medical excursions. Elsewhere, I have treated his knowledge of medical semiotics, especially indications – medical signs that point to specific conditions and therapies.[38] Via semiotics, he becomes aware of what might be called "medical time," the progress of distemper towards its crisis. As part of an excursus on the "medical month," an astrological period devised in order to better discern "Decretory or Criticall dayes," Sir Thomas Browne notes that the crisis of an illness is the point at which "there ensueth a sensible alteration, either to life, or death."[39] Calculated by the position of the moon in the zodiac and, in Donne's terms, the "time of the Patients lying downe," the *decubitus*,[40] crisis occurs on the "7, 14, 20, or 21, 27, 28 or 29. dayes of a sicknes."[41] Disease has two temporal registers: its own course, including its critical days, and its relationship to an individual's "*Climactericall years.*"[42] When in the *Devotions* his physicians observe that maculae appear on a critical day, physical crisis yields a spiritual trial; he then uses medical terms to envision his illness conforming to the hexameral week. His final day, the day of judgement, "is truely, and most literally, the *Critical*, the *Decretory day.*"[43] Decretory is a legal term for decree, final judgement; Nicholas Culpeper argues that the notion of crisis itself is "taken by a Metaphor from the Judiciall Court to the Art of Physick."[44] As Donne himself observes on the cusp of relapse: medicine's uncertainty means we "stand at the same *barre*," unsure of diagnosis or the signs by which it is warranted.[45]

Among the many other ways in which Donne retails his medical knowledge, two related concerns focus the rest of this chapter: hygiene and medicine's purpose. A "long & a regular work,"[46] health is a state in accordance with nature; disease is contra-natural, a disturbance of the balance of humours and qualities in the body. The ideal is the *neutrum*.

Derived from scholastic and humanist commentaries on Galen's *Ars med-ica*, this complex term denotes either balance in temperament, itself exceedingly rare, or simply somatic conditions and dispositions; it is epistemological – an abstract, normative state of well-being – rather than practical, except perhaps as a term for nosologically complex illnesses, like cachexia. As Donne writes, we are "born ruinous": "There is no health: physicians say that we, / At best, enjoy but a neutrality" (*The First Anniversary*, 95, 91–92). In a c.1609 letter, he offers the same view, which he elaborates in a 1618 sermon.[47] Still, there was broad agreement, from antiquity on, that the dual purpose of medicine was the preservation and restoration of health. As the physician Giovanni Argentario put it in 1610, physic's prime offices are conservative and curative.[48] Donne echoes this notion – "the true and proper use of physick, is to *preserve* health, and, but by accident to restore it"[49] – but he is interested in means as well as aims. "We study *Health*, and we deliberate upon our *meats*, and *drink*, and *Ayre*, and *exercises*."[50] Among things conducive to well-being, he mentions the non-naturals, "*eating*, and *sleeping*, and other such."[51] Learned and popular attention to the non-naturals focussed on the ways in which health is perverted, in Burton's words, "in offending in some of those six non-natural things."[52] Dearth or excess in any one regulatory field courts disease, but Burton, like many of his contemporaries, was sharply appre-hensive about the passions. Distraction, akrasia, "want of government," "our facility ... in giving way to every passion and perturbation of the mind" overthrow our constitutions.[53] For Donne, too, intemperance per-verts, as "God would not have the body corrupted and attenuated, shrunk and deformed with incontinency and licentiousnesse."[54] A "sober and temperate life" is a warrant of faith.[55] Sobriety, in its broadest sense, assumes a central place in early modern discussions of longevity; as Thomas Cogan writes, "it is better to preserve health by sobriety, and temperance, than by surfet and misorder, to make the body weak and sickly, and odious both to God and the world."[56]

Recent scholarship has begun to explore the connections between the passions and health, positing an early modern "medicine of the mind," treating the harmful, even fatal, effects of vehement passion, under the broad rubric of hygiene. "Emotional health" fell within a physician's pur-view: for example, cures for sorrow enjoin sufferers to embrace the "hol-some counsayles" in scripture and "bokes of morall doctrine."[57] Since soul and body are united, remedying physical suffering means "care must be taken, to sweeten and abate the troubles of the mind with pleasing words ... *A good speech is a Physitian for a sick mind*."[58] In order to cure "spirituall sicknesses," physicians must "invent and devise some spirituall pageant to fortifie and help the imaginative facultie, which is corrupted and depraved," imprinting "wise or foolish" conceits "in the Patient's braine."[59] The corrupt "imaginative facultie" must be healed by "invention," strengthened in order to relieve suffering. A sick person "is to be wrought into an Imagination quite contrary" to the offending passions that accompany or intensify distemper.[60] Here, Galenic strictures – cure by opposites – organize psychological intervention, itself devoted to inspiring *metriopatheia*. "Due temper" funds moral action (*The First Anniversary*, 89), and frequently virtue itself is figured as constancy, as moderation of the passions.

The contrariness of psychic cure appears in a 1608 letter that explores Donne's own passions. Our three parts, "Soul, and Body, and Minde," partake of "thoughts and affections and passions, which neither soul nor body hath alone, but have been begotten by their communication." While we can reach a kind of moral certainty with respect to physical illness, in "diseases of the minde, there is no *Criterium*, no Canon, no rule; for, our own taste and apprehension and interpretation should be the Judge, and that is the disease it self." For his own passional distemper, Donne's remedy is contrary: "when I finde my self transported with jollity, and love of company, I hang Leads at my heels; and reduce to my thoughts my fortunes, my years … when sadness dejects me, either I countermine it with another sadnesse, or I kindle squibs about me again, and flie into sportfulnesse and company."[61] As I have argued before, recognising that affective response as well as conditioned character, early moderns endorsed four main techniques in the face of vehement or prolonged passion: counsel might be sought from a trusted friend or advisor; reason, prudence, or meditation might inure one against such turbulence; diversion or redescription might assuage or occlude immoderate feeling; or, Donne's method, one passion might be used to "master" another. The latter is "of special use in moral and civil matters" in which one "faction" is set against another in the "government within."[62] The physician Timothy Bright recommends "alteration of the passion by the contrarie affection."[63] But, for Donne, remedies falter, for they are as diverse as the "variety of mindes" that employ them; perhaps that is why he urges God to restrain his affections.[64] This aretology is tested during his 1623 illness, and the problem is fear.

For Donne, bedridden and melancholy, fear is the "*busiest* and *irksomest affection*." Like "*wind* in the body," it counterfeits "every action, or *passion* of the *mind*."[65] In fear, the blood and spirits withdraw from the heart, "the minde is troubled," the spirits "inflamed";[66] it "disorders in the soule, filling it with such confusion, as shee leaues him neither memory, nor iudgement, nor will, to encounter any danger that threatens his ruine."[67] And physical strength and vitality are "dissolved" by "the sudden recourse of Heat, Blood, and spirits, into the outward parts" or its opposite, rendering the limbs and face pale.[68] Fear can kill.[69] It affects most "sick and impotent persons,"[70] and those with intermittent fever should "refraine perturbations of the minde, specially, anger, feare, sorrow, and such like."[71] Most of all, excessive fear is unbecoming to "a connstant, and valiaunt man, who shoulde alwayes bee reddie to suffer all things patiently, without signe of a troubled mind."[72] In contrast, moderate fear is "natural Wisdom," a means of defence, a spur to deliberation;[73] yet even this "natural" fear should be "subdued to our feare of God and his goodnesse."[74] Donne interrupts his own disquisition by claiming that God occasions licit passion "as a ballast to carry us steadily in all waters," and he prays for "tender, and supple, and conformable affections." As humiliation tastes of consolation, so passions aid the sufferer and mollify the experience of sickness;[75] one passion might drive out another, and "wee may correct in our selves one disease by another."[76] In the throes of passion, of "vaine imaginations," Donne seeks moderation, a "middle heart," broken by contrition, immured against overmuch confidence in "morall Constancie."[77] Constancy is steadfastness, "a right and immoveable strength of the minde," in the words of Flemish neostoic Justus Lipsius, "neither lifted up, nor pressed downe with externall or casuall accidents."[78] Fear impugns moral constancy, autonomy, self. Without a "disciplinary life," a fearful man, Donne writes, "fals from his morall and Christian constancy" into anxiety, incertitude, irresolution. Still, our "natural" selves, our affections, may aid in salvation, "if we resist them" and let them consume themselves.[79]

At stake in Donne's conception of affliction, in his use of medical thought, is the very thing that suffers: the self is precisely what must be either "discharged," cured with divine physic, or lost. Various afflictions punish with discomfort or solitude, but in sickness, Donne insists, "I lack my *self*."[80] Like others in his period, Donne pursued the ancient dictum *nosce teipsum* with robust armaments drawn from medicine and moral inquiry – moderation, regimen, *metriopatheia* – in order to understand his self, in part, medically. Guarding against physical and spiritual distemper meant apprehending one's "constitution, and bodily inclination to *diseases*."[81] This "new culture of pathology"[82] preoccupied him until his death. In what is likely his final letter, mentioning poor appetite, fitful sleep, coughs and deafness, Donne concludes that he "never had good temper."[83] He was not alone.

Notes

1. Edward Herbert, *The Life of Edward Lord Herbert of Cherbury* (London, 1770), 31–37.
2. Josephus Quersitanus, *The Practice of Chymicall and Hermeticall Physicke, for the Preservation of Health*, trans. Thomas Timme (London, 1605), sig. B2v.
3. John Donne, *Letters to Several Persons of Honour* [1651], introd. by M. Thomas Hester (New York: Scholars' Facsimiles, 1977), 135.
4. Donne, *Letters to*, 134–35.
5. Donne, *Letters to*, 31–32, 71–72, 98.
6. Richard Sugg, *Murder After Death: Literature and Anatomy in Early Modern England* (Ithaca, NY: Cornell University Press, 2007), 154.
7. Sugg, *Murder*, 151.
8. Stephen Blankaart, *A Physical Dictionary* (London, 1684), 263.
9. Donne, *Essayes in Divinity* (London, 1651), 10–11, 50–51.
10. Walton, *Lives*, 88.
11. Everard Maynwaring, *Tutela Sanitatis* (London, 1663), 46.
12. Daniel Sennert, *The Institutions or Fundamentals of the Whole Art, Both of Physick and Chyurgery*, trans. N. D. (London, 1656), 371.
13. John Stuteville, January 12, 1656, in *Memoirs of the Verney Family*, ed. Frances Parthenope Verney, 3 vols. (London: Longman, 1892–99), 3:200.
14. *Sermons*, 2:76.
15. *Barrington Family Letters, 1628–1632*, ed. Arthur Searle (London: Royal Historical Society, 1983), 191–92.
16. See *Women, Science, and Medicine 1500–1700: Mothers and Sisters of the Royal Society*, eds. Lynette Hunter and Sarah Hutton (Stroud, UK: Sutton, 1997); and Monica H. Green, *Women's Healthcare in the Medieval West: Texts and Contexts* (Aldershot, UK: Ashgate, 2000).
17. Margaret Pelling, *Medical Conflicts in Early Modern London: Patronage, Physicians, and Irregular Practioners, 1550–1640* (Oxford: Clarendon Press, 2003), 342–43.
18. Donne, *Biathanatos*, ed. Ernest W. Sullivan II (Newark: University of Delaware Press, 1984), 43.
19. Ambroise Paré, *The Works . . .*, trans. Thomas Johnson (London, 1634), 5.
20. Nancy Siraisi, *Medieval and Early Modern Renaissance Medicine: An Introduction to Knowledge and Practice* (University of Chicago Press, 1990), 104–6.
21. Lucinda McCray Beier, *Sufferers and Healers: The Experience of Illness in Seventeenth-Century England* (London: Routledge and Kegan Paul, 1987), 31.
22. Galen, *Galen's Method of Physick*, trans. Peter English (London, 1656), 195.
23. Paré, *Works*, 5.

24. Galen, *Galen's*, 195–96.

25. Roy Porter, "The Rise of the Physical Examination," in *Medicine and the Five Senses*, eds. W. F. Bynum and R. Porter (Cambridge University Press, 1993), 182.

26. Juan Huarte, *Examen de Ingenios. The Examination of Mens Wits (1594)*, trans. Thomas Carew, ed. Carmen Rogers (Gainsville, FL: Scholars' Facsimile, 1959), 180–82.

27. Thomas Cogan, *The Haven of Health* (London, 1636), 278–95.

28. E. Ruth Harvey, *The Inward Wits: Psychological Theory in the Middle Ages and the Renaissance* (London: Warburg Institute, 1975), 23–24, 27.

29. *Sermons*, 4:357–58.

30. Sir Thomas Elyot, *The Castel of Helth* (London, 1541), sig. 12r.

31. Sennert, *Institutions*, 12–13.

32. *Sermons*, 2:262.

33. Jean Fernel, *The* Physiologia *of Jean Fernel (1567)*, trans. John M. Forrester (Philadelphia, PA: American Philosophical Association, 2003), 285ff.

34. Donne, *Devotions upon Emergent Occasions*, ed. Anthony Raspa (Oxford University Press, 1987), 93.

35. Kate Gartner Frost, *Holy Delight: Typology, Numerology, and Autobiography in Donne's* Devotions upon Emergent Occasions (Princeton University Press, 1990), 8.

36. See Donne, *Devotions*, 119.

37. Charles Monroe Coffin, *John Donne and the New Philosophy* (New York: Columbia University Press, 1937), 277.

38. Stephen Pender, "Essaying the Body: Donne, Affliction, and Medicine," in *John Donne's Professional Lives*, ed. David Colclough (Cambridge: Brewer, 2003), 215–48.

39. Thomas Browne, *Pseudodoxia Epidemica* (London, 1646), 213.

40. *Pseudo-Martyr*, 26.

41. Nicholas Culpeper, *Semeiotica Uranica, or an Astrological Judgment of Diseases* (London, 1651), 5, 17, 37.

42. Donne, *Devotions*, 71, 73, 97–98.

43. Donne, *Devotions*, 76.

44. Culpeper, *Semeiotica*, 17.

45. Donne, *Devotions*, 121–22.

46. Donne, *Devotions*, 7.

47. Donne, *Letters to*, 30; *Sermons*, 2:80.

48. Heikki Mikkeli, *Hygiene in the Early Modern Medical Tradition* (Helsinki: Academia Scientiarum Fennica, 1999), 48.

49. *Sermons*, 2:76.

50. Donne, *Devotions*, 7.

51. *Sermons*, 2:79.

52. Robert Burton, *The Anatomy of Melancholy*, 3 vols. (London, 1886), 1:181.

53. Burton, *Anatomy*, 1:182.

54. *Sermons*, 6:268–70.

55. *Sermons*, 7:107.
56. Cogan, *Haven*, 228.
57. Elyot, *Castel*, sig. 64v.
58. Levinus Lemnius, *The Secret Miracles of Nature*, trans. T. N. (London, 1658), 65.
59. William Vaughan, *Approved Directions for Health, Both Naturall and Artificiall: Derived from the Best Physicians as well Modern as Ancient* (London, 1612), 90.
60. Johannes Jonstonus, *The Idea of Practical Physick*, trans. Nicholas Culpeper (London, 1657), 21.
61. Donne, *Letters to*, 70–72.
62. Francis Bacon, *The Works of Francis Bacon*, eds. James Spedding et al, 12 vols. (London: Longman, 1857–74), 3:438.
63. Timothy Bright, *A Treatise of Melancholy* (London, 1586), 245.
64. Donne, *Essays*, 75.
65. Donne, *Devotions*, 122, 29.
66. Philip Barrough, *The Method of Physicke* (London, 1583), 173.
67. Nicholas Coeffeteau, *The Table of Humane Passions, with Their Causes and Effects*, trans. Edward Grimeston (London, 1621), 469–70.
68. Jonstonus, *Idea*, 20.
69. Coeffeteau, *Table*, 452.
70. Thomas Rogers, *A Philosophicall Discourse, Entituled The Anatomie of the Minde* (London, 1576), sig. 36r.
71. Barrough, *Method*, 183.
72. Rogers, *Philosophicall*, sig. 30v.
73. Coeffeteau, *Table*, 472.
74. Thomas Cooper, *The Mysterie of the Holy Government of our Affections* (London, 1620), sig. 39v.
75. Donne, *Devotions*, 32, 34, 39.
76. Donne, *Biathanatos*, 171, margin, citing Hippocrates.
77. Donne, *Devotions*, 10, 59.
78. Justus Lipsius, *Two Bookes of Constancie*, trans. Sir John Stradling, ed. Rudolf Kirk, comm. Clayton Morris Hall (New Brunswick, NJ: Rutgers University Press, 1939), 79.
79. *Sermons*, 6:105–11.
80. *Sermons*, 2:80.
81. Donne, *Devotions*, 119.
82. Michael Solomon, *Fictions of Well-Being: Sickly Readers and Vernacular Medical Writing in Late Medieval and Early Modern Spain* (Philadelphia, PA: University of Pennsylvania Press, 2010), 95–96.
83. Donne, *Letters to*, 316–17.

CHAPTER 21

Science, Alchemy, and the New Philosophy

Margaret Healy

And new philosophy calls all in doubt.

–John Donne

Donne's famous line referring to 'new philosophy' (205) in *The First Anniversary* seems to invite speculation: what did our poet mean by this intriguing phenomenon that – for him at least – called 'all in doubt'? What was it that was so 'new' and unsettling, and how did it differ from the old? Traditional natural philosophy denoted the study of the natural world and of man's place within it: it examined organic and physical change, including motion, as well as the heavens (cosmology), the earth's atmosphere (meteorology), and the earth itself (minerals, plants, animals, and human beings). Natural philosophy also addressed metaphysical questions such as the nature of the soul and the relation of God to creation.[1] It was dominated by the ancient Aristotelian and (in medicine) Galenic textual wisdom taught in the scholastic syllabus of the universities, but, under the aegis of humanism in the Renaissance, it absorbed other approaches to nature derived predominantly from Platonic, Neoplatonic, Neopythagorean, Hermetic, and Stoic sources.[2] Furthermore, for the Christian individual in early modern times, the intensive study of the Book of Nature – God's created world – was increasingly perceived as a crucial means, alongside the Bible, through which to come to know God.

Dangerous controversies arose in this period when novel theories about nature appeared to contradict biblical wisdom; less heretical, but almost as problematic, were new ideas – increasingly based on experience, eye knowledge, and mathematical advances – which undermined the key Greek and Roman textual authorities, especially Aristotle. William Harvey's 'Letter to Doctor Argent', prefacing his 1628 treatise *De Motu Cordis* which details his theory about the circulation of the blood, succinctly captures the troubling tension that had arisen by the early seventeenth century between tradition and that which he termed 'Truth': 'True Philosophers, aflame

with love of truth and wisdom ... suffer not themselves to become
enslaved and lose their freedom in bondage to the traditions and precepts
of any, except their own eyes convince them. Nor, while swearing allegiance to mistress Antiquity, do they openly abandon Friend Truth and
desert her in sight of all.'[3] Like many early modern philosopher-empiricists
– those whom today we might term scientists – Harvey strove to adopt and
articulate a middle way in which 'industry and diligence' in the practice of
dissection and experimentation could build respectfully on the knowledge
of prior, textual authorities.

   In early modern times, 'science' (Latin *scientia*) did not have its current
meaning but was a much more general term for a body of knowledge;
indeed, theology belonged to *scientia* – it was the 'queen of sciences'.[4]
The *scientiae mediae* included the mathematical disciplines of arithmetic
and geometry as well as astrology, astronomy, optics, harmonics, and
mechanics; these disciplines were distinct from the 'mechanical arts',
which included practical applications of this knowledge in fields such as
architecture, navigation, clock making, and engineering.[5] However, the
meaning of 'science' was shifting: as the words of the physician John
Securis reveal, it was becoming increasingly aligned with a particular
type of study of the natural world that certainly involved Harvey's notion
of 'diligence and industry'. His medical book declared, 'Science is
a habit ... [a] ready, prompt and bent disposition to do any thing
confirmed by long study, exercise, and use'.[6] For Securis, science was
a mental outlook and a practical pursuit associated with proof and application; it was not owned by any specific philosophy of the body or the
universe. In *The Jewel House: Elizabethan London and the Scientific
Revolution*, Deborah Harkness has convincingly argued that from the
sixteenth century the term was increasingly associated with 'a manipulation of the natural world for productive and profitable ends'.[7] Diverse
pursuits were particularly linked with this term, including medicine,
anatomy, alchemy, mining, brewing, viniculture, dyeing, metallurgy, and
the type of applied mathematics associated with astronomy and navigation.
In these fields, experiment, observation, and recording – empirical
method – were being brought together with, and even privileged over,
traditional book learning. Harkness's study presents us with a compelling
vision of England's capital city bustling with quasi-scientific projects, its
residents busying themselves in shops, houses, and gardens, 'in cramped
backyards over furnaces and smelting ovens, and operating out of store-
fronts in the Royal Exchange': 'hundreds of men and women engaged in
the work of science, medicine and technology'.[8] Exploring the buzzing

metropolis of Hugh Plat's London – which was also Donne's London – *The Jewel House* uncovers a populace hungry for invention and profit, making the type of discoveries conducive to the development of a more thoroughgoing scientific and technological culture that would be nurtured by overseas exploration and two important London institutions: Gresham College (1597) and its famous offshoot, The Royal Society (1660) – 'a Colledge for the Promoting of Physico-Mathematicall Experimentall Learning'.[9]

'Scientist' was not an operative term in this period, but talented empiri-cists had certainly emerged on the European scene and Donne appears to have been familiar with many of their ideas. Their discoveries were of fashionable interest so it is not surprising that a witty poet writing for an educated, elite audience would engage with them. But what exactly did Donne's enigmatic reference to the 'new philosophy' in his eulogy of Elizabeth Drury signify, and why did it – rather startlingly – call 'all in doubt'?:

> And new philosophy calls all in doubt,
> The element of fire is quite put out;
> The sun is lost, and th'earth, and no man's wit
> Can well direct him where to look for it.
> And freely men confess that this world's spent,
> When in the planets and the firmament
> They seek so many new.   (205–11)

These playful lines take us unmistakably into the realm of the new astronomy which was shaking the firm ground of the world and causing havoc in the heavens. The brilliant mathematicians who were together responsible for this disruption were Nicholas Copernicus (1473–1543), Tycho Brahe (1546–1601), Johannes Kepler (1571–1630), and Galileo Galilei (1564–1642).[10] That the earth had shifted position and been shot into the heavens is a clear reference to Copernican theory; in *De Revolutionibu Orbium Coelestium* (1543) Copernicus had set out the mathematics under-pinning his sun-centred cosmology, which effectively dethroned the earth as the focus of planetary orbits and undermined the entire Ptolemaic system. In a sermon of later years, Donne again made clear reference to this: 'We wonder, and justly, that some late Philosophers have removed the whole Earth from the Centre, and carried it up, and placed it in one of the Spheres of Heaven'.[11]

Tycho Brahe (*Progymnasmata*) was one of several philosophers to argue that the element of fire did not exist ('is quite put out') and he was among the first to see the new stars that had appeared suddenly (while some old ones mysteriously vanished) in 1572 and 1604.[12] These were recorded by his assistant Johannes Kepler (*De Stella Nova*, 1606) who went on to prove that the orbits of the planets were elliptical and to demonstrate the motion of Mars through new mathematics (*Astronomia Nova*, 1609). When Donne alludes in *The First Anniversary* to 'Such diverse downright lines, such overthwarts' (256) in relation to the 'perplexed course' (253) of the heavens, he is undoubtedly seeking to convey the tension between traditional Aristotelian cosmology and the new physics with its revised mathematical calculations that were throwing everything out of kilter. Robert Burton captured this confusion brilliantly in *The Anatomy of Melancholy*: 'our latter mathematicians have rolled all the stones that may be stirred: and, to solve all appearances and objections, have invented new hypotheses, and fabricated new systems of the world, out of their own Daedalian heads'.[13]

A year before *The First Anniversary* appeared, Galileo published his amazing observations of stars and planets viewed through a revolutionary new telescope (*Sidereus Nuncius*, 1610).[14] Donne would not have had to read Galileo himself to be aware of his shattering astronomical discoveries. His friend Sir Henry Wotton, Ambassador to Venice, writes to Lord Salisbury (March 13, 1610) about 'the Mathematical Professor at Padua' who with the help of 'an optical instrument' has 'discovered four new planets rolling about the sphere of Jupiter, besides many other unknown fixed stars' and so has 'overthrown all former astronomy'.[15] Wotton was in frequent letter contact with Donne, but the two men could have also discussed this directly because he was back in London by 1611.

In fact both *Anniversary* poems excel in their glances at divers 'new philosophy'. The following lines, for example, seem to record an awareness of W. Gilbert's work on the magnetic compass published in *De Magnete* (1600): 'She that had all magnetic force alone, / To draw and fasten sundered parts in one' (*The First Anniversary*, 221–22). Similarly, Donne appears mindful of current controversies about the heart and blood – 'Know'st thou how blood, which to the heart doth flow, / Doth from one ventricle to th'other go?' (*The Second Anniversary*, 271–72) – and may well have attended William Harvey's public lectures detailing his experiments on animal hearts. The Roman physician Galen (AD 129–c. 212) had maintained that there were passages through the interventricular septum that separated the ventricles of the heart through which thin blood could pass. By means of a series of experiments and arithmetical calculations Harvey refuted this, detailing the blood's pulmonary circulation from the veins to the right ventricle of the heart to the lungs, then back to the left side of the heart and onward, via the arteries, around the body.

The *Anniversary* poems allude several times to shifts in medical philosophy – the 'new physic' (*The First Anniversary*, 160). *The Second Anniversary* illuminates the nature of the challenge to traditional humoral medicine:

> Have not all souls thought
> For many ages that our body's wrought
> Of air, and fire, and other elements?
> And now they think of new ingredients.   (263–66)

The 'new ingredients' undoubtedly refer to the alchemical model of the body introduced by the iconoclastic Swiss-German physician Paracelsus in the sixteenth century. In Galenic humoral medicine taught in the universities, each humour – yellow bile, black bile, blood, phlegm – corresponded to an element. According to Paracelsus, however, there were no humours; in his competing paradigm, bodies were composed instead of three substances – sulphur, mercury, and salt. The body's metallic constitution necessitated mineral cures produced by the purifying techniques of alchemy; in fact, Paracelsus was responsible for a new era of iatrochemistry, or chemistry applied to medicine.[16] Donne refers in a letter to the world-changing nature of this new physic: '*Galen* ... taught them the qualities of the four Elements, and arrested them upon this, that all differences of qualities proceeded from them. ... we see the world hath turned upon new principles which are attributed to *Paracelsus*'.[17]

Indeed, Paracelsus's heterodox medicine, together with the 'burgeoning Neo-platonism of the Renaissance' fuelled initially by Marsilio Ficino's fifteenth-century translations of Plato and the Hermetic writings, helped to shift alchemy from its marginal position as 'a discipline concerned mainly with mineralogy, metallurgy, and the products of chemical technology to the centre of the European stage', where it became the basis for a comprehensive theory of matter and spirit – it became 'the *idée fixe* of the learned'.[18] Several centres of alchemical experimentation emerged in England in the late sixteenth century: Gresham College in London, John Dee's Mortlake home, and Ralegh's Durham House. Ralegh's 'set' included figures such as the 'wizard Earl', Henry Percy, Ninth Earl of Northumberland (whose own library boasted a fine collection of Paracelsian volumes), and the mathematician Thomas Harriot.[19] All these locations were associated with literary visitors including Sidney, Donne, Chapman, and Marlowe.[20]

Contrary to a widespread misapprehension, early modern alchemy was not solely invested in attempts to transmute base metals into gold. In fact the latter activity was often derided by alchemists who sought to distance themselves from this covetous practice. Practical alchemy might more accurately be characterized as proto-chemistry involving experiment and application in a diverse range of pursuits including metallurgy, dye and pigment manufacture, brewing, and pharmacy. As Donne's 'mummy' suggests, the pursuit of gold was increasingly understood as an elusive quest, 'as no chemic yet th'elixir got' ('Love's Alchemy', 7); however, along the way chemical research was discovering useful things, including new drugs ('some odoriferous thing, or medicinal', 10). By the turn of the seventeenth century there were many practising alchemical physicians in London, and, in spite of professional rivalries, Galenic practitioners were increasingly embracing the new mineral pharmacy alongside traditional cures.[21] George Puttenham's *The Art of English Poesy* notably advocates Paracelsian physic, declaring that 'the noble poets' sought by their art 'to remove or appease, not with any medicament of a contrary temper, as the Galenists use ... but as the Paracelsians, who cure *similia similibus* making one dolor to expel another'.[22] While Galenic medicine had traditionally cured by contraries, like cured like in the Paracelsian schema. Puttenham's words suggest that 'dolor' witnessed through 'poesy' (such as in tragedy) could eradicate or reduce more significant suffering experienced in real life.

Indeed, the alchemical vogue of the early modern period manifests itself in some unlikely places that can help to illuminate Donne's substantial creative use of its lexicon and symbolism. In the early sixteenth century Martin Luther had given his blessing to the art, declaring, 'The science of alchemy I like very well ... I like it not only for the profit it brings in melting metals ... I like it also for the sake of the allegory and secret signification, which is exceedingly fine ... even so God, at the day of judgment, will separate all things through fire'.[23] God is imagined here as a divine alchemist, and purification through fire is associated with spiritual renewal and resurrection: alchemical purification could thus have both material (exoteric) and spiritual (esoteric) implications. In keeping with this, Paracelsian medicine envisaged a Christocentric universe in which suffering, prayer, and meditation – particularly upon Christ's Passion – could purify and regenerate the sick soul. Notably, in Donne's 'The Cross', 'spiritual crosses' are likened to 'extracted chemic medicine' (27): the poem affirms that you can be 'your own physic, or need none, / When stilled or purged by tribulation' (29–30). Thus alchemical techniques of healing are imagined as applicable to matter and spirit – outer and inner nature, soma and soul. In seeking to 'enrol' the 'fame' (*The First Anniversary*, 474) and celebrate the extraordinary spiritual purity of Mistress Drury, Donne again enlists this understanding, describing the process of driving out the 'poisonous tincture' of original sin as 'true religious alchemy':

> She in whom virtue was so much refined
> That for alloy unto so pure a mind
> She took the weaker sex; she that could drive
> The poisonous tincture, and the stain of Eve
> Out of her thoughts and deeds, and purify
> All by a true religious alchemy.   (177–82)

The alchemist's 'limbeck' (distillation vessel) is consistently a symbol of regeneration in Donne, and sometimes it is the grave that refines bodies in preparation for the resurrection (as in 'Elegy on the Lady Markham', 23). In the poem 'Resurrection, Imperfect' Christ is the philosopher's stone, the 'gold' distilled to 'tincture' through the resurrection, which can transmute 'Leaden and iron wills to good' (13, 14, 15). This is the transmutation that the poet desires for himself in 'A Litany': 'From this red earth, O Father, purge away / All vicious tinctures, that new fashioned / I may rise up from death before I'am dead' (7–9). In his sermons, Donne frequently uses terms from alchemy and metallurgy to detail the steps in the process of salvation and to define and ground the stages of a metaphysical process resulting in spiritual perfection. Donne's sermon *Preached upon the Penitentiall Psalmes* provides a prime illustration of this:

> Therefore David who was metall tried seven times in the fire, and desired to be such gold as might be laid up in God's treasury, might consider, that in the transmutation of metals, it is not enough to come to a calcination or a liquefaction of the metal . . . nor to an Ablution, to sever drosse from pure, nor to a Transmutation, to make it a better metall, but there must be a Fixion, a settling therof, so that it will not evaporate into nothing, nor returne to his former state.[24]

On Easter Monday 1622 his sermon affirmed: 'God can work in all metals and transmute all metals: he can make . . . a Superstitious Christian a sincere Christian; a Papist a Protestant'.[25] Spiritual alchemy and divine love were notably not, however, dissociated from erotic love; on the contrary biblical Solomon had long been co-opted by alchemists as a gifted practitioner, and in 1609 Joseph Hall's commentary on the *Song of Songs* interpreted 'this whole Pastoral-marriage song' as an alchemical allegory 'where the deepest things of God are spoken in riddles'.[26] Philosophical alchemy often expressed its mysteries through erotic symbolism such as the kiss and copulation, and this provides an additional lens through which to ponder some of Donne's more alchemically-tinged love poetry.

Donne certainly appears sufficiently well informed about the new natural philosophy of his age for it to serve as a rich reservoir of symbolism for his elaborate metaphysical conceits. But what was his opinion of it? It is doubtful that he was personally much disturbed by Copernicanism for in a letter of 1609 he reflects, 'Copernicism in the mathematics hath carried Earth farther up from the stupid centre, and yet not honoured it nor advantaged it, because, for the necessity of appearances, it hath carried Heaven so much higher from it'.[27] More tellingly, on one occasion he used the experience of his own sickness, which made him stumble dizzily across a room, seemingly to endorse Copernican theory: 'why may I not believe, that the *whole earth* moves in a *round motion*, though that seeme to mee to *stand*, when as I seeme to stand to my *Company*, and yet am carried, in a giddy, and *circular motion*, as I *stand*?'[28] It is striking to find, however, that in the satire *Ignatius His Conclave* (1611) he places Copernicus and Paracelsus on an equal footing in Hell vying with Machiavelli and the Jesuit Ignatius Loyola for the accolade of 'having been the innovator whose works have caused most confusion in the world, thereby aiding the Devil in his task of leading Mankind to damnation'.[29] It would be easy to assume that Donne had a highly negative apprehension of the 'new philosophy'; however, this would be an erroneous reading. It is crucial to observe that this is a Papal version of Hell in which the papists have foolishly extended the name and the punishment of heresy almost to everything; in fact the target of this playful satire is Jesuit stupidity and intolerance. As Joseph Mazzeo observes, 'there is ... more praise than blame for these two innovators in this witty piece'.[30] This view would seem to be supported by Donne's tract on suicide, *Biathanatos* ('death by violence'). Here, in the course of his discussion, Donne disputes the idea that the longevity of a belief could be urged in its defence, citing St Augustine's opposition to divorce as an example:

> are not Saint Augustine's Disciples guilty of the same pertinacy which is imputed to Aristotle's followers who, defending the heavens to be inalterable because in so many ages nothing had been observed to have been altered, his scholars stubbornly maintain his proposition still, though by many experiences of new stars, the reason which moved Aristotle seems now to be utterly defeated?[31]

On balance, then, Donne would seem to be on the side of the innovators, championing experiential discoveries over stubborn and blind adherence to outworn beliefs and traditions.

Notes

1. Katharine Park and Lorraine Daston, "Introduction," in *The Cambridge History of Science, Volume 3: Early Modern Science*, eds. Katharine Park and Lorraine Datson (Cambridge University Press, 2006), 4.
2. See Anna Blair, "Natural Philosophy," in *Cambridge History*, 365–406.
3. William Harvey, "To Doctor Argent, President of the London College of Physicians," in *The Circulation of the Blood and Other Writings*, ed. Andrew Wear (London: J. M. Dent & Sons Ltd, 1990), 5.
4. Park and Daston, "Introduction," 3.
5. Park and Daston, "Introduction," 4.
6. John Securis, *Detection and Querimonie of the Daily Enormities and Abuses Committed in Physic* (London, 1566), sig. B4v.
7. Deborah E. Harkness, *The Jewel House: Elizabethan London and the Scientific Revolution* (New Haven, CT: Yale University Press, 2007), xv.
8. Harkness, *Jewel House*, 9.
9. On November 28, 1660, the committee of 12 announced the formation of The Royal Society in these terms. See https://royalsociety.org/.
10. William Donahue, "Astronomy," in *Cambridge History*, 562.
11. *Sermons*, 6:265.
12. See *The First Anniversary*, "And in those constellations there arise / New stars, and old do vanish from our eyes" (259–60).
13. Robert Burton, *The Anatomy of Melancholy*, ed. Holbrook Jackson (London: J. M. Dent & Sons, 1932), 56.
14. John Haffenden, "Introduction," in *William Empson: Essays on Renaissance Literature, Volume One: Donne and the New Philosophy* (Cambridge University Press, 1993), 25–26.
15. Sir Henry Wotton, *Life and Letters*, ed. Logan Pearsall Smith, 2 vols. (Oxford, 1907), 1:486–87.
16. John Read, *Through Alchemy to Chemistry* (London: G. Bell and Sons, 1961), 24.
17. *Letters*, 13.
18. William R. Newman, "From Alchemy to 'Chymistry,'" in *Cambridge History*, 497–517, 498, 497, 499.
19. See Charles Nicholl, *Chemical Theatre* (London: Routledge, 1980), 17.
20. Lyndy Abraham, *Marvell and Alchemy* (Aldershot: Scolar Press, 1990), 2–3.
21. See Margaret Healy, *Shakespeare, Alchemy and the Creative Imagination* (Cambridge University Press, 2011), 32–35.

22. George Puttenham, *The Art of English Poesy by George Puttenham: A Critical Edition*, eds. Frank Whigham and Wayne A. Rebhorn (Ithaca, NY: Cornell University Press, 2007), 136–37.

23. Martin Luther, *The Table Talk of Martin Luther*, trans. William Hazlitt (London: G. Bell, 1902), DCCCV.

24. *Sermons*, 5:19. Discussed in James R. Keller, "The Science of Salvation: Spiritual Alchemy in Donne's Final Sermon," *Sixteenth-Century Journal* 23:3 (1992), 491.

25. *Sermons*, 4:110.

26. Joseph Hall, *An Open and Plaine Paraphrase, upon the Song of Songs, which is Salomens* (London, 1609), sig. N2v.

27. *Letters*, 102.

28. Donne, *Devotions upon Emergent Occasions*, cited in John Stubbs, *John Donne: The Reformed Soul* (New York: W. W. Norton & Company, 2006), 404.

29. Cited in J. V. Field, "John Donne and 'New Philosophy,'" Literary Londoners: A Series of Lectures Given at Gresham College in 1995, www .gresham.ac.uk, 43.

30. Joseph Mazzeo, *Renaissance and Seventeenth-Century Studies* (New York: Columbia University Press, 1964), 61.

31. John Donne, *Biathanatos*, eds. Michael Rudick and M. Pabst Battin (New York: Garland Publishing, 1982), 140.

CHAPTER 22

Donne and Skepticism

Anita Gilman Sherman

Skepticism appears to be a contrarian way to approach John Donne's thought and art. After all, how can a man as religious as the Dean of St. Paul's, the author of sermons and works like the Holy Sonnets and the *Devotions upon Emergent Occasions*, be a skeptic? It is implausible only if we mean by skepticism (as many do today) a loose synonym for disbelief or disenchantment. In the sixteenth century, however, skepticism meant doubting whether it was possible to have true and certain knowledge about the world.[1] If we go back to the Greek origins of the word – *skeptikos* means questioning, which is related to the verb *skeptesthai*, to look out or consider – we discover that it refers to a process of intellectual inquiry that does not preclude religious faith and can occur alongside it. While Donne dissociates himself from the Greek skeptics on the rare occasions he mentions them, he nevertheless finds aspects of their philosophy of investigation congenial.[2] Skepticism offers him a structured way to think about the disjunction between his own roving curiosity with its appetite for novelty and his longing for certainties. Skepticism also allows him to prize doubt. Skeptical doubt operates for Donne not only as a symptom of the crisis of knowledge precipitated by the Renaissance and Reformation, but also as a therapeutic cure for it.

When Donne writes in "Satire III," "doubt wisely; in strange way / To stand enquiring right is not to stray" (77–78), he is speaking of the search for "true religion" and of the quandary of the believer in a post-Reformation world where Christian sects abound. Donne himself struggled with his religious allegiance, eventually abandoning the Catholic faith in which he had been raised and converting to Protestantism. "Satire III" attests to the conflicting emotions of such a struggle. The poet resents that he "Of force must one, and forced but one allow; / And the right" (70–71), signaling with his repetition the coercion of having to choose a religion when everything – salvation itself – is at stake in picking the right one. "Fool and wretch," he says, addressing himself, "wilt thou let thy soul be tied / To man's laws, by which she shall not be tried / At the last day?" (93–95). In his protest against the power of the state to compel religious belief, he argues that doubt is the avenue to truth and thoughtful inquiry the most heroic stance for the truth-seeker. "Satire III" imagines the believer's search for religious truth as a quest:

> On a huge hill,
> Cragged and steep, Truth stands, and he that will
> Reach her, about must, and about must go;
> And what the'hill's suddenness resists, win so.   (79–82)

The circling labor of conquering the hill is the mind's equivalent of knightly valor: "Hard deeds, the body's pains; hard knowledge too / The mind's endeavours reach" (86–87). Skepticism here is about the mind's endeavors, a restless striving for religious truth.

If skepticism in "Satire III" is about the intellectual courage of doubting wisely and keeping faith with one's own conscience, elsewhere the mood of Donne's skepticism differs. Sometimes it takes a mournful turn, as if a new uncertainty had entered the world, shaking its foundations. In *The First Anniversary*, for example, when he writes that the "new philosophy calls all in doubt" (205), Donne confronts the Copernican Revolution. By "new philosophy" he means the new astronomy. The "all" eroded by doubt gestures both to the past and the future: grieving the loss of traditional understandings of the universe and anticipating its far-reaching consequences. The poem continues:

> And freely men confess that this world's spent,
> When in the planets and the firmament
> They seek so many new; they see that this
> Is crumbled out again to his atomies.
> 'Tis all in pieces, all coherence gone;
> All just supply and all relation.   (209–14)

Somehow the new science is both cause and symptom of a world that is falling apart, rendering "just" relations elusive. At other times, however, Donne's mood is playful, as if skeptical inquiry were a pleasurable self-indulgence. In a 1619 sermon, for example, he observes that "the mind of a curious man delights to examine it selfe upon Interrogatories, which, upon the Rack, it cannot answer, and to vexe it selfe with such doubts as it cannot resolve."[3] Doubt functions here as a voluptuous form of self-inflicted torture or masochistic compulsion. But regardless of his mood – whether viewing doubt as a bad habit to be overcome, as the cataclysmic end of tradition, or as a chivalrous trait to be cultivated – Donne favors the thought-experiment as a skeptical strategy.

The term thought-experiment usually refers to the philosophical practice of imagining hypothetical situations that test the limits of an issue and
map its frontiers. René Descartes is famous for devising thought-
experiments like the scenario that issues in his famous dictum, *cogito ergo
sum*. Donne performs something like Cartesian investigations when he
gives his mind free rein and permits himself to pursue a line of inquiry to its
outermost limit. Like Descartes, who hoped to vanquish doubt and isolate
truth by methodically doubting everything, Donne engages in thought-
experiments designed to arrive at metaphysical truths. The metaphysical
wit for which he is known enlivens his poetic forays to the edges of the
knowable. Take, for example, "The Relic," a poem at once deeply religious
and light-heartedly skeptical that sketches various moments in a possible
afterlife. The first stanza sets the parameters of the thought-experiment:

> When my grave is broke up again
> Some second guest to entertain
> (For graves have learned that woman-head
> To be to more than one a bed),
>   And he that digs it spies
> A bracelet of bright hair about the bone,
>   Will he not let'us alone,
> And think that there a loving couple lies,
> Who thought that this device might be some way
> To make their souls, at the last busy day,
> Meet at this grave, and make a little stay?   (1–11)

At least three futures are projected: the speaker's own burial, a disinterment
further off in time uncovering two bodies, and a fleeting rendezvous on
the Day of Judgment. The past surfaces at the stanza's midpoint when "a
bracelet of bright hair" evokes a former gift or love-token now deemed by
the poet a "device" that will help the pair find one another in the chaos of
the general resurrection. The poet dwells on the interpretation of the
gravedigger, guessing the questions he will ask. This fits with Donne's
predilection for imagining the mind-set of third parties witnessing his love.
He develops his fantasy in the second stanza, picturing a world that has
reverted to Catholicism and its "mis-devotion:"

> If this fall in a time or land
> Where mis-devotion doth command,
> Then he that digs us up will bring
> Us to the bishop and the king
>   To make us relics; then
> Thou shalt be'a Mary Magdalen, and I

> A something else thereby;
> All women shall adore us, and some men;
> And since at such time miracles are sought,
> I would have that age by this paper taught
> What miracles we harmless lovers wrought.   (12–22)

Donne fantasizes that "he that digs us up" will recognize their physical remains as "relics" worthy of adoration. He spins out the thought to a heretical extreme, appending the word "I" and adding an extra syllable to the stanza's central line, before likening himself (it is implied) to none other than Jesus. Since all this will happen when "miracles are sought," the speaker feels obliged – in a mood both pedagogical and meta-poetical – to instruct those future people "by this paper" the miracles "we harmless lovers wrought." The third stanza lists the lessons of their exemplary love, surprising us with the couple's chastity as a way of backing off from the dangerous suggestion lodged in the second stanza that Mary Magdalen and Jesus enjoyed erotic intimacy:

> First, we loved well and faithfully,
> Yet knew not what we loved, nor why;
> Difference of sex no more we knew
> Than our guardian angels do;
>   Coming and going, we
> Perchance might kiss, but not between those meals;
>   Our hands ne'er touched the seals
> Which nature, injured by late law, sets free.
> These miracles we did, but now, alas,
> All measure, and all language, I should pass,
> Should I tell what a miracle she was.   (23–33)

The third stanza reverts to the past tense, wistfully recalling the miracles of *agape*, even while suggesting that but for "late law" things might have been otherwise. The poem closes by pondering the limitations of language such that "the word *miracle* becomes harder and harder to read, and yet a place to dwell and an idea to dwell upon."[4] If the poem memorializes a miraculous relationship, its mode of celebration adopts the skeptical strategy of the thought-experiment. Its hypothetical scenarios skirt the edges of blasphemy with its joyously narcissistic fantasy of shared sainthood.

Donne engages in these skeptical investigations not only in his poetry but also in his prose and in his sermons. For example, in his treatise *Biathanatos* he explores suicide in various times and places. In it he entertains the idea that Jesus himself was a suicide, thereby making self-slaughter acceptable. While this work is by turns macabre and melancholy, it too evinces the skeptical temper of Donne's mind: his need to question and test received truths. In 1619, on the eve of a trip, Donne sent a manuscript copy to his friend Sir Robert Ker for safe-keeping, distancing himself from the work by saying it was "a Book written by Jack Donne, and not by Dr. Donne."[5] He imposed a retrospective narrative on his life, separating his libertine youth from his maturity as a responsible man of the cloth. Many critics (among them, Izaak Walton, Donne's first biographer) follow this account, assuming that Donne dropped his skeptical tendencies once he became a minister. While it is true that Donne worked hard to govern his skepticism in his later years, mobilizing rhetorical and psychological strategies to contain it, in my view this effort reveals the dialectical quality of his skepticism rather than its abeyance. Donne may labor to relinquish his skepticism – for example, by modeling himself retrospectively on the Augustinian pattern of conversion – but his attempts belie him since his questions and hunger for answers continue unabated.

Skepticism not only has moods, but also a dialectical rhythm, veering from despair to detachment to faith and back again. Because it involves "dissatisfactions with finitude" (to borrow the phrase of the contemporary American philosopher Stanley Cavell), skepticism is no mere philosophical pose, but rather a way of experiencing the world.[6] It is an existential condition prone to fluctuation – inconstancy, Donne might call it – and yearnings for perfect knowledge. It does not issue in the peace of mind that the Greek skeptics claimed followed from skeptical inquiry. On the contrary, doubt produces unappeasable desire. As a young man, Donne is consumed with his "Hydroptique immoderate desire of humane learning and languages."[7] Likewise, in his old age he describes his "desire to learne" and "the restlesnesse, and irresolution of the Soule," declaring that "the soule of man cannot bee considered under a thicker cloud, then Ignorance, nor under a heavier weight, then desire of knowledge."[8]

In his Easter sermon of 1628, Donne meditates on the intertwining of skepticism and Christianity, selecting the verse from Paul's first Letter to the Corinthians: "For now we see through a glass, darkly; but then face to face: now I know in part; but then shall I know even as I am known" (13:12). Donne's metaphysical wit is on full display in this sermon. He opens soberly by parsing individual words and phrases, but soon the Pauline language becomes a vehicle for Donne's interpretive riffs on reason, faith, belief, and knowledge. The words *now, then, see, glass, light, sight,* and *darkly* (as a translation for *in ænigmate*) become occasions for rhetorical dilation, even as Donne delights in paradox, saying of God, "All other sight

is blindnesse, all other knowledge is ignorance."[9] What begins as an
explication of the Biblical text grows into a joyous exercise of semantic
proliferation as metaphors and questions multiply. As he does in
"The Relic," Donne fathoms future times and possible afterlives, confi-
dently ventriloquizing other voices from a "Basilisk" and a "Slowe-worme"
to a "bestiall Atheist" and to Jesus, although stopping short of God himself.
He even conjures up the darkness of Hell. The skepticism of this sermon
has nothing to do with religious doubt. It has to do with Donne's central
concern: the varieties of partial understanding that define our existence in
this world. He contrasts inadequate forms of sight and knowledge in this
life with exalted forms of sight and knowledge in heaven. To illustrate the
imperfections of worldly sight, he adapts tropes from Greek skepticism.
"But how doe we see in a glasse? Truly, that is not easily determined," he
notes before canvassing "the old Writers in the Optiques" whose contradictory opinions he deems "a uselesse labour . . . to reconcile." Then he
introduces an ancient skeptical commonplace: "This glasse is better then
the water; The water gives a crookednesse, and false dimensions to things
that it shewes; as we see by an Oare when we row a Boat."[10] The crooked
oar underwater is a sign of unreliable perception and has a long and
distinguished history. It appears, for example, in Plato's *Republic* (X.602.
d), in Cicero's *Academica*, in Augustine's *Against the Academicians*, and in
Sextus Empiricus's second-century codification of skeptical philosophy
where it serves to illustrate the fifth Mode of Anaesidemus.[11] My point is
that Donne draws on skeptical commonplaces in his recital of different
degrees of dissatisfaction with finitude.

In another sermon, he also alludes to Aneasidemus's bent oar: "And as
under water, every thing seems distorted and crooked, to man, so does man
himself to God, who sees not his own Image in that man, in that form as he
made it."[12] Here the stymied knower is God, prevented by human sin from
seeing his creature face to face. In this early sermon from 1618, the thought-
experiment has traveled so far out that we are made privy to God's
thoughts. But in his 1628 Easter sermon, Donne reins in his investigations.
When he asks, "What shall we see, by seeing him so, *face to face?*" he
criticizes Gregory the Great for his too "wild speculation" on the subject
and pulls back, preferring to "rest we in the testimony of a safer witnesse,
a Councell."[13] Rather than speculating about what that exalted vision
might encompass, Donne concentrates instead on an epistemological
analysis of faith: "Faith is a blessed presence, but compared with heavenly
vision, it is but an absence; though it create and constitute in us
a possibility, a probability, a kinde of certainty of salvation, yet that

faith, which the best Christian hath, is not so far beyond that sight of God which the naturall man hath, as that sight of God which I shall have in heaven, is above that faith which we have now in the highest exaltation." Possibility, probability, a kind of certainty – these intuitions of faith fall short of knowing God. As he puts it, "the knowledge which I have of God here (even by faith . . .) is but a knowledge in part."[14] Donne's longing for complete knowledge depends on his skeptical awareness that knowledge in this life is, at best, partial. Although he had long disavowed his skeptical phase as Jack Donne, when he sat down in the spring of 1628 to write a sermon on Paul's verses from 1 Corinthians, Donne found himself once more conveying the dialectical rhythms of skepticism with its extremes of despair and deferred ecstasy.

In other words, skepticism in Donne has to be approached in two seemingly contradictory ways. The first involves an intermittently alienated way of being-in-the-world that manifests itself in "passionate utterance," which Stanley Cavell describes as "an invitation to improvisation in the disorders of desire."[15] Skepticism, one might say, invites Donne to improvise on the disorders of desire: his passionate desire for truth alternates with frustration over the impossibility of complete knowledge. The second approach is less psychological and more historical. It involves the books Donne read and the practices of the Renaissance schoolroom. Like many well-educated Europeans, Donne was familiar not only with classical works of skepticism, many of them newly translated, but also with contemporary texts. Donne cites Michel de Montaigne's *Essays*, for example, arguably the most important skeptical text of the sixteenth century. He was also acquainted with the work of his fellow Londoners, Francis Bacon, William Cornwallis, Sir John Davies, John Florio, and Fulke Greville, among others – all of whom read Montaigne and discussed skepticism. Besides Sextus Empiricus, whose *Outlines of Skepticism* had been translated into Latin in 1562, Donne knew the skeptical dialogues of Lucian of Samosata, translated by Erasmus, and *The Lives of the Philosophers* by Diogenes Laertius with its amusing account of Pyrrho, founder of the Pyrrhonist school of skepticism. At the turn of the seventeenth century, many intellectuals, including Donne, grappled with skeptical philosophy and its implications.

Alongside his library of skeptical texts, Donne internalized skeptical practices from the rhetorical training he received formally as a student and informally as a reader. The key here was the skeptical emphasis on arguing both sides of a question – *in utramque partem*. The model of the Ciceronian dialogue, the declension of the medieval *quaestio*, the technique of the Senecan *controversia*, the habit and aesthetic of *copia*, the *paragone* pitting the arts against one another, and the tradition of humanist debate – all these rhetorical structures were imparted to young minds.[16] They encouraged pupils to inhabit different points of view and to impersonate different voices, even as they elicited problems of choice. Pyrrho and Sextus advised the skeptic to suspend judgment (*epochē*) and thereby attain tranquility (*ataraxia*), since it was impossible to know the truth of things. But some Renaissance skeptics found that seeing two or more sides of a question did not produce tranquility. Although Donne tries to convince himself in "Satire III" that doubting wisely is the best option, the poem eloquently shows the agitation accompanying a stance of principled detachment. Donne's skepticism, with its openness to other beliefs, endows him with an acute sensitivity to ethical pressures and the stakes of action.

Donne's skepticism may not offer him serenity, but it does contribute to the crafting of his unmistakable poetic voice and his unerring sense of the important issues of his time. Religious pluralism, the scientific revolution, liberty of conscience, erotic love, the costs of conformity, political tyranny, the fear of death, the hope of salvation – these are his preferred themes. Donne elaborates on them and their attendant paradoxes – the clash of private and public, the intertwining of the sacred and the profane, the loneliness of a puzzling universe – in keeping with the dialectical temper of his skeptical mind. Luckily for his readers, Donne's profound dissatisfaction with finitude leads to experiments and improvisations on the disorders of desire that seduce us still, four centuries later.

Notes

1. Charles B. Schmitt, *Cicero Scepticus: A Study of the Influence of the* Academica *in the Renaissance* (The Hague: Martinus Nijhoff, 1972), 8.
2. See Donne, "Paradox 3," and Sermon 7 in vol. 1 and Sermon 4 in vol. 2 of *Sermons*.
3. *Sermons*, 2:84.
4. Kenneth Gross, "The Survival of Strange Sounds: Forms of Life in Lyric Poetry," *Yale Review* 103:2 (2015), 41.
5. Carey, *Mind*, 209.
6. Stanley Cavell, *Philosophy the Day after Tomorrow* (Cambridge, MA: Harvard University Press, 2005), 44.
7. *Letters*, 44.
8. *Sermons*, 8:258.
9. *Sermons*, 8:220.

10. *Sermons*, 8:222–23.
11. See Julia Annas and Jonathan Barnes, *The Modes of Scepticism: Ancient Texts and Modern Interpretations* (Cambridge University Press, 1985).
12. *Sermons*, 2:114.
13. *Sermons*, 8:234.
14. *Sermons*, 8:229.
15. Cavell, *Philosophy*, 19.
16. Anita Gilman Sherman, *Skepticism and Memory in Shakespeare and Donne* (Palgrave Macmillan, 2007), 13.

CHAPTER 23

The Metaphysics of the Metaphysicals

Gordon Teskey

A specter haunts English literary history of the seventeenth century, the specter of *metaphysical poetry*. This is perhaps as it should be, for metaphysics – the abstract science of being and of first principles such as time, space, substance, and motion – is the most spectral of disciplines, existing in a middle state between the tangible and the wholly transcendent, between the physical world and theology. But we are assured that the term *metaphysical*, applied to poets of the early seventeenth century, and preeminently to Donne, has nothing to do with metaphysics as a philosophical discipline. It means nothing more than abstract, over-subtle, and ingenious to a fault.

To begin at the beginning. In the mid-1590s, between the first and second installments of Spenser's *Faerie Queene* (1590 and 1596), John Donne began to write an aggressively new, anti-Spenserian kind of verse. The new verse employed scholastic knowledge as a substitute for classical myth; displayed what Francis Bacon, speaking of the scholastic philosophers, would call "infinite agitation of wit"; and invented strikingly unnatural, unintuitive, unexpected comparisons.[1] Moreover, to contemporaries, Donne made a new sort of sound: his meter is deliberately rough – Jonson would say he deserved hanging for not keeping accent – and his voice is self-assertive, even aggressive. Spenser's *Amoretti* 75 begins, "One day I wrote her name upon the strand, / but came the waves and washèd it away" (1–2).[2] The meter and phrasing are equitonal, a smoothly repetitive oscillation, gently rising and falling, like a sine wave. Donne opens "The Sun Rising" as follows: "Busy old fool, unruly Sun, / Why dost thou thus, / Through windows and through curtains call on us?" (1–3). The meter of every line is different, and complex, and the tone is hurried, breathlessly annoyed; the effect, in contrast with the Spenserian sine wave, is jagged. Spenser's voice is that of the generalized and ennobled poet, at ease in the universe and not entirely distinct from it, being in harmony with all things, with the *musica universalis*. Donne's voice is utterly individual and a law to itself – hence the delightful and, we should have thought, spectacularly inappropriate epithet of the sun: *unruly*. The sun always keeps to its rule: it comes up in the morning and goes down in the evening. Donne's speaker will make the sun conform to *his* rule, not to its own: "This bed thy centre is, these walls, thy sphere" (30). This is not a voice that affirms its harmonious and authoritative belonging to the world, as Spenser's does. It is a voice fighting for power. Its will is always opposed to another, here, the will of the sun.

In the standard account, metaphysical poets of the seventeenth century are a loosely defined group, the members of which, stretched over three generations, were not conscious of belonging to any such classification, although they were all conscious of moving beyond the aureate, mythopoeic, and euphonious style of the great Elizabethans. The more prominent figures after Donne are George Herbert (1593–1633), Thomas Carew (1595–1640?), John Cleveland (1613–1658), Abraham Cowley (1617–1618), Andrew Marvell (1621–1668), Henry Vaughan (1622–1695), and Thomas Traherne (1636–1674). But many more could be included in the group, including Katherine Philips (1632–64), as they were in the modern anthology by Donne's great editor, H. J. C. Grierson, published in 1921, *Metaphysical Lyrics and Poems of the Seventeenth Century*.

The metaphysical poets wanted two things: to be as like Donne as possible, and to be as different from the great Elizabethans as possible. In pursuit of these goals their ingenuity was applied to alienating themselves from all the familiar pathways of thought that earlier poets had worn through that world, the familiar comparisons and clichés, consecrated by time. How to be absolutely new? Physically separated but spiritually united lovers are a pair of stiff twin geometrical compasses; the distinction between a man's love and a woman's is the difference between angelic intelligence and the pure, crystalline heavenly sphere that this intelligence governs (this, at least, a truly metaphysical conceit); the soul separated from the body is a bullet fired from an exploding, rusty gun; God's love is the cement between stones on the church floor; human restlessness is a pulley, the contrivance of God's prevenient grace; mowers are Israelites passing through the steep sides of a sea of grass; and fishermen carrying their leather boats on their heads are antipodean monopods, shading their heads with one shoe. As in Donne, there is not a single classical image or allusion among these examples, classical myth having been the *parole* of poets for two thousand years. New imagery, new ways of feeling emotion more keenly by comparison to the ostentatiously other, must be found.

Grierson's anthology was reviewed in *The Times Literary Supplement* (1921) by T. S. Eliot, in a classic essay that set the metaphysical poets on course to become an academic field, and *metaphysics* to mean the immediacy of thought as sensuous experience: "a thought to Donne was an experience; it modified his sensibility ... [like] the noise of the typewriter or the smell of cooking; in the mind of the poet these experiences are always forming new wholes."[3] We have come a long way from Dr. Johnson's use of the word *metaphysical* for thoughts that are abstract and unnatural. The metaphysical in poetry – for Eliot, it was possible in thirteenth-century Italy and nineteenth-century France, as well as in seventeenth- and twentieth-century England – is the unmediated transmission of thought into the physical world, into sounds and smells.

The adjective *metaphysical* would be fastened on the poets of the seventeenth century toward the end of the following century, in Samuel Johnson's "Life of Cowley" (1779), the first of his *Lives of the Poets* (1779–1781), in which Johnson speaks of a "race" of "what may be termed metaphysical poets" appearing "about the beginning of the seventeenth century." They operate by "a kind of *discordia concors*; a combination of dissimilar images, or discovery of occult resemblances in things apparently unlike." As a result, their thoughts are "often new, but seldom natural; they are not obvious, but neither are they just; and the reader, far from wondering that he missed them, wonders more frequently by what perverseness of industry they were ever found." With cautious approbation on one point, Johnson says that to write in this over-ingenious style it was at least necessary to read and think.[4] Poets deserving the term *metaphysical* in a more rigorous sense are Margaret Cavendish (1623–73) and Lucy Hutchinson (1620–81).

Johnson has his impressive term for these poets from John Dryden, writing at the end of the seventeenth century:

> [Donne] affects the metaphysics, not only in his satires, but in his amorous verses, where nature only should reign; and perplexes the minds of the fair sex with nice speculations of philosophy, when he should engage their hearts, and entertain them with the softnesses of love. ... Their wish was only to say what they hoped had never been said before.[5]

Dr. Johnson's use of *metaphysical* is casually descriptive, as was Dryden's before, but Dryden is a little more precise in contrasting the term *metaphysical* with *nature*. The *metaphysics*, as Dryden calls them in the plural, with his awareness of Greek (*ta meta ta physika*), are abstracted from nature, for they consist in the "nice" or subtle distinctions that are made in speculative philosophy about such things as being, quality, genesis, and change, and also about the immortal substance of the heavenly bodies, a question of particular interest to Donne.

As with specters of any kind, opinion has swung wildly back and forth between enthusiastic credulity and wise-in-its-own-conceit skepticism as to the existence of a school of metaphysical poets separable from individuals (this question – whether entities are to be multiplied beyond necessity – is itself a metaphysical question). Are there any metaphysical poets? Is Donne *sui generis* and his followers hardly to be accounted anything more than a fashionable mimicry? Is there a defined school, or "race," bearing a family resemblance, where some members share traits with some others who in turn share different traits with yet others, but no common trait runs through the whole? Are all poets of the seventeenth century, or at least of the century's first two thirds, possessed by metaphysical tendencies? Is the entire century, or the first two thirds of it, in some occult sense *metaphysical?*

* * * *

For Aristotle, the discipline of inquiry that would after him be called *metaphysics* (*meta* "across, alongside, beyond" + *physis* "nature," that which grows, changes, and decays), is "first philosophy" (*hê prôtê philosophia*). It is concerned with the first and most fundamental question, that of "being and not being" (*on kai mê on*). What is the foundation, the ground of being? Aristotle described such knowledge as "theological" (*theologikê*), and differentiated it on the one hand from the "mathematical" (*mathematikê*) and on the other hand the "physical" (*physikê*). Mathematical knowledge – for example, geometry – concerns things that have freedom from change (the sum of the angles of a triangle does not decay over time) but lack independent being: triangles must be represented contingently on physical things, for example, on paper. Physical knowledge – for example, biology – concerns things that have independent being (bodies exist in themselves) but lack freedom from change: bodies die. "Theological" knowledge – knowledge of the heavenly bodies above the moon – concerns things that suffer neither of these deficiencies.[6] These are free from change and have independent being, and are thus closer to "being" in itself, as opposed to "not being." At least this seemed to be so until supernovas were observed in the heavens, the course of the planets, especially Mars, seemed "out of square," and Edmund Spenser composed *The Mutabilitie Cantos* (1609), his great poetic meditation on metaphysical decay, that is, on change above the sphere of the moon.

Donne famously refers to the same phenomenon in *The First Anniversary*, the "new philosophy" (i.e., science) that "puts all in doubt" (205). But more often he refers to the old, Ptolemaic and Aristotelian cosmology and its adjustments because of its usefulness to poetry as an image of perfect, non-decaying, immutable being. In particular, he refers often to the perfect substance, or "metal" of the nested, crystalline spheres enclosing the earth at successive distances, spheres on which the planets are the only part visible to us, like the point of light on a soap bubble. When he says, "So thy love may be my love's sphere" ("Air and Angels," 25) and "Let man's soul be a sphere" ("Good Friday, 1613," 1), he is referring to metaphysical objects, things that are free of decay and have independent being. They are perfect, or teleological, things since they are what every independent being wants to be: existing in eminence, and everlasting. They are also an image of divine Creation before the Fall, when the substance of the material world was perfect. In our day, powerful telescopes allow us to look back in time, into the noise and primordial light of the original universe. In Donne's day, when Galileo's discoveries were just becoming known, it seemed possible, by looking up into the heavens, to look back in time at the substance of the world as it was when God made it, before Eve and Adam fell.

Medieval theology added entirely spiritual beings – beings above these teleological things – to the array of possible beings, such as angels, or, as they are also called, "intelligences." Angels are assigned to move the celestial spheres – one angel per sphere – but they have their home above the visible heavens, in the supercelestial realm, such as we see in the later parts of Dante's *Paradiso* when we have passed beyond the sphere of the fixed stars. For this reason medieval theology, which includes the theory of angels, is distinct from and higher than metaphysics.

Here, then, is a theological question. Since angels are spiritual beings wholly distinct from physical beings, such as humans who have bodies, how do angels become visible to humans, as they do in the Bible to Abraham and to the Virgin Mary? How does an angel kill the firstborn of Egypt, or the Assyrian host? The answer of Thomas Aquinas is that angels clothe themselves in bodies made of the most rarified element, that of air, which is highest in nature (air, it was supposed, reaches up to the moon) and which is closest to the metaphysical realm of unchanging bodies. Hence, Donne can write, "Then as an angel, face and wings / Of air, not pure as it, yet pure doth wear" ("Air and Angels," 23–24). This intermediate and transactional region of *disparity* between purely spiritual and the purest material things fascinates Donne: "Just such disparity / As is

'twixt air and angels' purity / 'Twixt women's love and men's will ever be"
("Air and Angels," 26–28).[7]

Angels put on visible bodies of compressed air, and angelic intelligences
move the crystal spheres in the heavens. As to the objects in the heavens –
the planets and their spheres plus, above them, the sphere of the fixed
stars – these are *supernaturalia* ("things above nature"), where the Latin
prefix *super* ("above") translates the subtler and more complex Greek prefix
meta; and Latin *natura* (a word related to birth, coming into being)
translates Greek *physis*, a word related to *phuo* ("to grow"). By this process
of translation and adaptation, metaphysics came to mean the supersubtle
science of universals, of permanent abstractions above physical particulars
(e.g., correlatives and contraries), and of the finer distinctions between
such abstractions, as seen in the most difficult of the late medieval philosophers, Duns Scotus, who not without reason was called the "subtle
doctor," and who was an important figure for Donne.

Once one has entered this mentally challenging, spectral realm of
scholastic philosophy, the more fundamental question of metaphysics –
the question of being and not being, and the question of the ground,
"what is Being?" (*ti to on?*) – falls out of sight. It falls out of sight *as
a question*. It does so because medieval science had an answer to it, one
that would hold until the metaphysical inquiries of Hobbes and
Spinoza in the seventeenth century. Being is two substances, matter
and spirit; but the former, matter, was created by the latter in its
highest form, that is, by God. Although being is divided between
matter and spirit, spirit is the ultimate ground of being because God
created matter itself out of nothing (*ex nihilo*). Being is divided
between spirit and matter, but spirit is prior to matter. As God,
Spirit is the productive *archê* or *principium*, the first principle for first
philosophy, that is, for metaphysics: *in principio erat Verbum* "in the
beginning was the Word" (John 1:1). For medieval, scholastic metaphysics, therefore, the ground of being is no longer a question. It has been
answered with a theological mystery that permits no further inquiry.
But later problems, such as whether souls exist eternally or are created
at each birth, and the relation of the immortal soul to the body – still
a live question for René Descartes – and whether universals exist, are
indeed open questions. The point is, they are questions that come later.
They are not, in the full sense, originative metaphysical questions but
rather technical problems flowing from unquestioned presuppositions.

Such questions – the relations between physical bodies, metaphysical
objects, and the spiritual world, and the possible relations between

disembodied souls (as in "The Ecstasy") – are continually worried and exploited in Donne, notably in the *Anniversaries*.

The result is a curious aesthetic paradox. By shunning classical myth in favor of outmoded, supersubtle, medieval cosmology and metaphysics, Donne manages to seem modern, smart, and up to date. The reason this tactic worked is that Donne uses medieval knowledge as others used classical myth: advancing no claim for its objective truth but making considerable claims for its subjective truth. Once this point has been appreciated, all questions concerning Donne's use of scholastic metaphysics become problems of annotation, of philology, in the same way and for the same reason that the ontological question, the question of first philosophy, became in the later Middle Ages a fantastic array of technical problems. The problems of annotation are, to be sure, challenging and demand professional skill. But they are not philosophical.

* * * *

But what of the side of metaphysics that scholastic philosophy forgets because it has an answer, the question of the ground? What is the ground of being for Donne *as a poet*, and for the poets that we call, by an accident, as it seems, *metaphysical*? That the ground of being for Donne as a man, and for the other metaphysical poets, was what it was for most people in the earlier seventeenth century – body and soul, matter and spirit – is true but uninteresting. This dualism, with the single principle of Spirit behind it at the beginning, had been the answer to the question of Being, of *esse*, throughout the Christian Middle Ages. None of the poets we call "metaphysical" was interested in the monism that made its appearance in the seventeenth century in Spinoza and, for poetry, in Milton.

But the question of the ground does open up for the metaphysical poets in the earlier seventeenth century. The "ground" in question, however, is not the ground of Being, but rather what we may name *the ontological ground of figurative language*. This is the unspoken and unseen basis of a poetry that speaks and sees because of it, performing such operations as *metaphor*, "a carrying across" (Gr. *meta* + *pherein*), by which the virtue of one thing is carried over to be absorbed in the force of another. That such operations are possible requires that there be in place first a ground of assumptions about the world (an analogy to it is the operating system on your computer), a ground that makes poetic expression possible in the first place. What are the conditions for the possibility of poetic expression for the Elizabethan poets? *What is there, what exists, to make poetry possible in the first place?* That is the metaphysical question for poetry, the site of its "first philosophy." Adapting it to the question in hand, we may ask, *What is, or what are, the metaphysics of the metaphysicals?*

Such a question implies that a new ground for poetry had to appear in the seventeenth century, if we may extend the century back into the 1590s, when the world itself seemed to be crumbling to its atomies, as we see, for example, in Hippolyta's great speech on decay in *A Midsummer Night's Dream* (2.2.88–114). Bad harvests, hailstones, climate change, plague, economic depression, dissolution of communities and of peoples, many of them streaming into London, and a suddenly old Virgin Queen whom time had surprised – all suggested that an older and more orderly world was falling apart. What was this more orderly, though imaginary, world? It is described in detail in two great and simple books by modern masters of criticism: E. M. W. Tillyard's *Elizabethan World Picture* (1943) and C. S. Lewis's *The Discarded Image: An Introduction to Medieval and Renaissance Literature* (1964). "World Picture" and "Image" translate the useful German word *Weltanschauung*, "how the world comes forth in appearance to people in particular circumstances at particular times."

How is the world composed and put together, of what does it consist in its various parts, and on what principles do its parts interact? In the sense we have examined *metaphysics* so far, these are subsequent or technical questions, not primordial ones; for as we saw, the primordial was no longer in question: God created the world, and created it perfectly. For our purposes, one idea underlies the Elizabethan world picture, which was stated most openly by the Florentine philosopher Pico della Mirandola in his *Heptaplus: de Septiformi Sex Dierum Geneseos Enarratione* (1490), an overwrought theoretical work on seven aspects of the six days of Creation, and an inspiration for Baudelaire's great sonnet, "Correspondances." It is that the world, being created by God in perfection, is woven together by innumerable correspondences and harmonies, so that when any single thing is evoked it chimes with other, similar things on different levels of being, or even on the same level of being. The most moving and complete expression of this worldview in the seventeenth century is Milton's "On the Morning of Christ's Nativity" (1629), when the nine crystal spheres of the cosmos are enjoined to "ring out" and make "full consort" with the song of the angels at the Nativity of Jesus (125, 132; the entire passage extends from lines 109–48). This music, called the *musica mundana*, "music of the world [cosmos]," or *musica universalis*, "universal music of the spheres" (where *universal* means "all turning into one"), was audible to Eve and Adam before the Fall, but is unheard thereafter. The premature hope of the singer of Milton's Nativity Ode is that the Incarnation of Christ will make this music audible again, as the chorus of angels is audible.

But that is not possible, yet, and will not be until the Apocalypse. The thought is still more fully expressed in Milton's "At a Solemn Music" (1633). Yet this music, once heard by our first parents, still sounds in the Heavens above the moon. "There's not the smallest orb which thou behold'st," says Shakespeare's Lorenzo to Jessica, as they lie on their flowery bank in the moonlight, "But in his motion like an angel sings." But, he adds, "whilst this muddy vesture of decay [the sinful body] doth close it [the soul] in, we cannot hear it" (*The Merchant of Venice* 5.1.67–68; 70–71).[8] If music is the expression of these correspondences above the moon, in their perfect form, poetry is the expression of these correspondences below.

What the poets imitate or "feign" is the hidden, inner ideal, which has its natural expression in metaphor, because metaphor is based on real affinities between things, such as the natural affinity between a lady and a rose, or between her eyes and the stars, or between Queen Elizabeth and the goddess Diana or Spenser's Belphoebe. These are not arbitrary signs but motivated symbols, tiny, momentary revelations of the harmonious interior of the natural world. Poets play upon this world as an organist plays on an organ. The world is a perfectly tuned instrument for poetic expression.

Spenser's *Mutabilitie Cantos* provided a vision, although it was a temporary one, of the muddy vesture of decay smeared across sky and blotting out the stars. Donne's *Anniversaries* show us a world in which nothing is certain anymore and all is in doubt. The loss of the Elizabethan world picture, of the acoustical "Image" of a harmonious universe underlying the one we experience, the universe as it came from God's hand at Creation, was of course caused by the rise of modern science. But another of its effects was the loss of the ontological ground for figurative language. The poets were alone, alienated from the universe and, so far as a common system of belief for making poetry was concerned, separated from one another as well. They could go their separate ways; they could be individuals. A deeper and more perilously isolated and factitious subjectivity is born.

This means that the metaphysics of the metaphysicals was not shared but plural. Setting aside the greater figures of Spenser, Shakespeare, and Milton, the finest poets in this age of so many fine poets are represented in three generations. In the first generation we have John Donne and Ben Jonson, both born in 1572; in the second George Herbert, born in 1593; and in the third Andrew Marvell, born in 1621. Ben Jonson is not traditionally included among the metaphysical poets but has instead been thought, in the bewhiskered histories of English literature, to stand at the head of another, contrasting school, that of the cavalier poets. But in the sense I am using the term *metaphysical* here – a sense different from Dr. Johnson's casual one – the term includes all poets of this period because all had to find a new ground for poetic expression, a new operating system underlying and legitimating poetic figurality and expression.

Here in brief is what it seems to me they are. For Donne, it is the *will*; for Jonson, *society*; for Herbert, *God*, or rather his relation to God; and for Marvell, *consciousness*, or rather his relation to his own consciousness. Consciousness becomes the ground of modern poetry, whatever else is involved, such as politics, and the path of consciousness as a ground leads – to pluck some leading figures out of the crowd – from Marvell to Mallarmé, Eliot, Stevens, Ashbery, Heaney, and Graham. Herbert's God is not the God of Creation or even, primarily, the God of the Bible, the God who made of the world a system of natural symbols. Herbert's symbols are arbitrary because his God is an entirely personal one, his Redeemer, the God of Hopkins and Merton. For Herbert, his relation to God is the continual revelation of the unbelievable fact of Redemption. For Donne, his relation to God is a contest of turbulent wills.

As for Jonson, in, for example, "To Penshurst" or "Inviting a Friend to Supper," in his best-known poems (although what I am speaking of is even more obvious in the less familiar ones) the ground of poetic expression is in a new concept, although the word for it is older, denoting what "good conversation" means now: *society*. Marvell uses it purely in this older sense when he says, "Society is all but rude, / To this delicious solitude" ("The Garden," 15–16).[9] Good conversation, the most civilized of pleasures (after poetry) is crude and dull, so says the speaker of Marvell's poem, in comparison to the solitary pleasures of the garden. In Latin, as in earlier English usage – and of course the meaning is still primary today – a *societas* is a professional association, one united for a clear common purpose, whether for trade, religion, or war. The modern, holistic, and totalizing sense of *society* as "a community ... having shared customs, laws, and institutions" does not appear to have come into use until 1670.[10] Society in Durkheim's sense is an entity to itself, one that underlies law, politics, culture, manners, and economy. It is "metaphysical" because, although one cannot point to it, it is taken to exist fundamentally, to have independent being, and always to be present where there are human beings living together and striving for a common good. The metaphysical character of the term was indicated, perhaps unintentionally, when Margaret Thatcher, responding to a minister's appeal to it, said "there is no such thing as society."[11] *Society* in our sense of the word, as an underlying common good, is a modern idea, and For Spenser and Donne, see William Empson, "Donne the Space Man," in *Essays on Renaissance Literature*, ed. John Haffenden (Cambridge University Press, 1993), 1:86; Yulia Ryzhik, "Complaint and Satire in Spenser and Donne: Limits of Poetic Justice," *ELH* 47.1 (2017): 110–35; and "Spenser and Donne Go Fishing," *Spenser Studies* 32 (2018): 417–37. Jonson is its first poet.

Notes

1. Francis Bacon, *The Advancement of Learning*, ed. Thomas Case (Oxford University Press, 1974), 32–33.
2. Edmund Spenser, *The Shorter Poems*, ed. Richard A. McCabe (London: Penguin, 1999), 424.
3. T. S. Eliot, "The Metaphysical Poets," in *Selected Essays*, 3rd edn (London: Faber, 1951), p. 287. See also T. S. Eliot, *The Varieties of Metaphysical Poetry*, ed. Ronald Schuchard (New York: Harcourt Brace, 1993).
4. Samuel Johnson, *The Lives of the Poets*, ed. John H. Middendorf, 3 vols. (New Haven, CT: Yale University Press, 2010), 1:23–24,25–26, 27.
5. John Dryden, "A Discourse Concerning the Original Progress of Satire," in *Essays of John Dryden*, ed. W. P. Ker, 2 vols. (Oxford: Clarendon, 1926) 2:19.
6. Aristotle, *Metaphysics* 1026a10–22, ed. W. D. Ross (Oxford: Clarendeon Press, 1924). See also *De Caelo* 270b14.
7. For angels wearing bodies of compressed air, see the note on "Aire and Angels," in *The Poems of John Donne*, ed. Herbert J. C. Grierson, 2 vols. (Oxford: Clarendon Press, 1912), 2:21–22.
8. *The Complete Oxford Shakespeare*, eds. Stanley Wells and Gary Taylor, et al. (New York: Oxford University Press, 1987).
9. *The Poems of Andrew Marvell*, ed. Nigel Smith, 2nd edn (Harlow, UK; New York: Pearson, 2007).
10. "society, n.," *OED Online*. The introduction to this entry (under etymology) gives 1670 as an approximate but probable date for the emergence of what would become the modern, holistic sense of *society*. The early witnesses under 7a and 9a – 1535, 1566, 1573, 1583 and 1639 – are partial, referring to law, politics, or the aristocracy (and in one, presumably misplaced instance, 1573, to logic). The first attestation of the modern sense is Ralph Cudworth's *True Intellectual System* (1678), in which *humane society* is offered as a new term and glossed as *common good*. In Locke's *Two Treatises of Government* (1690), with its reference to "all those of that society," we have something still closer to the modern and, as I have argued, metaphysical sense of the term.
11. "society, n.," 7a, *OED Online*.

CHAPTER 24

Controversial Prose

Andrew Hadfield

It is easy to agree that Donne's three major prose treatises are controversial. *Pseudo-Martyr* is an outspoken attack on the cult of Catholic martyrdom; *Ignatius His Conclave* is a satirical work in a similar vein that shows the malign effects of the Jesuits who are in league with Satan; and *Biathanatos*, the most controversial of all, defends the right of individuals to commit suicide. I would like to suggest, however, that they have sometimes been misconceived, principally because the significance of *Pseudo-Martyr*, usually regarded as the most tedious of Donne's writings, has been down-played and the work treated as if it were a detour or self-interested plea for preferment. As a result, *Biathanatos* is read as if it were just about suicide and was therefore an eccentric experiment in reasoning by a maverick figure.[1] What links Donne's controversial works is a sustained plea for toleration of the individual conscience in religious matters, best achieved through the establishment of a secure but distant central authority. Donne, exceptionally keen on paradoxical thinking, argues that the best way to protect religious belief is to limit the hold that religious institutions could have over individuals and to ensure that everyone took an oath to obey the secular authority. This does not make him, as some critics have argued, an absolutist.[2] Rather, it shows the complex interaction between religion, secularism, and toleration in early modern England and suggests that Donne's religious beliefs were very much in tune with a policy that did not want to look too deeply into men's souls.

Pseudo-Martyr was published in 1610, and may well have had some form of official sanction as it seems very close to the writings of James I, and it is possible that, as Anthony Raspa claims, *Triplici Nodo* (1607), James's defence of the Oath of Allegiance, 'inspired Donne to write *Pseudo-Martyr*'.[3] Donne argues, in an uncontroversial way, that 'all power is from God' (79), but he is clear that this is secular authority, a central

---

* I am grateful to Shanyn Leigh Altman for reading and commenting on this essay.

power that devolves government to the magistrates to run the country. While the basis of kingly authority is godly, the reality of monarchical rule is not: 'Nor is secular authority so *mediate*, or dependent upon men, as that it may at any time be extinguished, but must ever reside in some forme or other' (78). For Donne, secular authority cannot and should not be challenged, a direct refutation of James's Catholic opponents like Robert Parsons who claimed that all secular figures and institutions were answerable to the church. And, indeed, Parsons is one of the key targets of *Pseudo-Martyr*.

The fear that monarchs would once again become over-mighty, assume titles that gave them religious as well as secular authority, start to insist on conformity, and even persecute their subjects in the name of religious unity is omnipresent throughout *Pseudo-Martyr*: 'All this I say, not to encourage princes to returne to those styles, which Christian humilitie hath made them dis-accustome, and leave off, and which could not be reassum'd without much scandal, but to shew the iniquitie and preversenesse of those men, who think great Titles belong to Kings, not as Kings, but as Papisticall Kings' (56). In the wake of the Gunpowder Plot, the Oath of Allegiance required every subject to swear loyalty to the monarch and to renounce the claims of the Pope to have any secular power over Catholics.[4] Donne praises this far-sighted policy as an obvious, practical solution for all James's subjects: 'If therefore the matter of this oath be so evident, as being Morall, & therefore constant and ever the same, that it can never neede his judgement, because it can in no case be sinne, the scruple which some have had, that by denying this power absolving, his spiritual power is endamaged, is vaine and frivolous' (254). The Oath, according to Donne, is simply sensible policy because it involves no need to think and cannot envelop the swearer in sin, thereby liberating men and women to act as they please and as their consciences see fit. Oaths, binding agreements that commit the swearer to follow or avoid courses of action, are vital to the functioning of Christian society, but they must not be abused. Donne acknowledges the need for oaths, but makes a telling contrast between the false oaths imposed by the Catholic Church and the necessary oath undertaken by the loyal subject of the British king:

> And at no time, and to no persons, can such *Oathes* be more necessary, then to us now, who have been awakened with such drummes as these, *There is no warre in the world so just and honourable, be it civill or forraigne, as that which is waged for the Romane Religion.* And especially in this consideration are *Oathes* a fit and proper wall and Rampart, to oppose against these men,

because they say, *That to the obedience of this Romane Religion, all Princes and people have yielded themselves, either by Oath, vow, or Sacraments, or every one of them*. For against this their imaginary oath, it is best, that a true, reall, and lawfull oath be administered by us. (242)

Donne draws a pointed contrast between the true and proper Oath of Allegiance, and the false and deluded oath of absolute loyalty demanded by the Catholic Church. In fact, the Oath demanded by the legitimate secular authority is a reaction to the wicked and destructive promise extorted by the Pope to fulfil his mistaken claims to hegemony over kings and their subjects. The Oath is a vital form of protection against claims that will encourage religious persecution and so undermine the fabric of religious and secular life. The worst confusion that can be wrought is to confuse and conflate these two forms of authority: 'Nor is there any thing more monstrous, and unnaturall and disproportioned, then that *spirituall* power should conceive or beget *temporall*: or to rise downwards, as the more degrees of height, and Supremacie, and perfection it hath, the more it should decline and stoope to the consideration of secular and temporall matters' (250). Donne again shows his delight in paradox: the more religion concerns itself with secular matters and claims supremacy over political powers, the less spiritual it becomes, sullying and diluting the sacred and undermining the legitimate authority of the prince. For Donne the crucial point is that we should all be responsible for our own souls and salvation, if permitted by earthly institutions and the authorities do not mislead us or force us to act against God's will:

> when all things are in such sort wel composed and established, and every subordinate Wheele set in good order, we are guilty of our owne damnation, if wee obey not the Minister, and the Minister is guilty of it, if hee neglect to instruct us, so is the Prince guilty of our spiritual ruine, and eternall perishing, if hee doe not both provide able men to give us spirituall foode, and punish both their negligence and our transgressions. (144)

The penalties for confusing the spiritual and the secular are catastrophic: not only is proper rule compromised and realms placed in unnecessary danger, but everyone concerned is in grave danger of eternal damnation.

Such passages remind us of the central point of *Pseudo-Martyr*, that death in the service of illegitimate authority is not merely futile, but diabolical, likely to imperil the soul of the victim rather than elevate him or her to heavenly bliss. It is the duty of authorities to facilitate the salvation of the subjects entrusted to their care, something best achieved by leaving them alone to make their own decisions rather than coercing them and so removing the power of choice. Worst of all are the Jesuits who press the men who have taken their oath to sacrifice themselves for the glory of the church. Chapter four details the failings of their doctrine, concluding 'That the desire of Martyrdome might be vicious, & that, as the Roman authors observe in the first times, it had been so; and, That by the Romane doctrine it must of necessity be so, we have added now, that the *Jesuites* more then any, inflame thereunto' (120).

Such comments show that Donne is invariably concerned to limit pointless and wasteful sacrifice, blaming deluded and aggressive authorities for sending men and women to their deaths under the guise of martyrdom. *Pseudo-Martyr* is central to our understanding of Donne's intellectual and religious beliefs during James's reign. It explains his loyal adherence to the monarch and – in part – his decision to pursue a career in the Church of England.[5] Donne had lived under the threat of imprisonment and possible execution throughout his life, but the Oath of Allegiance provided a means of safety and squaring conscience. Donne particularly abhors wasted life and pointless death, which helps to explain why *Biathanatos* needs to be read as a companion piece to *Pseudo-Martyr*. I would argue that this second treatise, which unlike *Pseudo-Martyr* had a complicated and problematic passage into print, is really concerned with the logic of false martyrdom and its consequences.[6]

In *Biathanatos*, Donne makes a strong link between suicide and martyrdom:

> None may justly say that all which kill themselves have done it out of a despaire of Gods mercy (which is the onely sinnefull despaire) we shall . . . finde many who at that act have been so far from despaire, that they have esteemed it a great degree of Gods mercy to have been admitted to such a glorifying of his name, and have proceeded therein as religiously as in a sacrifice.[7]

If the treatise is read with this connection in mind, it becomes less a serious or frivolous defence of self-slaughter and more an exploration of relative values and the possibility that there may indeed be many things worse than suicide, namely the abuse of individuals by religious authorities who send them to death and damnation through a false belief in the ways and means of salvation. Donne, perhaps following Spenser's representation of Despair tempting the Red-Cross Knight to end his troubles by committing suicide, suggests that this is only one route to the false lure of easeful death.[8] Far more prevalent and dangerous is the lure of martyrdom.

Throughout the short treatise Donne compares forms of death to suicide and worries at the differences assumed by authorities between the two. In doing so he displays a sceptical, even hostile, understanding of the doctrines, teaching, and records of the Catholic Church. He discusses the cases of a number of martyrs, such as Saint Pelagia, a fifteen-year-old virgin who jumped to her death rather than be violated by soldiers during Diocletian's persecutions:

> The memory of *Pelagia*, as of a virgin and Martyr, is celebrated the ninth of *June*. And though the History of this woman suffer some perplexity, and give occasion of doubting the truth thereof, (for *Ambrose* says that she and her Mother drownd themselves, and *Chrysostome* that they flung themselves downe from a house top; and *Baronius* saw this knot to be so hard to unentangle, that he says, *Quid ad hac dicamus, non habemus* [We do not have anything to say about this]) yet the Church, as I said, celebrates the Act, as though it were glad to take any occasion of approving such a courage in such a cause, which was but preservation of Chastity. *Their Martyrdome*, saith Saint Augustine, *was ever in the Catholique Church frequented* Veneratione Celeberrima [With most honoured veneration] [Rhodes's translations]. (72–73)

Donne explores here the moral difference between pseudo-martyrdom and suicide, and the clear implication is that there is very little to choose between them. Catholic political thinkers argued that while they had the Church to guide them when they felt obliged to resist the secular authorities, Protestants had to rely on their own conscience, a terrifying prospect that opened the way for madmen to act unchecked.[9] Here Donne is indicating that the Catholic tradition may not be as secure as its apologists claim; that accounts of martyrdom are contradictory and confused; and that some historians simply refuse to verify what others claim. An authority is assumed but it rests on shaky foundations. The Catholic Church celebrates its martyrs without question even though the historical record does not support or justify what they believe. Accordingly, many may well be pseudo-martyrs held up as examples to encourage yet more pseudo-martyrs, very close to, if not actually, a case of mass suicide.

Donne's target in *Biathanatos* is tyranny, especially that of institutions overstepping the mark in order to assert their power over people, driving them not merely to their deaths but also to probable damnation. The individual soul should be sacrosanct, but the assumption of supreme religious authority and the right to command absolute obedience invariably has terrible consequences as the political and the religious are combined in toxic ways. Arguing that there are religious laws that cannot be violated, such as the prohibition of idolatry, Donne concludes:

> By which Rule, if perchance a publique, exemplary person, which had a just assurance that his example would governe the people, should be forced by a Tyrant to doe an act of Idolatry, (although by circumstances he might satisfie his owne conscience that he sinned not in doing it) and so scandalize and endanger them, if the matter were so carried and disguised, that by no way he could let them know that he did it by constraint, but voluntarily, I say perchance he were better kill himselfe. (76)

The argument is a powerful but also a subtle one, again forging a strong link between suicide and pseudo-martyrdom. The reason why the imagined figure is better off committing suicide rather than performing the act of idolatry is because of the effect that his actions are certain to have on others. Donne creates a situation in which the victim has no chance of letting witnesses know that he is acting under constraint so that they will assume he has acted in accordance with his free will. Many will follow the example of a leader they respect and so endanger themselves as well as others, leading to a domino effect which will do so much harm that the public figure is better off taking his own life.

Donne performs a sleight of hand and leaves out a key stage of the argument in not exploring what is also likely to happen, i.e., that the exemplary person behaves in an exemplary fashion and publicly speaks out against idolatry. The consequence of his action is likely to be his own death, making him a martyr rather than a pseudo-martyr. This then raises the problem of the distinction between types and choices of death and martyrdom. Of course, it would be best to act heroically – confront the tyrant, denounce his demands, and so face a painful death. But if that is exemplary action then might we also argue that simply committing suicide, while not as heroic, is still more heroic than taking the line of least resistance, performing the act of idolatry, and so preserving one's life while imperilling the souls of others? Then again, if we are arguing about the need to preserve more souls – which is, after all, the point of the tradition of martyrdom, the death of the faithful serving to inspire the faith of others – then might it not be better to commit suicide and so not imperil the souls of those who have to put the exemplary figure to death?

Some of these conclusions are implicit within the argument, not explicitly stated. What we should concentrate on, I would like to argue, is the cause of the situation, which leaves the exemplary person with an impossibly difficult choice. It is the tyrant who creates this dilemma, assuming a right to demand absolute obedience from his subjects, a wilful usurpation of legitimate authority and an assumption that everything is subject to his commands. Tyranny was defined in careful and precise terms in early modern Europe. Tyrants were unable to control their appetites and had surrendered all rational control, making themselves subject to their whims, desires, and imagination. They had no respect for the rule of law or their subjects' rights and so took what they wished, most significantly their subjects' wives and property. The Old Testament in particular provided endless examples of tyrants and tyrannous behaviour, such as Ahab and Jezebel's murder of Naboth in order to seize his vineyard, and David's sending Uriah the Hittite to his death in battle in order to disguise his affair with Bathsheba. More seriously still, tyrants had no respect for religious belief and imposed their own false beliefs on their subjects. Accordingly, both Catholics and Protestants accused their opponents of tyranny.[10]

Donne argues that tyranny goes even further than people imagine, destroying the lives of the subjects who are oppressed by its power. Tyranny mixes, confuses, and undermines the distinction between religious and secular authority to such an extent that seemingly abhorrent moral distinctions collapse, and what might seem to be the most heinous of crimes, self-murder, becomes a viable option for those placed in an impossible situation. However, Donne does not advocate for suicide in *Biathanatos*, nor does he diminish the awful significance of such an act. Rather, he points out that when having to deal with the aggressive actions of a tyrant, suicide may be a logical choice and a decision that has to be condoned. And he questions, in particular, the false authority of the Catholic Church, which is prepared to sanction the effective suicide of its most committed supporters.

Ignatius His Conclave, the last of Donne's controversial prose works to be written, was published in 1611. The slightest of the three, it is a robust, polemical satire of the Jesuits.[11] Donne has an 'extasie' and his soul is transported to Hell where he meets the forces of evil who surround Lucifer. These include Pope Bonniface III, who established papal power in the seventh century, Muhammad and Saint Ignatius Loyola (1491–1556), the founder of the Jesuits, who outwits the devil and establishes himself at the end of the work as the chief innovator who has distorted and inverted true religion. So much does the devil fear Ignatius that he sends him off to colonise the moon where he will be less threatening to the master of evil.

Ignatius is similar in substance to *Pseudo-Martyr* and *Biathanatos*, repeating many of their arguments and aiming at the same target. Donne again argues that the confusion of political and religious authority has particularly disastrous consequences. Probably the most interesting passage in the satire is the exchange between Machiavelli, the arch-exponent of political ruthlessness, and Ignatius, who adopts even more ruthless principles in furthering his religious empire. Machiavelli delights in killing, stating that he enjoys the different types of death that his authority can generate and that he has a connoisseur's appreciation of the distinction between forms of slaughter: 'For I my selfe went always that way of bloud, and therefore I did euer preferred the sacrifices of the *Gentiles,* and of the *Iewes,* which were performed with effusion of bloud (whereby not only the people, but the Priests also were animated to bold enterprises) before the soft and wanton sacrifices of *Christians*'.[12] Machiavelli craves rivers of blood, showing him to be one of the old pagan idols (perhaps like the one that the 'exemplary figure' is forced to worship in *Biathanatos*?) who are really devils in Hell.

Machiavelli is a devil and well worth the high esteem he receives in Hell. However, his labours to confuse political and religious authority and so damn the souls of those foolish enough to listen to him are negligible compared to those of the greater master, Ignatius, who points out his superiority in a disdainful speech. Arguing that the Pope is able to define his own authority as supreme pontiff, Ignatius claims they have nothing to learn from his new-fangled doctrines:

> This then is the point of which wee accuse *Machieull,* that he carried not his Mine so safely, but that the enemy perceiued it still ... yet I doe not obstinately say, that there is nothing in *Machieuls commentary*, which may bee of vse to this Church. Certainely there is very much; but we are not men of that pouerty, that wee neede begge from others, nor dignify those things with our prayers, which proceede not from our selues. (74–75)

As Ignatius points out, the church has a long history of duplicity and deception that renders Machiavelli's ideas virtually redundant, which is why he is damned with such faint praise. In particular, Ignatius pours scorn on Machiavelli's discovery of lying as a strategy, showing that the church has a long history of far worse behaviour from Herod to the Jesuit doctrine of equivocation: 'The libertie of lying, is neither new nor safe as almost all *Machiauells* precepts are ... stale and obsolete' (77–78). The Catholic Church does not need such allies – even though they are reprehensible enough – because it can do much better if left to its own devices. The Jesuits have already found more than enough ways to lure the unwary to their doom. In doing so they simply reveal themselves as the natural culmination of all that is Satanic in Catholicism, creating a series of plausible but false doctrines designed to cause death and damnation, the most pernicious of which is the need for the pseudo-martyr.

Notes

1. An exception is Adam H. Kitzes, "Paradoxical Donne: *Biathanatos* and the Problems with Political Assimilation," *Prose Studies* 24 (2001), 1–17.
2. See Debora Shuger, "Donne's Absolutism," in *OHJD*, 690–703.
3. *Pseudo-Martyr*, xxxv. All subsequent references to this edition are in parentheses in the text.
4. Roger Lockyer, *James VI and I* (London: Longman, 1998), 128.
5. David Nicholls, "The Political Theology of John Donne," *Theological Studies* 49 (1988), 65.
6. *Biathanatos* was not published until 1646, fifteen years after Donne's death. See Ernest W. Sullivan, II, "The Paradox: *Biathanatos*," in *OHJD*, 153–57.
7. John Donne, *Biathanatos*, in *Selected Prose*, ed. Neil Rhodes (Harmondsworth, UK: Penguin, 1987), 64. All subsequent references to this edition are in parentheses in the text.
8. See Paola Baseotto, *"Disdeining life, desiring leaue to die": Spenser and the Psychology of Despair* (Stuttgart: Verlag, 2008).
9. William Allen, *A True, Sincere and Modest Defence, of English Catholiques that Suffer for their Faith both at Home and Abrode* (Rouen, 1584), 84–85.
10. See Robert M. Kingdon, "Calvinism and Resistance Theory, 1550–1580," in *The Cambridge History of Political Thought, 1450–1700*, eds. J. H. Burns and Mark Goldie (Cambridge University Press, 1995), 193–218; and J. H. M. Salmon, "Catholic Resistance Theory, Ultramontanism, and the Royalist Response, 1580–1620," in *Cambridge History*, 219–53.
11. See Anne Lake Prescott, "Menippean Donne," in *OHJD*, 168–72.
12. John Donne, *Ignatius His Conclaue* (London, 1611), 35. All subsequent references to this edition are in parentheses in the text.

CHAPTER 25

Devotional Prose

Brooke Conti

In the best-loved and most frequently excerpted passage from *Devotions upon Emergent Occasions*, John Donne describes the wide embrace of the Church in lines that are frequently misread as a more general statement about the mutual dependence and interconnectedness of the human race. The opening of Meditation 17 makes the context clear, although its potentially divisive character is easily overlooked. Donne begins, "The *Church* is *Catholike, universall*, so are all her *Actions; All* that she does, belongs to *all*." A few sentences later he has moved to "All *mankind*," which he claims is "of one *Author*, and . . . one *volume*," before eventually concluding that "No Man is an *Iland*, intire of it self."[1] Donne says something similar in his earlier work of devotional prose, *Essays in Divinity*, where he argues that "Synagogue and Church is the same thing" and "*Roman* and *Reformed* . . . [are] but one Church, journying to one *Hierusalem*."[2] As expressions of Christian universalism, both passages have an appeal not limited to the works' twenty-first-century readers. The fantasy of Christian unity – whether experienced as nostalgia for the pre-Reformation church or hope for a harmonious Protestant future – exerted a powerful hold over many early moderns.

But while Donne's broad-based and accommodating church participates in this fantasy, it does not speak to all parties equally. In both works, Donne's ideal church is set in stark contrast to more exclusionary definitions of Protestantism, and by the time he writes the *Devotions*, his open and accommodating vision is quite clearly tied to a single church, the Church of England. In reading Donne's devotional prose, then, we do well to understand it as an outgrowth of his brief career as a polemicist. Partly rejecting and partly continuing both the debates and the methods of *Pseudo-Martyr* and *Ignatius His Conclave*, the *Essays* and *Devotions* show Donne not so much setting controversial matters aside as moving his consideration of the after-effects of the Reformation to a new genre.

Sometimes said to include almost any popular religious work that is not theological or polemical, devotional prose is a capacious and miscellaneous category united chiefly by its focus on the inner spiritual life of the faithful reader. Of course, the way one approaches God, confronts death, or finds consolation in hard times can be heavily shaded by an author's own doctrinal positions, and many devotional works are at least implicitly theological. However, devotional literature's focus on enduring spiritual and existential problems frequently allows such works to transcend denominational divides, and their meditative style encourages readerly assent and identification.

Donne's devotional prose both fits this model and stretches it, placing private spiritual experience in the service of larger political ends. The *Essays* and *Devotions* deal with broadly Christian concerns, such as the meaning of God's creation and how to worship the Creator in it; why God often seems to speak in riddling messages in scripture; the nature of and reason for sickness and death; and how to live in a fallen condition. Although the two works touch on some of the differences between the churches of England and Rome, as well as some of the devotional and ecclesiological issues disputed within the English Church itself, their tone is moderate and at times even startlingly tolerant, especially when contrasted with the two prose works that immediately preceded *Essays*, the explicitly polemical *Pseudo-Martyr* and *Ignatius His Conclave*. Indeed, Donne's devotional works go out of their way to criticize the methods of religious controversy. However, Donne's devotional prose is not a straightforward rejection of his polemical career. Rather, using the different resources of devotional literature, Donne continues to work through questions about the history, nature, and shape of the Christian Church, and to promote the version that he finds most intellectually and emotionally satisfying. As we shall see, the *Devotions* is somewhat more successful at this than the *Essays*, but both works give Donne a means of avoiding the polarizing pitfalls of polemic while still pursuing some of polemic's ends. In other words, what devotional prose allows Donne is an opportunity to argue without arguments.

Although the *Essays* and *Devotions* were written approximately a decade apart and at very different moments in Donne's life (and only one was published during his lifetime) they are both shaped by religious conflict. The *Essays* is more obviously tied to controversial culture, not least because of its composition date: the work was written between 1611 and 1614, which places it between *Ignatius His Conclave* and Donne's ordination. There is no evidence that the work's composition was directly related to Donne's preparation for the priesthood (as his son claims in the note to the reader that prefaces the work's posthumous publication), but by the early 1610s Donne had been thinking and writing about the differences between the churches of Rome and England for some years. According to *Pseudo-Martyr*, Donne's conversion was preceded by serious theological investigations; Donne's work as a controversialist required more of the same; and we may presume that being urged to take Holy Orders inspired yet further study. Whatever its immediate impetus, then, the *Essays* is indisputably a part of the process that helped Donne refine his thinking about the characteristics of the church in which he was born and that in which he would later be ordained.

The *Essays* appears to have been intended as a series of meditations and prayers on the first line of each book of the Bible, but the work as we have it treats only Genesis and Exodus. Within the confines of this structure, Donne ranges over a wide variety of subjects, giving sustained attention to the question of how one interprets scripture and what kind of guidance it provides in doctrinal, ecclesiological, and devotional matters. This in turn brings him to the fierce intra-Christian wrangling on the subject. Donne allows that "there be proper use of controverted Divinity for Medicine" (13), but he adds that we should be cautious in claiming certitude in doctrinal or devotional affairs: "there are some things which the Author of light hides from us, and the prince of darkness strives to shew to us; but with no other light, then his firebrands of Contention, and curiosity" (16). Donne's ambivalence about the field of religious controversy is clear: it *can* serve as an antidote to erroneous beliefs, but it also contains temptations to certitude, pride in one's own arguments, or contention for contention's sake.

Donne returns to this metaphor of a light that does not illuminate later in the work, in a description of the tendentious ways controversialists employ the Bible for their polemical ends. "[M]any lights," he says – meaning, many biblical expositors – "cast many shadows, and since controverted Divinity became an occupation, the Distortions and violencing of Scriptures, by Christians themselves, have wounded the Scriptures more, then the old Philosophy of *Turcism*" (45). Although there is no reason to suppose that Donne is repudiating his own contributions to controversial literature, this and Donne's other references to religious polemic give the impression of someone weary of those battles. In turning his pen to reflections on the first line of each book of the Bible, Donne may be attempting to do what he claims controversialists do not: take the text on its own terms, a full sentence at a time, rather than

chop it up into "incoherent" fragments to serve a predetermined controversial agenda (47).

Reflecting on the Bible in this way brings Donne to its many mysterious
contradictions, such as the fact that both Esau and Moses's father-in-law
are called by different names at different times. This first leads Donne to
the conclusion that there are no easy answers to the kinds of questions that
preoccupy controversialists, and then to the speculation that God may
have *intended* the confusion to illustrate this very point: "I encline to
think," Donne writes,

> that God in his eternall & ever-present omniscience, foreseeing that his
> universal, Christian, Catholick Church ... should in her latter Age suffer
> many convulsions, distractions, rents, schisms, and wounds, by the severe
> and unrectified Zeal of many, who should impose necessity upon indifferent
> things, and oblige all the World to one precise forme of exterior worship,
> and Ecclesiastick policie; averring that every degree, and minute, and
> scruple of all circumstances which may be admitted in either belief or
> practice, is certainly, constantly, expressly, and obligatorily exhibited in
> the Scriptures ... his Wisdome was mercifully pleas'd, that [we] ... should
> from this variety of Names in the Bible it selfe, be provided of an argument,
> *That an unity and consonance in things not essentiall, is not so necessarily
> requisite as is imagined.* (55–56)

This passage intensifies Donne's critique of the methods of religious
controversy: not only is it foolish to think that every facet of worship or
church government needs to have a clear warrant from scripture, but
arguing over such trivialities divides and wounds God's church. For the
first time, the precise target of Donne's criticisms is clear: he objects to the
approach of fellow Protestants, and specifically those of a more zealous or
Puritan bent. Donne thus both criticizes religious polemists and, ironically, responds to them in kind: in making his case for tolerance, he too
uses the Bible as a proof-text and a weapon against his opponents.

It might not be surprising that the Donne who was so recently engaged
in a more overt form of polemic should continue a version of that practice
here; what *is* surprising, coming from the author of *Pseudo-Martyr* and
Ignatius His Conclave, is that Donne's negative descriptions of polemicists
(and his own polemical energies) are directed almost exclusively at other
Protestants rather than Catholics. Donne does not discuss Catholic controversialists at all, and while he does refer to the failings of the Catholic
Church, his criticisms are noticeably muted. He describes the Roman
Church as "that Church from which we are by Gods Mercy escaped"
and boasts that "our reformed Christian Religion" is "the thriftiest and

cheapest that ever was instituted … now that we have removed the
expensive dignifying of images, and relicks" (56, 72–77), but he stops
noticeably short of the usual polemical charges of idolatry and vanity.
About the Roman "[a]dditions" to the foundations laid by Christ and the
apostles, he is equivocal, labeling them "of so dangerous a construction,
and appearance, and misapplyableness, that to tender consciences they
seem'd Idolatrous, and are certainly scandalous and very slippery, and
declinable into Idolatry" (56). Donne begins the sentence fiercely enough,
but by the end he is pulling his punches: the additions made by the
medieval church may be scandalous and slippery, but they only *seemed*
idolatrous to the Reformers, or will only *potentially* lead there.

Donne continues backing away from any overly harsh critique of the
Catholic Church as the passage continues, describing it as "concur[ring]
with us in the root, and suck[ing] her vegetation from one and the same
ground, *Christ Jesus*"; and adding that as long as "they keep their right foot
fast upon the Rock Christ, I dare not pronounce that she is not our Sister"
(56–57). Finally, he concludes, "we [shall] best conserve the integrity of our
own body, of which she is a member, if we laboriously build upon her, and
not tempestuously and ruinously demolish and annull her; but rather
cherish and foment her vitall and wholsome parts" (57). Donne's frank
assertion of the genealogical relationship between the Protestant and
Catholic Churches will not surprise anyone who has read *Pseudo-Martyr*,
which, for all its hostility toward the Jesuits, the Pope, and much of post-
Tridentine Catholicism, expresses considerable tolerance for what Donne
regards as traditional Catholicism. However, in a work so critical of fellow
Protestants, the circumspect and even conciliatory language Donne uses
toward Catholics indicates that something else is afoot.

Donne is clearly not interested in returning to Rome, but he seems
undecided about what form Reformed religion should take, especially the
question of how many divisions and purifications are necessary to reach
a true, apostolic religion. On the evidence of the *Essays*, Donne's preference
is for fewer divisions and a bigger church. This leads him to the potent and
provocative fantasy that I alluded to earlier, which is also inspired by the
diversity of names in the Hebrew Bible: "if *Esau, Edom*, and *Seir* were but
one man; *Jethro* and *Revel*, &c. but one man … so Synagogue and Church
is the same thing, and of the Church, *Roman* and *Reformed* … but one
Church, journeying to one *Hierusalem*, and directed by one guide, Christ
Jesus" (58). Donne presumably does not believe in a literal equivalence
between Jews and Christians, and he probably does not literally mean that
the Roman and Reformed churches are equally viable paths to salvation.

However, Protestants *did* believe in an unbroken line of faith from the Old Testament patriarchs up to their own day, and Donne's ecstatic vision might appeal, at least as a bit of literary hyperbole, to the desire of many early modern Christians to see their own church as the universal one. Even the hotter sort of Protestants insisted that unity and continuity were their goals – they simply demanded purity as their precondition.

Donne acknowledges that some might see his own desire for unity as "inordinate," but adds, "I do zealously wish, that the whole catholick Church, were reduced to such Unity and agreement, in the form and profession Established, in any one of these Churches (though ours were principally to be wished) which have not by any additions destroyed the foundation and possibility of salvation in Christ Jesus"; under those circumstances, he adds, wistfully, "the Church, discharged of disputations, and misapprehensions, and this defensive warr, might contemplate Christ clearly and uniformely" (58). Despite Donne's parenthetical reference to his preference for the English Church, neither in this passage nor elsewhere does the *Essays* take a strong stand for the Church of England; Donne seems to be seeking an end to Protestant in-fighting, so any form of worship that all could agree on would be satisfactory, and preferable to a diversity of forms. The *Essays* promotes the cause of Christian unity by imagining a Protestantism that will heal the rifts of the Reformation – if not *with* the Catholic Church, then as a corrected alternative to it. It is an appealing vision, but one whose vagueness means it remains a fantasy. The *Essays* criticizes the divisive nature of polemic while trying to yoke some of its methods to the more expansive and exploratory mode of devotional prose. But without a specific church or form of worship to argue for, the work's controversial energies have nowhere to go.

* * * *

Approximately a decade after Donne set aside his *Essays* he wrote his more celebrated work of devotional prose, the *Devotions upon Emergent Occasions*. Although the precise circumstances of the *Essays'* composition are unknown, the same is not true for the *Devotions*: Donne's descent into and recovery from a near-fatal illness in late 1623 provide both the work's impetus and its subject. A longer, more elaborate, and more polished work than the *Essays*, the *Devotions* consists of twenty-three devotions (each one divided into a meditation, an expostulation, and a prayer) that appear to follow the actual course of Donne's sickness. Unlike the *Essays*, Donne chose to publish the *Devotions*, albeit for reasons that remain somewhat mysterious: never a fan of print, Donne rushed the work to press while still not completely recovered. One explanation for Donne's eagerness might be found in the work's mingling of the personal and the political. The *Devotions* is not just a devotional work: it is also an insistent declaration of Donne's allegiance to the Church of England and a defense of that church against the same over-zealous reformers Donne inveighed against in the *Essays*.

I have argued elsewhere that Donne's performance of obedience seems motivated by sickbed doubts about his own orthodoxy, but for our present purposes the reason for Donne's performance is less important than its method and effects.[3] As in the *Essays*, Donne argues for a more tolerant and accommodating church (while also criticizing those he sees as insufficiently accommodating), but in the *Devotions* his polemical positions are folded more smoothly into the work's devotional form. Donne never mentions the field of religious controversy explicitly, as he did in the *Essays*, but in enacting his identity as a member of the Church of England, Donne actually speaks from a more clearly polemical position. In this work the unified, stable Protestantism that Donne celebrates is linked to the English Church, and when he criticizes more reform-minded Calvinists he now does it from a position of authority. More fully than he did in the *Essays*, Donne continues to convert the stuff of religious controversy into the stuff of religious devotion.

Like all devotional works, the *Devotions upon Emergent Occasions* is surely designed for private, individual use, but its meditations, expostulations, and prayers repeatedly emphasize the social and communal nature of religion. Donne laments the fact that his illness isolates him from others, describing solitude as the greatest misery of humankind and fretting that his disease prevents him from attending or officiating at services (25, 17). However, it is not only the congregation that he misses; he longs for "the Instruments of true comfort, [found] in thy Institutions, and in the Ordinances of thy *Church*" (18). These might seem peculiar things to miss, but the *Devotions* is full of references to the Church's "ordinances" and "officers" and the security, stability, and comfort they provide. Donne assures God that he seeks an understanding of scripture "not from *corners*, nor *Convenventicles*, nor *schismatical singularities*, but from the assotiation, & communion of thy *Catholique Church*, and those persons, whom thou hast always furnished that *Church* withal," later reiterating that he "hearken[s] after *thy voice, in thine Ordinances* ... not a *whispering in Conventicles*" (39, 113). Whatever private spiritual benefits the *Devotions* may provide, the work insists that true worship is communal, public, and undertaken in the established church. Inserted into seemingly private colloquies with or prayers to God, the polemical thrust of the above lines is less obvious than similar claims made in a controversial work, but arguably more effective for being so. Donne places all who object to the church's ordinances and officers outside the recognized church: their preferences are "schismatical" and their associations "conventicles."

In addition to his more general celebrations of the established church, Donne mentions several specific, potentially contentious issues in passing, including the use of religious images, the observance of feast days, the "uncharitable *disputations*" over the relative importance of faith and works, controversies over the ontological status of the Eucharist, and (more obliquely) the Book of Common Prayer and the benefits of a set liturgy (84, 73–74, 106, 75, 99). However, the devotional practice that gives Donne the most scope for advancing his case for the English Church and for criticizing nonconformists is the ringing of bells for the sick or recently deceased. For Donne the bells he hears from his sickbed are a means of "bring[ing] the *Congregation* together, and unit[ing] *God* and his *people*" (83), and he dismisses the objections of more zealous reformers more or less out of hand. Donne acknowledges the basis for these objections – bells were used by pagans and Catholics, and the practice does not have an adequate scriptural warrant – but he never fully engages with these objections. Rather, he first says that these reasons are not compelling enough, given the manifest value of bell-ringing, and then he demonstrates that value by showing the spiritual uses to which a bedridden sick man might put these bells.

This long portion of the work makes a twofold case against Donne's anti-ceremonialist opponents. In praying that "[Christians] not breake the *Communion of Saints*, in that which was intended for the *advancement* of it" (84) and implying that his opponents are dissentious, Donne is wrong-footing his imagined interlocutors, insisting that "In *Ceremoniall things* . . . any *convenient reason* is enough" to justify the ceremony (93). But by far his stronger case is made through his evocative, semi-autobiographical first-person devotions, which *show* the benefits of these devotional practices. Thus, when Donne eventually gets to his stirring vision of a single church and a mutually interdependent humanity in Meditation 17, it functions as both a celebration of that church and as a rebuke to the small-minded zealots who would limit its inclusive embrace. As in *Essays*, Donne presents himself and his ideal church as tolerant and broad-based, but here that church is unquestionably the Church of England in its most ceremonial form. Its would-be reformers are cast as not just wrong-headed, but potentially disloyal to both church and state.

In highlighting the more controversial moments in the *Devotions*, I am not trying to reduce the work to those moments; the polemical stances taken by Donne are woven into a work that is chiefly a meditation on sin, sickness, and repentance. That, however, is my point: in the *Devotions* as in the *Essays*, Donne has found a way of fusing the devotional and the controversial. Both works present an open and broad-based church, one that is antagonistic toward no one except those who are antagonistic toward *it*. Rather than arguing at length for or against any specific practices or ecclesiological model, Donne allows the appeal of the church he describes to do its own convincing. In the *Essays*, Donne appears still to be thinking through the methods of religious controversy, for he refers to them explicitly even as he tries to move past them. However, in that work his ideal church is still relatively nebulous; Donne seems not yet to have made up his mind about its precise shape and form of worship. In the *Devotions*, Donne has a church to hang this fantasy upon, and he makes a quietly polemic case for its virtues and against those who seek further purifications and divisions. As such, the work is less overtly engaged with polemic, but better at employing it.

Having said that, I am not suggesting that Donne is deliberately or subversively employing devotional literature for polemical ends; rather, we might see its form and content as mutually constitutive. Just as the form taken by much of Donne's verse is an idiosyncratic response to the demands of its content, so too with Donne's devotional prose. If Donne's controversial writings allow him to draw some sharp distinctions between the Protestant and Catholic Churches, the calmer register of devotional prose permits him to do something similar with the intra-Protestant disputes over worship and ecclesiology. As Donne attempts to define his ideal church and distinguish it from what he considers inappropriately exclusionary models, he is able to take a more generous tone and avoid the appearance of overt conflict with his co-religionists. We have every reason to suppose that Donne is sincere. However, devotional prose, as a genre, does tend to inspire charitable readings.

Notes

1. John Donne, *Devotions upon Emergent Occasions*, ed. Anthony Raspa (Montreal: McGill-Queen's University Press, 1975), 86–87. All subsequent references to this edition are in parentheses in the text.

2. John Donne, *Essayes in Divinity*, ed. Anthony Raspa (Montreal: McGill-Queen's University Press, 2001), 58. All subsequent references to this edition are in parentheses in the text.

3. See Brooke Conti, *Confessions of Faith in Early Modern England* (Philadelphia, PA: University of Pennsylvania Press, 2014), 50–73.

CHAPTER 26

The Sermons

Lori Anne Ferrell

I am not all here, I am here now preaching upon this text, and I am at home in my Library considering whether *S. Gregory*, or *S. Hierome*, have said best of this text, before. I am here speaking to you, and yet I consider by the way, in the same instant, what it is likely you will say to one another, when I have done. You are not all here neither; you are here now, hearing me, and yet you are thinking that you have heard a better Sermon somewhere else, of this text before; . . . you are here, and you remember your selves that now yee think of it, this had been the fittest time, now, when every body else is at Church, to have made such and such a private visit; and because you would bee there, you are there.

—*Sermons*, 3:110

"Here" was the chapel at Lincoln's Inn in 1620, where John Donne addressed the audience of students, lawyers, and city folk that populated its pews. His choice of text, Job 19:26 – "And though, after my skin, worms destroy this body, yet in my flesh I shall see God" – was mordant, but given the sensibilities of the man, not outrageously so, and, given the times, not inappropriately so. Donne, the most eloquent preacher to grace the pulpits of a Church already plentifully supplied with golden-voiced talent, had "opened," or explicated, this passage to answer the ageless, anxious question *what happens to us after we die?* The query led him on: not straight to the grave, nor even to heaven or hell, but after the lively, wandering minds of his laypeople – and their preacher.

This passage reveals not only the singular way Donne crafted his sermons, but also their – and his – place in a long and vigorous Christian tradition. Preaching is an art that springs from the particularities and purpose of its genre. Though they can sound like them, sermons are not scriptural commentaries; neither are they devotional meditations, works of systematic theology, or catechisms. They are written for pulpits. Like their closest secular counterpart, theatrical plays, sermons are

266

amalgams of word and action – *proclamation, exhortation, declaration* – designed to inhabit purpose-built spaces; even issued on the page, their impact as well as their format depend on the professional fact of their specialized location. A good early modern preacher leavened an exacting study of scripture and theology (patristic and contemporary) with acute observations of human nature; he then cast his findings in rigorous generic form and committed them to memory. If he wished his words to be listened to, he spoke them with rhetorical passion. If he wished them to be famous, he hoped to deliver them from influential pulpits. And if he wished them to be remembered, he, or someone else, made certain they were preserved in manuscript and issued in print.

By all these reckonings, John Donne was a remarkably successful early modern preacher. During his lifetime, the rather modest course of his career as a poet stood in marked contrast to his later success as a preacher – a prosaic fact that can surprise modern readers (who assume that their literary tastes influence those of the past). Donne's evident talent for sermon writing, actorly relish for dramatic delivery ("like an Angel from a cloud," reported his dazzled friend Izaak Walton[1]), and near-perfect alignment with the multifaceted and shifting religious politics of early Stuart England meant he filled a number of very high-profile pulpits, attracting the audiences of a lifetime.[2] He gained the attention of posterity, however, with the sermons that went to press. This essay concentrates on John Donne's career as a preacher, a vocation entirely conducted under the authority of the Jacobean and Caroline Churches of England. It places his sermons in professional and literary context: the ecclesiastical and generic constraints *within* which, the times *in* which, the occasions *on* which, and the pulpits *from* which he preached.

The Church

A convert from a stubbornly recusant family (Donne's younger brother Henry was prosecuted for harboring a priest in the 1590s), Donne entered and left university early, never taking the formal degree: students over sixteen years of age as well as all graduates were required to subscribe to the articles of religion and the royal supremacy of the Church of England. He then read, but did not practice, the law. With nothing but late-awarded honorary degrees (an MA in 1610 and doctorate in 1615), Donne finally took clerical orders at age 43.

This late-in-life vocation suited both Donne and the times. King James I liked his clergy witty, learned, and skilled in the parry and feint of confessional controversy. Donne, who had been seeking governmental preferment since his twenties, mostly without notable success, had commended himself to the king in 1610 with a political tract designed to intervene in the Oath of Allegiance controversy. *Pseudo-Martyr* was a learned and skillful text, as were the prose works on religious subjects that followed. In them the evidence of Donne's informal apprenticeships – in canon law, casuistry, and the pursuit of public life in a Protestant world – came to brilliant light. Little in them, however, hinted at the depth and eloquence of the sermon-writer to come.

Here it is essential to remember that what might seem most unusual, or unseemly, about Donne's qualifications to be a Protestant minister – his familial recusancy, educational vagaries, and literary worldliness – posed no particular barrier to a professional career in the post-Reformation Church of England. In seventeenth-century England, the practice of religion was as much a matter of legislative statute and outward profession as it had been in the reign of Henry VIII. All subjects were enjoined to testify publicly to their conversions – not of their hearts, so unfathomable and inviolate, but instead to the established Church's confession of faith, in acts openly accountable – and so, when we read of "conversion" in this period, we are rarely if ever encountering the Damascene version.

Modern literary critics have had difficulties reconciling the older Donne's ardent spiritual gifts – what Peter McCullough has called his evident "astonishment at the duty and power of his office to proclaim nothing less than God's salvation to his hearers"[3] – with his equally avid ecclesiastical careerism. This literary-critical disquiet largely stems from a basic misunderstanding of and discomfort with the nature of the pre-modern Church of England, which functioned as a visible branch of civil, if not secular, government (the closest equivalent today would be universal public education – but only if none were allowed to choose private schooling as an alternative). With its royal appointment system and massy ranks of episcopal hierarchs, the Church was as tailor-made for strivers and self-starters as it was for the soulful, a juxtaposition that neither Donne nor his contemporaries found particularly jarring. The Church offered the nearest thing to meritocracy in a world otherwise designed by primogeniture, and under King James, it employed a wide range of talented, learned, sincere, and undoubtedly ambitious preachers. Like his fellow churchmen, Donne was called not only by the King to serve the church but also by God to proclaim the gospel. Both senses of vocation – the worldly and the otherworldly – existed comfortably within the structure of the Jacobean Church.

In the early Stuart Church, then, preaching licenses were not granted for personal piety or inward conviction. Licensing, like the awarding of university degrees, was contingent upon a candidate's formal subscription to the doctrinal articles of the Church, his submission to the monarch's earthly supremacy over Church matters, and his acceptance of the liturgical mandates of the Book of Common Prayer. To all these Donne assented to the satisfaction of John King, Bishop of London, who in 1615 ordained him deacon and priest. Soon thereafter he was licensed to preach, awarded a number of benefices, and appointed as one of James I's chaplains. The success that eluded the poet had found the preacher.

Genre

The considerable task of the sermon in post-Reformation England was to proclaim the truth of a radical, confusing, and multivalent Bible without recasting its Church's fundamental commitment to unity, uniformity, and liturgical order, and not every minister was up to the job. Preachers, like print, required not only licensing but ongoing oversight; in any case, only the most learned and most highly placed English clergy were encouraged to pen their own sermons (others were commanded to read from official books of homilies, an order some lesser clergy took with a grain of salt and many others with a sigh of relief). England's Church government by bishops and archbishops was well placed and long suited to the responsibilities of oversight; furthermore, the office of the Bishop of London was charged with approving all sermons that went to press.[4]

Thus, before they put pen to page, preachers had already confronted requirements that governed not only the function, but also, inextricably, the form of the sermon. What distinguishes Donne's preaching is how widely, creatively, and dexterously he was able to range through points of doctrine, scripture, politics, and human nature in this age of confessional volatility, governmental caution, episcopal authority, and faith by statute. Like his peers, Donne consulted the rules of classical oratory when composing sermons. In his warmly approving memoir, Izaak Walton detailed how his friend "usually preached once a week, if not oftener, so after his Sermon he never gave his eyes rest, till he had chosen out a new Text, and that night cast his Sermon into a form, and his Text into divisions; and the next day betook himself to consult the Fathers, and so commit his meditations to his memory, which was excellent."[5] Walton's description of Donne's employment, even the commitment to memorize a text that could last more than an hour in the pulpit, was not exceptional for a preacher of Donne's rank. To prove, or *explicate*, their own points, ministers collected examples of patristic scriptural commentary, organizing them by means of the medieval scholastic method called *divisio*; these observations, or *meditations*, were then subjected to the Reformation method known as "doctrine and uses" – the idea that the Bible must not only be *explained* but also *applied* to human life. But Walton's amplifying asides – "if not oftener"; "that [same] night"; "the next day" – introduce us to the sheer intellectual *and* physical energy Donne put into that standard work, even to the point of ocular exhaustion.

Scripture

Donne had long been fascinated by and occupied in the study of religious controversy and canon law, and dabbled with biblical exegesis in his *Essays in Divinity* (c. 1614), but his sustained and passionate engagement with the Bible dates from his ordination and its concomitant requirement that he preach for his living. The sermons testify to Donne's rapt enthrallment with the biblical text; generations of editors have noted what George Potter and Evelyn Simpson, in 1955, termed Donne's "general indebtedness to the scriptures."[6] As befit their liturgical status, the Psalms, the Gospels, and the Epistles regularly served as sermons texts for Donne. As a cathedral dean he was not constrained by preaching license – nor did he feel personally confined – to one particular version of English scripture: his sermons contain references to the Coverdale Bible (1535), Henry VIII's "Great Bible" (1539), the Geneva Bible (1560), Elizabeth I's "Bishop's Bible"(1568), and the Bible commissioned by James I (1611).[7] The seeming promiscuity merely reflected the fact that he served a Church regulated by statute, one wherein Bibles were "authorized" only insofar as they were ordered to be purchased to be used in worship and copies "set up" in churches and cathedrals; private reading, as well as sermon preparation, knew no such restriction.

Nor, however, was Donne (or any other university-educated preacher) restricted to the vernacular: perhaps given his Catholic upbringing, Donne was not only as conversant, but also as apt, with the Latin Vulgate as he was with Englished scripture. In this, he was probably representative of the English ecclesiastical elite, whose educations were classical, whose theologies were continental, and whose intellectual comfort zones remained Latinate. As he was to explain, he could never disapprove of most of the Vulgate's content; it was the Council of Trent's soul-crushing insistence on its sole orthodoxy that he deplored.

Donne was captivated with the exegetical possibilities offered by Greek and, especially, Hebrew, languages he pursued with more enthusiasm than skill in the great polyglot Bibles of the day: the Alcala Complutensian (1514–17) and the Antwerp Montanus (1571–73). These, plus the great Hebrew-to-Latin translation of Tremellius, allowed Donne not only to immerse himself in the humanist study of the Old Testament, but also to compare its words side-by-side with Greek, Aramaic, and Latin parallels. Donne's indebtedness to a wide range of scripture editions and translations may account for the occasional looseness of his translations: he quoted freely, from memory, and with a fine disregard for strict accuracy. A forgivable trait, perhaps: as it can never be exact, translation invariably plays a bit rough with the original. For Donne, the possibilities suggested *by* translation, more so than the actual act *of* translation, offered compelling exegetical themes.[8]

Location

Donne's ultimate task was to apply those words of scripture and the insights they afforded to the condition of his audience and the circumstances of the day. The requirement of *decorum*, the process by which any preacher assessed the "persons, the time and the place" of his sermon and made certain that it was both applicable and appropriate to the social and political condition of their congregants, explains why the sermons vary, in style and in substance, according to the places in which he preached. At a time when clergymen regularly and quite licitly collected pulpits in plural but preached in few of these, Donne was a extraordinarily diligent preacher to (among others) his London parish, St Dunstan's-in-the-West; the chapel at Lincoln's Inn; St Paul's Cathedral, where he was dean, as well as in its outdoor preaching place known as "Paul's Cross." He delivered sermons to private households and in the chapels royal of James I and his son Charles I. To reckon up his many appointments – cathedral dean, royal chaplain, Inns of Court lecturer, priest – is to understand that Donne served many earthly masters. Thus to know where and to whom Donne preached is essential, if we are to understand the import of his words.

In 1626, a quarto pamphlet was printed for Thomas Jones for the purposes of sale at the Sign of the Black Raven in the Strand, London. Its title enumerates its contents:

> *Five Sermons upon Speciall Occasions,*
> [*viz.*]

1. A Sermon Preached at Pauls Crosse.
2. To the Honorable Virginia Company.
3. At the Consecration of Lincolnes Inne Chappell.
4. The first Sermon preached to K. Charles at St. James, 1625.
5. A Sermon preached to his Maiestie at White-hall, 24. Feb. 1625

By John Donne, Deane of Saint Pauls, London.

The title serves as *curriculum vitae*: in the decade between Donne's consecration and licensing, he had managed to fill a complement of important pulpits in and around his decanal base in London. Donne spoke to disparate audiences both between and within his many venues. An influential, if socially diverse, urban cohort made up the St Paul's Cathedral auditory: mayors, aldermen, members of the corporation of the city of London. Paul's Cross, the popular outdoor preaching space next to Paul's, attracted an even more diverse audience of politicos, court observers, foreign visitors to London, MPs in town for sittings of Parliament, and assorted locals. Lincoln's Inn, one of the best-remunerated lectureships in London, boasted a well-educated auditory of barristers and students. St Dunstan's, a parish also in the heart of London's legal district, had a congregation made up of judges, lawyers, and printers, as well as the well-off citizens of the nearby parish of St Clement Danes. But to preach "at court" was to preach anywhere the monarch was, and also before those whose job or ambitious pleasure it was to be near the king and his privy council; the chapel royal was thus the most public of private venues. Donne preached there at the behest of two kings, whom he served (along with a rota of others, who, at least under James I, represented an impressively disparate range of theological opinion) as chaplain-in-ordinary. James's successor Charles I extended the same regard, and ordered Donne's Lent sermon, preached to him in 1626, published. It was his fourth sermon to attain the afterlife of print.

Occasion

Timeless, time-bound, and timely, early modern sermons are occasional: composed to order, marking specific works and days. Donne preached on ecclesiastical holidays and seasons in their everlasting round: Lent, Easter, Whitsun (the second-ranking festival in the liturgical year, marking the end of the Easter season), Christmas, Candlemas. He preached to fulfill particular assignments: Donne held the prebend of Chiswick, and thus was a member of the cathedral chapter, which required him to recite and meditate upon the Psalms daily.[9] And he preached by command on politically oriented topics: in that most public and popular of all official preaching venues, Paul's Cross, Donne was ordered to explicate and defend the "Directions to Preachers" issued by James I in 1622. The Directions forbid the airing of controversial topics from English pulpits, thus making Donne yet another of the early Stuart preachers whose ironic brief it was to preach against preaching.

The Times

Donne's career spanned the most politically fragile and religiously fraught period in England before its civil wars of the 1640s: an era marked by the death of James I (March 27, 1625) as well as the increasingly controversial early reign, and first year of personal rule, of Charles I. Donne was an observant and cosmopolitan man, and his sermons frequently gave subtle (and sometimes not-so-subtle) voice to England's increasing political and social instability. Much of this disaffection was religious in nature: by the early 1620s the Church of England's equilibrium, always delicate, had begun to tilt perceptibly towards an ecclesiastical faction with liturgical, theological, and ecclesiological designs to thwart the ambitions of the doctrinal majority in its ranks, after the Synod of Dort (1618) had failed to secure a Calvinist consensus in the episcopate at home.

In the final years of Donne's life, other sermons preached in influential pulpits by men who would come into unprecedented (if not exactly unexpected) power under Charles and his archbishop William Laud took an increasingly bold and openly bellicose tone towards predestinarian Calvinism, now equated openly with Puritan "sectarianism." Many of these sermonic opinions later took on more substantial life in print, making an indelible impression (whether true or not) that the Church had finally become irrevocably divided over Protestant doctrine as well as Protestant practice. While at least one of his sermons was examined by Laud for evidence of heterodoxy (or, more likely, disloyalty to the new ecclesiastical regime), John Donne's sermons always took the measured part in this arena of religious dispute. Unlike many equally ambitious fellow churchmen, he believed in the pastoral as well as the intellectual validity of *via media*, not manipulating the idea of a golden mean into baldly partisan advocacy of Laudian ritual innovation.[10]

Amidst the roiling set of political and ecclesiastical controversies that marked the later reign of James I and the opening years of the reign of Charles, Donne's personal life also took its own fearful turns: in 1617, when his wife Ann died in childbirth; in the winter of 1623–24, as he battled the illness that was to form the organizing principle of his *Devotions upon Emergent Occasions*; during the resurgence of plague that not only felled him but effectively emptied London in the summers of 1625, 1626, and 1627; in his final decline and fatal illness. All, including this last, to the amazement of his hearers, formed themes that reliably surfaced in poignant ways in his writing and preaching. Indeed one *leitmotiv* punctuating contemporary accounts of Donne's career is wonder: at his capacity and willingness to push himself past physical limits, especially in times of personal illness and grief – as he was himself dying in 1631, at his wife's own funeral in 1617 – preaching *in extremis* being one great, perhaps *the* one great, source of his remarkable charisma in the pulpit.

Conclusion

Sermons were the primary tools of debate in the domains we consider "official" and "public" in this age – parliament, court, and church – and they were disseminated in media we also recognize as "public" – words not only voiced ephemerally, but also committed to ongoing lives in print publication and manuscript circulation. In the sermons of John Donne we have the personal, the political, and the prophetic allied in singular sermonic performance. The man revealed in these sermons was not to be bound by occasion, even as he discussed it thoughtfully and with rare passion: he was, at heart, a talented prose stylist, a skilled biblical exegete, and a subtle Christian theologian.

These literary traits and spiritual gifts allowed John Donne to transcend, in a way few early modern English preachers have done, an imprisoning early modern timeliness, but having such a great number of his sermons go into print in the three decades following his death in 1631 also sustained Donne's reputation as a preacher as well as a poet. Documented in the memoirs of his contemporaries, in ecclesiastical records, and in official and personal correspondence, the trajectory of Donne's religious career is nonetheless mainly to be traced in long, representative runs of his printed sermon texts like the omnibus volumes published posthumously in 1640's *LXXX Sermons*, 1649's *Fifty Sermons*, and 1660–61's misleadingly titled *XXVI Sermons* (which in fact contains twenty-three sermons). In all, six sermons went to print in Donne's lifetime and another seven soon after his death, including several editions of his best-known effort, *Deaths Duell*, in which, according to Walton, "Dr. Donne *had preach't his own Funeral Sermon*."[11]

In subsequent centuries, Henry Alford edited Donne's Works in six volumes in 1839, wherein sermons claimed the lion's share of page space. But it was George Potter and Evelyn Simpson, while stubbornly insisting that it was "as a poet" that Donne held "and will continue to hold his place in English literature," who edited the first great modern critical edition of the sermons in the early 1950s: one hundred and sixty sermons, with scholarly introductions and critical apparatus, reprinted in ten volumes.[12] Since then, scholars have discovered more manuscript evidence against which to assay the currency of the extant print sources, and an updated, enlarged, and richly annotated edition of the complete sermons is forthcoming from Oxford University Press. Students of John Donne's writings now consult a richly diverse archive of sermon sources as they assess the career of this celebrated preacher in the post-Reformation Church of England.

Notes

1. Walton, *Lives*, 49.
2. See Bald, *Life*.
3. Peter McCullough, "Donne as Preacher," in *CCJD*, 176.
4. See Lori Anne Ferrell, "Religious Persuasions: Teaching the Early Modern Sermon," in *Teaching Early Modern Prose*, eds. Suzanne Brietz Monta and Margaret W. Ferguson (New York: MLA, 2010), 61–70.
5. Walton, *Lives*, 67.
6. *Sermons*, 10:295.
7. David Colclough, "Donne, John (1572–1631)," in *Oxford Dictionary of National Biography*, eds. H. C. G. Matthew and Brian Harrison, www.oxforddnb.com/.
8. Lori Anne Ferrell, "The Preacher's Bibles" in *The Oxford Handbook of the Early Modern Sermon*, eds. Peter McCullough, Hugh Adlington, and Emma Ratigan (Oxford University Press, 2011), 29–30; *Sermons*, 10:307, 328.
9. *Sermons*, 6:30, fn. 70.
10. See Lori Anne Ferrell, "Kneeling and the Body Politic," in *Religion, Literature, and Politics in Post-Reformation England*, eds. Donna Hamilton and Richard Strier (Cambridge University Press, 1996), 70–92.
11. Walton, *Lives*, 75.
12. *Sermons*, 1:83.

CHAPTER 27

The Self

Nancy Selleck

To explore conceptions of "the self" in early modern English culture is to enter a complex and fascinating territory that belies the ease with which we use that simple phrase today. Prevailing models of selfhood in the Renaissance were different from modern notions of the autonomous individual. Indeed, they often present an opposite conception of selves – as contingent and context-embedded. The discursive conventions of identity in early modern England tended to make selves material rather than abstract, relational rather than individual, protean rather than stable. As scholars have often noted, Donne's writings are full of especially vivid examples of these various models of embodied, relational, or mutable selves. To be sure, early modern culture also saw an increasing emphasis on inward experience – in religious introspection, medical self-knowledge, poetic self-speaking, and other cultural practices. Yet the basic paradigms and conceptions of soul, body, and mind in the period – from humoral theories of assimilation and digestion to literary tropes of lovers' exchanged hearts and selves – still suggest a profound imbrication of self and world. As Donne and his contemporaries seem keenly aware, to turn inward, then, is to discover not a private solitude but a space always already penetrated from without.

And if early modern notions of identity often differed from our own, they were also themselves in flux. Looking closely at the ways writers in the period render selfhood, scholars have found a multiplicity of ideas in play and in tension with each other, sometimes even within the same text.[1] Many texts register not only competing ideas, but a sense of paradox in the effort to formulate what a "self" might be – a struggle with meaning evident even in the use of that word in early modern English. While "self" appears only rarely as a full-fledged noun in the late sixteenth century, its initial uses are surprisingly varied as well as vexed. In literary texts, they range from a complex "inward selfe" in Spenser (Sonnet 45, 3), to Jonson's notion of a "gathered self" (Epigram 98, 10), to a Shakespearean "kind of self resides with you" (*Troilus and Cressida* 3.2.135). The only consistent substantive use of "self" in the period is a trope that refers, paradoxically, not to oneself but to a highly significant *other* whom one calls "my self" or "my other self." This trope is especially popular among poets in the 1590s, who are quick to question the very properties of a "self" – its self-propriety, for instance, or its boundaries – that later speakers and writers would take for granted.[2] Donne uses the trope in "The Legacy," a poem about the aftermath of lovers' parting, when the speaker tells his beloved "that myself (that is you, not I) / Did kill me" (10–11). As the fulcrum in that poem's exploration of the vicissitudes of a self in love, this radically decentered "self" throws the whole idea of an inward locus of personal identity up for grabs. Combined with the related trope of lovers' exchanged hearts, Donne's other-self conceit creates an entanglement that takes many forms at once – physical, emotional, volitional, legal, moral – and that leaves the lovers mutually embedded, but still not "true."

Such complex experiments with the meaning of "self" are common among early modern English writers, and they often constitute a debate over the ethical dimensions of selfhood as well. Donne engages vigorously in such debate in both verse and prose, showing a deep knowledge of the theoretical controversies within the religious, political, and philosophical discourses of his day and arguing strenuously about their implications for selfhood. Often his arguments emphasize the context-dependency of, and connection between, selves – for instance, when he claims in the *Devotions* that "no man is an island unto himself" and insists that "there is no Phoenix, nothing singular, nothing alone."[3] Of course, such a vehement rejection of autonomy also confirms that that was another possible model of selfhood in the period. The presence of so much debate implies that the meanings and parameters of selfhood were not yet clear or given. Tracing Donne's engagement in such debates can help us discern some of the varied and competing conceptions of selfhood – inward and otherwise – with which he and his contemporaries lived and wrestled.

Material Inwardness

Early modern English speakers used "soul" more than "self" to signify inward being, and it was not only a religious concept. "Soul" in the sense of "psyche" had material dimensions, comprising a physio-psychological system that included vegetal, sensible, and rational souls. Among the key elements of this system informing everyday conceptions and

representations of persons are the understanding of the heart as the
physical locus of sense impressions and the notion of "spirit" as
a physical substance – a subtle vapor arising in the blood and linking
body and soul.[4] Such theory informs Donne's own emphatically material
conception of persons – his repeated insistence that soul and body are one,
that "the body makes the mind,"[5] and that "all that the soule does, it does
in, and with, and by the body."[6] His frequent assertions of the interde-
pendence of soul and body, while based on widely accepted faculty
psychology, are yet in tension with some philosophical efforts in the period
to distinguish body and soul. Neoplatonic theorists, for instance, recognize
the material bases of sense and imagination but also stress the soul's
capacity to transcend its material world. Adapting Plato's theory of love,
Marsilio Ficino sees the contemplation of beauty as a means by which the
soul can leave behind its physical sense impressions and attain a more
abstract knowledge of true forms, thereby raising the soul "up to the
angelic or contemplative life."[7] Such highly theoretical discourses are
more widely disseminated through works such as Castiglione's
The Courtier, which culminates in a stirring version of this theory of the
soul's transcendence via its contemplation of pure beauty. Closing the
debate on courtly self-fashioning, Bembo describes how the mature courtier should avoid the torment of physical love and "enjoy beautie without
passion," using his physical sense of the beloved's body only "as a stayer (as
it were) to clime up" to a higher form of love and of being.[8] If the courtier
ultimately frames that beauty "within his imagination *sundred from all
matter*," his soul (figured as female) can turn "to the beholding of her owne
substance" and "coople herselfe with the nature of Aungelles."[9]

English poets show interest in this theoretical model of the self's transcendence through the distanced contemplation of "beautie without passion," but often they are testing and critiquing the model rather than
merely adopting it. In Donne's "The Ecstasy," for instance, we seem to
begin with a Neoplatonic conception of the immateriality of true lovers'
souls, which are "so by love refined" (21) that their connection is only
minimally physical. Yet Donne's version of this higher love keeps joining
rather than distancing the lovers. Using the plural "we" throughout the
poem, the speaker emphasizes the ways that love "Interanimates two souls"
(42) rather than exalting one of them. The sense of the lovers' mutuality is
striking – "both meant, both spake, the same" (26) – and it soon appears
that the movement of these refined souls is less *upward* than *outward*. It is
the movement of literally *ec-static* souls that are "gone out" toward each
other and hang suspended between – an expansion also figured in the

imagery of mixing, redoubling, and multiplying (34–40). The poem does acknowledge a striving toward immateriality, noting that "our blood labours to beget / Spirits as like souls as it can" (61–62). But as readers have noted, it also insists on the opposite trajectory, *toward* the material body, stressing that the "subtle knot which makes us man" (64) is the *connection* between physical and spiritual selves.[10] The climax of the poem deliberately inverts (and subverts) the Platonic model of transcendence by insisting that pure lovers' souls

> must . . . *descend*
> T'affections and to faculties,
> Which sense may reach and apprehend,
> Else a great prince in prison lies.
>
> (65–68, emphasis added)

Thus for Donne, the body is what frees us rather than what we must escape. The ecstasy of "interanimation" is love's great achievement, and the poem's last lines cast this "dialogue of one" as little different from sexual union: the lovers' appearance will show "Small change, when we'are to bodies gone" (75–76).

Donne's insistence on the material dimensions of the self often explicitly reflects another key theoretical context: that of humoral physiology, the ancient medical theory in which the fluctuating balance of the body's humours – produced by the process of digestion – determined both physical and mental conditions. As Michael Schoenfeldt has shown, the paradigms and practices of humoral theory offered Renaissance speakers and writers a rich and "near-poetic" language of identity as concrete, visceral inwardness.[11] Humoral theory entails a profound reciprocity of mental and physical functioning that distinguishes it from post-Cartesian conceptions of a more abstract inwardness or a self based in *thinking*. Whereas Descartes's *cogito* isolates as its definitive mode of being an inward, thinking subject explicitly stripped of any physical or social context, humoral inwardness is necessarily a function of the body, and that body is radically subject to its environment. In humoral physiology, the person is literally made and remade by what the body takes in – air, food, spirits – and assimilates or digests. Thus humoral being entails a subtle but constant permeation by one's surround. This "ecological" model of self takes the confounded soul and body and confounds them further with the external world.[12] And that material engagement with context includes the social world as well, for humoralism makes inward experience available to others by rendering the deep makeup of the self *legible* on the surface.[13]

With the language of humoralism very much part of everyday speech and conceptions of living in the body and in the world, all kinds of writers take up its implications for selfhood. Some texts offer the possibility of self-improvement (via physical regimen), while others promise knowledge of both self and others through understanding "the foure Complexions . . . and their externall Intimates."[14] Some stress the openness and vulnerability of the humoral person, so unremittingly subject to "externall spirites recoursying into hys bodye and mynde,"[15] or emphasize the person's necessary context-dependency: "Such is the air, such be our spirits; and as our spirits, such be our humours."[16] Donne's assertion that "Men are sponges which to pour out, receive" recognizes and applies this paradigm of the humoral body as a general principle of the ineluctable engagement of self with context.[17]

The humoral model of an always-penetrable self – permanently subject to influence from without and therefore in constant need of external "correctives" as well – resembles many of the images of Donne's religious writings. In Holy Sonnet 10, the already "usurped" speaker longs to be broken and ravished by divine penetration. Or in Holy Sonnet 19, the bodily imagery likens the spiritual instability of the speaker's "devout fits" (12) to "a fantastic ague" (13), which also constitutes a cure – "Those are my best days when I shake with fear" (14). Increasingly, Donne is fascinated by the humoral concept of *digestion* as the process by which the self is continually reconstituted, and he repeatedly applies the idea to spiritual matters. In a 1619 sermon he explains that "good digestion brings alwaies assimilation, certainly, if I come to a true meditation on Christ, I come to a conformity with Christ."[18] And a sermon on the doctrine of resurrection uses the humoral idea of assimilation as the model for an ultimate *physical* participation and union in God: "As my meat is assimilated to my flesh, and made one flesh with it; as my soul is assimilated to my God, and *made partaker of the divine nature*, and *Idem Spiritus*, the same Spirit with it; so, there my flesh shall be assimilated to the flesh of my Saviour, and made the same flesh with him too."[19] Again, the idea of mutual *participation* is paramount for Donne, and he often uses humoral imagery to render that crucial sense of the self's material connection with God.

Relational vs. Individual Being

Notable in these examples is the way that Donne's imagery is not only physical but relational – that is, his preoccupation with the body is simultaneously a preoccupation with the other. That relational mode of being is broadly characteristic of the language and many of the constructs of early modern selfhood. The word "person" in sixteenth-century usage denoted relational rather than individual being, "personal" signifying not what was private (as the word does today) but what belonged to one's physical appearance or social role. One's outward habit or "guise" spoke one's identity, as did one's humoral "complexion." The pervasiveness of hierarchy in the culture helped to cast selves as relational rather than independent entities, making identity a function of place or position within social or political structures. Humanist pedagogy emphasized commonplace knowledge as well as imitation or "following." And the centrality of rhetoric in early modern education also promoted a sense of relational identity in the model of a rhetorical self constituted in its engagement with an audience. The thrust of persuasion is toward the minds of others, and thus rhetorical training instills a deeply dialogized consciousness, as evidenced in the many early modern texts that repeatedly stress the importance of adapting one's speech to one's particular listeners. Such factors contribute to a cultural milieu in which Donne can readily assert the self's social embeddedness, as when he claims in the *Devotions* that "any man's death diminishes me, because I am *involved in* mankind."[20]

But in arguing thus, Donne also resists some contrary ideas in play at the time. Part of his social critique in *The First Anniversary* concerns the diminished value of such relational identity in a world where "all coherence" and "all relation" are gone: "Prince, subject, father, son, are things forgot, / For every man alone thinks he hath got / To be a phoenix, and that there can be / None of that kind, of which he is, but he" (213–18). Here social hierarchies signify connection for Donne as much as status, and this phoenix is a negative image for an individualized self. That individual model also carries the danger of solipsism, which Donne often describes as fatal to the self: "I must not be alone with my selfe ... I am a reciprocall plague ... and I am the Babylon that I must goe out of, or I perish."[21] Donne shows a similar concern about the discourse of "conscience" – an increasingly individual idea in early modern culture. Etymologically rooted in the classical Latin *conscientia* (meaning a holding of knowledge in common), "conscience" had gradually replaced the older Anglo-Saxon "inwit" and for a while combined both senses of inward thinking and shared moral knowledge before developing the more private sense signifying "an individual entity."[22] This individual conscience carries significant implications for the nature of identity that are sometimes queried or resisted by early modern writers.[23] In a 1622 sermon, Donne admits the principle that one should not go against conscience, yet he also claims "many men flatter themselves too far" with that principle and suggests that it is "a greater sin, not to labour to recover the conscience" when it "be in an error," and to divest it of wrong suspicions by seeking the advice of knowledgeable others.[24] In another sermon, he insists on the importance of "assisting" one's conscience with "more witnesses": "Serve not thy selfe with that triviall, and vulgar saying, As long as my conscience testifies well to me, I care not what men say of me."[25] And still later, preaching at Whitehall, he says flatly, "never make thy private conscience the rule of publique actions; for to constitute a Rectitude, or an Obliquity in any public action, there enter more circumstances, then can have fallen in thy knowledge."[26] Here Donne reminds his listeners (including the king) of the insufficiency of any single perspective and the need for consensual validation and dialogue.[27]

Donne's persistent focus on the need for dialogue – or more generally on the self's inherent need to go beyond itself – also shows in his engagement with another significant discursive convention of early modern culture: the classically based Renaissance discourse of same-sex friendship or "amity" that attracts so many writers of the period.[28] Focusing on the importance for the self of an especially intimate other, discussions of friendship are among the earliest places the popular trope of one's "other self" emerges in English. As one sixteenth-century translation of Cicero's *De Amicitia* puts it, "he is a freend, which is (as it were) an other himselfe."[29] Early modern writers also highlight the process of such friendship as a fundamental exchange and mingling of souls without boundaries. Montaigne, for instance, describes how friends' souls "entermixe and confound themselves one in the other, with so universal a commixture, that they can no more finde the seame that hath conjoyned them."[30] Donne is conscious of this "commixture" effect particularly in writing to friends, as he explains in a verse letter to Sir Henry Wotton that begins, "Sir, more than kisses, letters mingle souls." And for Donne, this all-important "mingling" of friends' souls also explicitly involves the soul's outward movement or "ecstasy." As he tells his friend Sir Henry Goodyer, "this writing of letters, when it is with any seriousness, is a kind of extasie, and a departure and secession and suspension of the soul, wh^ch doth then communicate itself to two bodies."[31] Such writings exemplify the way that friendship discourses share the language of lovers' confounded souls and selves – as when Donne begins "The Storm," a poem to Christopher Brooke, "Thou which art I." This intense identification of friends is also explicitly dialogic – not a mere merger but an encounter with a distinct interlocutor. As Ramie Targoff shows, Donne often theorized about letters as an active dialogue between friends: "Donne understood his letters as 'mutual communicating' and depended upon his friends to 'inanimate' and re-inanimate" their meaning in reading them.[32] Like the wider discourse of friendship in which they participate, Donne's addresses to friends strive to articulate the essential role of others in the makeup of the self.

Protean Identity

Also looming large in early modern representations of identity is the self's capacity for change. Whether dreaded or celebrated, the protean nature of persons is a ubiquitous topic in the period, and perhaps understandably, given the seismic changes and pressures within early modern European culture. The religious upheavals of the Reformation, challenges to traditional cosmology, and the movement from a feudal to a more mercantile economy are just a few of the larger factors producing the prospect of more fluid social, spiritual, and class identities. Explorers' encounters with unfamiliar cultures began to broaden awareness of different ways of being. For many, the expansion of knowledge and experience – through the rapid development of print culture, increase in travel, and new opportunities for middle-class education – likely added to the sense of potential mobility and transformation of identity. In England the presence of women on the throne for half a century was also among the factors helping to generate questions and debates about gender roles and contributing to a growing fascination with the nature and parameters of gender identity. In this moment of vast social change, the question of protean identity – an oxymoron for us – becomes an important topos.

Indeed, "identity" in the sense of self-sameness is not a term that belongs to the Renaissance. The abstraction it later comes to signify – a property of persistent being over time – seems much less a given at this time. The early modern English term for self-sameness is "constancy" – certainly a crucial idea in the period, but not a term that denotes an inherent aspect of persons (as the later "identity" does). On the contrary, constancy is rooted in behavior and is something one has to achieve, while inconstancy is at least as "proper" or natural to persons – an always-implicit potential in the discourses of constancy. Moreover, those discourses tend to have a specific and concrete focus – sexual constancy, for instance, or religious faithfulness, to cite two issues sometimes seen as linked in Donne's poetry. References to the shape-shifting Proteus often express anxiety about the self's potential for mutability in the form of hypocrisy or false appearances or betrayal.

Although sexual inconstancy is often broadly attributed to women, writers can also make it a male attribute – as Shakespeare does in his Proteus and other "giddy" male characters. Many early modern texts also show irritation with the self's potential "humorousness," whether in the sense of the humoral body's inherent instability or the fashion for "affecting a humour" or outward style of behavior. Such "humorousness" is widely satirized – for instance in Jonson's humours plays, or by Donne in his "Satire I," "Away thou fondling motley humorist" (1).

But early modern writers can also embrace the self's mutability, exploring the possibilities of transformation in more playful and positive terms. The prevalence of cross-dressing narratives in romance and on the stage reflects persistent interest in transgressing the boundaries of identity, as does the surging interest in theatre itself. The protean self was also the product of introspection, especially in the mode of lyric poetry. The emphasis of Petrarch and his many imitators on the exploration of inward, subjective experience – minutely following the speaker's own shifting thoughts and passions – helped open new ways of speaking about a more variable self. Many poets embrace with great imaginative energy an Ovidian model of the self's continual transformation in love, exploring its richness and vitality as well as its pitfalls. Donne's "Change" seems to capture both sides of the early modern ambivalence toward the protean self. It begins with the speaker's dread of his beloved's potential inconstancy, but then shifts gears and accepts – or rather celebrates – such infidelity as the source of freshness and purity. Denigrating constancy as "captivity" (29), the poem turns to an image of flowing waters which, "when they kiss one bank, and leaving this / Never look back, but the next bank do kiss, / Then are they purest" (33–35). And if that imagery still seems tinged with irony, the closing lines do not: "Change'is the nursery / Of music, joy, life, and eternity" (35–36).

Whether positive or negative, the early modern concern with constancy renders selfhood an ethical category – a point that applies to most of the models of selfhood this brief essay has been able to address. Because they are neither self-contained nor abstract, such selves are not safe from social or material contingencies. As a result, writers like Donne must struggle with the necessary imbrication of self and other, self and material world, and thus with an idea that cannot be reduced to a discrete individual. And those are possibly also the factors that make early modern writers' representations of self so rich, so fraught, and so endlessly interesting to readers today.

Notes

1. See, for instance, Mary Thomas Crane's analysis of Hamlet in *Shakespeare's Brain: Reading with Cognitive Theory* (Princeton University Press, 2001), 116–55.
2. On the history of the language of selfhood in the Renaissance, see Nancy Selleck, *The Interpersonal Idiom in Shakespeare, Donne, and Early Modern Culture* (New York: Palgrave Macmillan, 2008), 21–55.
3. Donne, *Devotions upon Emergent Occasions, and Severall Steps in my Sicknes*, ed. John Sparrow (Cambridge University Press, 1923), 98, 23.
4. Marsilio Ficino, *Three Books on Life*, trans. and eds. Carol V. Kaske and John R. Clarke (Binghamton, NY: Medieval and Renaissance Texts and Studies, 1989), 111.
5. Donne, *Paradoxes and Problems* (Oxford: Clarendon Press, 1980), 6.
6. *Sermons*, 4:358.
7. Marsilio Ficino, *Commentary on Plato's Symposium on Love*, trans. Sears Jayne (Dallas, TX: Spring Publications, 1985), 7.1.
8. Castiglione, *The Book of the Courtier*, trans. Sir Thomas Hoby (London: J. M. Dent & Sons, 1948), 357–58.
9. Castiglione, *Courtier*, 357–60, emphasis added.
10. On the poem's Aristotelian emphasis and "forceful reversal" of the Platonic model, see Ramie Targoff, *John Donne, Body and Soul* (University of Chicago Press, 2008), 53–59.
11. Michael Schoenfeldt, *Bodies and Selves in Early Modern England* (Cambridge University Press, 1999), 3.
12. Gail Kern Paster, *Humoring the Body: Emotions and the Shakespearean Stage* (University of Chicago Press, 2004), 18.
13. Selleck, *Interpersonal*, 61–65.
14. Thomas Walkington, *The Optick Glasse of Humors* (London, 1639), title page.
15. Levinus Lemnius, *Touchstone of Complexions*, trans. Thomas Newton (London, 1576), sig. 21v–22r.
16. Robert Burton, *The Anatomy of Melancholy*, eds. Thomas C. Faulkner, Nicolas K. Kiessling, and Rhonda L. Blair (Oxford: Clarendon Press, 1997), 1.2.2.5.
17. "To Sir Henry Wotton ('Sir, more than kisses')", 37.
18. *Sermons*, 2:212.
19. *Sermons*, 3:112–13.
20. Donne, *Devotions*, 98, emphasis added.
21. *Sermons*, 9:311.
22. "conscience, n.," *OED Online*.
23. See, for instance, Shakespeare's extended meditation on the nature of conscience in *Richard III*.
24. *Sermons*, 4:222.
25. *Sermons*, 7:250.
26. *Sermons*, 7:408.

27. On the communal nature of conscience in Donne see Ceri Sullivan, *The Rhetoric of Conscience in Donne, Herbert, and Vaughn* (Oxford University Press, 2008), 231.

28. On friendship discourses see Jeffrey Masten, *Textual Intercourse: Collaboration, Authorship, and Sexualities in Renaissance Drama* (Cambridge University Press, 1997), 28–62; and Laurie Shannon, *Sovereign Amity: Figures of Friendship in Shakespearean Contexts* (University of Chicago Press, 2002), 17–53.

29. Cicero, *Fowre Seuerall Treatises of M. Tullius Cicero, Conteyninge His Most Learned and Eloquent Discourses of Frendshippe*, trans. Thomas Newton (London, 1577), sig. 34r.

30. Michel de Montaigne, *The Essayes of Montaigne: John Florio's Translation*, ed. J. I. M. Stewart (New York: Modern Library, 1933), 149.

31. *Letters*, 10.

32. Targoff, *Body and Soul*, 48.

CHAPTER 28

Portraits

Sarah Howe

The first edition of Donne's *Poems* (1633) lacks the frontispiece portrait that would help lend the second, smaller-format edition of 1635 an aura of his resurrected presence. Yet the volume's front matter calls out for such a portrait even in its absence. The book opens with Donne's own voice – dated August 16, 1601, thirty years before his death – ringing through the introductory epistle to his *Metempsychosis*, a poem, fittingly, about the transmigration of souls: 'Others at the Porches and entries of their Buildings set their Armes: I, my picture; if any colours can deliver a minde so plaine, and flat, and through light as mine.'[1] Placed at the head of the volume by a canny printer or publisher, Donne's words invoke the superior 'colours' of rhetoric, as though to summon a verbal portrait of the poet for a print readership. The passage shows Donne's knowledge of the *paragone* between the arts – the topos that painted portraits, unlike poems, struggle to capture their subject's intangible 'mind' – while also playing with the idea of perspective, the illusion of depth on a two-dimensional surface. In the following epistle, the printer Miles Fletcher goes on to quote Donne's famous lines from 'The Storm' in praise of the Elizabethan miniaturist Nicholas Hilliard: '*A hand, or eye, / By* Hilyard *drawne, is worth a history / By a worse Painter made.*'[2] Fletcher argues that 'a scattered limbe of this Author' is worth more than another's entire corpus, just as a palm-sized portrait by Hilliard might outshine a grand history painting. His preface makes explicit the metonymy by which physical books came to stand for their authors' absent presence – a lack the frontispiece portrait was, through the course of the seventeenth century, increasingly called on to fill.

Donne was fascinated by his own image and its recording in paint. Across four decades, he sat for his portrait at least five times – a total equalled among the period's poets only by the aristocratic Sir Philip Sidney, himself keenly interested in painting. From his writings, Donne was as familiar with Dürer on perspective as he was with the debate surrounding the role of images in worship. Freshly contentious in the political climate of the late 1620s, the terms of the iconoclastic controversy marked Donne's preaching of the period. But the sermons, with their sophisticated analogies drawn from painterly technique, also reveal Donne's sensitivity to the visual arts.[3] Donne's own modest activities as a collector were fostered by friendship with connoisseurs such as Sir Henry Wotton. From the legacies to friends recorded in his will, we know about the twenty-five or so paintings, mainly of religious subjects, that hung in his Deanery at St. Paul's until his death in 1631. That his 'Picture of the blessed Virgin Marye' has since been identified as a Titian, which later belonged to Charles I, suggests the refinement of his eye.[4] While not large by the standards of a Penshurst, or the Stuart nobility's burgeoning long galleries, his collection was sufficient 'to have filled nearly every corner of Donne's little world with imagery'.[5]

Commissioned at very different points in his career, Donne's portraits open a window onto his changing self-presentation. They shape our sense of his life's distinct phases, as well as its various 'conversions'. The poses he inhabits in the surviving pictures range from young gallant, to melancholy lover, to solemn divine, suggesting Donne's preoccupation with his identity as a thing repeatedly refashioned. We should certainly see his intentions reflected in the design of these portraits. Donne's degree of involvement can be glimpsed perhaps in Izaak Walton's remarkable tale of him posing for his minutely stage-managed deathbed sketch. Donne's portraits testify to what Louis Martz has called his lifelong practice of 'creating fictional roles out of aspects of his being'. In his portraits, no less than his poems or sermons, 'the complex personality that we call "Donne"' is fashioned out of a 'continually shifting series of dramatic moments'.[6]

Donne's first portrait, painted aged 18, survives only in the frontispiece already noted, from his posthumous *Poems* of 1635 (Figure 1). The image, dated 1591, represents Donne during a period of his life that remains the subject of biographical speculation. In the two years before he entered the Inns of Court in 1592, it has been suggested he may have travelled in Europe for a spell, prior to enrolling at Thavie's Inn for a year's preparatory study.[7] The frontispiece engraving by William Marshall is usually said to preserve a lost miniature by Nicholas Hilliard. However, the attribution depends more on Donne's poetic praise for Hilliard's work than on any stylistic evidence beyond the picture's format.[8] The workmanlike Marshall was the same engraver responsible for the portrait Milton derided on the frontispiece of his *Poems* (1645). Its crude drawing and oddities of scale – the tiny foreground hand makes its gripped sword feel comically

Figure 1: Frontispiece portrait engraved by William Marshall, from Donne's *Poems* (1635), based on a lost original possibly by Nicholas Hilliard. Reproduced by permission of Cambridge University Library.

ineffectual – suggest we cannot take Marshall's Donne as a faithful tran-
scription of its source, at least in terms of technique. Nevertheless, the
resemblance of this youthful portrayal to Donne's next portrait, the so-
called 'Lothian', suggests the likeness is probably a fair one. If we were to
credit the attribution to Hilliard, it would say something important about
Donne's early connections to the Court: painter to the highest ranks of
English society, Hilliard did not usually include fledgling law students
among his sitters.[9]

Whether its original was a limning or a full-sized painting, the oval
portrait is framed to create the impression of a (gilt-edged?) miniature
resting on a dark background. Identified only by an *impresa*-like motto,
the portrait seems designed to reproduce the miniature's aura of
intimacy, but for a print readership. Like the initials 'I.D.' pointing
elliptically to the author's identity on the title-page, the frontispiece
evokes the social exclusivity of a coterie audience, who would possess
the keys to such enigmatic tokens. In its setting on the 1635 frontispiece, the Marshall portrait presents Donne as a dashing, courtly figure
in the vein of Sidney, whose verse was similarly loosed into the wider
world of print only after his death. The youth's clasped sword hilt –
raised perhaps in an oath of fidelity to his mistress – styles him as
a love poet who is also a man of action.

The verses that sit beneath the portrait were contributed for the purpose
by Donne's first biographer, Izaak Walton. Walton's text seeks to direct
our interpretation of the image along the same lines as his hagiographical
agenda in the *Life of John Donne* (1640). The lines chart Donne's trajectory
from 'youths Drosse' to his 'last, best Dayes' as penitent divine: 'Witnes
this Booke, (thy Embleme) which begins / With Love; but endes, with
Sighes, & Teares for Sins.' For Walton, the Marshall engraving – like the
book as a whole – is an 'Embleame' in the double sense that it combines
image and text, while also supplying readers with a moralizing example.
However, other elements in the portrait's design tug against Walton's
edifying gloss. In the top right-hand corner, just above the coat-of-arms
claiming descent from the Welsh Dwns of Carmarthenshire, sits an
inscribed scroll. Its Spanish motto, '*Antes muerto que mudado*' ('Sooner
dead than changed'), is taken from a song in Jorge de Montemayor's
popular romance, the *Diana*. Adapted by a change of gender to apply to
the portrait's male sitter, the line comes from the *Diana*'s first song, where
it comments ironically on a fickle mistress: she is as constant as the sand on
which the poem is traced.[10] Walton notably misconstrues the motto in his
Life, skewing his translation so as to turn it into the teenage Donne's

premonition of his later conversion from profane to sacred love: 'How much shall I be chang'd / Before I am chang'd.'[11]

When read as a male lover's boast of constancy, the motto lends the Marshall portrait a youthful swagger, softening its stern mouth with the hint of a smile. However, recent critics have been prompted by another detail in the engraving – the cross dangling from Donne's right ear – to recognize in the motto's insistence on fidelity a religious dimension. Helen Gardner takes the earring to be simply a fashionable accessory.[12] But it is now agreed its cruciform shape was not just a piece of foppish styling, but rather a sign, boldly displayed, of the young Donne's continuing commitment to Catholicism. An unthinkable adornment for an Elizabethan Protestant given Reformist attitudes towards the display of the cross, the portrait's earring, read together with the motto, was 'the equivalent of declaring a preference for martyrdom over apostasy'.[13] But as the motto's built-in ironies ruefully hint, Diana will be unfaithful and Donne will be changed.

Donne's second image, the 'Lothian' portrait, dates from around 1595, during his time at the Inns of Court (see Book Cover Image: NPG 6790, John Donne by Unknown English artist (the 'Lothian' portrait). Oil on panel, circa 1595. © National Portrait Gallery, London). It is the same portrait Donne described in his will as 'that Picture of myne wch is taken in Shaddowes and was made very many yeares before I was of this profession'.[14] Separated out from the will's briefer entries on the other paintings, this picture seems to have held a special significance for Donne. Left by him to his friend Robert Ker, Earl of Ancram, the portrait's 'melancholie posture' was noted by William Drummond of Hawthornden shortly after its arrival in Scotland.[15] It was believed lost until 1959, when John Bryson made fresh enquiries with Ker's descendants, the Marquesses Lothian. He discovered that, early in the eighteenth century, one of the picture's corners had been labelled 'John Duns'. This caused it to be recorded in inventories as a portrait of Duns Scotus, the medieval scholastic theologian, concealing Donne beneath this unlikely alter-ego for the next two centuries.[16]

When Bryson uncovered the painting in 1959, it was in poor condition. Still visible in the right foreground were 'Traces of books and a quill' which later vanished, to the consternation of the literary scholars who began to re-examine the picture in 1993.[17] These signs of Donne's writerly vocation are clearly discernible in a photograph dated 1959, in the Heinz Archive & Library, National Portrait Gallery, London.[18] Jane Eade, Associate Curator at the gallery, which has been the painting's home since its acquisition in

2006, informed me that the book, quill, and inkstand (as far as can be discerned from the photograph) have the look of later additions. They are cramped within the crook of Donne's left arm and out of proportion with the rest of the composition. Though details of the actual treatment were not recorded, it appears they were removed as non-integral during conservation work undertaken in 1961, since they are no longer visible in a photograph taken that year.[19]

Nor was it clear, until another phase of extensive conservation between 2011 and 2012, exactly how enveloping its distinctive shadows had been in Donne's vision of the painting. Removing at least three layers of discoloured varnish and overpaint, restorers uncovered subtle gradations of tone in the background, as well as a rich red lake pigment in Donne's sleeves.[20] Analysis also revealed as original an enigmatic detail – the pale vertical plume that rises from Donne's chest to his collar – which some have argued represents 'the vapour of melancholy' as described in the *Devotions* (1623).[21] While it is tempting to see in it a visible sign of Donne's fascination with the intertwining of body and spirit, the curious brushstroke might simply be a poorly blended highlight.

That his will describes it as 'taken in shadows' supports the notion Donne had a role in determining the design of the picture, whose striking *chiaroscuro* is so unusual among Elizabethan portraits. Despite the painting's Italianate elements, its technique is currently thought to be characteristic of an English painter.[22] Several aspects of its composition anticipate later portraiture, including the grey *trompe l'oeil* frame – one of the earliest recorded English uses of such a device – that creates a second, illusory threshold through which Donne gazes.[23] Donne's apparent fondness for the contrivance (repeated in the portrait of 1620 with its feigned circular frame) calls to mind his own poetic play with perspectival illusion.[24] With a black cloak pulled moodily around his body and a wide-brimmed hat tilted on his brow, Donne's self-conscious adoption of a role looks forward to the later Stuart trend of sitting for portraits 'in character'. The part Donne plays in this picture is that of the melancholy lover, a fashionable type in the period's drama and one explicitly associated with poetic activity.[25] Bryson notes a close visual parallel on the title-page of Burton's *Anatomy of Melancholy* (1628), where the lovesick 'Inamorato' stands with arms folded, face almost obscured by his broad, floppy hat.[26] Donne's unusual cross-armed pose, with its air of truculent resistance, might even glance back to his earlier portrait's cruciform earring.[27]

Donne's fashionably triple-layered lace collar lies open, its ties trailing in a state of artful dishabille that might suggest a pun on his name ('unDonne').[28] The figure's full lips heighten the portrait's impression of amorousness – in the sombre-hued image their sensuous pink draws the eye. This erotic charge is sustained in the Latin inscription, '*Illumina tenenbr[as] nostras domina*' ('Lighten my darkness, Lady'), which arcs over the sitter's head like a profane nimbus. Behind this plea to a secular mistress lies a religious prayer, blasphemously parodied. With a shift of gender, Donne adapted his motto from the pre-Reformation service of Compline, '*Illumina quesumus domine deus tenebras nostras*' – a passage echoed in the third collect of Anglican Evensong, 'Lighten our darkness, we beseech thee, O Lord.'[29] Tarnya Cooper suggests the portrait may have been painted as a gift or a plea to a lover.[30]

The handful of seventeenth-century reports of the painting – which hung for a time in private chambers at Lincoln's Inn – linger on its shadowed setting and risqué motto, but tend to misremember slightly the motto's wording. Dr. Thomas Morton, Bishop of Durham, remarked how Donne's portrait was 'all envelloped with a darkish shadow, his face and feature hardly discernible', but forgot about the ironic change of gender in the 'ejaculation and wish written thereon'.[31] In addition to the mentions by Morton and Drummond, Alison Shell has more recently brought to light another allusion to the Lothian portrait, in a controversial pamphlet of 1613 by the Jesuit John Floyd. Arguing for the legitimacy of religious images, Floyd turns to attack a 'creature of *Dunne* colour' – a certain 'I.D.' – for his lascivious worship of 'the picture of his Mistresse, which he kept in his Chambers, with this prayer unto it, *Illumina tenebras meas*, before which he did not omitt to doe morning and evening devotions'.[32] Floyd seems to misremember the Lothian portrait as a picture of Donne's mistress; either that, or he is condemning (or satirically inventing) some kind of parodic idolatrous practice on Donne's part, to which the Lothian motto might also have alluded. We might imagine such a picture becoming an embarrassment to Donne in his later years, but his will shows that it remained a lifelong possession. Perhaps the self it portrayed held a lingering fascination for Dr Donne, or its prayer for illumination found a holier object.

Unsurprisingly no portraits date to the difficult years following Donne's clandestine marriage in 1601, so we have no record of his face during that period's gruelling search for secular employment. Donne's next two portraits show him in the early stages of his ministry. In 1616, the year after he entered the priesthood, Donne sat for a miniature by Isaac Oliver, Hilliard's former pupil (Figure 2). Depicted in gown and ruff, his beard neatly trimmed, Donne's appearance is newly formal, in a manner befitting the royal Chaplain to James I. The portrait appears, reversed, in Matthäus

Figure 2: Miniature by Isaac Oliver, watercolour and bodycolour on vellum laid on card, 1616, Royal Collection Trust. © Her Majesty Queen Elizabeth II 2013.

Merian's engraved frontispiece to Donne's *LXXX Sermons* (1640) (Figure 3). The page's elaborate architectural edifice transforms Oliver's miniature into the centrepiece of a public monument.

By 1620, and the painting of his fourth portrait, Donne was well established in the Church. It shows him during his tenure as reader in divinity at Lincoln's Inn, a few months before his election to Dean of St. Paul's (Figure 4). Depicting Donne not in ecclesiastical dress but in the classical drapery of a Roman orator, the painting suggests he had not put aside his fondness for staging his image in costume. Jonathan Post sees in the portrait's classicizing tendency a hint that Donne's 'worldly and spiritual identities were beginning to converge'.[33] Its circular *trompe l'oeil* frame echoes the tondo format popular in Renaissance Italy, as well as the

Figure 3: Frontispiece portrait engraved by Matthäus Merian, from Donne's *LXXX Sermons* (1640), based on the miniature by Isaac Oliver. Reproduced by permission of Cambridge University Library.

Figure 4: Portrait in roundel format, oil on canvas, 1620, Deanery of St. Paul's
Cathedral, London. © The Chapter of St. Paul's Cathedral.

medallion reliefs of Roman sarcophagi.[34] Two versions of the portrait exist:
Roy Strong pronounces the version still in the Deanery at St. Paul's to be
the primary one, and the Victoria and Albert Museum's the copy.[35]
Differences include the slight elongation of the St. Paul's version, and
the direction of Donne's gaze, which in the V&A copy is directed subtly
upwards. This portrait was the source for Pierre Lombart's engraved
frontispiece, converted to an oval, from Donne's *Letters* (1651) (Figure 5).
    Donne's emaciated final portrait – that of his funerary monument in
St. Paul's and its associated engravings – is a stark contrast to his earlier
likenesses. As it now stands in Wren's cathedral, the stone effigy depicts
Donne standing on an urn, wrapped in a shroud which is drawn back to
reveal his face (Figures 6 and 7). The statue is enclosed within a shallow

Figure 5: Frontispiece portrait engraved by Pierre Lombart, from Donne's *Letters*
(1651), based on the roundel portrait of 1620. Reproduced by permission of
Cambridge University Library.

Figure 6: Marble funeral monument to Donne by Nicholas Stone the Elder, 1631,
St. Paul's Cathedral, London. © The Chapter of St. Paul's Cathedral.

black niche, with an epitaph set on a tablet above. Donne's monument was
the only one to survive the Great Fire of 1666, escaping with only minor
scorch damage and the urn's broken left handle.[36] The full-length effigy
can be seen in the frontispiece (engraved once again by William Marshall)
to the 1634 and 1638 editions of the *Devotions* (Figure 8).

Figure 7: Detail of Stone's funeral monument to Donne. © The Chapter of
St. Paul's Cathedral.

Another engraving of Donne in his shroud, by Martin Droeshout, was
prefixed to the 1632 edition of Donne's last sermon, *Deaths Duell*
(Figure 9). Its oval frame reveals only the figure's head and shoulders.
Below the oval is engraved a Latin motto, '*Corporis haec Animae sit Syndon,
Syndon Jesu*' ('May this shroud of the body be the shroud of the soul: the

Figure 8: Donne in his shroud, frontispiece portrait engraved by William Marshall, from the *Devotions* (1638). Reproduced by permission of Cambridge University Library.

Figure 9: Donne in his shroud, frontispiece portrait engraved by Martin Droeshout, from *Deaths Duell* (1632). Reproduced by permission of Cambridge University Library.

shroud of Jesus'), which Gardner believes Donne wrote for the image during his final illness.[37] Despite the sunken eyes, gaunt cheeks and deeply furrowed brow, Donne's features are still recognizable from his earlier portraits. The Droeshout engraving's pinched and hollowed visage is quite different from the smooth features of the St. Paul's effigy, whose idealized fullness perhaps suggests a body on the way to resurrection.[38]

Donne's funeral portrait has generally been read alongside Walton's famous account of its creation. Walton tells how, in the midst of his preparations for death, Donne was persuaded by his friend and physician, Simon Fox, to have a monument constructed for himself. Donne then called for a 'Carver' to supply a board the same height as his body, along with a wooden urn of specific dimensions. This prop obtained, Donne 'without delay' summoned a 'choice Painter' to create the image that would, after his death, be 'carved in one entire piece of white Marble'. The unknown painter took the ailing Donne's likeness as he stood atop the urn. 'Charcole-fires' were prepared in the 'large Study' to prevent the invalid from catching a chill as he posed. Stripped of his clothes, Donne was wrapped in a winding sheet with 'so much of the sheet turned aside as might shew his lean, pale, and death-like face, which was purposely turned toward the East, from whence he expected the second coming of our Saviour'. When the portrait was finished, Donne had it placed at his bedside, where it became 'his hourly object till his death' – after which it passed to his Executor, Dr. King.[39] From King it presumably went to Nicholas Stone and his assistants, the carvers engaged to create the monument.[40]

Gardner counsels against taking Walton's account at face value, since this final performance would have demanded extraordinary control from a man on his deathbed. The passage appears only in the 1658 edition of Walton's *Life*, which much embellished the text of 1640.[41] Gardner agrees with Walton, however, that Donne penned the inscription placed above the statue. This epitaph ends with Donne's hope for resurrection: '*Hic licet in occiduo cinere / aspicit eum Cuius nomen / est Oriens.*'[42] Nigel Foxell points out that the standard translation given by Bald fails to capture Donne's double meanings: 'here, though in falling [western] ashes, he looks towards Him whose name is rising [the east].'[43]

The fact that Donne consented at all to the erection of an elaborate monument could be read as a gesture in support of Laud's ceremonialism.[44] However, it is uncertain how far the monument's execution reflected Donne's own wishes. Its symbolism seems contradictory and thus difficult to interpret. For example, the way the folds of the stone shroud fall, clinging close to the body, would be more apt in a recumbent figure. By contrast, the winding sheet in the Droeshout engraving hangs straight down, as it would on an upright body. Donne's eyes are closed in the sleep of one awaiting the Last Trumpet, yet its erect stance, knees slightly bent, suggests the statue is on the point of springing from the grave. By way of explanation, Gardner proposes that Stone's original commission was to carve a recumbent effigy to lie on an altar tomb, but that it was converted to stand in a niche because of a lack of space. This change of plan is reflected perhaps in the incongruity – naturalized only by the image's familiarity – of Donne's corpse being perched atop an 'absurdly small' urn.[45]

The prefatory verses in Donne's *Poems* (1633) look back on the recent frontispiece to *Deaths Duell* and Donne's statue in St. Paul's:

> I See in his last preach'd, and printed booke,
> His Picture in a sheete; in *Pauls* I looke,
> And see his Statue in a sheete of stone,
> And sure his body in the grave hath one:
> Those sheetes present him dead, these if you buy,
> You have him living to Eternity.[46]

Playing on the St. Paul's monument's own symbolism, these prefatory verses – attributed to the volume's publisher, John Marriot – hold out a different kind of resurrection for Donne's posthumous image. The winding sheet of Donne's last portrait transforms, via the pun in the penultimate line, into the sheets of paper on which the volume's poems are printed. In the octavo of 1635, Marriot's verses sit a few pages away from the frontispiece portrait, which shows not the decaying Dean of St. Paul's, but the face of Jack Donne aged 18, as though rejuvenated by his words printed across the ensuing pages.

Notes

1. John Donne, "Infinitati Sacrum," *Poems, by J.D.* (London, 1633), sig. A3r. My account of the 1633 front matter is indebted to Leah S. Marcus, *Unediting the Renaissance: Shakespeare, Marlowe, and Milton* (London: Routledge, 1996), 192–98.
2. Donne, *Poems*, sig. 2A1v.
3. Annabel Patterson, "Donne in Shadows: Pictures and Politics," *JDJ* 16 (1997), 1–35.
4. Bald, *Life*, 563; W. Milgate, "Dr. Donne's Art Gallery," *Notes and Queries* 194 (1949), 318–19.

5. Ernest B. Gilman, *Iconoclasm and Poetry: Down Went Dagon* (University of Chicago Press, 1986), 121.

6. Louis Martz, *From Renaissance to Baroque: Essays on Literature and Art* (Columbia, MO: University of Missouri Press, 1991), 16.

7. David Colclough, "Donne, John (1572–1631)," in *Oxford Dictionary of National Biography*, eds. H. C. G. Matthew and Brian Harrison, www .oxforddnb.com/.

8. Dennis Flynn, "Donne's First Portrait: Some Biographical Clues?" *Bulletin of Research in the Humanities* 82 (1979), 7–8.

9. Dennis Flynn, *John Donne: Man of Flesh and Spirit* (London: Continuum, 2001), 5.

10. See Catherine J. Creswell, "Giving a Face to an Author: Reading Donne's Portraits and the 1635 Edition," *Texas Studies in Literature and Language* 37 (1995), 3–9.

11. Walton, *Lives*, 79.

12. Donne, *The Elegies and the Songs and Sonnets*, ed. Helen Gardner (Oxford: Clarendon Press, 1965), 266.

13. Flynn, *Flesh*, 4; Patterson, "Shadows," 8.

14. Bald, *Life*, 567.

15. Qtd. in Donne, *Elegies*, 267.

16. John Bryson, "Lost Portrait of Donne," *The Times* 13 October 1959, 13, 15.

17. Bryson, "Lost Portrait," 13.

18. Heinz Archive Registered Packet 6790. The 1959 photograph is unnumbered; the 1961 photograph is Reference Negative No. 10179.

19. Private correspondence, October 2013. I am grateful to Jane Eade and Charlotte Bolland for their help in unpicking this puzzle.

20. Charlotte Bolland, "John Donne Back on Display," *National Portrait Gallery*, 22 January 2013, www.npg.org.uk/blog/john-donne-back-on-display.php.

21. Nick Davis, "Melancholic Individuality and the Lothian Portrait of Donne," *American Notes and Queries* 26 (2013), 5–12.

22. "Notes on Likely Authorship and Justification" from NPG technical report (see note 20 above).

23. Tarnya Cooper, "Professional Pride and Personal Agendas: Portraits of Judges, Lawyers, and Members of the Inns of Court, 1500–1630," in *The Intellectual and Cultural World of the Early Modern Inns of Court*, eds. Jayne E. Archer, Elizabeth Goldring, and Sarah Knight (Manchester University Press, 2011), 173.

24. See Ernest Gilman, *The Curious Perspective: Literary and Pictorial Wit in the Seventeenth Century* (New Haven, CT: Yale University Press, 1978), 176–88.

25. Roy Strong, "The Elizabethan Malady: Melancholy in Elizabethan and Jacobean Portraiture," in *The English Icon: Elizabethan & Jacobean Portraiture* (New York: Paul Mellon Foundation for British Art, 1969), 352–54.

26. Bryson, "Lost Portrait," 15.

27. Jonathan F. S. Post, "Donne's Life: A Sketch," in *CCJD*, 7.

28. Tarnya Cooper and Jane Eade, *Elizabeth I & Her People* (London: National Portrait Gallery, 2013), 181.
29. Martz, *From Renaissance*, 8.
30. Tarnya Cooper, *A Guide to Tudor & Jacobean Portraits* (London: National Portrait Gallery, 2008), 25.
31. Qtd. in Donne, *Elegies*, 268.
32. From *Purgatories Triumph Over Hell*. Qtd. in Alison Shell, "Donne and Sir Edward Hoby: Evidence for an Unrecorded Collaboration," in *John Donne's Professional Lives*, ed. David Colclough (Cambridge: D. S. Brewer, 2003), 121–22.
33. Post, "Donne's Life," 14.
34. David Piper, *The Image of the Poet: British Poets and Their Portraits* (Oxford: Clarendon Press, 1982), 28.
35. Roy Strong, *Tudor & Jacobean Portraits*, 2 vols. (London: National Portrait Gallery, 1969), 1:66.
36. Richard S. Peterson, "New Evidence on Donne's Monument I," *JDJ* 20 (2001), 8.
37. Helen Gardner, "Dean Donne's Monument in St. Paul's," in *Evidence in Literary Scholarship: Essays in Memory of James Marshall Osborn*, eds. René Wellek and Alvaro Ribeiro (Oxford: Clarendon Press, 1979), 34.
38. Nigel Foxell, *A Sermon in Stone: John Donne and His Monument in St. Paul's Cathedral* (London: Menard Press, 1978), 5.
39. Walton, *Lives*, 78.
40. Gardner, "Donne's Monument," 31.
41. Gardner, "Donne's Monument," 29–30.
42. Gardner, "Donne's Monument," 34. For the full inscription, see Peterson, "New Evidence," 20–21.
43. Foxell, *Sermon in Stone*, 10.
44. David Norbrook, "The Monarchy of Wit and the Republic of Letters: Donne's Politics," in *Soliciting*, 26.
45. Gardner, "Donne's Monument," 41–44.
46. "*Hexastichon Bibliopolae*," in *Poems* (1633), sig. [A2]v.

CHAPTER 29

Donne in the Seventeenth and Eighteenth Centuries

Nicholas D. Nace

> Donne himself, for not being understood, will perish.
>
> – Ben Jonson[1]

Donne *did* perish. Not immediately upon his death in 1631, not precisely for the reasons Jonson predicted, and not in a way that kept him from constituting a reference point – often the *ne plus ultra* – in the increasingly turbulent history of "wit." But as the distancing effect provided by the Stuart Restoration began to push poets toward a practice of active poetic modernization, the "last age" of poets, as Dryden called it, quickly began to appear more than a generation apart. Donne in particular seemed to the anonymous author of the 1676 "Session of the Poets" as "an Ancient grave Wit, so long lov'd and fear'd,"[2] a relic of what Donne himself called the "age of rusty iron" ("Satire V," 35). Neither Donne, nor the less "fear'd" Caroline poets who could be classified as minnows in the "School of Donne," continued to be read much past the 1670s. During and after the Restoration, what demand there was for Donne's poetry could be satisfied by a single edition. Only a decade on from 1660, Henry Herringman, publisher of Dryden's epoch-defining royalist panegyric *Astrea Redux*, released what would be the century's final edition of Donne's poetry, and the only edition, save one by Jacob Tonson in 1719, to be published within the next 100 years.

Individual Donne poems continued to appear as anthology pieces. However, by the eighteenth century the poet formerly praised in lavish funeral elegies as "incomparable" could not be distinguished from his imitators. In 1721 a verse collection titled *The Grove* proclaimed on its title page the inclusion of Donne, suggesting some benefit in trading on the Donne name. However, it printed only John Hoskyns's "The Absence," an unevocative rehash of "A Valediction Forbidding Mourning," on the mistaken assumption that it was a discovered manuscript poem by Donne. Even after John Bell returned Donne's poems to print in 1779 as part of his 109-volume *Complete Edition of the Poets of Great Britain* series, Donne's fiercely individual verse was read mostly by antiquaries. As Reverend Vicesimus Knox believed, such new editions of Donne were fit only for "filling a vacancy on the upper shelf of some dusty and deserted library."[3] In the eighteenth century, none but the Oxford don Walter Harte, an intimate of Alexander Pope, predicted that Donne one day would be resurrected. Donne might be "forgotten now," Harte said in 1730, "yet still his fame shall last."[4] For nearly everyone else, Donne was a formidable wit whose body of work illustrated the way *not* to write poetry.

Herringman's edition, still used by readers as late as Charles Lamb and Samuel Taylor Coleridge, reveals this duress in its very title. From the first collected edition in 1633 onward into popular editions through the 1650s, the title had been, quite simply, *Poems, by J.D.* The fortified title of Herringman's edition, *Poems, &c. By John Donne late Dean of St Pauls*, reflects in its sites of expansion ("&c," the poet's full name – now disambiguated from Dryden's – and his prestigious ecclesiastical office) a lack of confidence in marketing a book based solely on Donne's reputation as a poet. Readers were now induced to Donne's poems expecting some elucidation of his non-poetic career, which had been the overwhelming emphasis of Izaak Walton's influential *Life of Dr. John Donne*, first published in the 1640 edition of Donne's *Sermons*.

Walton's hagiography continued to divide and eclipse its subject throughout the eighteenth century. Walton himself devotes only two paragraphs, two-thirds of the way into *Life*, to the poetry by which Donne primarily is known today, designating all but his "high, holy, and harmonious Composures" as merely "the Recreations of his youth."[5] Walton's reprinting of only "A Valediction Forbidding Mourning" appears to have established Donne as the preeminent poet of distance and departure, of "interassured minds" ecstatically defying physical presence, a context in which Katherine Philips, Andrew Marvell, and Rochester would seek him. While "Honest Izaak" proves accurate in chronology, and faithful to Donne's own sense of the greater importance of his ecclesiastical career, he allows Donne the cleric to pull away from Donne the poet. Thus we get the enduring narrative of Jack Donne always on the way to becoming Dr. Donne, which was reiterated by Giles Jacob in 1719, the year of Tonson's edition, as a move from "eminent Poet" to "more eminent divine."[6] As a favorite book of Samuel Johnson, Walton's *Life* loosely served as an archetype for the kind of "little lives" of estimable authors that comprised *Lives of the Most Eminent English Poets*, a series that would not include Donne, though would offer, in its leadoff "Life of Cowley," the most enduring assessment of him and the "metaphysical" style he inaugurated.

By the dawning of the Age of Sensibility, Donne the poet is effectively de-canonized. Such arbiters of taste as Oliver Goldsmith obligingly quantify for us the precise amount of canonicity certain poets possess at mid-century, at which point Donne has already fallen off the charts. In Goldsmith's "A Poetical Scale," a system of point values given to such qualities as "Genius" and "Versification," Donne's scores appear too low to bother calculating – lower, evidently, than Waller or Drayton, both of whom score a mere 50 out of 80 compared with Milton and Dryden, who are tied for first place at 69. Goldsmith demotes Donne to a "man of wit" who unfortunately "seems to have been at pains not to pass for a poet."[7] Whether the criteria was sonority and "keeping of accent," or argumentative consistency and natural-ness of conceit, Donne's poems no longer fit the category of poetry.

So what happened?

One might attribute Donne's near oblivion simply to the vagaries of taste: the emergent preference for the snap and fluency of dapper Augustan wit, the belief that consistency of meter must be the fixative of experience, the increasing tendency to equate poetry with public argument and not private expression. However, some scholars view Donne as an aberration, a wit with no desire to adopt the habit of a poet, the product of critical desires. Ben Saunders has scrutinized the unexpressed agendas of those who would suppress Donne's poetry on metrical grounds, and Kevin Pask, drawing from Donne's construction in such life narratives as Walton's, argues that Donne's association with a notion of aristocratic libertinage accounts for his increasingly shadowy presence.[8] Yet part of the reason for Donne's rejection was his cultivation of uniqueness and emotional precision, which has been occluded by the insistence on a "School of Donne," the demise of which can be dated to its failure ever to have coalesced beyond a shared taste for *discordia concors*. The "School of Donne" indeed has been inscribed around a widespread scatter. The Herberts, whom Donne seals into his tribe through the intimate presentation of his Christ and Anchor seal, show the strongest family resemblance. Edward, Lord Herbert of Cherbury, displayed a fondness for the echo conceit that he and his younger brother adapted from a line in Donne's 1624 sermon on Matthew 19:17; and Cherbury's "Parted Souls" condenses, over the course of its three stanzas, the argument of Donne's "A Valediction Forbidding Mourning." The younger Herbert, George, echoes Donne less directly, but follows him in seeking the metaphorical habits of the divine. From there strains of Donnean wit can be found in the proto-Romanticists Henry Vaughan and Thomas Traherne, as well as the Neoplatonists Katherine Philips and Andrew Marvell. Even Thomas Carew, Donne's most Donnean elegist, and "smooth" Edmund Waller demonstrate strategic uses for Donne while acknowledging their predecessor's uniqueness.

To ascribe fully to the notion of a "School of Donne," as Alfred Alvarez did in 1961, presents the early seventeenth-century field cleanly but inaccurately, turning many distinguished poets into epigones of only one of their influences. The case of Carew most clearly illustrates the need, felt by many Caroline poets, to please two poetic fathers: Donne and Jonson. Robert Herrick's "Fain would I kiss my Julia's dainty Leg / Which is as white and hair-less as an egge," with its comparison of objects that share, in only one dimension, a startling similarity, could not have been composed by strict adherence to the idiom of the "Tribe of Ben."[9] Henry Vaughan wrote few new poems after 1660, largely satisfying his meditative bent through his study of Hermeticism. Only Richard Crashaw takes Donne's extravagance as a course of action, ending up, literally, on the continent. Even Abraham Cowley, Samuel Johnson's "metaphysical" *bête noire* who not only followed Donne but, as Dryden believed, "copied him to a fault," continued in political exile to develop and refine the style he adapted from Donne in *The Mistress* (1647).[10] Cowley found in Pindar's odes a way to develop Donnean expression within a commodious classical idiom. The English "Pindarick" ode – a "crude cousin" in Alvarez's estimate to "metaphysical" verse – therefore develops, in the work of Aphra Behn and others, more in the image of Donne than Pindar, making a virtue of Cowley's "various and irregular" meter, "harsh and uncouth" tone, and "enthusiastical manner."[11]

T. S. Eliot, who followed and eclipsed Sir Herbert Grierson in what now seems a concerted effort at resuscitating Donne in the twentieth century, offered perhaps the grandest explanation for Donne's rejection, a paradigm shift he referred to, ominously, as "the transition." This shift signaled nothing less than a crisis in Western culture: "In the 17th century," Eliot claimed, "a dissociation of sensibilities set in, from which we have never recovered." About the date of this rupture, Eliot is neither precise nor consistent, but he posits it began around "the time of Donne and Herbert of Cherbury," citing Donne's ability to fully experience thought and "devour any kind of experience" through any and all complexities and emotions of indigestion as the *terminus ad quem* of integrated thought and emotion.[12] At least at its front end, this narrative easily accords with standard political periodization: Donne's "monarchy of wit," as Carew called it ("Elegy," 96), appears to have been overthrown and executed along with Charles I, and, like the monarchy, would not return in a recognizable form.

What Eliot proves clearer about are the culprits, Dryden and Milton – Goldsmith's two highest ranked poets. Their notion of poetic refinement separated out and ultimately relinquished the genre's cherished claims on feeling and offered little place for "metaphysical" explorations of how thinking and feeling collude in the emergence of specific emotional complexes. Thinking and feeling came to be cordoned off from one another, contained within irreconcilable agendas that aimed, respectively, at either solemn lucidity or unbridled enthusiasm. What comes to be sacrificed is the poetic authority of the emotional pressures of wit, what Coleridge called "transient feeling," which can produce the frisson that George Williamson in the 1920s termed a "metaphysical shudder."[13]

The intense affect of the shudder reached its apotheosis with Donne. Just several months after praising Cromwell in his "Heroic Stanzas," Dryden takes the opportunity of the Stuart Restoration, when "the muses stand restored," to proclaim in the self-consciously old fashioned "To My Lord Chancellor" that with the exile of Charles, "Wit and religion suffered banishment."[14] Yet Dryden's use of Donne's wit illustrates the emotional domestication poetry would need in the new age. He leaches the menace from "Batter my Heart" to praise the captivating yet liberating beauty of his earliest patroness in "To the Lady Castlemaine." And when he wishes to cast off the oppressive role of public poet and free his "wantonness of wit" in his panegyric *Eleonora*, he openly mimics the intimacy of Donne's *Anniversaries*, but orchestrates it all in the service of his deeply ingrained monarchism. Dryden esteemed Donne the "greatest wit, though not the best poet," acknowledging the losses of wit in his "present age" as a victory for poetry: "if we are not so great wits as Donne, yet certainly we are better poets."[15] As Johnson would point out about all of his "metaphysical poets," those critics "who deny them to be poets, allow them to be wits."[16]

Pope's definition of wit as "What oft was thought, but ne'er so well exprest," gauges success in psychological terms that Johnson would adapt in his condemnation of metaphysical poetry in favor of "just" wit, which seeks to be "at once natural and new."[17] Seen as a poet of unnatural wit, Donne had no place in the age that focused relentlessly on the appropriateness, not the emotional discoveries, of wit. The historian John Oldmixon, whom Pope would later fit into his translation of Donne's "Satire IV" as the prevaricating Jovius, demonstrates his revulsion at

Donne's ability to "subtilize" his language and "turn wit into point."[18] Wit became relegated strictly to the procedures of *inventio* and could not maintain a constitutive authority in *dispositio*, where distanced reflection reigned. As Matthew Prior believed, when Donne's verse became "too dissolute and wild," it came "too near prose" and therefore needed the supplement of prospective design.[19] The otherwise untrappable emotions captured in the alignments of Donne's conceits often came across as beside the point, a prolegomenon to a work never finished, an abandoned cathexis. The abrupt improvisatory shifts, so much part of Donnean wit, could not be held still within neoclassical frames without violence.

By the time of *The Compleat Angler* (1653), Walton recognized that Donne's "irregular" style was coming to be seen as an impediment rather than a means of expression. Walton's voluble woodsman, Venator, possesses the keen eye to recognize that Donne's knotted lines were intentional, citing the free flowing, end-stopped verses of "The Bait" as a counterexample "made to show the world that he could make soft and smooth verses, when he thought smoothness worth his labor."[20] But disharmony still could not be fathomed as an emotional correlative, particularly when the syllable count remained consistent. Donne embraces the "durus componere versus" that Horace ascribes to Lucilius, but finds nonsatiric uses for it as well. Donne's verse epistle to Samuel Brooke ("To Mr S.B.") rejects soft but perilous "Siren-like" (9) inspirations by acknowledging his "harsh" (10) inducements in the form of "articulate blasts" (14) that fan the "bright sparks" (12) of Brooke's talent. In the neoclassical idiom, sincerity could not coexist with inconsistency, metrical or other. Johnson, who admired Dryden's "flowing" and "sonorous" diction, felt that Donne's "numbers" or meter consisted of no greater harmony than meeting "a certain quantity of syllables." For Johnson, Donne "stood the trial of the finger better than of the ear."[21]

But not every poet found Donne's meters inhospitable. Despite his reputation for writing with "ease," Rochester adapted Donne's metrical innovations in his love poems as well as his philosophical satires. Rochester's "Upon His Leaving His Mistress" follows the stanzaic form of "The Good Morrow" but condenses the pentameters to tetrameters while simultaneously alluding to Elegies III and V, as well as to "Song ('Sweetest love, I do not go')." Yet, as he adapts "The Ecstasy" in his famous "Imperfect Enjoyment," Rochester separates out the sensuality from the spirituality while retaining the speculative distance that for Donne joined the two. The tendency to stamp Donne's poetry as "metaphysical," with its implications of tenebrous scholarship, was brought into the debate by Drummond of Hawthornden when he chides Donne's "metaphysical ideas and scholastical quiddities."[22] Dryden picks the term up when he worries over how Donne's poetry "affects the metaphysics" – a forgivable fault, perhaps, in satire, but wholly inappropriate in "amorous verses," where "nature only should reign."[23] Unaffected metaphysics might be most applicable to Marvell and Rochester, who grasped most fully Donne's use of symbolic imagery to analyze individual states of thought and feeling and fit them into a pattern of philosophical thought. Yet the Restoration poet most obviously indebted to Donne may be John Oldham, whose famous *Satyrs upon the Jesuits* (1678) points to the generically heterogeneous nature of Donne's *Poems* in defense of his own collection, without mentioning the obvious debt to *Ignatius His Conclave*. Oldham's satiric voice drew from Donne even when translating Horace and Juvenal. The inserts between the lines of his translation of Horace's Satire I.9 owe a great deal to Donne's "Satire IV," as does the whole of the first version of his "Satyr on the Times." Pope's version of Donne's "Satire IV" – titled "The Impertinent, or A Visit to the Court" on its first appearance in 1733 – appears in a lineage running from Horace, to Donne, to Oldham, to Pope, to Cowper's "Description of an Impertinent."

One accomplishment that Donne could not be denied was his resurrection of the Roman genre of numbered formal verse satires. It was one instance in which Donne's reading of classical antiquity showed, even if the poems produced in this vein were directly connected to the "harshness" that would echo throughout Donne's reception history. His five satires, taken together, embrace the taunting obscurity of Persius, the febrile indignation of Juvenal, and, less often, the smiling *urbanitas* of Horace. For Donne, however, the formal verse satirist's dual civic aim of *laus et vituperatio* does not exclude from examination the satirist himself. The satires are, then, the precursor to both the louche, offensive satires of Oldham and the frequently rebarbative self-analysis we find extending from the eschatological dilemmas of the Holy Sonnets to George Herbert's articulation of the self's "wretchedness," neither of which we typically find in Scriblerian satiric *vers d'occasion*.

As a preface to his 1693 edition of Juvenal, Dryden's "Discourse Concerning the Original and Progress of Satire" was addressed to his lampoonist patron, Charles Sackville, Earl of Dorset, and it was Dorset's own satirical flytings that Dryden praised through a comparison with Donne: "Donn[e] alone, of all our Countrymen, had your Talent; but was not happy enough to arrive at your Versification."[24] In Dryden's compendious history of satire, however, Donne is not alone in being rejected for his lack of ease. Dryden denounced Persius in particular on terms nearly identical to those routinely leveled against Donne by the Augustans: "his diction is hard; his Figures are generally too bold and daring; and his Tropes, particularly his Metaphors, insufferably strain'd."[25] When Dryden translated Persius, his approach to making his satires more readable involved expanding them, in nearly every case, to double the length of the original. While the language itself was the initial difficulty, as with Donne, the efforts to make that language correct reveal the problem to be structural as well. Though he does not choose to improve Donne's satires, Dryden believes them corrigible, though still liable to fall short of Augustan grandeur: "were he Translated into numbers, and English, he wou'd yet be wanting in the Dignity of Expression."[26] Alexander Pope would perform precisely this service.

Held to the steady light of eighteenth century wit, Donne's smoldering satires were, like Persius's, considered dense, opaque, claustrophobic – in need of aeration. Pope recognized the problem early. In an April 1705/6 letter to William Wycherley, Pope elucidates his editorial aims in a series of revisions of some of Wycherley's own poems – contracting and redacting them, focusing and pruning – so that they be "turned more into poetry" (an approach Coleridge would later, in his own practice of correcting Donne, refer to as applying "the filter").[27] "Donne," Pope said, "had infinitely more wit than he wanted versification."[28] In order to allow Donne's prodigious wit to breathe, Pope's answer was to "versify" two of the earlier poet's works (Satires II and IV) and encourage Thomas Parnell to perform the same service to another ("Satire III"). Pope's first attempt, in 1713, he termed a "translation"; then as part of his full-dress 1735 *Works* he presented his versifications *en face* with Donne's original for parallel reading.

The comparison Pope enables reveals the ways Donne's satires needed emotional restraint as much as they needed the procrustean labors of stretching or clipping the lines by the standard of Augustan measure. Even more than Juvenal, Donne aims for the full-throated and searching expression of emotion in his satire. Donne's satires, particularly the famous third, register his youthful speaker's inability to locate his emotions within the spectrum of affect for which language provided adequate expression. Nor would simple affective fusion suffice – even the rough composite "Kind pity" finds itself emotively unavailable from one direction by a conflict with "spleen" (echoing Persius's "sum petulanti splene"), and stifled from tearful expression by "brave scorn" ("Satire III," 1). Yet while the speaker's emotion may be restrained, his expression of it is briny with indignant anger. The erratic, outraged, impatient speaker refuses to be mystified at the promise of stability. Donne's raw emotion proved no more assimilable to eighteenth-century taste than the tartness of his metrical liberties. As revised by Thomas Parnell, Donne's third satire is reduced to an *ars satirica* in which "Compassion" stands in for "kind pity," and "scorn" loses its bravery to fit the meter and the taste. What for Donne was a genuine quagmire of maintaining truth amidst the distortions of ideology, for Parnell becomes a buoyant apostrophe to Satire.

Donne was perfectly happy to diminish rhyme's prominence when it stood in the way of his verse's expressive force. To take one particularly clotted, irregular stretch of Donne's "Satire IV," we find the enjambment that caused George Jeffreys to see in them the tendency to "stand stock still":[29]

> As prone to'all ill, and of good as forget-
> ful, as proud, as lustful, and as much in debt,
> As vain, as witless, and as false as they
> Which dwell at court, for once going that way.   (13–16)

Compare Pope's "English'd" version:

> As prone to *Ill*, as negligent of *Good*,
> As deep in *Debt*, without a thought to pay,
> As *vain*, as *idle*, and as *false*, as they
> Who *live* at *Court*, for going once that *Way*!   (20–23)[30]

Donne was free from the anxiety of sequence that Pope's more refined, stately pacing reveals. Pope's poised, metrically circumspect verse may be thick with "nameless graces," but in its neoclassical order it moves steadily and predictably. The intimate connection between the uneasy emotions of Donne's satires and their equally uneasy numbers appears to have been unfathomable to Pope. Donne is aloof, perhaps, but not precisely detached; he is a resident of the world he satirizes, even if he fantasizes otherwise. Pope, by contrast, cultivates or assumes an authoritative poise. Pope recognized that "*Sound* must seem an *Eccho* to the *Sense*," but he appears to have disregarded the ways that rhythm, too, must adequate itself to sense, including emotion.[31] In Pope's desire to "versify" Donne's satires, what seems like an unsubtle form of belittlement in fact appears as an earnest response to a perceived problem of reception. Donne felt little need to subordinate style to the needs of the social.

Dryden's worry that Donne "perplexes the minds of the fair sex with nice speculations of philosophy" seems to have constituted a *casus fœderis* for female wits, who continue after Donne's death to read him with the "fastidiousness" that Thomas Zouch, Walton's own biographer, thought necessary.[32] Katherine Philips, who has been called "Donne's last and best heir and innovator," transformed Donne's most famous conceit, that of the twin compasses, into a celebration of female friendship.[33] Anne Finch's "On my being charged with writing a lampoon at Tunbridge" incorporates Donne's language of satiric affect, while praising him as England's answer to Juvenal. Margaret Cavendish, who fluidly moves from microcosm to macrocosm, reworks *The First Anniversary* in "The World in an Ear-ring." "The Ecstasy" was found by one contributor to *The Female Tatler* to be "so unforc'd" that the author "must feel the Fire he Paints."[34] If there was a metaphysical school that extended wit's complex emotive possibilities into the eighteenth century, it was composed of the female writers who felt the "metaphysical shudder."

If, as Johnson claims, Donne expands lovers' "tears" into entire "worlds," those new worlds are still grounded in the realities of emotion, rendering them more, not less, valuable to modern readers precisely when their "figures" do not easily "reconcile to the understanding."[35] This proves to be a core tenet of the "metaphysical" style, though Dryden's enduring claim that Donne "affects the metaphysics" tells with its verb a slightly different story about Donne's reception history. The affections could not be moved with affectation, so the Augustans felt; emotion could not be legitimate without the twin restraints of realism and regularity. Just as much as the term "metaphysical" clings to Donne even to the present day, the more damning notion of "affectation" has never been far behind: Joseph Spence attacked Donne's "puerile affectation," Lewis Theobald decried his "ostentatious Affectation of abstruse Learning," which produced only a "Heap of Riddles," Thomas Birch found his style "affected and obscure," Richard Hurd lamented his "affectation for pleasing," and Vicesimus Knox noted that he "affected a rugged style."[36] What appears to have left Donne most vulnerable to temporary oblivion was less his "harsh numbers" or "slender conceits" than the sense that both were a product of "ingenious absurdity" in which sentiment could not override its artificial origins in wit.[37]

Notes

1. Ben Jonson, *Conversations of Ben Jonson with William Drummond*, ed. Philip Sidney (London: Gay and Bird, 1906), 25.

2. *Poems on Several Occasions: By the Right Honorable, the E. of R–* (Menston, UK: Scolar Press, 1970), 102.
3. *Critical Heritage*, 247.
4. Walter Harte, *The Amaranth* (London, 1767), 126.
5. Walton, *Lives*, 60–61.
6. Giles Jacob, *The Poetical Register* (London, 1719), 47.
7. Oliver Goldsmith, *Literary Magazine*, January, 1758, 423.
8. Ben Saunders, *Desiring Donne: Poetry, Sexuality, Interpretation* (Cambridge, MA: Harvard University Press, 2006); Kevin Pask, *The Emergence of the English Author: Scripting the Life of the Poet in Early Modern England* (Cambridge University Press, 1996).
9. *The Poetical Works of Robert Herrick*, ed. L. C. Martin (Oxford: Clarendon Press, 1956), 139.
10. *The Works of John Dryden*, eds. H. T. Swedenberg Jr. et al., 20 vols. (Berkeley, CA: University of California Press, 1974), 4:7.
11. Alfred Alvarez, *The School of Donne* (New York: Pantheon, 1961), 142; *The English Writings of Abraham Cowley*, ed. A. R. Waller, 2 vols. (Cambridge University Press, 1905–06), 1:157.
12. T. S. Eliot, *Selected Essays* (London: Faber & Faber, 1932), 287–8.
13. See George Williamson, *The Donne Tradition* (Cambridge, MA: Harvard University Press, 1930).
14. Dryden, *Works*, 1:38.
15. Dryden, *Works*, 4:6–7.
16. Samuel Johnson, "Life of Cowley," in *The Lives of the Poets*, ed. John H. Middendorf, 3 vols. (New Haven, CT: Yale University Press, 2010), 1:24.
17. *The Poems of Alexander Pope*, ed. John Butt (New Haven, CT: Yale University Press, 1963), 153; Johnson, *Lives*, 1:19–20.
18. *Critical Heritage*, 190.
19. *Critical Heritage*, 70.
20. Izaak Walton, *The Compleat Angler* (London, 1653), 184.
21. Johnson, *Lives*, 1:24.
22. William Drummond, "A letter on the True Nature of Poetry" in *Poems and Prose*, ed. Robert H. McDonald (Edinburgh: Scottish Academic Press, 1976), 192.
23. Dryden, *Works*, 4:7.
24. Dryden, *Works*, 4:6.
25. Dryden, *Works*, 4:51.
26. Dryden, *Works*, 4:6.
27. Samuel Taylor Coleridge, *Poetical Works*, ed. J. C. C. Mays, 3 vols. (Princeton University Press, 2001), 1:115.
28. *Alexander Pope: Selected Letters*, ed. Howard Erskine-Hill (Oxford: Clarendon Press, 2000), 11.
29. *Critical Heritage*, 157.
30. Pope, *Poems*, 680.
31. Pope, *Poems*, 155 (l. 365).

32. Dryden, *Works*, 4:7; Izaak Walton, *Life of Donne*, ed. Thomas Zouch (York, 1796), xiii.

33. Paula Loscocco, "Inventing the English Sappho: Katherine Philips's Donnean Poetry," *The Journal of English and Germanic Philology*, 102.1 (2003), 59.

34. Qtd. in Donald W. Rude, "John Donne in *The Female Tatler*: A Forgotten Eighteenth-Century Appreciation," *JDJ* 18 (1999), 153–66.

35. Johnson, *Lives*, 1:21.

36. *Critical Heritage*, 196, 197, 210, 241, 247.

37. Johnson, *Lives*, 1:21.

CHAPTER 30

Donne in the Nineteenth and Twentieth Centuries

James Longenbach

Let's say you want to write a poem that, within its first four or five syllables, establishes itself as an urgently spoken utterance, a poem that makes its readers feel instantly engaged with an interlocutor, perhaps even making readers feel that they're late to the party – that the conversation is well underway.

You might begin with an imperative that fills out a single iambic pentameter line, the majority of the stressed syllables registering changes on a single vowel (*God, hold, tongue, love*): "For God's sake hold your tongue, and let me love" ("The Canonization," 1). Or you might offer a charged exclamation, a string of punchy monosyllables overriding the iambic rhythm, the majority of those syllables sharing no consonant with any other (*he, stark, mad*): "He is stark mad" ("The Broken Heart," 1). Or you might ask a question, an aggressive enjambment dividing subject from predicate and throwing extra pressure on the syllable (the first person pronoun) with which the pentameter both begins and ends: "I wonder by my troth, what thou and I / Did, till we loved" ("The Good Morrow," 1–2).

No English-language poet is more thrillingly efficient than John Donne at establishing the immediate illusion of a speaking subject. The robust syntax of Shakespeare's blank verse generates the illusion as well ("Soft you! A word or two before you go," *Othello* 5.2.338), but it was Donne's achievement to have harnessed such dramatic energy within the compass of a lyric poem, and one feels the lasting influence of Donne's strategies in the opening lines of poems by poets as different as Robert Browning – "But do not let us quarrel any more" ("Andrea del Sarto," 1) – and Marianne Moore: "Why so desolate?" ("Is Your Town Nineveh?," 1).[1]

We can't know for sure what Ben Jonson meant when he called Donne "the first poet in the World in some things,"[2] but Donne remains to this day the first poet of lyric presence. In the twilight years of the twentieth century, one find his strategies in poets as different from each other as John

Ashbery – "Time, you old miscreant!" ("I Asked Mr. Dithers," 1) – and Louise Glück: "Go ahead: say what you're thinking" ("Daisies," 1).[3] When we say that a poem presents us with a strong sense of a speaker, we're often saying the poem sounds like Donne.

There are many other ways to sound, of course, and if we associate a successful lyric poem with a strong sense of voice, it is in large part because of the lasting influence of the New Critical differentiation of a poem's speaker from its author – a differentiation that depended on the central place that Donne's poems occupied in so many New Critical analyses. But it's important to remember that poems don't really have voices, that what we're hearing in Donne's opening lines is the masterfully abrupt construction of an illusion – as if a painter had created a recognizable human face with two or three slap-dash brush strokes. When we refer to a poem's speaker, we're making a highly metaphorical (if useful) statement about the poem, one that automatically makes us think about poems in one way rather than another, one that makes us imagine ourselves as intimate listeners rather than more distanced readers. We might just as plausibly refer to the writer of the poem, in distinction to its author, and if we did so, we'd be more apt to think of poems as strategic deployments of various kinds of syntax, diction, rhythm, and sonic echo (which poems are), rather than as strategic constructions of a voice implying the immediate presence of a speaking subject (which poems may or may not be).

"The world was filled with broken fragments of systems," said a prominent reader of Donne in 1927, and "a man like Donne merely picked up, like a magpie, various shining fragments of ideas that struck his eye, and stuck them about here and there in his verse."[4] The word *merely* seems damning, especially because the author of this sentence is T. S. Eliot, who made Donne's achievement central both to modernist poetry and to the mode of literary criticism, the New Criticism, that modernist poetry provoked. But whatever his power as a taste-maker, Eliot never set out merely to change taste; he set out to write poems, the best poems he could muster, and in the 1920s Eliot's relationship to Donne's achievement changed radically as his aesthetic goals changed. Or, to describe this transformation in a different way, Eliot's relationship to the idea of a poem's speaker changed. Today, if we're still grappling productively with Donne, we're also grappling with Eliot.

    ...always maintained, correctly, that he was not himself respon-
        ... Donne's reputation. While Donne had fallen out
            e compressed lyric poem more generally,
            century, many prominent writers reclaimed

him as tastes changed in the early decades of the nineteenth century. In England, Coleridge annotated the poems copiously, discovering in them a precedent for poems that dramatize the act of thinking.[5] By championing the poems in America, Emerson created a taste for Donne that was (as Dayton Haskin has shown in his history of Donne's reception) unhampered by the question of Donne's relationship to his national church.[6] A large-scale edition of Donne begun by James Russell Lowell was completed by Charles Eliot Norton, and in 1895 Norton's colleague at Harvard, Le Baron Russell Briggs, began featuring Donne in a large lecture course taken by most freshmen. It was there, in 1906, that Tom Eliot first read Donne.[7] Fifteen years later, when Eliot reviewed Herbert Grierson's *Metaphysical Lyrics and Poems of the Seventeenth Century* in the *TLS* (imagine the prescient editor who assigned this review to a young poet from Missouri), Eliot was bringing the American Donne home.

This 1921 review, which became the much-reprinted essay "The Metaphysical Poets," was not Eliot's first impassioned discussion of Donne. Two years earlier, writing in the *Egoist* about poetic diction, Eliot quoted Wordsworth ("the meanest flower that blows"), commenting that the daffodil is presented "for its own sake, not because of association with passions specifically human." In Donne's line "a bracelet of bright hair about the bone," in contrast, "the emotion is definitely human, merely seizing the object in order to express itself."[8]

Given the far more well-known remarks about the "impersonal theory" of poetry in "Tradition and the Individual Talent" (originally published around the same time as "Reflections"), Eliot's praise for the emotive Donne, in contrast to the more austerely impersonal Wordsworth, may seem surprising, but in fact Eliot never objected to personality in art as such. As his famous remark about the "dissociation of sensibility" in "The Metaphysical Poets" suggests, what mattered to Eliot was the relationship of human emotion to other elements in the poem, to precisions of diction, observation, or thought: "the ordinary man's experience is chaotic, irregular, fragmentary," but in the mind of a poet like Donne "experiences are always forming new wholes."[9] In another uncollected essay written around this time, Eliot was shrewdly self-conscious about why Donne's powers of synthesis should appeal to the maker and the audience of a poem like *The Waste Land*:

> Ethics having been eclipsed by psychology, we accept the belief that any state of mind is extremely complex and chiefly composed of odds and ends in constant flux manipulated by desire and fear. When, therefore, we find

a poet [like Donne] who neither suppresses nor falsifies, and who expresses complicated states of mind, we give him welcome.[10]

How was the author of these sentences capable, just a few years later, of chastising Donne for being a poet who was incapable of forming new wholes, a poet who "merely picked up, like a magpie, various shining fragments of ideas"?

Behind this question lie more fundamental questions, questions about the way in which poetic language may be understood to construct the illusion of human presence – the qualities we gesture towards when we use words like *emotion, personality, voice,* and *speaker* to talk about a poem. The Eliot who wrote about Donne in the early twenties was a poet who, like so many others, had learned from Donne how to establish the illusion of a speaking presence in just a few syllables: "Let us go then, you and I" ("The Love Song of J. Alfred Prufrock," 1); "Here I am, an old man in a dry month" ("Gerontion," 1); "My nerves are bad to-night. Yes, bad. Speak to me" (*The Waste Land*, III).[11] The first of these two poems are easily identifiable as dramatic monologues, but the dynamic unity of *The Waste Land*, which is not, also depends upon the swiftly established illusion of the spokenness of its constituent pieces, an illusion that grips us long before we have time to puzzle out the intricate connections between those pieces. The poem won't allow us to say that the line "My nerves are bad to-night" is uttered by the same *speaker* as the lines "I was neither / Living nor dead, and I knew nothing" (39–40) or "I can connect / Nothing with nothing" (301–2), but we feel, despite the lack of the unifying energy of a single speaker, the dramatization of a struggle towards a unified utterance, a struggle that constitutes simultaneously the poem's thematic business and our readerly experience of the poem. To borrow from Eliot's description of Donne, his poems up to *The Waste Land* are poems of *psychology*, poems that dramatize *states of mind composed of odds and ends in constant flux manipulated by desire and fear.*

But in the years following the publication of *The Waste Land* in 1922, as Eliot accumulated the fragments he would eventually bring together to make *The Hollow Men* three years later, a different kind of poem began to emerge – a poem that does not encourage us to feel that it is spoken by a discrete human subject with a particular psychology. If the tone is still anguished, it is not self-dramatizing, as it is in "Prufrock" or "Gerontion"; the utterance feels oracular, dislocated, as if it were emerging not from within but from beyond human experience:

> Here the stone images
> Are raised, here they receive
> The supplication of a dead man's hand
> Under the twinkle of a fading star.
>
> ("The Hollow Men," 41–4)[12]

The author of these lines has no more use for Donne, a poet who now seems to have perpetuated the dissociated sensibility, rather than mending it. The author of these lines has even less use for the poet of "Prufrock."

For many years, it was difficult to describe this sea-change in Eliot's relationship to Donne, for the major critical endeavor in which he expressed it, the Clark Lectures delivered at Cambridge University in 1926 ("On the Metaphysical Poetry of the Seventeenth Century with Special Reference to Donne, Crashaw and Cowley"), was not published until 1993. Throughout these lectures, Eliot depends on a distinction between the *psychological* poet, such as Donne, and the *ontological* poet, such as Dante. While the psychological poet "is imprisoned in the embrace of his own feelings," his language always gesturing toward the self that the poem constructs, the ontological poet is interested "not in the world of floating ideas" but "in the outside world," especially when the object of attention in the outside world is worthy of religious devotion. Donne remains for Eliot a "true poet, perhaps even a very great poet," but his poems, unlike Dante's, are held together by "what we call unsatisfactorily the personality of Donne."[13] Eliot no longer wanted to be that kind of poet.

Such suspicion of psychology, a suspicion not only of the narrow space of the mind but of the lyric's propensity to seduce us into the illusion of that space, is not unique to Eliot. One feels it in poets of a certain strain of the American avant-garde, poets from Louis Zukofsky writing in response to Eliot in the 1920s to Susan Howe writing today; the variety of poets who became associated with the magazine $L=A=N=G=U=A=G=E$ in the 1970s were more or less united by their desire to write poems that could not be imagined as being spoken. While Eliot's swerve away from Donne was driven in part by the Christianity he embraced publicly in 1927, the rejection of the possibly pernicious illusion of the self-determining human subject was driven in these poets by the double onslaught of Marxism and post-structuralism.[14]

These debates are now part of our literary past, not the present; Donne has survived them, just as he survived the censure of Pope and Johnson in the eighteenth century. But the value of these debates is that they don't allow us to take for granted the kind of work that Donne has accomplished; that is, we're made to consider the precise formal mechanisms through which the illusion of a poem's speaker is constructed, rather than assuming that poems have speakers, the way people have tongues. How did Donne do it?

Despite Donne's reputation for what the romantic poet Walter Savage Landor called "verses gnarl'd and knotted,"[15] Donne's diction is most typically colloquial and his syntax limpid, unruffled by the shapes of even his most complicated stanzas. The eleven-line stanza of "The Relic" consists of four tetrameter lines rhymed *aabb*, four alternating trimeter and pentameter lines rhymed *cdcd*, and three concluding pentameters rhymed *eee*, but the syntax of the single sentence that constitutes the poem's first stanza proceeds as if in placid ignorance of the formal obstacle course from which it is extruded. Donne was of course a great writer of prose as well as verse, and just the rhymes marking individual clauses and phrases in his prose may be highlighted by printing the prose in lines –

> We die in the light,
> in the sight
> of God's presence,
> and we rise in the light,
> in the sight
> of his very Essence.[16]

– so may the effortlessly elegant syntax of his poetry be highlighted by printing lines from "The Relic" as prose:

> When my grave is broke up again some second guest to entertain ... and he that digs it spies a bracelet of bright hair about the bone, will he not let'us alone, and think that there a loving couple lies, who thought that this device might be some way to make their souls, at the last busy day, meet at this grave, and make a little stay? (1–11)

Yet the natural ease of this syntax is only heightened by the self-conscious delight with which it also fulfills the requirements of the stanza's meter and rhyme scheme: the sentence feels driven by the momentum of its emerging occasion, as if the voice or self we presume to be driving the utterance were not given but emergent. This tension constitutes the drama of spokenness to which the poem directs its readers, who feel themselves consequently to be listeners, engaged in seductively intimate conversation.

The first stanza of "The Canonization" also consists of one elegant sentence, its many phrases linked characteristically by *or* rather than *and*, the resulting choices enhancing our sense that the poem is in process: "Observe his honour, or his grace, / Or the King's real, or his stamped face" (6–7). But in the second stanza, Donne follows this syntactical performance, in which line is always overridden by sentence, with a string of one-line sentences, the imperative mode superseded by the interrogative:

> Alas, alas, who's injured by my love?
>   What merchant's ships have my sighs drowned?
> Who says my tears have overflowed his ground?
>   When did my colds a forward spring remove?   (10–13)

These characteristic shifts between sentences that alternately confirm or conflict with the stanza's lineation, between sentences that shift abruptly from one mode or tense to another, highlight the illusion of spokenness by once again making us feel that the poem progresses by means of a swift succession of choices – as if the utterances were not premeditated but were happening in the time it takes to read them.

As a result, the surprising conclusions of Donne's poems may also seem witheringly inevitable, long before the logic of the argument becomes clear. "The Canonization" begins by enjoining the listener to stop talking ("hold your tongue"), but it concludes, after so craftily dramatizing its utterance as a spoken event, by transforming its listener into a speaker, who is made to address the poem's lovers in the second person:

>   you whom reverend love
>   Made one another's hermitage,
>   You, to whom love was peace, that now is rage,
>   Who did the whole world's soul contract, and drove
>   Into the glasses of your eyes
>   So made such mirrors, and such spies,
>   That they did all to you epitomize,
>   Countries, towns, courts, beg from above
>   A pattern of your love.   (37–45)

What has happened here? The sentence is an imperative, the listener addressing the poem's speaker and the speaker's lover ("you"), but the predicate is delayed for so long by a sequence of parallel modifying clauses ("whom reverend love / Made one another's hermitage" – "who did the whole world's soul contract" – "who drove / into the glasses of your eyes") that when the predicate finally appears ("beg"), it is so syntactically satisfying that the poem's weirdly startling conclusion feels irrefutable: the poem's indomitable speaker has been humbled, enjoined to beg. This speaker is great, says "The Canonization," but the listener, who in this final sentence becomes a participant in the poem's unfolding action, is even greater, a voice who may enjoin the lovers to beg from above.

This drama, explicit in "The Canonization," is everywhere implicit – not only in Donne's poems but in any poem that invites its readers to participate in the dramatic illusion of lyric presence. Like the beloved addressed in "A Valediction of My Name in the Window," who is asked to see herself in a glass engraved with her lover's name, we listeners discover ourselves in the other: "Here you see me, and I am you" (12). We learn to speak Donne.

Notes

1. Robert Browning, *The Poetical Works*, ed. Ian Jack and Margaret Smith, 15 vols. (Oxford: Clarendon Press, 1983–2010); Marianne Moore, *The Poems*, ed. Grace Schulman (New York: Viking, 2003).
2. *Critical Heritage*, 69.
3. John Ashbery, *Chinese Whispers* (New York: Farrar, Straus, and Giroux, 2002); Louise Glück, *Poems 1962–2012* (New York: Farrar, Straus, and Giroux, 2012).
4. T. S. Eliot, *Selected Essays* (New York: Harcourt, 1960), 118.
5. See *Critical Heritage*, 266.
6. Dayton Haskin, *John Donne in the Nineteenth Century* (New York: Oxford University Press, 2007), 196–233.
7. Eliot recorded his debt to Briggs in "Donne in Our Time," in *A Garland for John Donne*, ed. Theodore Spencer (Cambridge: Harvard University Press, 1931), 3, and in "To Criticize the Critic," in *To Criticize the Critic* (London: Faber, 1965), 21.
8. T. S. Eliot, "Reflections on Contemporary Poetry I," *Egoist* 4 (Sept. 1917), 118.
9. Eliot, *Selected Essays*, 247.
10. T. S. Eliot, "John Donne," *Nation & Athenaeum* 33 (9 June 1923), 332.
11. T. S. Eliot, *Complete Poems and Plays* (New York: Harcourt, 1971).
12. Eliot, *Complete Poems*.
13. T. S. Eliot, *The Varieties of Metaphysical Poetry*, ed. Ronald Schuchard (New York: Harcourt, 1993), 114, 88, 155.
14. See Charles Bernstein, *Content's Dream: Essays 1975–1984* (Los Angeles: Sun & Moon, 1986).
15. *Critical Heritage*, 339.
16. *The Works of John Donne*, 6 vols. (London: John W. Parker, 1839), 3:485.

CHAPTER 31

Donne in the Twenty-first Century:
Thinking Feeling

Linda Gregerson

In the heyday of modernism, T. S. Eliot made John Donne the patron saint of an electrifying experimentation with poetic form and a fervent postulate about the amalgam of thinking and feeling, what Eliot called the "direct sensuous apprehension of thought."[1] Both Eliot and modernism have endured a thousand slings and arrows ever since, but the vast majority of poets working in English today take the integration of thinking and feeling for granted, at least as an aspiration, and the best of them understand form as an instrument for discovery and the working-through of apprehension in the broadest, most variable sense. I take much of this to be the poetic and spiritual legacy of John Donne. In a lengthier essay, I would wish to make the case for the robustness of that legacy by considering the work of poets whose indebtedness is not explicit at all, poets who may not even be consciously aware of their own indebtedness. The most potent forms of poetic influence, after all, are those that break free of thematics, those that so colonize the ear and the imagination that they seem to be the native cadence or temperament of the (present) age. In the pages below, however, I will confine myself to poets whose debt is overt.

In the poetry of Kimberly Johnson, especially in her 2008 volume *A Metaphorical God*, homage to Donne is blazoned and sustained. Like Donne, and like his mentor Augustine, Johnson works obsessively at the paradox of transcendence in a universe condemned to mortal time. Her poems are a species of god-hunger, and an urgent, erotic, utterly contemporary calling-out to godhead saturates them all. For a representative example, consider the following "holy sonnet":

> O God my God, would you were an Abelard
> bowing each long midnight in your close cell
> over paper, quilling so fervent strokes
> to tear the page *My sister, my spouse.*
> Would you brooded on the wide between us
> unmanned with love, and in a florid hand

hatched assignations, which I in secret
bosomed up, panting for the hour. Constant
then and sure I'd be, as heaven-centered
as an astrolabe. But I can't fathom
your love-letters: libertine troth to the
second-person plural, dry *agape*,
and all your woo is *Touch me not.* My Lord my flesh
your tablet make. Inscribe *desire* in me.

("The Story of My Calamities," 1–14)[2]

The poem includes an epigraph taken from Augustine's commentary on the 64th Psalm, "*Misit ad nos epstolas et totam scripturam, / quibus nobis faceret amandi desiderium*," which Johnson translates as follows: "God sends the whole of scripture to us as a love-letter, / by which to provoke in us a longing to love him." But Johnson's speaker wants the letter hotter, the love more personal, than anything she can find in holy scripture, and so she dares her God to be more like the dangerously entangled lover of Heloise. In juxtaposition to the calm confidence of Augustine's commentary, the title of Johnson's poem invokes the turmoil of Abelard's autobiography: "The Story of My Calamities." Impassioned apostrophe, transgressive conflation of sexual passion and longing for the divine, flagrant opposition at the heart of that conflation: Kimberly Johnson boldly reconfigures John Donne's most characteristic moves as part of a twenty-first-century, re-gendered, mixed-diction address.

Less explicit in its debt to Donne is Alice Fulton's "Cascade Experiment" (later renamed "Shy One" in her *Selected Poems*) from her collection *Powers of Congress*. The title of the book is taken from the language of constitutional law: prescriptive language, public language, cleansed, one might suppose, of personality and private passion. But within that language, Fulton forges both an intimate address and a distinctly erotic valence: even as she evokes the civic and legislative realm, she also evokes the varied positions of bodies and minds in the realm we sometimes refer to as sexual congress. Furthermore, the poet's insistence upon the double nature of collective apprehension, the kernel of epistemological passion at the heart of all our efforts at objective truth, is the central claim and insight of her poetry:

Because faith creates its verification
and reaching you will be no harder than believing
in a planet's caul of plasma,
or interacting with a comet

in its perihelion passage, no harder
than considering what sparking of the vacuum, cosmological
impromptu flung me here, a periphrasis, perhaps,
for some denser, more difficult being,
a subsidiary instance, easier to grasp
than the span I foreshadow, of which I am a variable,
my stance is passional toward the universe and you.   (1–11)[3]

Fulton's work has always been characterized by athletic intellection, virtuosic wordplay, infatuation with all the new currents of science, and, above all, with the conspicuous, brazen display of wit – Donnean qualities all. And like John Donne, she grants a "passional" urgency (think sex as well as the Passion of Christ) to thought by casting it in the form of direct address to an intimate *you*, who is at once the lover, the reader, and the ever-elusive principle of unity (think deity) behind creation:

Because faith in facts can help create those facts,
the way electrons exist only when they're measured,
or shy people stand alone at parties,
attract no one, then go home to feel more shy,
I begin by supposing our attrition's no quicker
than a star's, that like electrons
vanishing on one side
of a wall and appearing on the other
without leaving any holes or being
somewhere in between, the soul's decoupling
is an oscillation so inward nothing outward
as the eye can see it.   (12–24)

As ever, the most urgent prompting to intellection – whether the speculative faculty finds its fittest vocabularies in astrophysics or metaphysics – is the radical No with which the universe confronts each one of us: the prospect of extinction. Common coin. And here we behold one of the great advantages of "thinking feeling": the poem is able to explore the ligatures between "naive" and "schooled" apprehension. In the fullest realms of apprehension, learning is never a linear process of replacing early imaginative templates with "corrected" models. Those early templates retain their resonance and strike echoing chords in all that comes later:

The childhood catechisms all had heaven,
an excitation of mist.
    Grown, I thought a vacancy awaited me.

> Now I find myself discarding and enlarging
>   both these views, an infidel of amplitude.   (25–29)

The locutions here – an excitation of mist, an infidel of amplitude – add a heady dose of Wallace Stevens to the Donnean athleticism: useful reminder that the "passional" quest for meaning may assume any number of phrasal and figurative habits. Useful reminder also that the transits of literary influence may in this regard resemble the transits of personal faith: what may look at first like abrupt discontinuity (between childhood's "heaven" and adulthood's "vacancy," between the turbulent eroticism of a seventeenth-century divine and the meditative metaphysics of an American insurance executive) may in fact bespeak a durable continuance. It sometimes takes a third instantiation (the "now" of personal meditation, for example, or the later poems that resonate with Donne and Stevens both) to make the concordances clear:

> Because truths we don't suspect have a hard time
> making themselves felt, as when thirteen species
> of whiptail lizards composed entirely of females
> stay undiscovered due to bias
> against such things existing,
> we have to meet the universe halfway.
> Nothing will unfold for us unless we move toward what
> looks to us like nothing: faith is a cascade.
> The sky's high solid is anything
> but, the sun going under hasn't
> budged, and if death divests the self
> it's the sole event in nature
> that's exactly what it seems.   (30–42)

Cognition is a transitive phenomenon, like poetry and prayer. And because this is true, Fulton is drawn, as Donne and Herbert are so often, to the optative mood:

> Because believing a thing's true
> can bring about that truth,
> and you might be the shy one, lizard or electron,
> known only through advances
> presuming your existence, let my glance be passional
> toward the universe and you.   (43–48)

Fulton finds the template for her epistemological meditation in a modern truism of experimental science: to observe a thing is to alter that thing. Donne's new science was rather different than our own, but he too found in it a stimulant to and icon of epistemological paradox:

> At the round earth's imagined corners, blow
> Your trumpets, angels, and arise, arise
> From death, you numberless infinities
> Of souls, and to your scattered bodies go . . .

(Holy Sonnet 4, 1–4)

The Book of Revelations told Donne that the Apocalypse would be announced by trumpeting angels at the four corners of the world. The new cosmology told him that the world was round. How to turn into a source of energy what would otherwise be intolerable contradiction? The earth is round: the instruments that tell us so, including and preeminently the human mind, are manifestations of the same deity that inspired Scripture. The earth's "corners" are the figures of imagination or, in the language of theology, of "accommodation," the willingness of an otherwise incomprehensible God to lend himself to the scale of human thought, and hence a kind of "love letter" to his fallible creatures. And, predicated on a devoutly-to-be-wished-for meeting place of the imagination, those four corners are solid enough to support the angels of the Apocalypse.

Christian Wiman writes no less urgently in "Every Riven Thing," but chooses the relative restraint of third-person meditation, building pressure by means of that very restraint and the tight *con*straint of repetitive syntax, variably parsed:

> God goes, belonging to every riven thing he's made
> sing his being simply by being
> the thing it is:
> stone and tree and sky,
> man who sees and sings and wonders why
>
> God goes. Belonging, to every riven thing he's made,
> means a storm of peace.   (1–7)[4]

Faith, for Wiman, is paradox under maximum pressure: a God who is both utterly immanent and utterly elusive, who means both absolute severance and absolute belonging, who brings a storm of peace. Forged to accommodate this faith is language under pressure: changes rung on words and clauses as if the conundrum of a present/absent god could be solved by way of a formal correlative:

> Think of the atoms inside the stone.
> Think of the man who sits alone
> trying to will himself into a stillness where

> God goes belonging. To every riven thing he's made
> there is given one shade
> shaped exactly to the thing itself: (8–13)

A decade ago, Christian Wiman was diagnosed with an incurable blood cancer. The poems in *Every Riven Thing* were written in the shadow of that illness and the often debilitating treatment designed to slow its progress. John Donne is not the only poet, of course, to have written some of his most intense work in the cauldron of bodily affliction, but the speaking position of afflicted embodiment is one that, in English poetry, shall evermore bear his stamp:

> under the tree a darker tree;
> under the man the only man to see
>
> God goes belonging to every riven thing. He's made
> the things that bring him near,
> made the mind that makes him go.
> A part of what man knows,
> apart from what man knows,
>
> God goes belonging to every riven thing he's made.   (14–21)

Faith is a circuit: it makes the mind that makes it go. And also: the God-made mind pursues a course that time and again makes God go missing. The knowing that makes God present is reiterative (a circuit in verse) and somatic (the riven body).

Very different prosodically, at almost the other end of the spectrum from Wiman's formalism, is a book from 2007 by the poet Mark Jarman. Taking the apostle Paul as its tutelary spirit, *Epistles* ventures to imagine not just the strenuousness of the individual will-to-believe, not just the psychological agon, but the corporate premise of faith. Its terms and methods are utterly contemporary, but its project is willfully contrarian, almost preposterous in the context of twenty-first-century literary secularism. What if the body of faith were authentically collective? What if the quarrel between skepticism and hope, the quarrel we call mindfulness, were conducted in the first person plural?

> We want the operation because we want the cure.
> We are naked and open unto his eyes, though draped in sterile cloth. He
> is quick and powerful, piercing even to the dividing of soul and spirit,
> though both choose amnesia.   ("We Want the Operation," 1–4)[5]

The prose poems of *Epistles* do not favor a testosterone-driven virtuosity. Their conceits are matters of patient explication rather than impacted conundrum:

> He separates them, even as he divides the
> joints and marrow, discerning the thoughts and intents of the heart in a
> small, vestigial, rooted, and determined thing.
>
> Later, he shows how the sick part was woven in . . .   (4–7)

If, on rare occasions, the imagery tilts toward an extravagance worthy of Crashaw ("An eye tips each of his bloody fingers"), the dominant effect is unsettling precisely because of its understatement. Something uncanny, for example, lurks in the juxtapositions of pastoral urging, passive voice, and blandly clinical description:

> . . . [F]irst the skin was shaved, then painted with antiseptic, the tomb
> jewel color of ochre. First the diagnosis was made. First the protocol and
> the procedure were recommended. We wanted the operation because we
> wanted the cure.   (19–22)

Christ the physician: by yoking the idioms and preoccupations of an ostensibly secular cultural realm – a realm in which we (falsely) imagine health to be a universal norm – to a more chastened sense of scale, Jarman finds the living tension in a venerable figure. "Thus God performs his surgery, closing and opening simultaneously, always with new reasons to go in" (28–29).

Rather than working the excitable juxtapositions we associate with metaphysical poetry, Jarman generates a troubling double consciousness: smoothest contemporaneity crossed with full frontal obsolescence. Sometimes the effect is a sort of deadpan: "When the thief comes in the night, it is mid-afternoon on a sunny day, with everybody at work" ("When the Thief Comes," 1–2). Sometimes it is authentically magical:

> It is nearing the time when one said to the dogwood where he was nailed,
> "I know you pity me. Never again will you grow like the oak and provide
> lumber for crucifixions. You will be slender, and your blossoms, two long
> and two short petals, will form a cross. At the tip of each petal, a wound
> where the nail bit, rusty with blood. At the heart of each flower, a crown
> of thorns. In this transformation, remembering me, you will be forgiven."
>   ("Forgive Me, Lord," 30–35)

Rhetorically, the poems of *Epistles* could scarcely be further from the lyric Donne. But like the lyric Donne, they are performative and flagrantly indifferent to accepted decorum. Not only do they appropriate the Pauline voice, but they dare to take seriously the Pauline mission. In this they are heir to the poet who preached at St. Paul's: "I send you this not knowing if you will receive it, or if having received it, you will read it, or if having read it you will know that it contains my blessing" ("If I Were Paul," 31–33).

To trace the Donnean in contemporary lyric I might almost have chosen any poem by Carl Phillips, and he has published fourteen books of them to date, because, whatever his ostensible subject, and throughout an ever-evolving exploration of poetic line and disposition-on-the-page, Phillips performs a Donne-like quarrel with syntax and metamorphic image:

> Meanwhile the sea moves uneasily, like a man who
> suspects what the room reels with as he rises into it
> is violation – his own: he touches the bruises at each
> shoulder and, on his chest,
>   the larger bruise, star-shaped,
> a flawed star, or hand, though he remembers no hands,
> has tried – can't remember . . .
>
> ("Radiance Versus Ordinary Light," 1–6)[6]

No poet writing in English today is more enamored of the noun clause: the naming that can only happen by way of an action. No poet is more profligate with the modifying clause: the adjectival or adverbial unit of such conceptual wholeness that it struggles against its own subordination:

>   That kind of rhythm to it,
> even to the roughest surf there's a rhythm findable,
> which is why we keep coming here, to find it, or that's
> what we say. We dive in and, as usual,
>   the swimming
> feels like that swimming the mind does in the wake
> of transgression, how the instinct to panic at first
> slackens that much more quickly, if you don't
> look back.   (6–13)

The swimming that the mind does in its quest for an ever acuter amalgam of thought and feeling is largely a matter of rhythm, mental process indistinguishable from somatic. The alternating tension and surrender of moving forward/looking backward is action in search of a subject. It is not sex exactly, though sex may be its best approximation. One knows only that the subject is elusive, and the search intensest when it feels like danger:

> Regret,
>   like pity, changes nothing really, we
> say to ourselves and, less often, to each other, each time
> swimming a bit farther,
>   leaving the shore the way
> the water – in its own watered, of course, version
> of semaphore – keeps leaving the subject out, flashing
> *Why should it matter now* and *Why,*
>   *why shouldn't it,*   (13–18)

Until the danger is how we know it's real: "as the waves beat harder, hard against us, until that's / how we like it, I'll break your heart, break mine" (19–20). For poets whose intellection is particularly visceral, the irreducible embodiment of imagination is also a form of soul-making. This phenomenon is not exclusive to Donne, of course. One hears, for example, a great deal of Herbert in Phillips as well. But the volume in which this particular poem appears grants pride of place to Donne: the book is titled *Riding Westward.*

Transgression sounds like ringing brass in Donne, whose syntactical extravagance is considerably more agitated than that of Phillips and relies on the conspicuous enjambment that rhyme and meter make possible:

> Batter my heart, three-personed God; for You
> As yet but knock, breathe, shine, and seek to mend;
> That I may rise and stand, o'erthrow me,'and bend
> Your force to break, blow, burn, and make me new.
>   (Holy Sonnet 10, 1–4)

By contrast, Phillips's syntactical divagations are unsettling precisely because of their surface calm: "like a man who / suspects what the room reels with as he rises into it / is violation – his own." In many of Phillips's poems the struggle between sado-domination and abjection is more explicit than in the poem reprinted here: bits and bridles, for example, muzzles and leashes. But always, the power of that struggle inheres precisely in its meditative composure, a very un-Donnean trait. In Phillips, transgression insinuates.

In Jericho Brown's first book, abjection and exorbitant eroticism become the stays of poetic address. Eschewing default nominatives, Brown makes the very title of his book a pleading expostulation: *Please.* "I saw some kids whip him with a belt while he / Repeated, *Please*" ("Track 5: Summertime," 20–21).[7] In poem after poem, the poet invites us to see the volatile tracks of sexual shame and familial violence inscribe themselves upon the substrate of consciousness. The devotional imperative may assume the form of a punishing father and a sacrificial son in a poem that calls itself a prayer:

> ... Father, I bear the bridge
> Of what might have been
> A broken nose. I lift to you
> What was a busted lip. Bless
> The boy who believes
> His best beatings lack
> Intention, the mark of the beast.
> Bring back to life the son
> Who glories in the sin
> Of immediacy, calling it love.
>
> ("Prayer for the Backhanded," 18–27)

It may surface in the shadow image of crucifixion:

> A man I tried to love
>   Handed me binoculars and
> Explained the shrike
>   Impales its victims on barbed wire
> And rusty nails.   ("Sean," 1–5)

Devotional templates may be narrativized:

> My father's embrace is tighter
> Now that he knows
> He is not the only man in my life.
> He ...
>   holds my hand hungry
> For a discussion of Bible scriptures
> Over breakfast ...
>   He begs forgiveness
> For anything he may have done to make me
> Turn to abomination ...   ("Like Father," 1–7, 11–13)

They may expand to constitute a book-length framework of incitement and resistance, as in Brown's most recent volume of poems and its frequent invocations of scripture:

> I will begin with the body,
> In the year of our Lord,
> Porous and wet, love-wracked
> And willing: in my 23rd year,
> A certain obsession overtook
> My body, or I should say,
> I let a man touch me until I bled ...   ("Romans 12:1," 1–7)[8]

Conflating the vocabularies of sexual longing and longing for the god who is and is not metaphorical, Donne rendered in verse the tumult of personal faith and the scandal of salvation that requires a crucified god. To this volatile mix, Jericho Brown has added the open (and political) thematics of sexual identity and race. In this he joins (and helps to lead) a strong cohort of younger American poets:

> As men
> Are wont to hate women,
> As women are taught to hate
> Themselves, they hate a woman
> They smell in me . . . my body,
> Dear dying sacrifice, desirous
> As I will be, black as I am.   (16–20, 23–25)

While explicitly religious vocabularies were tacitly excluded from the great preponderance of twentieth-century English-language poetry, the lyric in its oxymoronic conflation of immediacy and subjection-to-form has been centrally defined, throughout its history, by a longing for some antidote to transience. The poet Frank Bidart has called this "Hunger for the Absolute." With equal durability, erotic love has long claimed pride of place as engine to the lyric poem. The conjunction is not accidental: there was always more at stake than sex alone. As Bidart himself has written in a recent poem, "*Someone wanted more from that bed / than was found there*" ("Name that Bed," 7–8).[9] And as the other voice in the poem is prompt to respond: "Name the bed that's not true of" (9). It is not, in other words, the conjunction of erotic and devotional preoccupations that distinguishes John Donne's poetry from lyric more broadly construed. Nor is his consequence for subsequent poetry limited to the extraordinarily vivid techniques he developed to articulate that conjunction: the cultivated dissonance among inherited vocabularies, the extravagance of figure and rhetorical proposition, the interlineations of virtuosity and abjection. His most sweeping legacy is also the simplest, albeit the most difficult: the sustained amalgamation of feeling and intellection. In his poetry, Donne construed this amalgamation not as a philosophical premise but as a mode of practical action. In a broad array of thematic and stylistic instantiations, it is a mode of action to which poets aspire today.

Notes

1. T. S. Eliot, "The Metaphysical Poets," in *Selected Prose of T. S. Eliot*, ed. Frank Kermode (New York: Harcourt Brace, 1975), 63.

2. Kimberly Johnson, *A Metaphorical God* (New York: Persea Books, 2008), 36. Johnson's other books of poetry are *Leviathan with a Hook* (2002) and *Uncommon Prayer* (2014).

3. Alice Fulton, *Powers of Congress* (Boston: David R. Godine, 1990). Fulton's other books of poetry are *Dance Script with Electric Ballerina* (1983), *Palladium* (1986), *Sensual Math* (1995), *Felt* (2001), *Cascade Experiment* (2004), and *Barely Composed* (2015).

4. Christian Wiman, *Every Riven Thing* (New York: Farrar, Straus and Giroux, 2010). Wiman's other books of poetry are *The Long Home* (1998), *Hard Night* (2005), and *Once in the West* (2014).

5. Mark Jarman, *Epistles* (Louisville: Sarabande Books, 2007). Jarman's other books of poems are *North Sea* (1978), *The Rote Walker* (1981), *Far and Away* (1985), *The Black Riviera* (1990), *Iris* (1992), *Questions for Ecclesiastes* (1997), *Unholy Sonnets* (2000), *To the Green Man* (2004), *Bone Fires* (2011), and *The Heronry* (2019).

6. Carl Phillips, *Riding Westward* (New York: Farrar, Straus and Giroux, 2006). Phillips' other poetry books are *In the Blood* (1992), *Cortège* (1995), *From the Devotions* (1998), *Pastoral* (2000), *The Tether* (2001), *Rock Harbor* (2002), *The Rest of Love* (2004), *Quiver of Arrows* (2007), *Speak Low* (2009), *Double Shadow* (2012), *Silverchest* (2013), *Reconnaisance* (2015), and *Wild is the Wind* (2018).

7. Jericho Brown, *Please* (Kalamazoo, MI: New Issues, 2008). Brown's other books of poems are *The New Testament* (2014), and *The Tradition* (2019).

8. Jericho Brown, *The New Testament* (Port Townsend, WA: Copper Canyon, 2014).

9. Frank Bidart, *Metaphysical Dog* (New York: Farrar, Straus and Giroux, 2013). Bidart's other books of poems are *Golden State* (1973), *The Book of the Body* (1977), *The Sacrifice* (1983), *In the Western Night* (1990), *Desire* (1997), *Star Dust* (2005), *Watching the Spring Festival* (2008), and *Half Light: Collected Poems 1965–2016* (2017).

Further Reading

Donne's Literary Career

Adlington, Hugh. "Do Donne's Writings Express His Desperate Ambition?" *OHJD*, 718–31.

Love, Harold. *Scribal Publication in Seventeenth-Century England* (Oxford: Clarendon, 1993).

Marotti, Arthur F. *Manuscript, Print, and the English Renaissance Lyric* (Ithaca, NY: Cornell University Press, 1995).

Stringer, Gary A. "The Composition and Dissemination of Donne's Writings," in *OHJD*, 12–25.

Wall, Wendy, "Authorship and the Material Conditions of Writing," *Cambridge Companion to English Literature 1500–1600*, ed. Arthur F. Kinney (Cambridge University Press, 2000), 64–89.

Donne's Texts and Materials

Beal, Peter et al. *Catalogue of English Literary Manuscripts 1450–1700*, www.celm-ms.org.uk.

Dobranski, Stephen B. *Readers and Authorship in Early Modern England* (Cambridge University Press, 2005).

Love, Harold. *The Culture and Commerce of Texts: Scribal Publication in the Seventeenth Century* (Amherst, MA: University of Massachusetts, 1998).

Sullivan II, Ernest W. *The Influence of John Donne: His Uncollected Seventeenth-Century Printed Verse* (Columbia, MO: University of Missouri Press, 1993).

Woudhuysen, Henry. *Sir Philip Sidney and the Circulation of Manuscripts, 1558–1640* (Oxford University Press, 1996).

Donne and Print

Eisenstein, Elizabeth L. *The Printing Press as an Agent of Change: Communications and Cultural Transformations in Early-Modern Europe*, 2 vols. (Cambridge University Press, 1979).

Erne, Lukas. *Shakespeare and the Book Trade* (Cambridge University Press, 2013).
Marotti, Arthur F. *Manuscript, Print, and the English Renaissance Lyric* (Ithaca, NY: Cornell University Press, 1995).
Saunders, J. W. "The Stigma of Print: A Note on the Social Bases of Tudor Poetry," *Essays in Criticism* 1 (1951), 139–64.
Wollman, Richard B. "The 'Press and the Fire': Print and Manuscript Culture in Donne's Circle," *Studies in English Literature, 1500–1900* 33 (1993), 85–97.

Language

Brooks, Cleanth. *The Well-Wrought Urn* (New York: Harcourt Brace, 1947).
Empson, William. *Seven Types of Ambiguity* (London: Chatto and Windus, 1930).
Lewalski, Barbara Kiefer. *Protestant Poetics and the Seventeenth-Century Religious Lyric* (Princeton University Press, 1979).
Martz, Louis L. *The Poetry of Meditation: A Study in English Religious Literature* (New Haven: Yale University Press, 1954).
Ogden, C. K. and I. A. Richards. *The Meaning of Meaning: A Study of the Influence of Language Upon Thought and of the Science of Symbolism* (London: K. Paul, Trench, Trubner & Co, 1923).

Donne's Poetics of Obstruction

Bernstein, Charles. "Artifice of Absorption," in *A/Poetics* (Cambridge, MA: Harvard University Press, 1992), 9–89.
Blasing, Mutlu Konuk. *Lyric Poetry: The Pain and the Pleasure of Words* (Princeton University Press, 2007).
Dubrow, Heather. *The Challenges of Orpheus: Lyric Poetry and Early Modern England* (Baltimore, MD: Johns Hopkins University Press, 2008).
Kerrigan, William. "The Fearful Accommodations of John Donne," *English Literary Renaissance* 4 (1974), 337–63.
Saunders, Ben. "Prosodic Pleasures and Metrical Fantasies: Donne's 'Irregularity,'" *The Yale Journal of Criticism* 12.2 (1999), 171–87.

Elegies and Satires

Baumlin, James S. "Donne's 'Satyre IV': The Failure of Language and Genre," *Texas Studies in Language and Literature* 30 (1988), 363–387.
Bradbury, Nancy Mason. "Speaker and Structure in Donne's *Satyre IV*." *Studies in English Literature* 25 (1985), 87–107.
Dubrow, Heather. "'No man is an island': Donne's Satires and Satiric Traditions," *Studies in English Literature* 19 (1979), 71–83.
Hester, M. Thomas. *Kinde Pitty and Brave Scorn: John Donne's Satyres* (Durham, NC: Duke University Press, 1982).
Patterson, Annabel. "Satirical Writing: Donne in Shadows," in *CCJD*, 117–31.

The Unity of the *Songs and Sonnets*

Carey, John. *John Donne: Life, Mind and Art* (Oxford University Press, 1981).
Eliot, T. S. *The Varieties of Metaphysical Poetry*, ed. Ronald Schuchard (San Diego, CA: Harcourt Brace, 1993).
Saunders, Ben. *Desiring Donne: Poetry, Sexuality, Interpretation* (Cambridge, MA: Harvard University Press, 2006).
Vickers, Brian. "The 'Songs and Sonnets' and the Rhetoric of Hyperbole," in *John Donne: Essays in Celebration*, ed. A. J. Smith (London: Methuen, 1972), 132–74.
Winters, Yvor. "Aspects of the Short Poem in the English Renaissance," in *Forms of Discovery: Critical and Historical Essays on the Forms of the Short Poem in English* (Chicago: Alan Swallow, 1967), 1–120.

Divine Poems

Cefalu, Paul. "Godly Fear, Sanctification, and Calvinist Theology in the Sermons and Holy Sonnets of John Donne," *Studies in Philology* 100 (2003), 71–86.
Guibbory, Achsah. "Donne's Religion," *ELR* 31 (2001), 412–39.
Kuchar, Gary. "Petrarchism and Repentance in John Donne's Holy Sonnets," *Modern Philology* 105 (2008), 535–69.
Shuger, Debora. *Habits of Thought in the English Renaissance: Religion, Politics, and the Dominant Culture* (Berkeley, CA: University of California Press, 1990).
Young, R. V. "The Religious Sonnet," in *OHJD*, 218–33.

Letters

Corthell, R. J. "'Friendships Sacraments': John Donne's Familiar Letters," *Studies in Philology* 78 (1981), 409–25.
Daybell, James. *The Material Letter in Early Modern England: Manuscript Letters and the Culture and Practices of Letter-Writing, 1512–1635* (New York: Palgrave Macmillan, 2012).
Gibson, Jonathan. "Significant Space in Manuscript Letters," *The Seventeenth Century* 12:1 (1997), 1–9.
Schneider, Gary. *The Culture of Epistolarity: Vernacular Letters and Letter Writing in Early Modern England, 1500–1700* (Newark, DE: University of Delaware Press, 2004).
Summers, Claude and Ted-Larry Pebworth, "Donne's Correspondence with Wotton," *JDJ* 10 (1991), 1–36.

Orality and Performance

Bakhtin, Mikhail M. *The Dialogic Imagination: Four Essays*, trans. Caryl Emerson and Michael Holquist, ed. Michael Holquist (Austin, TX: University of Texas Press, 1981).

Furniss, Graham. *Orality: The Power of the Spoken Word* (New York: Palgrave Macmillan, 2004).

Herz, Judith Scherer. "Reading and Rereading Donne's Poetry," in *CCJD*, 101–15.

Marotti, Arthur F. *John Donne, Coterie Poet* (Madison: University of Wisconsin Press, 1986).

Ong, Walter J. *Orality and Literacy: The Technologizing of the Word* (London: Routledge, 1988).

Reading and Interpretation

Blair, Ann. *Too Much to Know: Managing Scholarly Information Before the Modern Age* (New Haven, CT: Yale University Press, 2010).

Craik, Katharine A. *Reading Sensations in Early Modern England* (New York: Palgrave Macmillan, 2007).

Ettenhuber, Katrin. "'Comparisons are Odious'? Revisiting the Metaphysical Conceit in Donne," *The Review of English Studies* 62 (2011), 93–113.

Lund, Mary Ann. *Melancholy, Medicine and Religion in Early Modern England: Reading "The Anatomy of Melancholy"* (Cambridge University Press, 2010).

Sharpe, Kevin. *Reading Revolution: The Politics of Reading in Early Modern England* (New Haven, CT: Yale University Press, 2000).

Education

Beales, A. C. F. *Education Under Penalty: English Catholic Education from the Reformation to the Fall of James II* (London: Athlone Press, 1963).

Cummings, Brian. *The Literary Culture of the Reformation: Grammar and Grace* (Oxford University Press, 2002).

Gwosdek, Hedwig. "Introduction," in *Lily's Grammar of Latin in English: An Introduction of the Eyght Partes of Speche, and the Construction of the Same*, ed. Hedwig Gwosdek (Oxford University Press, 2013), 1–27.

Hudson, Elizabeth K. "The Colloquies of Maturin Cordier: Images of Calvinist School Life and Thought," *The Sixteenth Century Journal* 9.3 (1978), 57–78.

Whitehead, Maurice. *English Jesuit Education: Expulsion, Suppression, Survival and Restoration, 1762–1803* (Farnham, UK: Ashgate, 2013).

Law

Baker, J. H. *An Introduction to English Legal History*, 4th edn (Oxford University Press, 2007).

Cormack, Bradin. *A Power to Do Justice: Jurisdiction, English Literature, and the Rise of Common Law* (University of Chicago Press, 2007).

Goodrich, Peter. *Oedipus Lex: Psychoanalysis, History, Law* (Berkeley, CA: University of California Press, 1995).

Raffield, Paul. *Images and Cultures of Law in Early Modern England: Justice and Political Power, 1558–1660* (Cambridge University Press, 2007).
Rhetoric and Law in Early Modern Europe, eds. Kahn, Victoria and Lorna Hutson (New Haven, CT: Yale University Press, 2001).

Donne's Prisons

Ahnert, Ruth. *The Rise of Prison Literature in the Sixteenth Century* (Cambridge University Press, 2013).
The Oxford History of the Prison: The Practice of Punishment in Western Society, eds. Norval Morris and David J. Rothman (Oxford University Press, 1995).
Pendry, E. D., *Elizabethan Prisons and Prison Scenes*, 2 vols. (Salzburg: Institut für Englische Sprache und Literatur, Universität Salzburg, 1974).
"Prison Writings in Early Modern England," eds. William Sherman and William Sheils [Special Issue], *Huntington Library Quarterly* 72.2 (2009).
Strauss, Paul. *In Hope of Heaven: English Recusant Prison Writings of the Sixteenth Century* (New York: Peter Lang, 1995).

Donne and the Natural World

Borlik, Todd A. *Ecocriticism and Early Modern English Literature: Green Pastures* (New York: Routledge, 2011).
Early Modern Ecostudies: From the Florentine Codex to Shakespeare, eds. Thomas Hallock, Ivo Kamps, and Karen Raber (New York: Palgrave Macmillan, 2008).
Ecocritical Shakespeare, eds. Lynn Bruckner and Dan Brayton (Farnham, UK: Ashgate Press, 2011).
Harvey, Elizabeth D. "The Souls of Animals: John Donne's *Metempsychosis* and Early Modern Natural History," in *Environment and Embodiment in Early Modern England*, eds. Mary Floyd-Wilson and Garrett A. Sullivan, Jr. (New York: Palgrave Macmillan, 2007), 55–70.
Tigner, Amy L. *Literature and the Renaissance Garden from Elizabeth I to Charles II: England's Paradise* (Farnham, UK: Ashgate Press, 2012).

Money

Anderson, Judith. *Translating Investments: Metaphor and the Dynamic of Cultural Change in Tudor-Stuart England* (New York: Fordham University Press, 2005).
Correll, Barbara. "Chiasmus and Commodificatio: Crossing Tropes and Conditions in Donne's Elegy 11, 'The Bracelet,'" *Exemplaria* 11.1 (1999), 141–65.

Deng, Stephen. *Coinage and State Formation in Early Modern English Literature* (New York: Palgrave Macmillan, 2011).

Freer, Coburn. "John Donne and Elizabethan Economic Theory," *Criticism* 38.4 (Fall 1996), 497–520.

Hawkes, David. *The Culture of Usury in Renaissance England* (New York: Palgrave Macmillan, 2010).

Sexuality

Bach, Rebecca Ann. "(Re)placing John Donne in the History of Sexuality," *ELH* 72 (2005), 259–89.

Bates, Catherine. *Masculinity, Gender and Identity in the English Renaissance Lyric* (Cambridge University Press, 2007).

Dubrow, Heather. *Echoes of Desire: English Petrarchism and Its Counterdiscourses* (Ithaca, NY: Cornell University Press, 1995).

Estrin, Barbara L. *Laura: Uncovering Gender and Genre in Wyatt, Donne, and Marvell* (Durham, NC: Duke University Press, 1994).

Low, Anthony. *The Reinvention of Love: Poetry, Politics and Culture from Sidney to Milton* (Cambridge University Press, 1993).

Donne and the Passions

Derrin, Daniel. "Engaging the Passions in John Donne's Sermons," *English Studies* 93 (2012), 452–68.

Passions and Subjectivity in Early Modern Culture, eds. Brian Cummings and Freya Sierhuis (Farnham, UK: Ashgate, 2013).

Selleck, Nancy. *The Interpersonal Idiom in Shakespeare, Donne, and Early Modern Culture* (New York: Palgrave Macmillan, 2008).

Smith, A. J. *The Metaphysics of Love: Studies in Renaissance Love Poetry from Dante to Milton* (Cambridge University Press, 1985).

Targoff, Ramie. *John Donne: Body and Soul* (University of Chicago Press, 2008).

Pain

Biss, Eula. "The Pain Scale," *Seneca Review* 35.1 (Spring 2005), 70–78.

Melzack, Ronald. *The Puzzle of Pain* (New York: Basic Books, 2003).

Merback, Mitchell B. *The Thief, the Cross and the Wheel: Pain and the Spectacle of Punishment in Medieval and Renaissance Europe* (University of Chicago Press, 1999).

Mills, Robert. *Suspended Animation: Pain, Pleasure and Punishment in Medieval Culture* (London: Reaktion, 2006).

Schoenfeldt, Michael. "Shakespearean Pain," in *Shakespearean Sensations*, eds. Tanya Pollard and Katharine Craik (Cambridge University Press, 2013), 191–207.

Medicine

Henry, John. "The Matter of Souls: Medical Theory and Theology in Seventeenth-Century England," in *The Medical Revolution of the Seventeenth Century*, eds. Roger French and Andrew Wear (Cambridge University Press, 1989), 87–113.

Religio Medici: Medicine and Religion in Seventeenth-Century England, eds. Ole Peter Grell and Andrew Cunningham (Aldershot, UK: Scolar Press, 1996).

Sawday, Jonathan. *The Body Emblazoned: Dissection and the Human Body in Renaissance Culture* (London: Routledge, 1995).

Siraisi, Nancy G. *Medieval and Early Renaissance Medicine: An Introduction to Knowledge and Practice* (University of Chicago Press, 1990).

Wear, Andrew. *Knowledge and Practice in English Medicine 1550–1680* (Cambridge University Press, 2000).

Science, Alchemy, and the New Philosophy

Blood Matters: Blood in European Literature and Thought, 1400–1700, eds. Bonnie Lander Johnson and Eleanor Decamp (Philadelphia, PA: University of Pennsylvania Press, 2017).

The Cambridge History of Science, Volume 3, Early Modern Science, eds. Katharine Park and Lorraine Daston (Cambridge University Press, 2006).

Gaukroger, Stephen. *The Emergence of a Scientific Culture: Science and the Shaping of Modernity, 1210–1685* (Oxford: Clarendon Press, 2006).

Shapin, Steven. *The Scientific Revolution* (The University of Chicago Press, 2008).

Webster, Charles. *Paracelsus: Medicine, Magic and Mission at the End of Time* (New Haven, CT: Yale University Press, 2008).

Donne and Skepticism

Gross, Kenneth. "John Donne's Lyric Skepticism: In Strange Way," *Modern Philology* 101.3 (2004), 371–99.

Hamlin, William M. *Montaigne's English Journey: Reading the Essays in Shakespeare's Day* (Oxford University Press, 2013).

Klause, John. "Hope's Gambit: The Jesuitical, Protestant, Skeptical Origins of Donne's Heroic Ideal," *Studies in Philology* 91.2 (1994), 181–215.

Spolsky, Ellen. *Satisfying Skepticism: Embodied Knowledge in the Early Modern World* (Aldershot, UK: Ashgate, 2001).

Strier, Richard. "Radical Donne: 'Satire III,'" *English Literary History* 60 (1993), 283–322.

The Metaphysics of the Metaphysicals

Foucault, Michel. *The Order of Things: An Archaeology of the Human Sciences* (New York: Pantheon, 1970).

Greenblatt, Stephen. *Renaissance Self-Fashioning: From More to Shakespeare* (University of Chicago Press, 2005).
Rivers, Isabel. *Classical and Christian Ideas in English Renaissance Poetry: A Student's Guide*, 2nd edn (London: Routledge, 1994).
Willey, Basil. *The Seventeenth Century Background: Studies in the Thought of the Age in Relation to Poetry and Religion* (London: Chatto and Windus, 1934).
Winny, James. *The Frame of Order: An Outline of Elizabethan Belief. Taken from Treatises of the Late Sixteenth Century* (London: Allen and Unwin, 1957).

Controversial Prose

Altman, Shanyn. "'An Anxious Entangling and Perplexing of Consciences': John Donne and Catholic Recusant Mendacity," in *Mendacity in Early Modern Literature and Culture*, eds. Ingo Berensmeyer and Andrew Hadfield (London: Routledge, 2016), 46–58.
Bushnell, Rebecca. *Tragedies of Tyrants: Political Thought and Theater in the English Renaissance* (Ithaca, NY: Cornell University Press, 1990).
Houliston, Victor. "An Apology for Donne's *Pseudo-Martyr*," *Review of English Studies* 57 (2006), 474–86.
Sullivan, Ernest. "Authoritative Manuscript Corrections in Donne's *Biathanatos*," *Studies in Bibliography* 28 (1975), 268–76.
Tutino, Stefania. "Notes on Machiavelli and Ignatius Loyola in John Donne's *Ignatius His Conclave* and *Pseudo-Martyr*," *English Historical Review* 99 (2004), 1308–21.

Devotional Prose

Frost, Kate Gartner. *Holy Delight: Typology, Numerology, and Autobiography in Donne's Devotions upon Emergent Occasions* (Princeton University Press, 1990).
Gray, Dave and Jeanne Shami. "Political Advice in Donne's *Devotions*," *Modern Language Quarterly* 50:4 (1989), 337–56.
Johnson, Jeffrey. "The Essay," in *OHJD*, 264–72.
Narveson, Kate. "Donne the Layman Essaying Divinity," *JDJ* 28 (2009), 1–30.
Strier, Richard. "Donne and the Politics of Devotion," in *Religion, Literature, and Politics in Post-Reformation England, 1540–1688*, eds. Donna B. Hamilton and Richard Strier (Cambridge University Press, 1996), 93–114.

The Sermons

The English Sermon Revised: Religion, Literature and History 1600–1750, eds. Lori Anne Ferrell and Peter McCullough (Manchester University Press, 2000).
Ferrell, Lori Anne. "Sermons," in *The Elizabethan Top Ten: Defining Print Popularity in Early Modern England* (Farnham, UK: Ashgate, 2013), 193–202.

Morrissey, Mary. "Interdisciplinarity and the Study of Early Modern Sermons," *Historical Journal* 42.4 (1999), 1111–123.
The Oxford Handbook of the Early Modern Sermon, eds. Peter McCullough, Hugh Adlington, and Emma Rhatigan (Oxford University Press, 2011).
Questier, Michael. *Conversion, Politics, and Religion in England: 1580–1625* (Cambridge University Press, 1996).

The Self

Greenblatt, Stephen. *Renaissance Self-Fashioning: From More to Shakespeare* (University of Chicago Press, 1980).
Rambuss, Richard. *Closet Devotions* (Durham, NC: Duke University Press, 1998).
Scarry, Elaine. "Donne: 'But yet the body is his book,'" in *Literature and the Body: Essays on Populations and Persons*, ed. Elaine Scarry (Baltimore, MD: Johns Hopkins University Press, 1988), 70–105.
Shuger, Debora Kuller. *The Renaissance Bible: Scholarship, Sacrifice, and Subjectivity* (Berkeley, CA: University of California Press, 1994).
Stallybrass, Peter. "Shakespeare, the Individual, and the Text," in *Cultural Studies*, eds. Lawrence Grossberg et al. (New York: Routledge, 1992), 593–610.

Portraits

Fumerton, Patricia. "Secret Arts: Elizabethan Miniatures and Sonnets," in *Cultural Aesthetics: Renaissance Literature and the Practice of Social Ornament* (University of Chicago Press, 1991), 67–110.
Howe, Sarah. "The Authority of Presence: The Development of the English Author Portrait, 1500–1640," *The Papers of the Bibliographical Society of America* 102 (2008), 465–99.
Hurley, Ann. *John Donne's Poetry and Early Modern Visual Culture* (Selinsgrove, PA: Susquehanna University Press, 2005).
Patterson, Annabel. "Donne in Shadows: Pictures and Politics," *JDJ* 16 (1997), 1–35.
Wendorf, Richard. *The Elements of Life: Biography and Portrait-painting in Stuart and Georgian England* (Oxford: Clarendon, 1990).

Donne in the Seventeenth and Eighteenth Centuries

Alvarez, Alfred. *The School of Donne* (New York: Pantheon, 1961).
Dodds, Lara. "Poor Donne Was Out: Reading and Writing Donne in the Works of Margaret Cavendish," *JDJ* 29 (2010), 133–74.
Mueller, Janel. "Women Among the Metaphysicals: A Case, Mostly, of Being Donne For," *Modern Philology* 87.2 (1989), 142–58.

Saunders, Ben. *Desiring Donne: Poetry, Sexuality, Interpretation* (Cambridge, MA: Harvard University Press, 2006).
Sullivan II, Ernest W. *The Influence of John Donne: His Uncollected Seventeenth-Century Printed Verse* (Columbia, MO: University of Missouri Press, 1993).

Donne in the Nineteenth and Twentieth Centuries

Brooks, Cleanth. *The Well-Wrought Urn* (New York: Harcourt, 1947).
John Donne: The Critical Heritage, ed. A. J. Smith (London: Routledge and Kegan Paul, 1975).
Eliot, T. S. "John Donne in Our Time," in *A Garland for John Donne*, ed. Theodore Spencer (Cambridge, MA: Harvard University Press, 1931), 1–19.
Eliot, T. S. *The Varieties of Metaphysical Poetry*, ed. Ronald Schuchard (New York: Harcourt, 1993).
Haskin, Dayton. *John Donne in the Nineteenth Century* (Oxford University Press, 2007).

Donne in the Twenty-first Century: Thinking Feeling

Bidart, Frank. *In the Western Night: Collected Poems, 1965–1990* (New York: Farrar, Straus and Giroux, 1990).
Fulton, Alice. *Felt* (New York: W. W. Norton & Company, 2001).
Herz, Judith Scherer. *John Donne and Contemporary Poetry: Essays and Poems* (New York: Palgrave Macmillan, 2017).
Jarman, Mark. *Unholy Sonnets* (Ashland, OR: Story Line Press, 2000).
Johnson, Kimberly. *Leviathan with a Hook* (New York: Persea Books, 2002).
Phillips, Carl. *Silverchest* (New York: Farrar, Straus and Giroux, 2013).
Wiman, Christian. *Once in the West: Poems* (New York: Farrar, Straus and Giroux, 2014).

Index

Abelard, 327
Abraham (Bible), 240
Academy of Complements, The, 27
Adam (Genesis), 36, 240, 243
adiaphora, 70
Ahab (Bible), 253
Alcala Complutensian, the (Bible), 271
alchemy, 76–78, 83n.19, 168, 218, 221–224
  spiritual, 222–224
Alcibiades, 66
Alford, Henry, 275
Allen, Don Cameron, 11, 12
Allsop, John, 96
Alvarez, Alfred, 309
anatomy, 197, 199, 200, 205, 207, 218
anatomy theaters, 205
angels, 43, 158, 237, 240–241, 243–244, 246n.7,
     267, 330
  coin, 168
Antwerp Montanus, the (Bible), 271
anxiety, 10, 59, 80, 94, 116, 125, 128, 185, 213, 283
Apocalypse/Armageddon, 188, 244, 330
Aquinas, Thomas, 123, 240
Argentario, Giovanni, 211
Ariosto, Lodovico, 44
Aristotelianism, 36, 205, 206, 217
Aristotle, 145, 146, 165, 167, 204, 217, 239
Ashbery, John, 245, 319
astronomy, 218, 219–220, 228
astrophysics, 328
Augustine (St.), 7, 11, 36, 123, 137, 186–187, 206,
     224, 231, 251, 327
  Against the Academicians, 232
  De Civitate Dei, 186

Bacon, Francis, 94, 97, 233, 236
  Novum Organum, 56
Bald, R.C., 103, 302
Bartlett, Lady, 102, 105
Bates, Catherine, 3
Bathsheba (Bible), 253

Baudelaire, Charles, 243
Beal, Peter, 96
beauty, 36, 62–63, 65–67, 185, 278, 310
Bedford, Countess of (Lucy Russell), 25, 97, 98,
     102, 103, 154, 162, 172–174, 185, 186
Bedford, Earl of, 21
Behn, Aphra, 309
Bell, Ilona, 3, 4, 84n.34, 96
Bell, John, 306
Bellarmine, Cardinal, 135
Bellay, Joachim du, 10, 44
Berger Jr., Harry, 62
Bible, 121, 217, 240, 245, 253, 258, 259, 260,
     270–271
  1 Corinthians, 36, 210, 231, 233
  Exodus, 258
  Genesis, 144, 258
  Hebrews, 65
  Isaiah, 165
  Job, 266
  John, 241
  Matthew, 308
  Psalms, 87–88, 153, 169, 270, 273, 327
  Revelations, 330
Bidart, Frank, 336
Birch, Thomas, 315
Bishop's Bible, 270
blazon, 64
Bodleian Library, 122
Bonniface III, Pope, 253
Book of Common Prayer, 42, 89, 263, 269
Boyle, Robert, 88
Brahe, Tycho
  Progymnasmata, 219–220
Braden, Gordon, 83n.28
Bridges, Grey, 103
Briggs, Le Baron Russell, 320
Bright, Timothy, 212
Brodsky, Joseph, 40, 47
Brooke, Christopher, 23, 149, 154, 282
Brooke, Samuel, 149, 311

Brown, Jericho, 335–336
Brown, Piers, 3
Browne, Sir Thomas, 78, 210
Browning, Robert, 318
Bryson, John, 291
Buckingham, Marquess of, 104
Bunyan, John, 86
Burton, Robert, 211
  The Anatomy of Melancholy, 220, 292
Bushnell, Rebecca, 3
Butteris, Simon, 27

Calvin, John
  sermons, 87
Calvinism, 86–90, 191, 262, 273
Cambridge University, 22, 134, 322
Campana, Joseph, 3
career, 6, 32, 134–135
  literary, 5–16, 37
    amateur vs. professional, 5–6, 9
career criticism, 6–7
Carew, Lady, 22
Carew, Sir Nicholas, 99
Carew, Thomas, 3, 15, 177, 237, 309
Carey, John, 5, 6, 94, 165, 168, 191
Carr, Sir Robert, Viscount Rochester & Earl of
    Somerset, 8, 96, 103, 150, 153, 173
cartography, 41, 45–47
Castiglione, Baldesar, 61, 65
  The Book of the Courtier, 58–63, 66, 278
Catholic Church, 248–249, 251, 253, 254,
    256–264; *See also* Church of Rome
Catholicism, 41–42, 122, 135–137, 149–150, 193,
    198–200, 229, 247–248, 251–253, 255,
    256–264; *See also* Donne and
    Catholicism
  anti-, 42, 131, 199
  English Catholics, 121
  poetics, 85–92
Cavell, Stanley, 231, 233
Cavendish, Margaret, 315
censorship, 21, 26, 27, 118
Chamberlin, Robert
  The Harmony of the Muses, 26
Chancery, the, 145–146
Chapman, George, 5, 51, 191, 221
charity, 186, 187
Charles I, King, 26, 101, 147, 271, 272, 273,
    288, 310
chastity, 62, 230, 251
Cheney, Patrick, 3
Christ/Jesus, 36, 43, 54, 153, 155, 187–188, 190,
    192–193, 202, 222–223, 230, 232,
    243–244, 260–261, 280, 328, 332
  death, 36, 124, 198, 202

sacrifice, 160
seal of, 104–105, 188, 308
suffering of, 198–199
Church of England, 5, 22, 42, 47, 48n.14, 70, 85,
    139, 250, 256–264, 267–269, 273
Church of Rome, 257–258, 260
Cicero, 206
  Academica, 232
  De Amicitia, 282
  De Oratore, 187
Circe, 61
Cleveland, John, 237
Cockayne, Anne, 99
Cogan, Thomas, 211
Cohen, Esther, 196, 197, 200
Coke, Edward, 140, 146–147
Coleridge, Samuel Taylor, 6, 40, 47, 177, 307,
    310, 313, 320
Colet, John, 132
Colie, Rosalie, 58
Collinson, Patrick, 59
compasses, 47, 191, 315
conceits, 21, 33, 43, 51, 52, 54, 55, 100, 124, 128, 129,
    161, 175, 177, 193, 224, 237, 311,
    315, 332
constancy, 44, 74, 127, 129, 205, 212, 213,
    283–284, 291
Conti, Brooke, 3
Cooper, Tarnya, 293
Copernican theory, 219, 224, 228
Copernicus, Nicholas, 224
  De Revolutionibu Orbium Coelestium, 219
Cordier, Maturin
  Colloquiorum Scholasticorum Libri Quatuor,
    131, 137n.1
Corkine, William
  The Second Booke of Ayres, 21, 31
Cornwallis, William, 233
Corpus Juris Canonici, 142–143
cosmology, 46, 80, 217, 242, 283, 330
  Aristotelian, 220, 240
  heliocentric, 219
  Ptolemaic, 36, 219, 240
coterie poet, 5, 7, 30, 32
Cotton, Sir Robert, 98, 102
Council of Trent, 270
Court, the, 290
courtiers/courtiership, 58–67; *See also*
    Castiglione, Baldesar, *The Book of
    the Courtier*
Coverdale Bible, 270
Cowley, Abraham, 237, 309
Cowper, William, 312
Crashaw, Richard, 309, 332
credit, 153, 165, 171–175

Cromwell, Oliver, 310
cross dressing, 114
Crucifixion, the, 105, 198, 202, 332, 335, 336
cynicism, 69, 70, 72, 73, 74, 76, 153

Daniel, Samuel, 5, 8
Dante, 322
  Paradiso, 240
Danvers, Sir John, 105
David, King (Bible), 169, 223, 253
Davies, Sir John, 34, 233
Davies, William, 95
Davison, Francis, 24
Daybell, James, 3
death, 15, 89–90, 116, 155, 185, 190, 196, 210, 234,
    249–255, 257, 302; *See also* Donne,
    death; martyrs/martyrdom
debt, 101, 150–151, 154, 171, 173–174
Dee, John, 221
Deloney, Thomas
  Strange Histories, 30
Dering, Edward, 99
Descartes, René, 229, 241, 279
desire, 66, 72, 75, 81, 129, 144, 234, 253, 261,
    308, 321
  communal, 175
  for knowledge, 134, 147, 231
  religious/spiritual, 55, 64, 66, 250
  sexual, 62–64
  for truth, 233
Devereux, Robert, Earl of Essex, 36, 102, 150
Devil, the/Lucifer, 224, 247, 253–254
Diana, 244
digestion, 276, 279, 280
Dijkhuizen, Jan Frans van, 198–199
DiPasquale, Theresa M., 12
dissections, 205, 218
divorce, 142, 224
Donne, Elizabeth (mother, née Heywood), 42,
    134, 149
Donne, Anne (wife). See More, Anne (wife)
DoBurton, Robernne, Henry (brother), 42, 133,
    149, 152, 267
Donne, John
  as a preacher, 5, 13, 21, 46, 123, 134, 266–275
  and Catholicism, 41–42, 85, 131–132, 133,
    136–137, 149–150, 227, 258, 267,
    270, 291
  dating/ordering of writing, 22–26, 68–82
  Dean of St. Paul's, 22, 143, 227, 270, 294, 303
  death, 274, 288, 299, 302–303
  difficulty in understanding, 1–3, 35–37, 50, 53,
    55, 118, 177, 178, 314
  as Dr. Donne, 5–6, 13, 20, 23, 179, 231, 293, 307

education, 22, 42–46, 137, 233–234, 270
emphasis of biography in criticim of, 6
employment, 32, 96, 103, 149, 172, 269, 293
influence on, 42–43, 66
inventiveness, 39, 40, 41, 53, 56, 190, 311
as Jack Donne, 5–6, 13, 23, 178, 196, 231, 233,
    303, 307
knowledge of foreign languages, 41, 133, 271
literary reputation, 1, 18, 97
marriage, 74, 76, 102, 104, 117, 134, 143,
    149–150, 154, 172, 174, 293
poetic legacy of, 326–336
poetics of, 50–57
portraits of, 287–303
in prison, 149
"School of Donne," 306, 308–309
travels, 99, 288
voice, 4, 236
will, 293
writing, poetry
  Divine Poems, 13, 85–92
    "The Cross", 202, 222
    "Goodfriday, 1613. Riding Westward",
      23, 25, 47, 88, 193, 202
    "A Hymn to God the Father", 21, 23, 192
    "Hymn to God my God, in my
      Sickness", 23, 36, 40, 88
    "The Lamentations of Jeremy", 87
    Holy Sonnets, 4, 10, 23, 24, 85, 86, 88–92,
      188, 227
      2 ("O my black soul"), 155, 193
      3 ("This is my play's last scene"),
        88–91, 190
      4 ("At the round earth's imagined
        corners"), 188, 330
      7 ("Spit in my face, you Jews"), 188
      8 ("Why are we by all creatures"), 160
      9 ("What if this present"), 43
      10 ("Batter my heart"), 40, 43, 44, 53,
        155, 188, 280, 334
      13 ("Thou hast made me"), 43, 190
      15 ("I am a little world"), 43
      18 ("Show me, dear Christ"), 54–55, 188
      19 ("O, to vex me"), 45, 280
    "Hymn to God my God, in my
      Sickness," 23, 36, 40, 88
    La Corona, 13, 85, 155, 190, 192
    "The Lamentations of Jeremy," 87
  Elegies, 10, 13, 58–59, 63–67
    "The Anagram," 24, 64, 65, 188
    "The Autumna," 11, 64–65
    "Change," 284
    "The Comparison," 64–65, 83n.19, 190
    "Elegy on the Lady Markham," 185, 223

"Elegy, On the Untimely Death of the Incomparable Prince, Henry," 14, 20, 31, 110

"Epitaph on Himself," 15

"The Expostulation," 59

"A Funeral Elegy," 8, 34

"His Picture," 63–67, 188

"Love's Progress," 11, 66, 76, 166

"Love's War," 155

"Nature's Lay Idiot," 59

"Obsequies upon the Lord Harrington, the Last that Died," 173

"On His Mistress," 63

"Sapho to Philaenis," 181

"To His Mistress Going to Bed," 21, 24, 27, 43, 46, 137, 188

"Variety," 181

Epicedes and Obsequies, 10

Epigrams, 10, 28

"The Juggler," 181

"A Lame Beggar," 30

"A Licentious Person," 31

Epithalamia, 10

Epithalamions

"Eclogue at the Marriage of the Earl of Somerset," 173

Poems by J.D. (1633), 6, 8, 11, 13, 15, 18, 21, 26, 28, 83n.32, 93n.10, 94, 95, 97, 110, 287, 303, 307

Poems by J.D. (1635), 6, 8, 11, 13, 24, 26, 68, 83n.32, 95, 125, 287, 288, 290, 303

Satires, 10, 23, 58–63, 314

"Satire I," 43, 59–60, 121, 181, 188, 284

"Satire II," 59, 123–124, 154, 313

"Satire III," 37, 59, 70, 185, 227–228, 234, 313–314

"Satire IV," 60–62, 154–155, 181, 310, 312, 313, 314

"Satire V," 59, 306

Metempsychosis, 11–13, 15, 33, 124, 155, 193, 287

" Upon Mr Thomas Coryat's Crudities," 11, 31

Songs and Sonnets, 10, 13, 23, 53, 68–82, 85, 111, 121, 129

"Air and Angels," 43, 66, 69, 240, 241

"Break of Day," 21, 27, 31, 43, 181

"Community," 70–71, 72

"Confined Love," 181

"The Anniversary," 81

"The Apparition," 188

"The Bait," 9, 21, 27, 160, 311

"The Blossom," 69, 74–76, 161–162

"The Broken Heart," 318

"The Canonization," 4n.3, 10, 14, 40, 43, 69, 78, 111, 112, 156, 174–175, 180, 183, 189, 318, 323–325

"The Curse," 113

"The Ecstasy," 40, 43, 69, 70, 78, 80, 180, 183, 185, 186, 209, 242, 278–279, 311, 315

"The Expiration," 21, 30, 186

"Farewell to Love," 54, 78, 83n.24

"The Flea," 43, 54, 68, 69, 190

"The Good Morrow," 44–45, 68, 69, 78–81, 111, 112, 115, 127, 128, 180, 311, 318

"The Indifferent," 72–73, 111–112, 113

"A Lecture upon the Shadow," 81, 111

"The Legacy," 189, 277

"Lovers' Infiniteness," 25, 43, 190

"Love's Alchemy," 76–78, 79, 81, 83n.24, 222

"Love's Deity," 73

"Love's Diet," 73–74, 75

"Love's Exchange," 69, 73

"Love's Growth," 69, 81

"Love's Usury," 69, 73, 188

"The Primrose," 46, 162

"The Prohibition," 188

"A Nocturnal upon St Lucy's Day, Being the Shortest Day," 31, 159, 190

"The Relic," 35, 40, 183, 229–230, 232, 323

"Self Love," 181

"Song" ("Go and catch a falling star"), 68

"Song" ("Sweetest love, I do not go"), 116, 117, 186, 311

"The Sun Rising," 43, 69, 81, 112, 114–115, 188, 190, 236–237

"The Triple Fool," 10, 21, 193, 201–202

"Twickenham Garden," 36, 127, 162–163, 188

"A Valediction Forbidding Mourning," 2, 27, 40, 47, 69, 81, 129, 192, 306, 307, 308

"Valediction of the Book," 14, 118, 183

"A Valediction of my Name in the Window," 15, 43, 44, 112, 116–118, 127–129, 180, 325

"A Valediction of Weeping," 46, 116, 180, 186, 192

"Witchcraft by a Picture," 43, 180, 192

"Woman's Constancy," 71–72, 78, 113–114, 181, 188, 190

dating/grouping/ordering of poems, 68–82

Donne, John (cont.)

The Anniversaries, 8, 10, 13, 14, 15, 20, 31, 34, 35–37, 86, 110, 242, 244, 310

The First Anniversary, 8, 11, 34, 35, 36, 45, 161, 211, 212, 217, 220–221, 223, 228, 240, 281, 315

The Second Anniversary, 8, 11, 15, 36, 155, 221

Verse Letters, 10, 15, 19, 22–23, 26–27, 94, 173, 181

"A Letter Written by Sir H.G. and J.D. alternis vicibus," 15, 161

"The Calm," 23, 193

"The Storm," 23, 154, 185, 282, 287

"To Mr B.B.," 9

"To Mr S.B.", 311

"To Sir Edward Herbert, at Juliers," 160

"To Sir H.W. at His Going Ambassador to Venice," 27

to Henry Wotton

"Sir, more than kisses," 111, 193, 194, 282

to Rowland Woodward

"Like one who'in her third widowhood," 193

"T'have written then," 154, 186

"To the Countess of Bedford, Begun in France but never perfected," 172

"To the Countess of Bedford, on New Year's Day," 15

to the Countess of Bedford (Lucy Russell)

to the Countess of Huntingdon

"Man to God's image," 36

"That unripe side of earth," 9

writing, prose

Biathanatos, 5, 21, 22, 24, 26, 47, 98, 124, 125, 144, 224–225, 230–231, 247, 250, 251–255

Cases of Conscience, 21, 99

The Courtier's Library, 22

Devotions upon Emergent Occasions, 4, 21, 26, 30, 67, 161, 199, 210, 211, 227, 256–257, 261–264, 274, 277, 281, 292, 298

"Meditation 17," 256, 263

Essays in Divinity, 21, 26, 256–262, 263–264, 270

Ignatius His Conclave (Conclave Ignatii), 21, 27, 30, 31, 32, 41, 42, 224, 247, 253–255, 256, 257, 259, 312

Juvenalia, 26

Letters, 22, 105, 125, 147, 173–174, 193, 204–205, 212, 224, 282–283

Letters to Severall Persons of Honour, 95, 97

Letters to Severall Persons of Honour (1651), 296

to George Garrard, 8

to Sir Edward Herbert, 98

to Sir Henry Goodyer, 6, 8, 23, 34

to Sir Robert Ker, 5

to Sir Thomas Egerton, 98

to the Countess of Bedford (Lucy Russell), 97

Paradoxes and Problems, 22, 25, 26, 124

Pseudo-Martyr, 21, 29n.20, 30, 31, 32, 42, 47, 98, 103, 121–122, 135–136, 144, 149, 247–251, 253, 256, 257, 258, 259, 260, 268

Sermons, 11, 19–21, 30, 92, 98–99, 105, 114, 122–123, 125–126, 152–153, 165, 168–170, 186–187, 192, 209, 211, 219, 223, 227–228, 230–233, 266–275, 280–282, 288, 308

A Sermon Preched at the Spittle upon Easter Monday, 136–137

Deaths Duell, 26, 274, 299, 303

of Easter 1628, 223, 231–233

Fifty Sermons, 26, 274

Five Sermons upon Special Occasions, 21, 271–272

Gunpowder sermon of 1622, 22

LXXX Sermons, 26, 274, 294–295

Preached upon the Penitentiall Psalmes, 223, 228

to the Virginia Company, 144–145

XXVI Sermons, 26, 274

Dowland, John

A Pilgrimes Solace, 27

Donne, John, the younger (son), 26, 95

Donne Variorum project, 3, 24

dramatic monologues, 69, 321

Drayton, Michael, 5, 6

Droeshout, Martin, 299

Drummond of Hawthornden, William, 27, 33, 50, 125, 291, 312

Drury, Elizabeth, 11, 20, 34–35, 161, 219, 223

Drury, Lady Anne, 96

Drury, Sir Robert, 23, 34, 96, 97, 99, 103, 173

Dryden, John, 310, 39, 238–239, 306–315

Dürer, Albrecht, 287

Durkheim, Émile, 245

Dutton, Elizabeth, 34

Eade, Jane, 291

eating, 139, 208–209, 211

Ebreo, Leone, 66

Edson, Margaret

W;t, 4

Egan, Gabriel, 159
Egerton, Sir Thomas, 32, 36, 96, 98, 102, 103, 104,
    111, 117, 135, 140, 145, 149, 150,
    152, 172
Eliot, T.S., 4, 6, 40, 41, 47, 75, 78, 178, 245,
    309–310, 319–322, 326
  "The Hollow Men," 322
  "The Metaphysical Poets," 39–40, 238, 320
  The Waste Land, 320–321
Elizabeth I, Queen, 22, 59, 243, 244
Elizabeth of Bohemia, Queen, 98
Elyot, Thomas
  The Boke Named the Governor, 158
embodiment, 104, 180, 276, 331, 334
Emerson, Ralph Waldo, 320
Empiricus, Sextus, 232–234
  Outlines of Skepticism, 233
Empson, William, 2, 68, 70, 74, 76, 81
English Parnassus, The, 27
enjambment, 36, 314, 318, 334
epic, 7
  classical, 12, 14, 114
  Virgilian, 11
Epicureanism, 200, 206
Erasmus, Desiderius, 233
eroticism, 10, 13, 20, 23, 44, 63, 68–69, 74, 77–78,
    81, 85, 117–118, 155, 175, 200, 223, 230,
    234, 293, 326–327, 329, 334, 336
Esau (Bible), 259
Ettenhuber, Katrin, 3
Eve (Genesis), 240, 243

faith, 227, 232, 330, 331
  personal, 336
Fall of Man, the, 240, 243
fame, 15, 18, 32
  literary, 7
favor, 149; *See also* patronage
  royal, 59
fear, 185, 212–213
  of death, 234
  of God, 187
Female Tatler, The, 315
Fernel, Jean, 204
Ferrabosco, Alfonso
  Ayres, 21, 30
Ferrell, Lori Anne, 3
feudal system, 141–142
Ficino, Marsilio, 66, 185, 221, 278
Finch, Anne, 315
Fineman, Joel, 180
Fish, Stanley, 61, 71, 179, 182, 183
Fitzgeffrey, Henry
  Satyres and Satyricall Epigrams, 31
Fletcher, John, 31

Fletcher, Miles, 287
Florio, John, 41, 233
Floyd, John, 293
Flynn, Dennis, 94, 95, 132, 133
Folger Shakespeare Library, 23
formalism, 331
Foucault, Michel
  The Order of Things, 159
Fox, Simon, 302
Foxe, John, 31
Foxell, Nigel, 302
Freitag, Johann, 204
friendship, 59, 175, 99–101, 282–283
Fulton, Alice, 329
  "Cascade Experiment," 327–329

Galen, 204, 206, 208, 211, 220, 221
Galenism, 198, 207
Galilei, Galileo, 219, 220, 240
garden/gardening, 159, 162–163
Gardner, Helen, 30, 68, 74, 76, 81, 84n.32, 86,
    291, 302, 303
Garrard, George, 8, 101, 103, 105
Garrard, Martha, 104, 105
Gascoigne, George, 50–52
gender, 180–183
  destabilizing, 114
  identity, 283
  performance of, 181–182
  shift in, 290, 293
Geneva Bible, 34, 270
genre, 3, 7, 9, 13, 59, 256
  patterning, 7, 11, 16
Gentili, Alberico, 143
Gerard, John
  Herbal, 159
Gerard, Sir Gilbert, 207
Germain, Christopher St., 146
Gilbert, Samuel, 159
Gilbert, William
  De Magnete, 220
Gilman, Ernst B., 199
Glück, Louise, 319
God, 43, 55, 89–91, 126, 137, 139–140, 153, 155,
    158–159, 162, 168, 172, 181, 186–189,
    202, 211–213, 217, 222–223, 231–233,
    237, 240–241, 243, 257, 259,
    262–263, 266, 268, 280, 326–327,
    330–332, 334
gold, 165–171, 223
Goldsmith, Oliver, 308, 310
Goodyer, Sir Henry, 8, 23, 24, 25, 27, 96, 98–99,
    100–102, 103, 105, 147, 150, 153,
    173, 282
Gordon, Andrew, 96, 102

grace
  Divine, 89–91, 188, 190, 237
  personal, 59, 62
Graham, Jorie, 245
Gratian, 142
Great Bible, 270
Great Fire of 1666 (London), 298
Gregerson, Linda, 1
Gregory I, Pope (The Great), 232
Gregory of Damascus (St.), 123
Gresham College, 219, 221
Greville, Fulke, 233
Grey, Lord, 32
Grierson, Sir Herbert, 19, 30, 39, 40, 237, 238, 309, 320
Grosart, A.B., 6
Grotius, Hugo, 143
Grove, The, 306
Gunpowder Plot, 42, 150, 248
Gunther, John
  Death Be Not Proud, 4

Hadfield, Andrew, 3
hagiography, 200
Hakluyt, Richard, 45
Hall, Bishop, 88
Hall, Joseph, 223
Hardy, Barbara, 73, 191
Harkness, Deborah, 218–219
Harley, Sir Robert, 104
Harrington, William, 42, 149
Harriot, Thomas, 221
Hart Hall, 42, 48n.14, 131, 133
Harte, Walter, 307
Harvey, Elizabeth, 12
Harvey, William, 206, 220
  De Motu Cordis, 217–218
Haskin, Dayton, 320
Hazlitt, William, 74
Healy, Margaret, 3
Heaney, Seamus, 245
Helgerson, Richard, 5, 6
Hell, 224, 232, 254, 266
Heloise, 327
Hemingway, Ernest
  For Whom the Bell Tolls, 4
Henry VIII, King, 132, 142, 268, 270
Henry, Prince, 14, 20
Herbert, Sir Edward (Lord Herbert of Cherbury), 96, 98, 105, 125, 204, 308, 309
Herbert, George, 86, 237, 244–245, 308, 312, 329, 334
Herbert, Lady Magdalen, 98, 100
Herendeen, W.H., 13

Hermeticism, 123, 217, 221, 309
Herod, 254
Herrick, Robert, 309
Herringman, Henry, 306, 307
Hertz, Judith Scherer, 6
heterosexuality, 178, 181–182
Heywood, Ellis, 132
Heywood, Jasper, 42, 132, 149, 151
hierarchy, 158, 159, 281
  social, 281
Hilliard, Nicholas, 287, 288–290
Hippocrates, 204, 206, 209
Histriomastix (William Prynne), 31
Hobbes, Thomas, 241
Hoby, Thomas, 58
Holy Spirit, 126, 209
Homer, 14
homoeroticism, 181, 282; *See also* friendship
homosocial, 181
Hooker, Richard, 139, 140, 144, 147
Hopkins, Gerard Manley, 245
Horace, 7, 10, 51, 59, 133, 187, 206, 311, 312
  "Satire 1.9," 60
Hoskyns, John, 306
Howard, Henry, Earl of Northampton, 96, 98, 103
Howard, Lady Frances, 150, 173
Howe, Sarah, 3
Howe, Susan, 322
humors/humoral theory, 198, 208, 210, 221, 276, 279–281, 284
Huntingdon, Countess of, 100, 174
Hurd, Richard, 315
Huygens, Constantijn, 27
hygiene, 207, 210–212

identity, 276, 283
idolatry, 86, 173, 183, 252, 260, 293
Ignatius of Loyola, 224, 253–255
  Spiritual Exercises, 42–44
illness/disease, 196, 210, 331
  Donne's, 212–214, 224, 261–264, 274, 296–302, 331
imperatives, 90, 114, 188–189, 318, 324
inconstancy, 71, 114, 231, 283, 284
infidelity, 127–129, 284
Inns of Court, 22, 23, 31, 45–46, 71, 82n.14, 131, 145, 271, 288, 291
intemperance, 211
inwardness, 276–280

Jacob, Giles, 307
James (VI and I), King, 34, 42, 46, 146–147, 247, 248, 250, 267, 268, 269, 270, 271, 272, 273, 293

"Directions to Preachers," 273
James, Thomas, 122
Jamestown, 46
Jarman, Mark
  Epistles, 331–333
Jeffreys, George, 314
Jerome (St.), 192
Jesuits, 41, 42, 87, 88, 121, 132, 133, 143, 149, 224,
    247, 250, 253, 254–255, 260, 293, 312
Jezebel (Bible), 253
Johnson, Kimberly, 3, 326–327
  "The Story of My Calamities," 327
Johnson, Samuel, 40, 160, 161, 238, 245, 307, 309,
    310, 311, 315
Jones, Thomas, 271
Jonson, Ben, 1, 5, 6, 7, 9, 10, 12, 18, 25, 35, 52, 55,
    118, 125, 150, 177, 191, 236, 244–246,
    276, 284, 306, 309, 318
  Tribe of Ben, 309
  Volpone, 20, 30
  Workes, 8, 19, 20, 125
Jovius, 311
Justinian, 142
Juvenal, 10, 59, 312, 313, 315

Kepler, Johannes, 27, 219–220
Ker, Sir Robert, Earl of Ancram, 5, 24, 97–99, 101,
    103, 231, 291
Ketteredge, Eric, 171
King, Dr. Henry, 302
King, John, 269
King's School Canterbury, 132
Kingsmill, Lady, 96, 97
Kneidel, Gregory, 3
knowledge
  arcane, 1–3
  yearning for complete, 231–233
Knox, Vicesimus, 307, 315

Laertius, Diogenes
  The Lives of the Philosophers, 233
Lamb, Charles, 307
Landor, Walter Savage, 323
Landreth, David, 3
Latour, Bruno, 159
Laud, William, 273, 302
laureate poets, 5–16
law, 139–147
  civil and canon, 139, 142–143, 268
  constitutional, 327
  English common, 139–147
  equity, 139, 145–147
  jus commune, 142–144, 145, 147
  Roman, 121
Legouis, Pierre, 69

Leinward, Ted, 83n.30
Leishman, J.B., 39
lesbianism, 181–182
Lewalski, Barbara, 86–88, 91
Lewis, C.S., 82n.4, 191, 196, 243
Liberties, the, 142
Lily, William, 132
Lincoln's Inn, 31, 45, 46, 121, 123, 131, 133, 134, 143,
    153, 266, 271, 272, 293, 294
Lipking, Lawrence, 6
Lipsius, Justus, 213
Littleton, Thomas
  Tenures, 142
Locke, Anne, 88
  Meditation of a Penitent Sinner, 85–86, 87
Lombart, Pierre, 296
Longenbach, James, 1
Lothian, Marquesses of, 291
love, 43, 45, 59, 63–67, 70–82, 85–86, 111–118,
    127–128, 162, 166, 175, 178–181, 183,
    185, 188–189, 202, 230, 237, 277–279,
    284, 291–292, 327, 335–336
  Divine, 237
  erotic, 223, 234, 336
  higher, 279
  mutual, 64, 78, 126, 179, 185
  of God, 186
  requited, 180
  self, 186–187
Lowell, James Russell, 320
Lowenstein, Joseph, 32
Lucan, 14
Lucian of Samosata, 233
Lucilius, 311
Luther, Martin, 222
Lyly, John, 132
lyric, 21, 23, 26, 53, 56, 68–70, 74, 78, 84n.36, 85,
    89, 110–112, 115, 117, 133, 177, 181,
    188–189, 191, 284, 318–319, 322, 325,
    332–333, 336

Macham, Samuel, 34
Machiavelli, Nicollo, 224, 254
macrocosm, 115, 159, 190, 315
Magdalen, Mary, 230
Magnusson, Lynne, 94, 189
Mallarmé, Stéphane, 245
manuscript/scribal publication, 5, 7–9, 14, 18–28,
    30, 31, 32, 35, 231; *See also* print
    publication
  Donne's preference for, 20
Marlowe, Christopher, 6, 9, 10, 16, 170, 222
  "The Passionate Shepherd to His Love," 9, 27
Marno, David, 3
Marotti, Arthur, 30, 35, 94, 191, 192

marriage, 55, 77, 142–143; *See also* Donne, marriage
Marriot, John, 26, 303
Marrow of Complements, The, 27
Marshall, William, 288–291, 298
Marston, John, 31–32
  The Fawn, 31
Marsyas, 66
martyrs/martyrdom, 135–136, 149, 247–255, 291; *See also* Donne, *Pseudo-Martyr*
Martz, Louis, 86, 88–89, 288
Marvell, Andrew, 86, 237, 244–245, 307, 309, 312
masochism, 200, 228
mathematics, 224, 239
Matthew, Tobie, 150–151
  Collection of Letters, 26, 95, 96
Matthew, Toby, 151
Maurer, Margaret, 94
May, Steven, 96
Mazzeo, Joseph, 224
McCullough, Peter, 21, 268
medical marketplace, 207
medicine, 45, 157, 166, 167, 197–198, 204–214, 218, 220–222, 258
  Galenic, 222
  Paracelsian, 222
meditation/s, 42, 85–91, 100, 118, 135, 162, 212, 222, 256, 258, 261–264, 266, 269–270, 280, 329–330; *See also* Donne, John, *Devotions upon Emergent Occasions*
melancholy, 208, 212, 231, 288, 291–292; *See also* Burton, Robert, *The Anatomy of Melancholy*
Merchant Taylors' School, 132
Merian, Matthaus, 294
Merton, Thomas, 245
metaphor, 40, 54–55, 116, 154, 156, 166, 191, 205, 242, 244, 313
metaphysics/metaphysical, 80, 95, 165, 167, 169, 217, 229, 231, 236–246, 328, 329
  poets/poetry, 10, 39, 41, 160, 161, 236–246, 308, 309, 310, 311–312, 315, 332
meter/rhythm, 27, 51, 53, 55, 59, 76, 78, 83n.26, 177, 201, 236, 308, 311, 314, 318–319, 323, 333–334
microcosm, 115, 159, 161–163, 190, 315
Middle Temple, 45
Middleton, Thomas, 40
Milgate, W., 30
Milles, Thomas, 20
Milton, John, 6, 8, 39, 86, 242, 244, 288, 308, 310
  "At a Solemn Music," 244
  "On the Morning of Christ's Nativity," 243
  Paradise Lost, 8

Mirandola, Pico della, 243
misogyny, 179
modernism, 326
Molyneux, Emery, 45
money, 165–175
  coins, 165–171, 174–175
  silver, 170–171
  value of, 166–168
Montaigne, Michel de, 69, 191, 282
  Essays, 233
Montemayor, Jorge de
  Diana, 290
Moore, Marianne, 318
More, Anne (wife), 23, 96, 104, 112, 117–118, 149, 172, 274
More, Robert (brother-in-law), 98
More, Sir George (father-in-law), 102, 104, 117, 149, 150, 152, 172
More, Sir Thomas, 31, 42, 136, 145, 149
Morris, David, 200–201
Morton, Thomas, 121, 293
Moses (Bible), 36, 259
Muhammad, 253
Muldrew, Craig, 171–172
Murray, Molly, 3

Naboth (Bible), 253
Nace, Nicholas, 1
narcissism, 160, 230
  specular, 180
National Portrait Gallery (London), 291
natural order, 158
nature/the natural world, 157–163
navigation, 218
Neoplatonism, 35, 74, 76, 118, 185, 217, 221, 278, 309
Neopythagoreanism, 217
New Criticism, 2, 319
New World, the/America, 45–46, 80, 144–145
Nicolson, Marjorie Hope, 161
Norton, Charles Eliot, 320

Oath of Allegiance, 121, 144, 247–250, 268
Oath of Supremacy, 133
objectification, 64
Odcombian Banquet, The, 31
Oldham, John, 312
Oldmixon, John, 310
Oliver, Isaac, 293
Oliver, P.M., 191
Ovid, 7, 10, 12, 44, 85, 133, 206
  Metamorphoses, 12
Oxford Handbook of John Donne, The, 4, 8, 9
Oxford University, 22, 45, 131, 133, 134, 143
Oxford University Press, 94, 275

pain, 196–202
  aesthetics of, 200
  language of, 197, 200–202
  in medieval Christianity, 197
  sexual, 200
panopticon, 151
Paracelsus, 161, 204, 205, 207, 221, 224
Paradise, 43, 162, 193
paradox, 6, 40, 231, 234, 242, 247, 276, 329, 330
Parnell, Thomas, 313, 314
Parsons, Robert, 121, 248
Pask, Kevin, 308
Passion, 188, 193, 199, 222, 328
passions, 185–194, 205–206, 208–209, 211–213
  and health, 211–212
  Donne's, 212–214
pastoral, 7, 32, 157–158
Patrizi, Francesco, 204
patronage, 19, 62, 126, 172–174
Patterson, Annabel, 94
Paul (apostle), 152, 186, 231, 233, 331, 333
Paul's Boys, 32
Pauline doctrine, 65, 210, 231, 333
Peacham, Henry, 187
Pebworth, Ted Larry, 19
Pelagia (St.), 251
penicillin, 83n.21
Pender, Stephen, 3, 198, 199
Penshurst, 288
Percy, Sir Henry, Earl of Northumberland, 102,
    150, 152, 153, 221
performance, 110–118, 191
  in letters, 94
  oral, 112–118
  in poetry, 181
  in sermons, 21
  of sexuality/gender, 182
  in song, 21–22
Persius, 10, 59, 312, 313
Petrarch, 7, 10, 66, 284
  Canzoniere, 62–63
  Rime Sparse, 44–45
Petrarchism, 7, 10, 44–45, 47, 58, 64, 67, 74–75,
    85–87, 111, 177, 186; *See also* sonnet,
    Petrarchan
Petty, Sir John, 27
Philips, Katherine, 307, 309, 315
Phillips, Carl, 333–334
  "Radiance Versus Ordinary Light," 333–334
Philosopher's Banquet, The, 27
philosophy; *See also* science
  first, 239, 241, 242, 243
  natural, 159, 161, 206, 217, 224
  the new, 45, 204, 206, 217–225, 228
Pindar, 14, 309

plague, 274
Plato, 221, 278
  Republic, 232
  Symposium, 67, 185
Platonism, 58, 63–64, 66–67, 78, 79, 83n.22, 217,
    279, 285n.10
Pliny, 36
poetic structure, 53–54
Pope, Alexander, 307, 310, 312–314
Pope, the, 248, 249, 254, 260
Pory, John, 102
Post, Jonathan, 294
Potter, George, 270, 275
prayers/praying, 42, 89–90, 126, 189, 192, 213, 222,
    258, 261–263, 293, 329, 334–335
print publication, 5–16, 18–22, 26–28, 30–37, 110
  Donne's attitude towards, 3, 5, 8–9, 20, 30–37,
    110, 261
Prior, Matthew, 311
prisons/imprisonment, 149–156
  Bridewell, 151
  Clink, the, 151, 152
  Counter, the, 150, 151
  in early modern London, 150–152
  Fleet, the, 149, 150, 152
  King's Bench, 151
  Ludgate, 151
  Marshalsea, 149, 151
  Newgate, 42, 133, 149, 151–152
  Poultry, the, 151
  Tower of London, 42, 132, 149–153, 155
  Westminster Gatehouse, 151
prosopopoeia, 187, 189
Protestantism, 41–42, 86, 150, 199, 227, 256–264
  poetics, 85–92, 160
Proteus, 283
psyche, 209, 278
Ptolemaic cosmology, 36, 219, 240
Puritans/Puritanism, 42, 85–86, 139–140, 147,
    202, 259, 273
Puttenham, George, 50–53, 222
Pyrrho, 233, 234
Pythagorean doctrine, 12

Quintilian, 206
  Institutio, 187–188

race, 336
Ralegh, Bess, 155
Ralegh, Elizabeth Throckmorton, 150
Ralegh, Sir Walter, 150, 152, 221
Ralph, Laura, 160
Ramelli, Agostino, 120
Raspa, Anthony
  Triplici Nodo, 247

Rastell, John, 42
reading, 110, 120–129
  in Donne's works, 120–129
  in sermons, 122–123
Red Lion Inn, 101
Reformation, 56, 70, 89, 122, 132, 183, 197–199,
    202, 227, 256, 261, 270, 283
  counter-, 86
  post-, 132, 202, 227, 268–269, 275
  pre-, 199, 256, 293
Reliquae Wottonianae, 27
repentance, 7, 188, 264
Restoration, 306, 310, 312
Rey, Rosaline, 197–198, 199
rhetoric, 187–191, 281
  auto-arousal, 187, 191
rhyme, 54–55, 59, 70, 76, 78, 83n.26, 87, 111, 201,
    314, 323, 334
Ridley, Thomas, 140, 146
Robbins, Robin, 4, 36, 193
Rochester (John Wilmot), 307, 311–312
Roe, Sir Thomas, 98
Rome, 131–132, 136–137, 193
Ronsard, Pierre de, 44
Royal Exchange, 218
Royal Post, 102
Royal Society, The, 219
Rundell, Katherine, 3

Sackville, Charles, Earl of Dorset, 313
sadism, 200
sado-masochism, 181, 334
saints, 43, 189, 199, 230, 263; *See also* martyrs/
    martyrdom
Salisbury, Countess of, 173
Salisbury, Earl of, 96, 220
Salvation, 88, 90, 196, 213, 223, 227, 233–234,
    249–250, 260–261, 268, 336
Sanchez, Melissa E., 3
Sanders, Wilbur, 69, 78, 79
satire, 58–63
Saunders, Ben, 179, 182
Sawday, Jonathan, 205
Scarry, Elaine, 197, 200
Schoenfeldt, Michael, 10, 198, 279
Schweizer, Harold, 200
science, 45–46, 134, 197, 204, 206–207, 217–225,
    240, 241, 244, 328, 330; *See also*
    philosophy
  medieval, 241
  the new, 160–161, 228, 329–330
Scotus, Duns, 241, 291
Secundus, Joannes, 10
Securis, John, 218
Selden, John, 150, 153

self, the/selfhood, 276–284
  protean nature of, 283–284
Selleck, Nancy, 3
Seneca, 153, 206
Sennert, Daniel, 204, 206, 209
Severinus, Petrus, 204
sex, 54–55, 66, 74–77, 81, 83n.27, 116–117, 178,
    200, 209, 230, 279, 283–284,
    327–328, 333, 336; *See also* eroticism,
    sexuality
  shame of, 334
sexual identity, 336
sexuality, 177–183
  instability of, 182–183
Seyle, Henry, 26
Shakespeare, William, 1, 6, 16, 18–19, 40, 92, 111,
    114, 157, 244, 276–277, 284
  plays
    The Merchant of Venice, 170, 244
    A Midsummer Night's Dream, 243
    Othello, 318
    Richard III, 285n.23
    Troilus and Cressida, 277
    Two Gentlemen of Verona, 284
  poetry
    The Rape of Lucrece, 19
    Sonnets, 180
      Sonnet 130, 64
    Venus and Adonis, 19
Shapiro, I.A., 94
Shell, Alison, 293
Sheppard, Samuel
    Merlinus Anonymous, 27
Sherman, Anita Gilman, 3
Shrewsbury School, 132
Shuger, Deborah, 198
Sidney, Sir Philip, 9, 10, 18, 52, 88, 97, 111, 132, 221,
    287, 290
Silenus, 66
Simpson, Evelyn, 270, 275
sin, 53, 60, 64, 89–90, 124, 187–188, 232, 248–250,
    252, 264, 284, 287, 333–334
  original, 193, 223
Skelton, John, 9
skepticism, 206, 227–234, 332
Smith, A.J., 13
Smith, Daniel Starza, 23
sobriety, 211
Society of Jesus, 132
Socrates, 66–67
solipsism, 282
Solomon (Bible), 223
sonnet, 10, 111; *See also* Donne, Holy Sonnets;
    Donne, *Songs and Sonnets*;
    Shakespeare, *Sonnets*

Petrarchan, 10, 62–64, 85–87, 92n.3, 111
soul, the, 11–12, 33, 33, 39, 43, 46–47, 55, 58, 62–64,
        66, 79, 89–90, 92, 127, 129, 154–156,
        166, 168, 185–187, 194, 205–206,
        208–213, 217, 222–223, 231, 237,
        241–242, 249, 251–254, 276–280,
        282, 287, 323–324, 334
Southwell, Robert, 86
Spanish Armada, 42
Spence, Joseph, 315
Spenser, Edmund, 5–10, 12–16, 18, 32, 35–36,
        38n.18, 96, 132, 191, 199, 236–237,
        244, 250, 276
    Amoretti, 236
    The Faerie Queene, 8, 18, 32, 236
    The Mutabilitie Cantos, 239, 244
spheres, 46, 189
    crystalline, 237, 240–241, 243
    earthly, 45
    heavenly, 219–220, 237
    of the moon, 239
    music of the, 77–78, 243
Spinoza, Baruch, 241, 242
spiritus, 209–210
sprezzatura, 58, 62
St. Clement Danes, 272
St. Dunstan's-in-the-West, 30, 271, 272
St. Paul's Cross, 21, 271–273
St. Paul's Cathedral, 22, 30, 271–272, 288, 296,
        303, 333
Stachniewski, John, 191
Star Chamber, the, 33, 145–146
Stein, Arnold, 54, 57n.14, 82
Stevens, Wallace, 245, 329
Stewart, Alan, 103
Stoicism, 194, 200, 206, 217
Stone, Nicholas, 302, 303
Strachey, William, 46
Strauss, Levi
    The Raw and the Cooked, 139
Strier, Richard, 3, 4, 63, 90
Stringer, Gary A., 8, 9
Strong, Roy, 162, 296
Stubbs, John, 4
Suárez, Francisco, 143
suicide, 21, 22, 98, 124, 224, 230, 247, 250–253; *See
        also* Donne, *Biathanatos*
Sullivan, Ernest W., 8
Summers, Claude J., 14
Swale, Richard, 143
Sylvester, Josuah
    Lachrymae Lachrymarum, 20, 31
Syminges, John (stepfather), 45
Synod of Dort, 273
syntax, 2, 80, 111, 318, 319, 323, 330, 333

Targoff, Ramie, 81, 92, 94, 283
Tasso, Torquato, 44
Taylor, John
    The Prayse and Vertue of a Jayle and Jaylers,
        151
Telesio, Bernadino, 204
Terence, 206
Tertullian, 123, 209
Teskey, Gordon, 3
Thatcher, Margaret, 246
Thavie's Inn, 45, 131, 133, 288
Theobald, Lewis, 315
theology, 41, 46–47, 55, 70, 87, 121, 123, 142, 144,
        198–199, 201–202, 205, 218, 236,
        239–241, 257–258, 266–267, 270,
        273, 330
Thirty-Nine Articles, 133, 267, 269
Thomas, Keith, 158
Tillyard, E.M.W., 158–159, 243
Tilmouth, Christopher, 3
Times Literary Supplement, 320
Tisdale, Roger, 13
Titian, 288
tolerance
    religious, 247, 257, 259, 260, 262, 263
Tonson, Jacob, 306, 307
Tossanus, Daniel, 122
Traherne, Thomas, 237, 309
transmutation, 208, 223
Tremellius, 271
Tremellius, Immanuel, 88, 271
Trevor, Douglas, 3
Trumbull, Sir William, 103
truth, 40, 58–62, 125, 217–218, 228–229, 231,
        233–234, 242, 314, 327, 329
    divine/religious, 62, 123, 269
Twickenham Garden, 162–163
tyranny, 234, 251–253

Ulysses, 61
Uriah the Hittite (Bible), 253

Valdesius
    *De Dignitate Regum Regnorumque
        Hispaniae*, 102
Vaughan, Henry, 237, 309
Vere, Edward de, Earl of Oxford, 32
Vere, Susan de, Countess of Montgomery, 98, 125
Vickers, Brian, 187
Victoria and Albert Museum, 296
Villiers, George, Duke of Buckingham, 95
Virgil, 7, 206
    Aeneid, 12
Virgin Mary, the, 35, 155, 240
Virginia Company, 46, 144–145

Wallace, Andrew, 3
Waller, Edmund, 309
Walton, Izaak, 6, 21, 24, 32, 33, 41, 99, 105, 205,
    231, 267, 269–270, 274, 288,
    290–291, 315
  Lives (Life of Donne), 33–34, 96–97, 133–135,
    291, 302, 307
  The Compleat Angler, 27, 33–34, 311
Watson, Robert, 157
Watson, Robert N., 157, 160, 162
Webster, John, 27, 40
Westminster Hall, 140, 142
Westmoreland, Earl of, 25
Whitehall, 153
Williamson, George, 310
Wilson, Thomas, 50
Wiman, Christian, 330–331
  "Every Riven Thing," 330–331
wit, 78, 114, 170, 190, 231, 236, 306, 310–311,
    313, 328

Donne's, 1, 16, 40, 141, 166, 168, 196, 229, 307,
    308–309, 310–311, 313
Woodward, Roland, 25
Woolf, Virginia, 202
Wordsworth, William, 320
Wotton, Sir Henry, 20, 96, 97, 124, 193, 194, 205,
    220, 282, 288
Woudhuysen, H.R., 119n.2
Wren, Christopher, 296
Wright, Thomas, 187
Wroth, Lady Mary, 111
Wyatt, Sir Thomas, 18, 177
Wycherley, William, 313

Yamamoto-Wilson, John R.,
    199–200
York House, 111, 117, 150

Zouch, Thomas, 315
Zukofsky, Louis, 322

For EU product safety concerns, contact us at Calle de José Abascal, 56–1°,
28003 Madrid, Spain or eugpsr@cambridge.org.